Ulrike Jessner, Claire Kramsch (Eds.)
The Multilingual Challenge

Trends in Applied Linguistics

Edited by
Ulrike Jessner
Claire Kramsch

Volume 16

The Multilingual Challenge

Cross-Disciplinary Perspectives

Edited by
Ulrike Jessner
Claire Kramsch

ISSN 978-1-5015-1628-3
e-ISBN (PDF) 978-1-61451-216-5
e-ISBN (EPUB) 978-1-5015-0031-2
ISSN 1868-6362

Library of Congress Cataloging-in-Publication Data
A CIP catalog record for this book has been applied for at the Library of Congress.

Bibliographic information published by the Deutsche Nationalbibliothek
The Deutsche Nationalbibliothek lists this publication in the Deutsche Nationalbibliografie;
detailed bibliographic data are available on the Internet at http://dnb.dnb.de.

© 2015 Walter de Gruyter, Inc., Berlin/Boston
This volume is text- and page-identical with the hardback published in 2015.
Typesetting: PTP-Berlin, Protago-T$_E$X-Production GmbH, Berlin
Printing and binding: CPI books GmbH, Leck

♾ Printed on acid-free paper
Printed in Germany

www.degruyter.com

Table of contents

Notes on the contributors —— vii

Ulrike Jessner and Claire Kramsch
Introduction: The multilingual challenge —— 1

Part I: Familial challenges

Li Wei and Zhu Hua
1 Challenges of multilingualism to the family —— 21

Maria Pilar Safont-Jordà
2 The promotion of multilingualism in a Catalan-speaking area. Familial challenges in the Valencian Community —— 39

Part II: Educational challenges

William Heidenfeldt
3 Conflict in the second language classroom: a teacher of Spanish facing the complicated dimensions of multilingualism —— 63

Claire Kramsch and Lihua Zhang
4 The legitimacy gap: multilingual language teachers in an era of globalization —— 87

Patrick K. Osterkorn and Eva Vetter
5 « Le multilinguisme en question ? » – The case of minority language education in Brittany (France) —— 115

Part III: Institutional challenges

Brian Lennon
6 Challenges to monolingual national literatures —— 143

David Gramling
7 Multilingual and intercultural competence on the threshold of the Third Reich — 161

Fabienne Baider and Marilena Kariolemou
8 Linguistic *Unheimlichkeit*: the Armenian and Arab communities of Cyprus — 185

Part IV: Scientific challenges

Georges Lüdi
9 Monolingualism and multilingualism in the construction and dissemination of scientific knowledge — 213

Geneviève Zarate, Aline Gohard-Radenkovic and Fu Rong
10 Le *Précis du plurilinguisme et du pluriculturalisme* : une recherche internationale, face aux défis d'une conception plurilingue et d'une traduction en anglais et en chinois — 239

Larissa Aronin and Ulrike Jessner
11 Understanding current multilingualism: what can the butterfly tell us? — 271

Part V: Professional and geopolitical challenges

Lisa McEntee-Atalianis
12 Language policy and planning in international organisations — 295

Elizabeth Ellis
13 Challenges within the ecology of multilingual interactions in Aboriginal cultural tourism in Central Australia — 323

Claire Kramsch
Afterword: Challenging multilingualism — 347

Index — 357

Notes on the contributors

Larissa Aronin is an Associate Professor at the Oranim Academic College of Education, Israel and is a research associate at Trinity College, Dublin, Ireland. She has published in a range of international journals on a wide array of topics connected with multilingualism. She is the co-author of *Multilingualism* (2012, John Benjamins), and co-editor of *The Exploration of Multilingualism* (2009, John Benjamins) and *Current Multilingualism: The New Linguistic Dispensation* (2013, De Gruyter Mouton).

Fabienne H. Baider graduated from the University of Toronto in 1999 and is Associate Professor in Linguistics in the Department of French and Modern Languages at the University of Cyprus. She works on semantics and discourse analysis from a socio-cognitivist perspective. Her work has been published in various journals such as the *International Journal of Lexicography, Modern and Contemporary France*. She co-directed several special issues and volumes, whether in discourse and gender ideology (2012, *Intersexion*) or in linguistic approaches to emotions (2013, Presses de la Sorbonne; 2014, John Benjamins). Her most recent research focuses on emotions and identity politics.

Elizabeth Ellis is a Senior Lecturer in linguistics at the University of New England in Armidale, NSW, Australia. Her research interests are in language in Central Australian tourism, bilingual family language maintenance, and plurilingual identities of teachers of English to Speakers of Other Languages. She has published in *TESOL Quarterly, Language Awareness* and *Current Issues in Language Planning*, and is the author of *The Plurilingual ESOL Teacher* to be published by De Gruyter Mouton in 2015.

Rong Fu is French Professor and Former Director of the French Department at Beijing Foreign Studies University, China. He received his Ph.D. in Languages and Cultures Didactics in 2001 from University Paris III. He is a member of the China National Commission for the higher French Education and the co-editor-in chief of *Foreign Languages Didactics Synergies China*.

Aline Gohard-Radenkovic is Associate Professor in the Department of Multilingualism and Foreign Language Learning and Teaching at the University of Fribourg (Switzerland). She has researched in the field of communication in foreign languages, in situations of migration or mobility. She was part of the team (2000–2003) that conducted the research project at the Council of Europe: *Médiation culturelle et didactique des langues/Cultural Mediation in Language Learning* *and Teaching* (2003/2004). She contributed to the research and editorial project (2004–2011): *Précis du plurilinguisme et du pluriculturalisme/Handbook of Multilingualism and Multiculturalism* (2008/2011*)*, now translated in Chinese. Since 1999, she has been the director of the multilingual and pluridisciplinary collection *Transversale*s by Peter Lang.

David Gramling has published extensively in the areas of multilingualism, German literature and film, and Turkish-German labor migrations. He is currently Assistant Professor in the Department of German Studies at the University of Arizona. He is co-editor, with Chantelle Warner, of the journal *Critical Multilingualism Studies*. He is also a working translator from Turkish and German to English. His forthcoming monograph is entitled *The Invention of Monolingualism*.

Ulrike Jessner has researched and published extensively in the areas of second language acquisition, third language acquisition, and bi/multilingualism. She is Professor at the English Department of the University of Innsbruck, Austria. She is founding member and former President of the International Association of Multilingualism. Among her numerous editorial activities, Jessner is founding co-editor of the *International Journal of Multilingualism*, and co-editor of the book series *Trends in Applied Linguistics* (De Gruyter Mouton) with Claire Kramsch (University of California, Berkeley).

Marilena Karyolemou is Associate Professor of Linguistics at the Department of Byzantine and Modern Greek Studies of the University of Cyprus. Her areas of interest are the sociolinguistics of the Cypriot variety, language policy and language planning, intra-family language policies and minority languages. She is founding member and current President of the Cyprus Linguistic Society, member of the Committee of Experts for the Revitalization of Cypriot Arabic and responsible for the creation of the Archive of Oral Tradition for Cypriot Arabic at the Ministry of Education and Culture. She is also the (co)organizer of *Med Conferences*, a series of conferences dealing with linguistic and sociolinguistic aspects of the Mediterranean world.

Claire Kramsch is Professor of German and Affiliate Professor of Education at the University of California, Berkeley. She has published extensively on issues of foreign language learning and teaching, language and culture, and multilingualism. Her most recent book is *The Multilingual Subject* (2009, Oxford University Press). She is the co-editor with Ulrike Jessner of the book series *Trends in Applied Linguistics* (De Gruyter Mouton) and with Zhu Hua of the series *Routledge Studies* *in Language and Intercultural Communication*. She is the current President of the International Association of Applied Linguistics.

Brian Lennon is Associate Professor of English and Comparative Literature at Pennsylvania State University. He is the author of *In Babel's Shadow: Multilingual Literatures, Monolingual States* (2010, University of Minnesota Press). He is currently working on a book entitled *Passwords: Philology, Security, Authentication*.

Lihua Zhang is a senior lecturer and the Chinese Language Program coordinator at the Department of East Asian Languages & Culture at the University of California at Berkeley, USA. She teaches both Chinese heritage and non-heritage Chinese language classes and has published in the areas of Chinese as heritage and as foreign language focusing on acquisition and pedagogy.

Li Wei is Professor of Applied Linguistics at the UCL Institute of Education. He has until recently been Pro-Vice-Master of Birkbeck College, University of London. His research interests are in the broad areas of bilingualism and multilingualism. Among his recent publications are *Translanguaging: Language, Bilingualism and Education* (with Ofelia Garcia, 2014, Palgrave) and *Applied Linguistics* (2014, Wiley). He is the Principal Editor of the *International Journal of Bilingualism* (Sage), Co-Editor of *Applied Linguistics Review* (De Gruyter), *Global Chinese* (De Gruyter) and *Chinese Language and Discourse* (Benjamins), and series editor of *Research Methods in Language and Linguistics* (Wiley). He is Chair of the University Council of General and Applied Linguistics (UCGAL), UK, and a Fellow of the UK Academy of Social Sciences.

Georges Lüdi is Professor Emeritus for French Linguistics, former Head of the Department of Languages and Literatures and past Dean of the Faculty of Arts at Basel University. He has researched and published extensively on linguistic aspects of migration, multilingualism, second language learning and educational language policy. From 2006 to 2011 he acted as deputy coordinator of the European DYLAN project. He has chaired the Swiss Linguistic Society and the Swiss Association for Applied Linguistics and has served as Member of the Executive Board of AILA. He has been awarded with the distinction of Officer in the Ordre national du mérite by the French Government.

Lisa McEntee-Atalianis lectures in Applied Linguistics and Communication at Birkbeck, University of London. She has published in the fields of aphasia, sign language/deaf studies and sociolinguistics. In recent years her research has focused on language use and identity in Cyprus, the Greek-Cypriot community in London, UK and the autochtonous Greek-Orthodox community of Istanbul, Turkey. Most recently she has undertaken an extensive investigation of language policy and diplomatic discourse within the International Maritime Organization (United Nations) in London and the United Nations in New York.

Patrick K. Osterkorn has studied French and German Philology in Salzburg, Paris and Vienna. He is involved in research projects at the Centre for Language Teaching and Learning Research at Vienna University. His research interests focus on applied linguistics with respect to multilingualism and language teaching and learning.

M. Pilar Safont-Jordà is Associate Professor of Sociolinguistics and Multilingualism and Director of the Multilingual Education Unit at the Universitat Jaume I in Castelló (Spain). Her research interests involve the development of pragmatic competence by third language learners of English, factors influencing third language use and early multilingualism. She has authored and co-edited a number of volumes published by Multilingual Matters, Springer, Peter Lang and Rodopi. She is also a reviewer of *TESOL Quarterly, the Modern Language Journal, International Journal of Multilingualism* and *Journal of Pragmatics*.

Eva Vetter is Professor of Language Teaching and Learning Research at the University of Vienna. She has published on multilingualism with respect to linguistic minorities, language policy, language teaching and learning and historical multilingualism. She is the co-editor of the *International Journal of Multilingualism* and President of the Austrian Association of Applied Linguistics.

Zhu Hua is Professor of Applied Linguistics and Communication and Head of Department at Birkbeck College, University of London. Her research interests include child development and intercultural communication. Her most recent book-length publications are *Exploring Intercultural Communication: Language in Action* (2014, Routledge); *Development of Pragmatic and Discourse Skills in Chinese-speaking children* (2014, John Benjamins, co-edited with Lixian Jin) and *The Language and Intercultural Communication Reader* (2011, Routledge). She is Reviews Editor of *International Journal of Bilingualism* (Sage) and joint Series editor for *Routledge Studies in Language and Intercultural Communication* (with Claire Kramsch).

Ulrike Jessner and Claire Kramsch
Introduction: The multilingual challenge

The idea of this book was given to Claire Kramsch by Fabienne Baider, who organized in June 2011 a conference in Nicosia, Cyprus on *Cognition, Emotion, Communication*. After the talk that Claire gave on "The emotional world of foreign languages", Fabienne exclaimed: "Mais Claire, tu parles toujours des bienfaits du plurilinguisme. Quand parleras-tu des cauchemars?" (Claire, you always talk about the benefits of multilingualism. When will you talk about the nightmares?). At a time when multilingualism is hailed as an instrument of political progress and social justice, e.g., through the inclusion of immigrant minority groups (e.g., Portes & Rumbaut 2001) and the validation of ethnic and regional languages (e.g., May 2012), and as an antidote against intra- and intercultural conflict (e.g., Clark & Dervin 2014:8ff, Cowley & Hanna 2013; however see Block's calls for caution), this book is an attempt to offer a more balanced view of research not only of the opportunities but also the difficulties faced by bi- and multilingual individuals as they manage the linguistic multiplicity of everyday life.

Within both the psycholinguistic and the sociolinguistic approaches to multilingualism the field is divided between those who applaud and strongly support the acquisition and use of different languages in schools, institutions, families and workplaces (e.g., for an overview see e.g. Baker 2011), and those who sound a note of caution and stress the challenges presented by linguistic multiplicity, both on the individual and on the societal levels (e.g., Jessner 2014; Kramsch 2014a).

In this book, we consider all approaches to be necessarily complementary. By seeing multilingualism as a complex and dynamic system we can concentrate on both the social and the psycholinguistic level of the phenomenon. The chapters in this book offer a variety of research perspectives which show how multilingual practices in families, schools, publishing houses, research teams, and international institutions are characterized by fuzziness and non-linearity. At the same time the realities or trajectories of the agents within the multilingual systems reflect representations of globalization and postmodern and sociolinguistic arrangements. From a complexity theoretical perspective, psycholinguistic systems are in constant interaction with – and therefore dependent on – social systems and vice versa, as also discussed by Larsen-Freeman and Cameron (2008).

Multilingualism in Applied Linguistics has been studied both as the individual process and practice of acquiring and using more than one language in everyday life, and as the collective and societal practice of using several languages in various domains of social and institutional life. In this book, we focus on multilingualism as both an individual and a social/cultural practice according to the broad definition given by Blommaert (2010: 102) and reproduced in Weber and Horner (2012: 3):

> Multilingualism ... should not be seen as a collection of 'languages' that a speaker controls, but rather as a complex of specific semiotic resources, some of which belong to a conventionally defined 'language', while others belong to another 'language'. The resources are concrete accents, language varieties, registers, genres, modalities such as writing – ways of using language in particular communicative settings and spheres of life, including the ideas people have about such ways of using, their language ideologies.

But this definition does not preclude other, more psycholinguistic definitions such as that given for example by Herdina & Jessner (2002: 52): "multilingualism... can be defined as the command and/or use of two or more languages by the respective speaker" or that proposed by Pavlenko: "bi- and multilinguals [are] speakers who use two or more languages or dialects in their everyday lives – be it simultaneously (in language contact situations) or consecutively (in the context of immigration)" (2005: 6).

1 Diversity as opportunity

During the last decades multilingualism has been seen mainly as an opportunity. Psycholinguists have generally identified three phases in the historic development of research on bi- and multilingualism. The first phase described the bilingual as a "social or cognitive Frankenstein", thereby measuring bilingual against monolingual proficiency (Hakuta and Diaz 1985: 320). An enthusiastic phase followed, triggered by the unexpected positive results of the Peal and Lambert study (1962), which showed that bilingual children outperformed their monolingual peers on both the linguistic and the cognitive level. Vildomec (1963) in one of the first books on multilingualism already pointed to the beneficial crosslinguistic influences between languages. The interest in the phenomenon of bilingualism increased immensely and the attitude towards bilingualism became more realistic due to numerous critical studies (Reynolds 1991; Skuttnab-Kangas 1984; De Bot and Clyne 1989). Most recently the work by Bialystok on cognitive advantages in bilinguals over the lifespan has definitely advanced our understanding of the bilingual mind (see also Pavlenko 2011). Due to the trained flexibility in the bilingual brain elderly bilinguals seem to be protected against the onset of dementia (for an overview see Bialystok 2011).

Although there are various definitions of multilingualism depending on the research background and theoretical orientation (for a detailed overview see Kemp 2009), the general attitude has been to embrace individual multilingualism as a cognitive and linguistic advantage. The bi- and multilingual norm in societal language use appears to have replaced the monolingual yardstick – at least in academia.

Today scholars are working with a number of definitions of multilingualism, as mentioned above. Some treat bi- and multilingualism synonymously, others treat multilingualism as an umbrella term for linguistic diversity. Terms that have been introduced range from plurilingualism introduced by the Council of Europe in 2005, polylingualism (Jørgensen et al. 2011), heteroglossia following Bakhtin (Blackledge & Creese 2014) to transmodality (Kress 2010), to name some of the well-known concepts. Multilingualism appears to be the most widely used.

From a psycholinguistic perspective multilingual development has been described as a dynamic and complex process by an increasing number of scholars applying dynamic systems theory or complexity theory to second language/bilingual development (e.g. Larsen-Freeman and Cameron 2008; De Bot 2008, Ortega 2009, 2014) and third language/multilingual development (Herdina & Jessner, 2002). Such an approach emphasizes change in systems and emergent properties as a result of a system's development.

Current work on multilingualism and multicompetence, in particular, has mainly been influenced by holistic ideas of bi- and multilingualism. Grosjean (1985; see also 2013) was the first to introduce a bilingual or holistic view of bilingualism. He compared the bilingual speaker to a high hurdler who combines his or her competences, jumping and sprinting, in one person, although he/she is not a specialist in hurdling or in high jumping. His approach opposes the monolingual norm assumption that interprets bilingualism as a kind of double monolingualism. This viewpoint has dominated most research on bilingualism and has given rise to portraying bilinguals as deficient monolinguals in each of their languages. Such an attitude has also been accepted by a large number of bilinguals who, although they function in both languages on a daily basis, criticize their own language competences and therefore are hesitant about referring to themselves as true or real bilinguals (Kramsch 2014b). The strong belief that a person can only be called truly bilingual if s/he is ambilingual, that is, is fully competent and therefore comparable to a monolingual native speaker in both languages, still seems to prevail among ill-informed politicians, academics and teachers.

Cook, who echoes the work by Grosjean in his concept of multicompetence (e.g. Cook 1991), defines multicompetence as "a supersystem" and argues that languages are displayed on a language integration continuum. This also implies that the relationship between the L1 and the interlanguage within one mind is different from that between the interlanguage in one mind and the L2, when the L2 has the status of an L1 in another mind (Cook 2003). In that sense, Cook's ideas are rather close to Grosjean's *language mode hypothesis*. According to Grosjean (2001) a trilingual person can function in a monolingual, bilingual or trilingual mode with various levels of activation. Activation of the various languages is strongly influenced, amongst other factors, by the speaker(s)' usual language mixing habits, language proficiency, socioeconomic status, the presence of mono- and bilinguals, the degree of formality etc.

In Herdina and Jessner's Dynamic Model of Multilingualism (Herdina & Jessner 2002) metalinguistic awareness or multilingual awareness has been identified as an emergent core factor of multilingual proficiency and is currently under investigation in an increasing number of studies on multilingual learning and teaching (Jessner, 2006; Moore 2006; De Angelis & Otwinowska 2014). In parallel and in contrast to traditional approaches, crosslinguistic influence is not only not considered a deficit but is viewed as a necessary part of the language learning process; in plurilingual approaches to language learning and teaching (e.g. Jessner 2008; Allgäuer et al. submitted) crosslinguistic awareness is considered a desirable and trainable trait.

All in all, discussions in Applied Linguistics point to moving away from the concept of transfer to interaction as a more dynamic term (e.g. De Angelis et al. 2015). This development of perspectives is linked to the starting alliance between socio- and psycholinguistics, that is bilingualism and SLA-studies on the one hand and the orientation towards multicompetence approaches on the other (for a detailed discussion see Jessner, 2008, 2015). By now translingual practice as code-switching and –meshing (Canagarajah, 2013) as well as translanguaging in classroom settings have entered the academic discourse in order to move away from monoglossic ideologies of bilingualism (see also May 2014). In fact **trans-** as in **trans**lingual/**trans**cultural competence have been used widely to denote in-between stages of competence or linguistic behavior on a continuum (Garcia and Li Wei 2014). Today in Applied Linguistics it is considered a fact that bi- and multilinguals use their languages in different domains and consequently develop what Blommaert (2010) refers to as " truncated multilingualism" (p. 23) or what Grosjean (2010) calls "the complementary principle" (p. 29–31), that is, they develop different levels of proficiency in each of their languages, depending on their perceived communicative needs. Applied to language education, such findings show that a multilingual pedagogy can enhance the participation, and hence the learning, of speakers of other languages.

From a purely sociolinguistic perspective, multilingualism has also been seen as an advantage. Language diversity can mean recognition of minority linguistic rights (May 2012). Claims for regional/ethnic identity can result in what is felt as social justice, thereby resisting English linguistic imperialism. Diversity can be seen as sociopolitical or as economic opportunity – the *sine qua non* for economic survival, professional mobility and success (Duchêne & Heller, 2011). In the recently established research field of linguistic landscapes (Gorter 2006; Shohamy and Gorter 2008; Huebner 2006) multilingualism has also been discovered as a sign of vitality. By studying the multiplicity of codes (Farsi, Hebrew, English), modes (writing systems, genres, registers) and modalities (written, visual or virtual signs) and their hybrid varieties displayed in public places, linguistic landscape researchers lay bare the power relations between different ethnic and linguistic groups within a given city or region (Shohamy 2006) and thus contribute to the democratization of the public sphere. In transnational networks, the ability to use various languages with various interlocutors has proved beneficial to immigrants and other expatriates around the world (Lam 2000). And the multilingual Internet (Danet & Herring 2007) has been hailed as having facilitated the dissemination of knowledge, the empowerment of minorities and even local popular uprisings with tremendous global consequences.

In sum: Current research on multilingualism has treated the phenomenon generally in a positive light:
(a) from a psycholinguistic perspective it has described the multilingual as a competent but specific speaker/hearer who develops linguistic and cognitive skills and abilities distinct from monolinguals, and thus draws benefits that go far beyond the sum of the distinct languages that constitute his/her repertoire;
(b) from a sociolinguistic perspective it has described language use by multilingual individuals as the integrated, flexible, and dynamic use of multiple symbolic and semiotic resources.

Both perspectives have enabled applied linguists to portray multilingualism as a dynamic, cognitively, emotionally and socially enriching process. The more languages one knows, the more one can see the world from different perspectives, communicate with a diversity of people, and expand one's understanding of oneself and others. So why question the advantages of multilingualism?

2 Diversity as challenge

Linguistic diversity, both individual and societal, has not always been a blessing. Despite the celebration of 'semiodiversity' (Halliday 2002) and the current fashion for embracing multilingualism in school curricula, workplaces and families, there is a dark side to linguistic diversity that has not been the object of enough attention in applied linguistics. While the majority of the world's population has always been multidialectal or multilingual in one way or the other without thinking twice about it, the increased mobility of the last century across geographical, social and political borders and the advent of the digital age have brought with them physical and emotional hardships that have made multilingualism a more complex phenomenon. Today's global rush to learn English as a Lingua Franca is only in part due to the desire to have a better job. It also has to do with the desire to escape the perceived nefarious effects of linguistic division and fragmentation and to construct instead the dream of a unified language, even though this monolingual dream is accompanied by the fear of losing one's cultural soul and one's unique historical identity.

Indeed, current efforts to promote multilingualism in Europe and to boost the teaching of foreign languages around the world are met with as much anxiety as enthusiasm. The benefits of multilingualism are for all to see: cognitive benefits of multilingual development over the lifespan, as discussed above (Bialystok 2011); greater professional opportunities; greater political and economic power; wider reach (Coupland 2010). The fears are related to the concerns about equity of access to knowledge, democratic fairness in civic participation, social and cultural identity and affiliation that multilingualism in itself does not ensure (see Duchene & Heller 2011; Moliner, Vogl & Hüning 2013; Grin & Gazzola 2013). A multilingual discourse order can also be seen as threatening the monolingual political discourse order that has been ours since the 19th century. Indeed, multilingualism can be seen as diversity itself: diversity of codes, discourses, registers, styles, modalities, systems of thought and worldviews. Behind all this diversity lurks the specter of the madness that Foucault contrasted with "civilization" and that threatens the very possibility of knowing anything at all (Foucault 1965, 2013).

The 'nightmares' of multilingualism that one is likely to experience today are not just related to individual crises of identity or subjective personal traumata experienced by individuals from multilingual families (Dorfman 1998, Lee 1995), feelings of imposture like those experienced by Eva Hoffman (1989), or suspicions of scientific disloyalty (Radosh & Milton 1997). They have to do with the much larger pervasive anxiety that is related to the transition, on the one hand, from a monolingual world of identifiable knowledge, predictable monolingual grammars, clearly recognizable authorities and gate-keeping mechanisms, disciplinary boundaries, attested forms of knowledge and certified channels of knowledge transmission, to, on the other hand, a multilingual world of multiple truths, multiple access to knowledge, and decentered sources of authority (academy, internet, webpages, Wikipedia, blogs, etc.), where people are no longer content to receive knowledge passively and respectfully, but want to participate, collaborate, manipulate, control and invent (Serres 2012).

Current multilingualism is much more than just a claim to know and master several linguistic systems and use them in global environments, nor even to learn and use the language of one's ancestors or cultural community, and to feel validated in one's cultural identity. It is part of a *general revolution against monolingualism and what it stands for,* namely: social and political centralization, social stratification, academic gate-keeping based on writing and print literacy (themselves policed by schools and educational institutions), belief in one universal truth held by the educated elite and belief in a universal scientific progress that can be expressed in any language. If monolingualism, ushered in by writing and print literacy, forms the bedrock of schooling, the nation-state, and the Academy (with its strictly delimited genres and disciplines), multilingualism is a return to the oral but now transformed by the digital. It is the characteristic of people who, for example, know only truncated forms of several languages, routinely code-mix and code-switch, and chat with one another online through the kind of metrolingualism identified by Pennycook (2007). It presages a form of participatory "democracy" that the young generation will have to invent and that is all the more unsettling as we don't know how it will look like.

Ever since Babel times, human beings have never ceased to dream of building a community of people who would understand each other effortlessly because they would all speak the same language. Every new technological advance – the invention of writing, of print, the steam engine, electric power and now electronic communication and the Internet, has been accompanied by dreams of a shared language and the hope of a shared language of dreams. As David Gramling reminds us (this volume), these dreams were particularly strong after the devastating experience of WWI. Today, they have been made stronger by the global spread of English and the global reach of networked computers. In fact, linguistic diversity has now been put at the service of a global vision of the world that speaks and dreams in English. Provided the language of communication remains English, we can now afford to indulge in the use of other languages as "languages of identification" (Hüllen 1992, House 2003). But is this all that these other languages are good for?

Block (2010) echoes Heller who argued that "the commodification of language means a shift from a valuing of language for its basic communicative function and more emotive associations – national identity, cultural identity, the authentic spirit of a people and so on – to valuing it for what it means in the globalized, deregulated, hyper-competitive, post-industrial "new work order" in which we now live... In other words, it means a shift from language as use-value to language as exchange-value" (Block 2010: 294–295). This division of linguistic labor has been accepted *de facto* by all those who organize and present at international research conferences held in English, and who publish or accomplish their business transactions in English. But ironically, the more convenient English becomes as a transactional language, and the more competitive the world becomes in the global knowledge economy, the more attractive the use of other languages becomes for other, equally valid forms of knowledge, from scientific insights to poetry slams, from historical archives to philosophical wisdoms. For example, being able to access other knowledges that are inaccessible to monolingual English speakers because they are expressed in languages other than English can give a researcher a competitive edge on the global market of scientific exchanges. So we have to ask: How much does mankind lose by conducting all legitimate scientific inquiry in English? But also: Who gets to lose by allowing other languages to claim the prerogatives that English enjoys?

The contributors to this volume clearly see multilingualism as providing a healthy counterbalance to the dominant monolingualism of much of applied linguistic research to date. They see multilingualism as contesting the dominance of the monolingual native speaker in second language acquisition research, the constraints of the monolingual nation-state in language policy and planning, and the monolingual hegemony of English as a global language of science, business and industry. They agree that multilingualism serves to decenter the sources of power by contesting the discourses of purity, normality and authenticity associated with monolingualism and by giving legitimacy to more hybrid forms of expression, across codes, modes and modalities (Kramsch 2014a). At the same time, they are aware of the perils of linguistic and semiotic diversity: the uncertainty of meanings, the constant negotiation of power, voice and identity, the conflicting demands of global reach and local trust. This book invites us to explore both the benefits and the challenges of multilingualism, become aware of what is at stake in linguistic diversity, and embrace the new challenges it presents.

3 Contents of the book

The contributors to this volume examine both the beneficial and the problematic aspects of multilingualism in various domains of private and public life.

3.1 Familial challenges

The first two chapters examine the challenges encountered by parents desirous to raise multilingual families in a context of immigration and in a bilingual context.

Li Wei and Zhu Hua discuss the challenges of linguistic diversity through a sociolinguistic ethnography of three transnational families, all from China, now living in Britain. Each of the three families uses various strategies as they struggle to maintain contact with both their former and their new "home" countries. The Korean family from China increasingly identified themselves over the years as Korean to distinguish themselves from the growing number of Chinese immigrants to the UK and replicated in Britain the duality "inside-the-family-language" (Korean) vs. "outside-the-family-language" (then Mandarin, now English) that they had maintained in China. The Cantonese-speaking Chinese family made a conscious effort to have their children learn Mandarin in order for them to have more opportunities for the future in a globalized economy. The elderly Chinese couple, fluent speakers of Mandarin and English, felt completely out of sync with the young generation of Mandarin speakers in their own family with whom they no longer shared any common "cultural memories" of China. Finding little in common with English speakers of their generation, who are mostly interested in gardening and taking walks, they reflect on their loss and isolation. The challenge of multilingualism in these three cases, as it is also for the Catalan-speaking parents studied by Safont (this volume), is indeed a constant "travel between memory and imagination" (Wei & Zhu Hua this volume).

Pilar Safont-Jordà focuses on a sociolinguistic setting, the Valencian Community in Spain, where the rapid decline of Catalan in favor of Spanish and the growing interest of parents to have their children learn English (instead of Catalan) offer a dramatic illustration of the multilingual challenge in Valencia. As English is perceived to be the gateway to global multilingualism, we have a paradoxical situation in which multilingualism presents a challenge to the hardwon Catalan-Spanish bilingualism. The spread of English in bilingual speech communities has promoted the interest for a kind of multilingualism associated with English, and, thus, for educational policies aimed at promoting English. However, parents often decide to prioritize English language learning over the community's minority language, Catalan, thus enabling the community to play a part in a global economy, but at the same time jeopardizing the sustainability of the whole Spanish-Catalan bilingual community. The ambiguous role played by English as both enabling and disabling minority languages is replicated in different ways in other contexts, e.g., in Cyprus (see Baider & Kariolemou, this volume).

3.2 Educational challenges

Chapters 3, 4 and 5 focus on the challenges that multilingualism represents with regard to traditionally monolingual school practices: monolingual heroes and heroines in language textbooks, monolingual native speakers of the target language in foreign language classes, monolingual immersion programs for endangered regional languages.

William Heidenfeldt explores the complex and dynamic linguistic and identity transformations of one multilingual teacher of secondary-level Spanish in the United States. Through the analysis of a classroom lesson on the role of *La Malinche* in the conquest of Mexico, the language teacher is shown responding creatively to the shifting linguistic and professional landscapes in her school. Not only is Cortez' mistress presented as a trilingual Nahuatl, Maya, and Spanish speaker, but as a major female player in the ambiguous world of the male Spanish colonization. Was *La Malinche* a translator or a traitor? Did she collaborate with the enemy of her people or did she give birth to a new people? Under the guidance of a feminist and multilingual teacher, the learning of Spanish becomes a challenge both to received versions of history and to traditional notions of what students should be learning in a foreign language classroom. By identifying with the historical figure, the teacher enacts the very challenge of multilingualism as she strives to enhance her students' historical and political awareness by not only teaching them the language of the colonizers but by making them reflect on what multilingualism has to do with love and betrayal, legitimacy and symbolic power.

Claire Kramsch and Lihua Zhang focus on the dilemma or "legitimacy gap" of language instructors who teach their native language and culture in monolingual institutional settings and who face the difficult task of mediating between two worlds that often seem historically, socially and culturally incompatible. Their chapter looks at how native language teachers experience day by day and deal with this cross-cultural gap by surveying 43 instructors of various western and non-western foreign languages at the college level throughout the University of California. They discover that native language teachers deal with that gap in imaginative and creative ways. However their multilingual expertise remains unrecognized and undervalued by academic institutions that are only interested in their monolingual skills as authentic 'native' speakers and in their in-depth acquaintance with the 'authentic' culture of their country of origin. Not only does the national identity of foreign language departments represent a challenge for the native instructors who are today multilingual global citizens, but the multilingual nature of the global world outside academia presents a formidable challenge to the traditional departmental and disciplinary boundaries within academic institutions. As the case of the Spanish instructor in Heidenfeldt's chapter shows, questioning those boundaries requires from the instructor a strong sense of educational mission and a multilingual view of history.

Patrick Osterkorn and Eva Vetter report on the Breton language medium schools in Brittany (France) called DIWAN schools (from *diwan* or seed in Breton), that were founded in 1977 as a reaction against monolingual language policy in France. These total immersion schools are based on an ideology of language revitalization, that aims to guarantee a secure Breton-only space within a national territory dominated by the French one language = one nation ideology. It thereby conforms to the 2002 demands of the European Council to recognize and validate regional languages within each of the European nation-states. But such a recognition creates its own challenges, as recounted in this chapter, that presents the results of a 3-month empirical study which combines language biographical, ethnographic approaches as well as linguistic landscaping. The theoretical concept of space on multiple scales provides an interesting lens to study the topographical and linguistic boundaries of the use of French and Breton in and out of the school grounds. Breton as language of education enables the students to successfully communicate in the educational domain but does not enable them to express themselves as teenagers with their peers. The tension between a cherished Breton heritage and an attractive French modernity plays itself out in schismatic verbal behaviors in the classroom and on the playground. Students develop astute strategies to circumvent the monolingual institutional space while at the same time contributing to its co-construction. This ambiguity reflects an ambiguous national language ideology that has prompted France to finally sign the Charter of Regional and Minority Languages in 1999, but without endorsing a societal multilingualism that is perceived to be a threat to the integrity of the French Republic. We find the same ambiguity in the language policies and practices of the UN (see Atalianis, this volume).

3.3 Institutional challenges

Chapters 6, 7, and 8 deal with the challenges that multilingualism presents for the institutional power of national publishing industries, national democratic institutions, and ethnolinguistic national identities.

Brian Lennon's chapter addresses a vexing challenge encountered by literary authors and scholars. How can works of literature represent the multilingual and code-switching speech practices of native and non-native speakers without having to resort to cumbersome glosses and translations that cancel their stylistic effects? And to what extent are mainstream Anglophone publishing houses willing to publish works written in multiple languages? Taking as examples Hemingway's *For Whom the Bell Tolls* and Ariel Dorfman's language memoir *Heading South, Looking North – A bilingual journey*, Lennon shows convincingly how Spanish is either trivialized by Hemingway through flawed Spanish grammar and exotic flavoring, or outright silenced by Dorfman who writes and publishes his bilingual journey exclusively in English. The disturbing question of the viability of a truly multilingual literature for an Anglophone readership finds no easy answer in a global world that prizes spoken linguistic diversity, but whose printed works of literature remain fundamentally monolingual. As we can see in the Zarate et al. chapter (this volume), if multilingualism poses a challenge to the publishers of monolingual national literatures, it is also because multilingual texts cannot be translated without losing their multilingual character.

David Gramling provides and analyzes data from programmatic, scholarly, and institutional texts that document the Third Reich's efforts to foreground multilingual and multicultural thinking in Europe – at the same time as its concentration camps were preparing a modernist prototype of transnational, translingual "inferno". He focuses particularly on the discourses of interculturality, translation, and translingual competence that were prevalent during the democratic Weimar Republic and that were appropriated by Adolf Hitler in his rise to power. This thought-provoking chapter argues that the Third Reich was one of the first modern visions of systemic globalization, founded as it was upon an anti-universalist discourse of cultural and linguistic diversity. While revisiting the multilingual rhetoric of the Third Reich might seem needlessly provocative, it serves to stress the complexity of the issues that were associated with internationalism and cosmopolitanism already in the 1920's and that are still with us today (see Atalianis, this volume).

Fabienne Baider and Marilena Karioleymou document through a series of interviews the complex ethnolinguistic identity of Armenian Cypriots/Arab-Cypriots or Maronites in Cyprus, an island already polarized between Greek and Turkish Cypriots. The Armenians, many of whom immigrated as a result of the Turkish massacres of 1915, speak Western Armenian and Cypriot Greek; all have an allegiance both to Cyprus and to the Armenian homeland. In addition, most of them speak English since they are connected to the Armenian diaspora in the UK and the US. Indeed, they chose to be interviewed in English. By contrast, the Maronites speak Sanna (a form of Arabic), Turkish and Greek and retain loose ties to

Lebanon. For each of these minorities on the island, multilingualism is associated with historical trauma and nostalgia, and with the extreme sensitivity of minority speakers to the symbolic value of different languages. The irruption of English as a global language in the Armenian Cypriot context redraws the age-old linguistic lines and, like in Valencia (see Safont-Jordà this volume), it serves at once to defuse and to exacerbate existing tensions.

3.4 Scientific challenges

The next two chapters focus on the challenges that both a common use of English as a Lingua Franca and the use of various national languages present to international research groups.

Georges Lüdi discusses the advantages and disadvantages of multilingual research teams, e. g. fruitful engagement with multiple perspectives and theoretical frameworks on the one hand, and, on the other hand, possible lack of creativity, loss of information, and the malaise not to be able to use one's own language. Instead of placing emphasis on an eventual clash between English and national languages, Lüdi reports on work that stems from data gathered in the Language Dynamics and Management of Diversity (DYLAN) project, looking for possibilities to create a balance between both, based on examples of good practice. At first reading, this chapter might seem to sing the praises of a multilingual approach to scientific discovery, which includes seeing English as a Lingua Franca itself as a "mixed plurilingual speech" that is not as standardized as assumed, but that changes and adapts to the thoughts of non-native speakers. But in the end, Lüdi reminds us that such multilingual conditions do not necessarily facilitate communication, on the contrary, they present an unexpected additional challenge (see also the chapter by Zarate et al.). What they increasingly require is circumspection and awareness that what researchers say in their various languages and what they write and publish in English might have different meanings that need to be questioned and problematized – multilingually.

Geneviève Zarate, Aline Gohard and Fu Rong discuss the challenges posed by the translation of the French *Précis du plurilinguisme et du pluriculturalisme* (Paris: Editions des archives contemporaines, 2008) into Chinese, under the scientific responsibility of Fu Rong (University of Foreign Languages, Beijing), following the publication of its English translation, *Handbook of Multilingualism and Multiculturalism,* in 2011. Researching the sensitive topic of plurilingualism in countries where the topic collides with monolingual national interests raises complex epistemological, methodological and political challenges. Researching such a topic multilingually, when the team of co-researchers is itself international and involves members who do not share the same language nor English as a Lingua Franca, is an additional challenge. As in the Lennon chapter, it highlights the difficult task of the translator called upon to translate the epistemologically or ideologically untranslatable. We find a similar concern with untranslatability in the work of the tour guides at Aborigines cultural sites in Australia (Ellis, this volume) and in the growing estrangement at the United Nations between those who speak and read English and those who don't (see Atalianis, this volume).

Larissa Aronin and Ulrike Jessner in the third chapter of this section attempt to explain the challenges multilingualism poses to researchers and practitioners working from a psycholinguistic perspective by showing how its very nature rests on complexity and they suggest some general ways of dealing with challenges of multilingualism from this perspective. They argue that perceiving the challenges of multilingualism, be it in the domain of language acquisition research or in the social sphere, as a function of its innate complexity would enable both scholars and practitioners to understand it better, and act more appropriately in various circumstances. In order to explain the fundamental differences between well-trodden paths in science and a complexity theory approach, Aronin and Jessner work with the assumption of traditional approaches, namely that languages are discrete, countable and therefore closed systems. They argue that a Dynamic Systems theoretical approach could be helpful to deal with the diversity resulting from developments on both the social and the individual level.

3.5 Professional and geopolitical challenges

The last two chapters focus on the challenges encountered in such international encounters as those of diplomats at the United Nations and those of international tourists and aboriginal Australians at sacred Aboriginal sites.

Lisa Atalianis discusses the complexity of multilingual practice within the International Maritime Organisation (IMO), an agency of the UN officially supporting the use of six official languages (Arabic, Chinese, English, French, Russian and Spanish) and three working languages (Spanish, English and French). Despite the *de jure* promotion of multilingualism, the reality is often the *de facto* practice of lingua franca communication in English. The author considers the nature of the UN's language policy, the practical and economic support given to its official languages, in addition to examining (via an ethnographic study, interviews and questionnaires) delegates' attitudes towards multilingual provision and actual language use. The study shows that 85% of participants, when given the choice, choose to contribute to discussions in English and 93% of the documents used are deliberately written in English – and that this trend is on the rise. And yet, a survey of 20 UN delegates reveals that they would not want the UN to abandon its multilingual mandate. How to deal with this contradiction without betraying the democratic mission of the United Nations as an inter-national institution (see Gramling, this volume)? The author discusses efforts by the UN to go beyond the dichotomy: economic/ pragmatic efficiency vs. democratic fairness and linguistic representation. As in the efforts made in the scientific community to diversify the code choices and linguistic needs of members of multilingual research teams (see Lüdi this volume; Zarate et al., this volume), the UN is looking into more flexible scenarios of interlingual practice that would meet UN members' needs as they arise, and would usher in greater international equity.

Elizabeth Ellis explores the sociolinguistic challenges of multilingual language use and interpreting in tourism services in two key Aboriginal-owned culturally significant sites: Uluru and Kata Tjuta of the Anangu people in Central Australia. In her study she focuses on the accuracy, cultural appropriateness and semantic nuances of information given to visitors in different languages by three kinds of guides. Indigenous tour guides, like Anangu elders, are concerned that visitors get the "right" information about the sacred nature of these sites and their people; they consider themselves to be "interpreters" and "translators" of these indigenous truths for non-Anangu visitors. The case is more complex with multilingual guides, i.e., residents of Central Australia who work with incoming groups in their first or second language(s). These guides pride themselves on extensive local knowledge of Aboriginal culture, geology, flora and fauna, and history as well as the broad knowledge of Australian society and institutions needed to answer tourist questions. They too interpret and translate, but in the linguistic sense, not in the indigenous sense. The real challenge comes from foreign tour leaders, who come from abroad, and who take on the role of translating for German or French tourists the Aboriginal culture mediated through the English of multilingual guides. This challenge is eloquently summarized by the author as follows:

> "Here we have a meeting of multilingual members of the world's oldest continuous culture (the Anangu) with tourists speaking multiple languages, catered for by both Australian-based multilingual tour guides and by foreign tour leaders with various language proficiencies and varying degrees of specialised local knowledge. These interactions are mediated via an English-speaking dominant host culture with a recognised monolingual mindset".

A multilingual challenge, indeed.

The book ends with an Afterword by Claire Kramsch that reflects on some of the main themes of this book.

References

Allgaeuer, Elisabeth, Hofer, Barbara and Jessner, Ulrike. under review. Emerging multi-/plurilingual awareness in educational contexts: From theory to practice.

Baker, Colin. 2011. *Foundations of Bilingual Education and Bilingualism*. Clevedon: Multilingual Matters.

Bialystok, Ellen. 2011. Reshaping the mind: The benefits of bilingualism. *Canadian Journal of Experimental Psychology* 65:4, 229–235.

Blackledge, Adrian & Creese, Angela (eds.). 2014. *Heteroglossia as Practice and Pedagogy*. Berlin: Springer.

Block, David. 2010. Globalization and language teaching. In Nikolas Coupland (ed.), *Handbook of Language and Globalisation*. 287–304. Oxford: Blackwell.

Blommaert, Jan. 2010. *The Sociolinguistics of Globalization*. Cambridge: Cambridge UP.

Canagarajah, A. Suresh. 2013. *Translingual Practice: Global Englishes and Cosmopolitan Relations*. New York: Routledge.

Clark, Julie & Dervin, Fred. 2014. Introduction. In Clark, Julie & Dervin Fred (eds.) *Reflexivity in Language and Intercultural Education. Rethinking multilingualism and interculturality*. (pp.1–42). London: Routledge.

Cook, Vivian. 1991. The poverty-of-the-stimulus argument and multi-competence. *Second Language Research* 7, 103–117.

Cook, Vivian. 2003. Introduction. The changing L1 in the L2 user's mind. In Cook, Vivian (ed.) *Effects of the Second Language on the First* (pp.1–18). Clevedon: Multilingual Matters.

Coupland, Nikolas. 2010. Introduction: Sociolinguistics in the global era. In Coupland, Nikolas (ed.) 1–28

Coupland, Nikolas (ed.). 2010. *The Handbook of Language and Globalization*. Oxford: Wiley-Blackwell.

Cowley, Peter & Hanna Barbara.2013. Anglophones, francophones, telephones. The case of a disputed Wikipedia entry. In Sharifian, Farzad & Jamarani, Maryam (eds.) *Language and Intercultural Communication in the New Era* (pp.198–221). Routledge.

Danet, Brenda & Herring Susan (eds.). 2007. *The Multilingual Internet. Language, culture, and communication online*. Oxford: Oxford U Press.

De Angelis, Gessica, and Otwinowska, Agnieszka (eds.). 2014. *Teaching and Learning in Multilingual Contexts: Sociolinguistic and Educational Perspectives*. Clevedon: Multilingual Matters.

De Angelis, Gessica, Jessner, Ulrike & Krésic, Marijana (eds.). 2015. *Crosslinguistic Influence and Crosslinguistic Interaction in Multilingual Langauge Learning*. London: Bloomsbury.

De Bot, Kees & Clyne, Michael. 1989. Language reversion revisited. *Studies in Second Language Acquisition* 11, 167–177.

Dorfman, Ariel.1998. *Heading South, Looking North. A bilingual journey*. New York: Penguin.

Duchêne, Alexandre & Heller, Monica (eds.). 2011. *Language in Late Capitalism. Pride and Profit*. Routledge.

Foucault, Michel. 1965. *Madness and Civilization*. New York: Vintage

Foucault, Michel. 2013. *Freedom and Knowledge. A hitherto unpublished interview*. Comment and edition by Fons Elders in collaboration with Lionel Claris. Amsterdam: Elders Special Productions BV.

Garcia, Ofelia. 2009. *Bilingual Education in the 21st Century. A Global Perspective*. Wiley-Blackwell, New York.

Garcia, Ofelia & Li Wei. 2014. *Translanguaging: Language, Bilingualism and Education*. New York: Palgrave Macmillan.

Gorter, Durk (ed.). 2006. *Linguistic Landscape: A new approach to multilingualism*. Clevedon: Multilingual Matters.

Grin, François & Gazzola Michele. 2013. Assessing efficiency and fairness in multilingual communication: Theory and application through indicators. In In A-C Berthoud, François Grin & Georges Lüdi (eds.), *Exploring the Dynamics of Multilingualism*. (pp.365–386) Amsterdam: John Benjamins.

Grosjean, Francois. 1985. The bilingual as a special but competent speaker-hearer. *Journal of Multilingual and Multicultural Development* 6:6, 467–477.

Grosjean, Francois. 2001. The bilingual's language modes. in: Janet Nicol (ed.), *One Mind, Two Languages:Bilingual Language Processing*. (pp.1–25). Oxford: Blackwell.

Grosjean, Francois. 2010. *Bilingual: Life and reality*. Harvard University Press, Cambridge, MA.

Grosjean, Francois. 2013. Bilingualism: A short introduction. in: Grosjean, Francois, Li, Ping, (eds.), *The Psycholinguistics of Bilingualism* (pp.5–25). London: Wiley-Blackwell.

Hakuta, Kenji & Diaz, Rafael. 1985. The relationship between bilingualism and intelligence: A critical discussion and some longitudinal data. In Katherine E. Nelson (ed.) *Children's Language* (pp. 319–344) Hillsdale, NJ: Lawrence Erlbaum.

Halliday, M.A.K. 2002. Applied Linguistics as an evolving theme. Plenary address to the International Association of Applied Linguistics. Singapore, December.

Herdina, Philip & Jessner, Ulrike. 2002. *A Dynamic Model of Multilingualism. Perspectives of change in psycholinguistics*. Clevedon, UK: Multilingual Matters.

Hoffman, Eva. 1989. *Lost in Translation. A life in a new language*. New York: Penguin.

House, Juliane. 2003. English as a lingua franca: A threat to multilingualism? *Journal of Sociolinguistics* 7:4, 556–578.

Huebner, Thom. 2006. Bangkok's linguistic landscapes: Environmental print, code-mixing and language change. *International Journal of Multilingualism* 3: 31–51.

Hüllen, Werner. 1992. Identifikationssprachen und Kommunikationssprachen. *Zeitschrift für Germanistische Linguistik* 20: 298–317.

Jessner, Ulrike. 2006. *Linguistic Awareness in Multilinguals. English as a third language*. Edinburgh: Edinburgh University Press.

Jessner, Ulrike. 2008. Teaching third languages: findings, trends, and challenges. *Language Teaching* 41:1, 15–56.

Jessner, Ulrike. 2014. On multilingual awareness or why the multilingual learner is a specific language learner. In M. Pawlak & L. Aronin, (eds.), *Essential Topics in Applied Linguistics and Multilingualism, Second Language Learning and Teaching* (pp.175–184), Wien, New York: Springer, 2014.

Jessner, Ulrike. 2015. Multicompetence approaches to language proficiency development in multilingual education. In O. Garcia & A. Lin (eds.), *Encyclopedia of Language and Education*, Vol 5.: Bilingual Programs. New York: Springer.

Jørgensen, Normann J., Karrebæk, Martha S., Madsen, Lian M. and Møller, Janus S. 2011. Polylanguaging in Superdiversity. *Diversities*. 2011, vol. 13, no. 2, pp., UNESCO. ISSN 2079-6595 www.unesco.org/shs/diversities/vol13/issue2/art2

Kemp, Charlotte. 2009. Defining multilingualism. In: Aronin, Larissa, Hufeisen, Britta (eds.), *The Exploration of Multilingualism* (pp. 11–26). Amsterdam: John Benjamins.

Kramsch, Claire. 2014a. Introduction. Teaching foreign languages in an era of globalization. *Modern Language Journal* 98:1, 296–311.

Kramsch, Claire. 2014b. A researcher's auto-socioanalysis: Making space for the personal. In Spolsky, Bernard, Inbar, Ofra & Tannenbaum, Michael (eds.) *Challenges for Language Education and Policy: Making Space for People* (pp.235–244). London: Routledge.

Kress, Gunther. 2010. *Multimodality. A social semiotic approach to contemporary communication*. London: Routledge.

Lam, Wan Shun Eva. 2000. L2 literacy and the design of the self: A case study of a teenager writing on the Internet. *TESOL Quarterly* 34:3, 457–482.

Larsen-Freeman, Diane & Cameron, Lynn. 2008. *Complex Systems and Applied Linguistics*. Oxford: Oxford U Press.

Lee, Chang Rae. 1995. *Native Speaker*. New York: Riverhead Books.

May, Stephen. 2012. *Language and Minority Rights*. 2d ed. London: Routledge.

May, Stephen (ed.). 2014. *The Multilingual Turn: Implications for SLA, TESOL, and Bilingual Education*. Oxford: Routledge.

Moliner, O., Vogl, U. & Hüning, M. 2013. Europe's multilingualism in the context of a European culture of standard languages. In A-C Berthoud, François Grin & Georges Lüdi (eds.). *Exploring the Dynamics of Multilingualism*. (pp.407–428) Amsterdam: John Benjamins.

Moore, Daniele. 2006. *Plurilinguisme et École*. Paris: Didier.

Ortega, Lourdes. 2009. *Understanding Second Language Acquisition*. London: Routledge.

Ortega, Lourdes. 2014. Experience and success in late bilingualism. Plenary Address at the AILA Congress in Brisbane, Australia, 11 August 2014.

Pavlenko, Aneta. 2005. *Emotions and Multilingualism*. Cambridge: Cambridge U Press.

Pavlenko, Aneta (ed.). 2011. *Bilingual Minds. Emotional experience, expression and representation*. Clevedon, UK: Multilingual Matters.

Peal, Elizabeth and Lambert, Wallace. 1962. The relation of bilingualism to intelligence. *Psychological Monographs* 76: 1–23.

Pennycook, Alastair. 2007. *Language as Local Practice*. London: Routledge.

Portes, Alejandro & Rumbaut, Ruben. 2001. *Legacies: The story of the immigrant second generation*. Berkeley: U of California Press.

Radosh, Ronald & Milton, Joyce. 1997. *The Rosenberg File*. New Haven: Yale University Press.

Reynolds, Alan (ed.). 1991. *Bilingualism, Multiculturalism, and Second Language Learning*. Hillsdale, NJ: Lawrence Erlbaum.

Serres, Michel. 2012. *La Petite Poucette*. Paris: Editions Le Pommier.

Shohamy, Elana. 2006. *Language Policy: hidden agendas and new approaches*. London: Routledge.

Shohamy, Elana & Gorter, Durk. 2008. *Linguistic Landscape: Expanding the scenery*. London: Routledge.

Skuttnab-Kangas, Tove. 1984. *Bilingualism or Not: The education of minorities*. Clevedon: Multilingual Matters.

Vildomec, Veroboy. 1963. *Multilingualism*. Leyden: A.W. Sythoff.

Weber, Jean-Jacques & Horner, Kristine. 2012. *Introducing Multilingualism. A social approach*. Clevedon, UK: Multilingual Matters.

Part I: **Familial challenges**

Li Wei and Zhu Hua

1 Challenges of multilingualism to the family

Abstract: Transnational and multilingual families have become commonplace in the 21st century. Yet few attempts have been made from an applied linguistics perspective to understand what is going on *within* such families; how their transnational and multilingual experiences impact on the family dynamics and their everyday life; how they cope with the new and ever-changing environment, and how they construct their identities and build social relations. In this chapter we start from the premise that bilingualism and multilingualism mean different things to different generations and individuals within the same family. Additive Bilingualism, which is often celebrated for the positive benefits of adding a second language and culture without replacing or displacing the first, is by no means universal. Using data gathered from a sociolinguistic ethnography of three multilingual and transnational families from China in Britain, we discuss the experiences of different generations and individuals in dealing with bilingualism and multilingualism and how their different experiences affect the way individual family members perceive social relations and social structures and construct and present their own identities.

Transnational and multilingual families are becoming more common in the UK as statistics suggest. In 2011, 31% of children born in the UK had either one or both parents from another country (Hall, 2013). In the same year, the census of England and Wales which records only the 'main' language of individuals showed that 4.2 million people (7.7% of the national population) spoke languages other than English as the main language (Office of National Statistics, 2013). Whilst there is considerable public interest in how transnational and multilingual families integrate into the broader British society (e.g. Brown, 2013; Phillips, 2013), especially how the children from transnational and multilingual backgrounds succeed or otherwise in the school system (e.g. Davies, 2012; Doughty, 2012; Royal Economic Society, 2013), there are few attempts to understand what is going on *within* such families; how their transnational and multilingual experiences impact on the family dynamics and their everyday life; how they cope with the new and ever-changing environment, and how they construct their identities and build social relations.

Corresponding Author: Li Wei, University College London, UK, li.wei@ucl.ac.uk

Family interaction has traditionally been viewed as 'private' or 'back-stage' of social life, to use Goffman's (1959) metaphor. Investigations of what is happening within the family, whilst having been done by anthropologists, psychoanalysts and others, are sometimes viewed as too detailed and trivial to the understanding of how society in the post-modern era works (see critiques in Budgeon and Roseneil, 2004; Roseneil and Frosh, 2012). Yet, it is precisely because of globalization, advancement of media and information technology, and transnationalism, all features of the post-modern society, that the boundaries between the public and the private, the front and back stages of social life have become blurred. There is an increased diversity, even superdiversity, of family structures. Different generations and individuals within the same family have vastly different sociocultural experiences. The impact of such different experiences of individual members of the family on how the family as a whole copes with the challenges of contemporary society remains largely under-explored.

This article starts from the premise that bilingualism and multilingualism mean different things to different generations and individuals within the same family. Additive Bilingualism (Lambert, 1974), which is often celebrated for the positive benefits of adding a second language and culture without replacing or displacing the first, is by no means universal. The experiences of different generations and individuals in transnational, multilingual families in dealing with bilingualism and multilingualism therefore are worthy of detailed investigation, not least because they impact on the family relations and dynamics as well as on the way individual family members perceive social relations and social structures and construct and present their own identities. We will focus on the experiences of three multilingual families from China living in Britain. Many aspects of their experiences, however, are shared by all transnational and multilingual families across the globe.

The article is structured as follows: We begin with a brief discussion of the main themes that have been discussed in the existing studies of multilingualism in transnational families. We then outline the methodological perspective of the present study. The main body of the chapter is devoted to an ethnographic account of three multilingual and transnational families from China in Britain and their experiences with multilingualism. The key issues emerging from the account and their implications for policy and practice are discussed in the final section of the chapter.

1 From language maintenance and language shift to transnational imagination

Most of the existing applied linguistic studies of transnational and multilingual families focus on the intergenerational language shift and the communicative difficulties that have been caused by such shifts (e.g. Lanza, 2007; Shin, 2005; Schecter and Bayley, 1997; Li Wei, 1994; Zhu Hua, 2008). The common recurrent pattern is that the first generation migrants find learning the languages of the new resident country is the most important and often challenging task, whilst their local-born children face the challenge of maintaining the home/heritage language. If there are grandparents joining the family in their new setting, they often take up the responsibility of childcare and interact primarily with other family and community members, and have relatively little opportunity for learning new languages. Members of transnational families have to face these different challenges together as a unit: the presence of monolingual grandparents is as much an issue to them as children not wanting or being able to speak the home language in their everyday family life. Transnational families also face the challenges of constructing new identities and fighting against prejudices and stereotypes, sometimes caused by their members not speaking the languages of the resident country.

Two issues have been highlighted by existing research of the changing sociolinguistic configurations in transnational families: necessity and opportunity. Yes, in most cases, it is necessary to have a good knowledge of the languages of the new resident country as it would enable members of the transnational family to access services, education and employment. Yet opportunities for learning the languages are not always readily available. In 2011, the coalition government in the UK announced a series of funding cuts to ESOL (English for speakers of other languages) provision including the introduction of fees for many students, a change in programme weighting, and the removal of a discretionary £4.5 million Learner Support Fund (Exley, 2011). The Ethnic Minority Achievement Grant which was used to fund bilingual teaching assistants in schools for pupils whose English is an additional language has been mainstreamed into the Direct Schools Grant covering everything, from buildings to stationery (NALDIC, online; NASUWT, 2012). With regard to the home/heritage languages, transnational families often find it necessary to maintain them for domestic communication, especially where there are monolingual grandparents around. But opportunities are not equally available across different home/heritage languages for the children to learn and maintain them. For example, some immigrant languages such as Bengali (150,000 speaker in the 2011 UK census) and Farsi (76,000 speakers) are taught in community schools and classes, while others such as Kashmiri (115,000 speakers), Tagalog (70,000 speakers) are not. Within the same ethnic community, there are better opportunities to learn and use some languages than others. In the Chinese community, for example, varieties of Chinese such as Mandarin and Cantonese are taught in heritage language schools. But no school teaches Hakka or Hokkien which also have significant numbers of speakers in the Chinese diaspora worldwide.

However, families' and individuals' motivations for learning, maintaining and using languages often go beyond necessity and opportunity. They are tied to the families' and individuals' sense of belonging and imagination. As scholars in diaspora studies point out, transnationals construct and negotiate their identities, everyday life and activities in ways that overcome the ethnic identity versus assimilation dilemma, suppressing or neutralising past differences and establishing commonality and connectivity in the building of a transnational imagination (e.g. Cohen, 1997). This imagination provides a site of hope and new beginnings (Brah, 1996: 193). Rather than looking back in a nostalgic effort of recovering or maintaining their identity, they discover or construct notions of who they are and where and what home is by essentially looking forward. Applied linguists have paid relatively little attention so far to the links between intergenerational language maintenance and language shift on the one hand and the transnational imaginations on the other amongst transnational family members both individually and collectively.

2 The present study

The present study is a sociolinguistic ethnography of three transnational families from China living in Britain. It is part of a larger, continuous ethnographic project of the Chinese community in Britain that began in the mid 1980s (Li Wei, 1997). The data for this chapter were gathered during 2006 and 2007. The research questions we set out to explore included how the families coped with issues such as family language policy, children's language socialization, linguistic ideologies, symbolic competence and changing linguistic hierarchies amongst the languages they lived with, and struggles and aspirations in maintaining contacts with both the former and new home countries. We followed a typical ethnography process of going from reflectivity to reflexivity, that is, from observation, description, introspection, to making connections between what's been observed in the present case and our knowledge of other cases. Whilst reflectivity emphasizes critical evaluation and analysis of the available evidence, reflexivity promotes the incorporation of the subjective, i.e. the analyst's own position, experience, and knowledge accumulated and synthesised through previous research in similar as well as different situations, in exploring the understanding or rationale related to questions of what, why, how and by whom. The actual fieldwork process involved the four core elements of ethnography LLTT, i.e. looking, listening, talking and thinking. As it is a family ethnography project, we paid special attention to spatial and temporal connectedness and 'relational thinking' (Enfield, 2013), including changes over generations, and contacts with extended relations living in other parts of the world.

The data we gathered include extensive field notes of observations, audio and video recording of family interaction, photography and samples of texts, and conversations with family members. The analysis follows the framework of Moment Analysis (Li Wei 2011; Li Wei and Zhu Hua, 2013), which was proposed in the context of studying multilingual creativity in everyday social interaction, with an aim to redirect the focus of analytic attention from the search of frequent and regular patterns in linguistic behaviour to spur-of-the-moment creative actions that have both immediate and long-term consequences. It is connected to Lefebvre's concept of rhythm in his 'rhythmanalysis' (e.g., 2004) which is concerned with various kinds of repetitions of actions of the human body and in daily life. But instead of measuring the intervals of repetitions, Moment Analysis focuses on what prompted a specific action at a specific moment in time and the consequences of the action including the re-actions by other people. Moment Analysis requires data from multiple sources. It is particularly important to have metalanguaging data, i.e., commentaries on the speaker's language practices as lived experience. This can be done by the speaker herself or by other interlocutors either during the interaction as it happens or afterwards on reflection. Metalanguaging data are useful because the process of individuals trying to make sense of their world, in this case, language users reflecting on the linguistic performances by themselves as well as the others they are interacting with, is an integral part of their cognitive processes surrounding the creative moment of action. From the analyst's point of view, the principal task is to focus on the way people articulate and position themselves in their metalanguaging, to detect any changes in the course of their self-reflection, themes and links that emerge from the narratives. These data are combined with observations and interpretations by the analyst of naturally occurring behaviour, resulting in what might be described as a double hermeneutic, i.e., "the participants are trying to make sense of their world; the researcher is trying to make sense of the participants trying to make sense of their world" (Smith and Osborn, 2008). In what follows, we present an account of the three families in turn.

2.1 Family 1: A Korean family from China

The first family we consider here is of Korean ethnic background from China. The Koreans are one of the largest *indigenous* ethnic minorities in China; *indigenous* in the sense that they are not migrants from the Korea peninsula and have always lived within the Chinese borders. In present-day China, many Korean families have connections with South Korea in particular. But these tend to be migrants *from* China *to* Korea rather than the other way round. There are Korean autonomous regions in the three northeastern provinces of China, and large Korean communities in major cities such as Beijing. The Koreans in China are known for their strong sense of ethnic identity; in large cities, they have clearly identifiable settlements; they maintain distinctive customs of food, dress, and marriage; and they have a high level of language maintenance including literacy. The vast majority of Koreans in China are bilingual in Korean and Mandarin Chinese (Guan, 2001).

The family we have studied came to Britain in the 1990s. The parents were professionals in their early thirties. They had one daughter who was born in China and 5 years of age when the family arrived in Britain. They all spoke fluent Korean and Chinese, and the two adults spoke good English. When we got to know the family shortly after they arrived in Britain, they were living and working in the northeast of England. As with most Korean families in China, this family's domestic interaction was mainly in Korean, with some Chinese words. They were Chinese passport holders and had never been to Korea before their migration to Britain.

Initially, the family's main concern was the daughter's learning of English. She attended a pre-school where nobody spoke Korean or Mandarin Chinese. The parents invested a great deal of time helping the daughter with her English outside school hours, by speaking English to her and reading bedtime stories in English. They did not send the daughter to Chinese complementary schools like other families from China do, because she already spoke Mandarin Chinese well. Her literacy level in both Korean and Chinese was age appropriate. The daughter's English developed fast. By the end of the first year at pre-school, she got a Very Good mark for her English. She began to mix some English words in her conversation with her parents. In the meantime, the amount of Mandarin Chinese she used was beginning to decrease.

Two and a half years after the family arrived in Britain, they had a new baby son, which became a key moment for their family language planning. The parents decided that their children should concentrate on using Korean and English, and the grandparents and other relatives in China all urged them to make sure that the new baby should know Korean. They had children's books in Korean sent by their relatives in China. And they displayed Korean cultural artefacts in the house. The birth of the son heightened their sense of being Korean. The parents spoke mainly Korean to the baby and Korean with English words with the daughter. Chinese seemed to have been abandoned. When asked about it, they explained that what they did was not much different from what they would do if they were living in China.

(1) KM: Father of the family. LW: researcher.

KM: 我们在家里都是说家里的话，外面就说家外的话。在中国在这里都是一样。
'At home we speak the 'inside-the-family' language, and outside the family, we speak the 'outside-the-family' language. It was the same when we were in China.'

LW: 家外的话就是汉语，中文。
'The 'outside-the-family' language is Chinese.'

KM: 是，中文。在这里就是英语。
'Yes, Chinese. It is English here (in Britain).'

It is particularly interesting to note their use of the term 家里的话, the 'inside-the-family' language, and 家外的话, the 'outside-the-family' language, and the change in what has been designated as the outside-the-family language from Chinese to English.

They also expressed a sense of loneliness amongst those 'from China' in Britain.

(2) KM: 从中国来的的确很多，而且越来越多。但像我们这样的没有。我们是少数民族。
'There are indeed many people from China (in Britain), and more and more are coming. But there isn't anyone like us. We are ethnic minority.'

They felt that they did not belong to the large and growing Chinese community in Britain. Their desire to maintain a distinctive ethnic identity, plus traditional practices of family interaction, led to the decision to continue speaking Korean with the children.

Another critical moment came when the family took a holiday in South Korea when the son was just over one year old. It was their first visit to Korea. But it proved to be a turning point for the family. It gave them first-hand experience with 'authentic' Korean culture and helped to legitimise their claim as Koreans. They had now been to places known to all Koreans in Korea and they felt that they could talk about Korea like those from Korea. Shortly after the trip, the family moved to the south of London, and chose to live in an area where there is a large Korean community. From then on, they did not tell people they were from China, but simply they were Koreans. When we visited them approximately a year after they moved south, they had made lots of friends with Korean families but only one Chinese family. They were interacting almost exclusively in Korean amongst themselves, with occasional English code-switching. By then, the son, who was three, did not understand Chinese, and told people that he was Korean. The daughter still understood some Chinese but did not speak it any more. Their neighbours knew them as Koreans, and they introduced us to their neighbours and friends as 'from China'. The parents did speak Chinese occasionally, but did not read Chinese newspapers or watch Chinese television programmes which were readily available. Instead, they had lots of Korean DVDs that they bought from China or Chinese shops in London.

Both children go to a Korean school at weekends. This, coupled with their decision to stop using Chinese in their daily interaction symbolises that they were moving away from their Chinese ties. In the first eight years of their life in Britain, they went back to China three times, each only for a couple of weeks. Recently, the family has begun to visit China more frequently, partly due to the grandparents getting older, and partly because they feel that they have acquired a new identity as Koreans in Britain. They are now British passport holders, and when asked about their ethnicity by strangers, they claim to be 'Koreans' in Britain. We noted that they use or code-switch to the English term *Korean* to describe themselves even when the conversation is primarily in Chinese. They never mention the term 鲜族 or 鲜族人, the terms used in China to refer to the Korean ethnic group. They do not talk about 韩国, the official Chinese term for the country of Korea, either. The English term provided them with an ambiguous but convenient label which was particularly useful in constructing a new identity for themselves.

When they were asked specifically whether they thought maintaining Chinese would give them and their children more opportunities now that China is becoming a world economic and political power, they gave the explanation that learning three different languages at once would be too much work for the children. But it seems clear to us that ethnic identity took priority over other considerations in their family language decisions.

2.2 Family 2: A British Chinese family

The second family we want to discuss is typical of many Chinese families in Britain today. They are a family of 2nd and 3rd generations of Chinese immigrants whose grandparents came from Hong Kong in the 1950s and 60s and were originally Hakka speakers. The grandfather who was the first in the family to settle in Britain came on his own in his twenties, and learned to speak Cantonese as a community lingua franca and English for wider communication. He ran a successful catering business before setting up a painting and decorating business. He married a Hakka woman in Hong Kong, who joined him in Britain three years after they got married and two years after she gave birth to their son. She knew Cantonese too but had very little English. We did not study the grandparents directly, although we met them during fieldwork and had conversations about their family history.

The parents and their children – the grandchildren generation of the family – are the main focus of our study. The mother is British-born to Hakka L1 parents, and the father came to Britain with the grandmother when he was around 2 to join the grandfather. They learned to speak Hakka at home, Cantonese outside the family within the Chinese community, and English beyond the Chinese community. They went to Chinese complementary schools when they were children and learned Cantonese only. There was, and still is, no Hakka school in Britain. They have two children – one boy and one girl – both British-born. The Grandfather passed away when the grandson was 4 and the granddaughter just over 1. Both grandchildren understood some Hakka, spoken by the grandma, and speak a mixture of Cantonese, a few Hakka words, and a lot of English, at home. The grandchildren attended a Cantonese complementary school over the weekend for a short while, but the parents decided that it would be more useful to learn Mandarin and moved them to a Mandarin weekend school. We had extensive discussions with the family over their decision to send the children to a Mandarin school. Here is an extract of a conversation with the mother.

(3) Lydia: The mother. LW: researcher.

LW: So you think it'll be better for them (referring to the children) to learn Mandarin.

Lydia: Because my Mandarin is so bad, 很糟糕，你都听不懂。
　　　　　　　　　　　　　　　　'Very bad. You can't understand it'

LW: 我听得懂。
'I can understand it.'

LW: (In Cantonese) 係咪？(Laugh.).
　　　　'Is that right?'

Lydia: I picked it up myself. No Mandarin when I was at Chinese school, you know. No Mandarin. Only Cantonese. And I wasn't even a Cantonese speaker.

LW: But you went to a Cantonese school.

Lydia: No choice. I couldn't learn Hakka. But now Mandarin is everywhere.

LW: So you think it's better for the children to learn Mandarin now.

Lydia: Yes, they have the opportunity now. They should seize the opportunity, don't you think? It'll be useful for them.

LW: In what way? Do you want them to work in China?

Lydia: Well, it will give them better opportunities in the future. Even if they are not going to China, they can find a job with Chinese. There are so many Chinese customers now. All the businesses want to work with China.

LW: So they can work here but use Chinese, Mandarin I mean.

Lydia: Yes, Mandarin is the future. China is the future.

LW: 你很乐观。
'You are very optimistic.'

Lydia: Am I? (laugh). I laugh a lot, don't I? (laugh)

Lydia confirms the changes to the sociolinguistic hierarchies amongst the different varieties of Chinese: Hakka has always had the status of a minority dialect within the Chinese community in Britain; Cantonese was once a community lingua franca; Mandarin is now the prestigious community language and is fast becoming the new lingua franca. This seems to be the trend in the Chinese diaspora worldwide (Li Wei and Zhu Hua, 2010). Different Chinese groups and individuals in different parts of the world communities respond to the changes differently as Li Wei and Zhu Hua's (2011) study illustrates. In the present case, Lydia has shown a particularly positive attitude towards the changes. It is noticeable that she repeats the word 'opportunity' several times in the short extract. She clearly associates Mandarin with opportunities for her children and for the overseas Chinese like herself. In the meantime, she often used phrases such as 返香港 (return to Hong Kong) in Cantonese, and 回国 (go back to the (home) country) in Mandarin when she talked about her holidays to Hong Kong and mainland China. What is interesting about her use of these phrases is the fact that she is British-born, and she does not visit Hong Kong and China often. When she does, it is usually for a very short period of time. For her to use phrases such as 'return' and 'go back' seems to us to reflect a typical diasporic mentality of living in one place and thinking of (living in) another place, feeling a sense of belonging somewhere else, and imagining the prospect of returning to the 'root'. Her positive, almost romantic attitude towards multilingualism and change is very likely to have been enhanced by her diasporic mentality.

In our conversations with the grandchildren, the third generation of the family, they showed no resistance to their parents' insistence that they should maintain their multilingualism and in particular, they seemed to be quite happy to attend Mandarin school at weekends. They have adopted their parents' discourse around learning Mandarin and used the word 'opportunity' on a number of occasions. The grandson in fact took part in a Mandarin Chinese competition organised by the Chinese schools association and won a free trip to China. It further boosted their positive spirit towards learning Mandarin and maintaining a high level of multilingualism.

It was also particularly noticeable that the family kept themselves very busy maintaining a huge and complex network of transnational connections. In addition to the contacts they have with the local Chinese families, they have relatives and friends in Hong Kong, China, the USA, Canada, Australia, New Zealand, the Netherlands and Spain, whom they talk to via Skype every weekend. They subscribe to Chinese satellite television channels, and regularly buy and read Chinese language newspapers and magazines. They live in a totally connected and highly multilingual world. Their family interaction is highly multilingual, involving constant codeswitching. When we asked them about their multilingual practice, they showed a very 'pragmatic' attitude. The mother, for example, said, 'I say whatever comes to my mind.' When further asked if she shared the view that mixing different languages would confuse the children, she said that she actually felt that it would help them maintaining all the languages.

2.3 Family 3. Grandparents at loss

The third family we consider consists of three generations. The parents are professionals, who were the first to come to Britain from China as postgraduate students in their late twenties. Our study focused on the two grandparents, who joined the family when the granddaughter was born about three years after the parents arrived in Britain. The two grandparents are highly educated academics who speak very good English. In fact the grandfather was a university professor of English and the grandmother was a teacher of English at a middle school in Beijing. They were retired by the time they came to Britain. In theory, they should find life in Britain fairly easy as they were already highly bilingual and could communicate with others with little difficulty. There was no specific language learning task for them. However, they felt very unhappy, which prompted us to talk to them in detail and study them as a case. We knew many Chinese families whose grandparents felt isolated because their children and grandchildren were busy with their routine jobs and studies and had very little time for them, and they themselves did not know English to make friends with non-English speaking neighbours. The Chinese community in Britain does not have identifiable, concentrated settlement, and Chinese families tend not to live close by with each other. Although there are community centres in the Chinatowns in large cities, it is not always easy and straightforward to get to them. Moreover, most of the Chinese community centres are run by Cantonese speakers. For those who do not speak Cantonese, socialising opportunities beyond the family can be restricted.

This retired bilingual couple whom we studied used a Chinese expression 百无聊赖 (bǎi wú liáo lài) to describe their existence in Britain. The four characters individually can be translated as 'hundred',' no', 'chat', 'reliance', meaning 'overcome with boredom'. They felt totally disconnected with the local Chinese community as the majority of the people of their age group were Cantonese speakers and they did not speak Cantonese. In fact, they could not find anyone of similar age with similar background, i.e. retired professionals from China who were bilingual in Mandarin and English. There was no meaningful social network support for their everyday interaction. When we asked them whether they tried to make friends with English people of their age, they said that the retired English people they knew were only interested in gardening or walking. They themselves were not so interested in such things, and felt little connection with other people. So the fact that they had the proficiency in the English language did not actually contribute positively to their life in Britain.

But what really intrigued us was their sense that after a few years in Britain, they felt a 'loss' of their Chinese. They told us that they could not understand what the young Chinese students they came across were saying; they even found some of the Chinese TV programmes hard to understand. We probed them on this topic on several occasions. They reflected on the fast-going changes in the Chinese society today. They found lots of new words and expressions in Chinese incomprehensible. Many were indeed new inventions, media-speak, and net-speak, used primarily by young people. The following exchange, which took place in their children's presence, provides some clue to their sense of the 'loss'.

(4) M: Grandfather; F: Grandmother; J: son of the older couple, in his thirties; LW: researcher:

LW: 您觉得跟他们（指在英国的中国学生）交流很难是吗？
'Do you think it is very difficult to communicate with them (re. Chinese students in Britain)?'

M: 对。
'Yes.'

LW: 那是文化差异还是语言问题？
'Is it cultural differences or a language problem?'

M: 文化差异当然也有了。不过真不知道他们在讲什么。
'There are certainly cultural differences. But we really don't understand what they are talking about.'

F: 似懂非懂，音懂意不懂，不知道到底他要表达什么。
'Half understood. Know the sounds, but not the meaning. Don't know what they want to say.'

J: 那你问不就完了嘛。
'Can't you just ask?'

F: 给我解释了，我也不会用。
'I don't know how to use it even if they explain it to me.'

M: 不懂、不会用、记不住。
'Don't understand it; don't know how to use it; and can't remember it.'

J: 你在国内不也一样？
'Isn't it the same if you were in China?'

M: Of course not the same.

J: Why not?

M: 环境不一样，身边各种各样的人都有，看人家怎么用，在什么场合用，慢慢的你就明白了，也会用。和你学英语一样。(对 LW)你说是不是？
Different environment. There are different kinds of people around us. If you can see how others use it, in what context, you can gradually understand it and use it. It's like you learning English. (To LW) Don't you think so?'

Whilst they agreed that generational cultural differences may have some effect on their apparent communication difficulties with the young people from China, they felt that the problems were caused mainly by their inability to understand the language the young people used. And this inability to understand the youth language is connected to the fact that they did not understand the context in which the words and expressions were used. Without understanding how the words and expressions were used in context, they themselves would not be able to use them, which frustrated them particularly. The 'loss' they were feeling is therefore not a loss of their language capacity, nor their capacity to ask questions, but a connection with the culture in which the new words and expressions are emerging and used. It is the language as a cultural practice that they felt they have lost, which added to their feeling of isolation in Britain. Even though they had the technical proficiency in both English and Chinese, they could not feel any real benefit; indeed, they feel 'loss' (of Chinese) without gain.

The parents, the old couple's children, told us a story which further illustrates the case. In 2009, the old couple went back to China for a short stay. They had some old friends visiting them one day, and they were catching up with each other's news. In the conversation, one of their friends used the phrase 打酱油 'to buy soy sauce' to describe the daughter of one of their mutual acquaintances. This caused a loud laugh amongst several of the visiting friends who competed in asking further questions and offering details of what happened to the young woman in question. The old couple of our study was very puzzled. They knew the literal meaning of the phrase, but they also realised that it was not the literal meaning that was intended in their friends' usage. Their friends had to explain to them that the phrase had by then acquired a new meaning of 'being involved in immoral behaviour'. The experience was quite a shock to the old couple, as it made them feel that they lost what they once knew and knew well, i.e. the 'cultural memory' (Erll and Nünning, 2008) of linguistic practices.

3 Summary and Conclusion

As we can see, whilst all three families we have discussed in this chapter come from China, their migration background and experiences are very different. The issues they face, linguistic and socio-cultural, are also very different. For the Korean family, maintaining, and indeed developing, a distinctive ethnic identity clearly takes priority. They are members of a minority (Koreans) within a minority (Chinese) in the British context. The shared connections between them and the large and growing number of Chinese immigrants from China in Britain are not enough for them to feel content and secure. They have found sufficient commonality with the Koreans in Britain to motivate their identification with that group. It is possible that being in a foreign country has strengthened their desire to make aspects of their identity clearer by aligning themselves with a relatively larger group. Their decision to be Koreans in Britain, as opposed to Koreans from China, goes hand in hand with their decision to maintain Korean within the family, developing their English abilities, and dropping Chinese. It is an interesting case of the complex relationship between language and identity in the context of migration.

For the second family, the main issues they are facing are the impacts of globalization and ongoing social changes within the Chinese diasporic community. As a family of second and third generations of immigrant background, maintaining a high level of multilingualism has enabled them to maintain and expand their transnational networks. Adapting themselves to the ongoing changes by, for example, acquiring new skills in Mandarin Chinese, has given them an advantage. The actual advantage is their capacity to develop new contacts with the Mandarin-speaking mainland Chinese and to acquire information and be part of the cultural flow that is mediated through Mandarin. Perhaps more importantly for this family, though, is the perceived, or imagined, advantage that there would be new opportunities, especially for the new generation, to work in the huge potential market of China-related business.

For the retired couple in the third family, having the right social network is clearly very important for their everyday life in Britain. In the meantime, losing the direct contacts with the spectrum of language users in China, and with the contexts in which communication occurs, has had an undesirable impact on their cultural memory of the Chinese language. They feel that the language is no longer theirs as they cannot understand it, remember it, or use it.

Taken together, these families represent the diversity of experiences of the Chinese transnationals worldwide. Like all diasporic families and communities, they travel between memory and imagination. For the Korean family, the emphasis is placed on where they are, rather than where they come from. For the second- and third-generation family, where they are now is also important. But they are more forward looking and more concerned with their future. In contrast, where they are now is less important than where they come from for the retired couple in the third family. They are more concerned with memory than imagination, although their concern is clearly related to the imagined future consequences of losing the memory.

As we said at the beginning of the chapter, studies of multilingual and transnational families have tended to focus on overall patterns of language maintenance and language shift and paid relatively little attention to the diversity of experiences with multilingualism within the families. Recognizing the diversity of transnational families and the experiences of different generations and individuals within the families has significant implications for policy, practice, and research. In making social policies and developing appropriate professional practices regarding transnational families, it is important to understand their experiences, histories, imaginations, why they feel the way they feel, and why they do things the way they do. Policies and practices should not be decided on some hypothetical uniform experience of transnational families. In research, bilingualism and multilingualism need to be studied as *experience*, and experiences need to be studied holistically and multidimensionally. Identifying overall patterns and analysing the details of interactional episodes are useful and necessary. But they need to be contextualised within the broader experiences of individuals, families and communities concerned. Whilst we celebrate the benefits of bilingualism and multilingualism, we should avoid romanticising them, or seeing them as universally positive experiences. Bilingualism and multilingualism are a reality in contemporary society. They are also a challenge to us all.

Acknowledgements

We are grateful to the families discussed in this chapter for allowing us to be part of their daily life. Without their trust, the research would never have been possible. We are grateful to the audiences in London, Manchester, Oslo, and elsewhere for listening to our presentations on the cases and giving us very useful feedback. We are particularly grateful to the editors of this volume for their support, patience and constructive criticism that have made the chapter much better.

References

Brah, Avtar. 1996. *Cartographies of Diaspora: Contesting Identities*. London: Routledge.
Brown, Christopher. 2013. Immigrants 'can do more to integrate into British culture'. *Bristol 24-7*, 17 October. http://www.bristol247.com/2013/10/17/immigrants-can-do-more-to-integrate-into-british-culture-16722/
Budgeon, Shelley, and Roseneil, Sasha (eds.). 2004. "Beyond the Conventional Family: Intimacy, Care, and Community in the 21st Century", special issue of *Current Sociology*, vol. 52. no. 2
Cohen, Robin. 1997. *Global diasporas: An introduction*. London: UCL Press.
Davies, Lizzy. 2012. Children from immigrant families 'face significant challenges' in UK schools. *The Guardian*, 11 September. http://www.theguardian.com/education/2012/sep/11/children-immigrant-families-uk-schools
Doughty, Steve. 2012. British schools fail our children say Eastern European immigrants who would rather return home than rely on the NHS. *The Daily Mail*, 9 May. http://www.dailymail.co.uk/news/article-2141974/British-schools-fail-children-say-Eastern-European-immigrants-return-home-rely-NHS.html
Enfield, Nick J. 2013. *Relationship thinking: Agency, enchrony, and human sociality*. New York: Oxford University Press.

Erll, Astrid and Nünning, Ansgar (eds.). 2008. *A Companion to Cultural Memory Studies*. Berlin: De Gruyter.
Exley, Stephen. 2011. ESOL cuts 'not thought through', claims NIACE. 18 February, 2011. http://www.tes.co.uk/article.aspx?storycode=6070629
Goffman, Erving. 1959. *The Presentation of Self In Everyday Life*. New York: Doubleday.
Guan, Xinqiu 关辛秋. 2001. 朝鲜族双语现象成因论 (On the causes of bilingualism in the Korean community). Beijing: 民族出版社 Minzu Press.
Hall, Melanie. 2013. Third of children born in England has foreign-born parent. *The Daily Telegraph*, 01 May 2013. http://www.telegraph.co.uk/news/uknews/10029547/Third-of-children-born-in-England-has-foreign-born-parent.html
Lambert, Wallace E. 1974. Culture and language as factors in learning and education. In Frances E. Aboud and Robert D. Meade (eds.), *Cultural Factors in Learning and Education*. (pp. 91–122) Bellingham, WA: Western Washington State University
Lanza, Elizabeth. 2007. Multilingualism and the family. In Peter Auer and Li Wei (eds.) *Handbook of Multilingualism and Multilingual Communication*. Berlin: De Gruyter, pp. 45–67
Lefebvre, Henri, 2004. *Rhythmanalysis: Space, Time and Everyday Life*. Continuum, London
Li Wei. 1994. *Three Generations Two Languages One Family*. Clevedon: Multilingual Matters
Li Wei. 2011. Moment Analysis and translanguaging space: Discursive construction of identities by multilingual Chinese youth in Britain. *Journal of Pragmatics*. 43, 1222–1235
Li Wei and Zhu Hua. 2010. Voices from the diaspora: Changing hierarchies and dynamics of Chinese multilingualism. *International Journal of the Sociology of Language*. 205, 155–171.
Li Wei and Zhu Hua. 2013. Translanguaging identities: Creating transnational space through flexible multilingual practices amongst Chinese university students in the UK. *Applied Linguistics* 34(5), 516–535.
NALDIC (online) http://www.naldic.org.uk/research-and-information/eal-funding.
NASUWT. 2012. Ethnic Minority Achievement. Birmingham: NASUWT.
Office of National Statistics. 2013. *2011 Census Analysis, Language in England and Wales*. http://www.ons.gov.uk/ons/rel/census/2011-census-analysis/language-in-england-and-wales-2011/index.html
Phillips, Melanie. 2013. My immigrant family were proud to assimilate. I despair that too many today expect Britain to adopt THEIR culture. *Daily Mail*, 7 May. http://www.dailymail.co.uk/news/article-2320940/MELANIE-PHILLIPS-Too-immigrants-today-expect-Britain-adopt-THEIR-culture.html
Roseneil, Sasha & Frosh, Stephen (eds.). 2012. *Social Research after the Cultural Turn*, Basingstoke: Palgrave.
Royal Economic Society. 2013. Immigrant children in schools have near-zero effect on educational results of native-born children. 23 August. http://www.res.org.uk/details/news/5129281/Immigrant-children-in-schools-have-near-zero-effect-on-educational-results-of-na.html
Schecter, Sandra R., & Bayley, Robert. 1997. Language socialization practices and cultural identity: Case studies of Mexican-descent families in California and Texas, *TESOL Quarterly*, Vol. 31, 513–541.
Shin, Sarah J. 2005. *Developing in two languages: Korean children in America*. Clevedon, UK: Multilingual Matters.

Smith, Jonathan & Osborn, Mike, 2008. Interpretative phenomenological analysis. In: Smith, Jonathan (ed.), *Qualitative Psychology*. 2nd edition. Sage, London, pp. 53–80.
Zhu Hua. 2008. Duelling languages, duelling values. Codeswitching in bilingual intergenerational conflict talk in diasporic families. *Journal of Pragmatics*, 40, 1799–1816.

Maria Pilar Safont-Jordà
2 The promotion of multilingualism in a Catalan-speaking area. Familial challenges in the Valencian Community

Abstract: The spread of English in bilingual speech communities has promoted the interest for multilingualism and, thus, the raise of educational policies aiming at this issue. Attitudes and beliefs towards languages and language learning have been examined in a number of bilingual contexts (Lasagabaster and Huguet 2007) with a specific focus on language learners and would-be teachers. Little is known about the opinions and feelings towards multilingualism of those people who are not directly linked to the language classroom, that is, those who are neither teachers nor learners. We would like to focus on a specific sociolinguistic setting, namely that of the Valencian Community in Spain.

A new educational law related to the *promotion* of multilingualism in schools has recently been approved. As argued by Wilton and Stegu (2011), policymakers influence the way in which a language is represented in a speech community. Decisions to include a minority language in the national curriculum may have a direct impact on the vitality and status of the language. Yet, we believe that decisions not to include that language may also have a direct impact on the language-related beliefs of society. On that account, we deal with parents' attitudes and specific challenges towards the promotion of their children's multilingualism. In so doing, we analyse their beliefs, and we focus on those actions that parents take in order to foster their children's multilingual development. Data for the present study were collected from a questionnaire and from observation of parent-child verbal interaction involving 100 parents whose children attend infant and primary schools in the Valencian Community. The questionnaire is an adapted version of the survey employed in Huguet and Lasagabaster's (2007) volume. In the analysis of verbal interaction in dyadic conversations, we focus on our participants' language choice. We also point to families' struggle in coping with their kids' multilingual development. Too often parents decide to prioritize the learning of English over the community's minority language, namely Catalan. Such a phenomenon may be a drawback for the multilingual sustainability of the whole community. We do agree with Wilton and Stegu (2011:1) on the priority and urgent need that policymakers be well informed by applied linguists on multilingualism and multilingual education.

Maria Pilar Safont-Jordà, Universitat Jaume I, Spain, mariapilar.safont@uji.es

1 Introduction

The raise of educational policies aiming at the promotion of multilingualism is a widespread phenomenon and Spain is not an exception. While research informs us on the advantages of being and becoming multilingual, the way in which educational authorities may tackle the issue, especially in bilingual communities with a majority and a minority language, presents a number of challenges for families. Our focus here is on one of these bilingual communities in Spain, and on the recent approval of educational reforms aiming at the promotion of multilingualism in children. We will particularly focus on parents' views and actions to achieve that linguistic target.

On that account, we shall first describe the sociolinguistic situation in the Valencian Community by paying special attention to current language practices, social status attributed to different languages and social reactions after recent educational reforms.

As it is our goal to deal with familial challenges, and examine their beliefs and behaviours regarding language choice and use, we shall next point to concepts like those of language attitudes, implicit metapragmatics and the role of parents in fostering their children's multilingualism. Next, we present our study in which we have examined parents' attitudes towards the three languages in contact from a quantitative and a descriptive viewpoint. Finally, we'll discuss our results which lead to the urgent need to transfer results from research to the general public and to educational authorities so that informed reforms may take place.

1.1 Sociolinguistic and educational situation in the Valencian Community

The Valencian Community is located in the Eastern Coast of the Spanish Peninsula. It was not until the early nineteenth century that it became part of Spain as it is known nowadays. The same happened to other regions, namely those of Basque Country and Catalonia. The map below shows the unity of these territories dating back to 1854.

Nevertheless, the Spanish language was already present in the region as it formerly belonged to Philip V empire (XVIIth century). In fact, at that time, the status of the Catalan language diminished and this language was often considered as inferior to Spanish. During most part of the XXth century, Catalan use was banned in official and public events. It was the time of the dictatorship and Spanish was the only language allowed even in education. Diglossia was a common phenomenon in society, Catalan was exclusively used at home or in informal situations. It was not until the late 80s (i.e. after the birth of the Spanish Constitution) that Catalan was present in education. In 1982, the *Estatut d'Autonomia* in the *Valencian Community* proclaimed the existence of Catalan and Spanish as official languages. This law gave rise to the *Llei d'Ús i Ensenyament del Valencià* in 1983, where the incorporation of Catalan in education was made compulsory. This law addressed the issue of the obligatory knowledge of Catalan for both teachers and students. In order to meet that goal, two language programs were created: a Catalan-based (PEV or PIL) and a Spanish-based (PIP) program. The Catalan-based or bilingual immersion program included Catalan as a means of instruction in all subject courses except for Spanish, while the Spanish-based program involved the use of Spanish as basis of instruction with the exception of the Catalan language.

Figure 1: Map of Spain in 1854. Source: *Biblioteca Nacional de Madrid*.

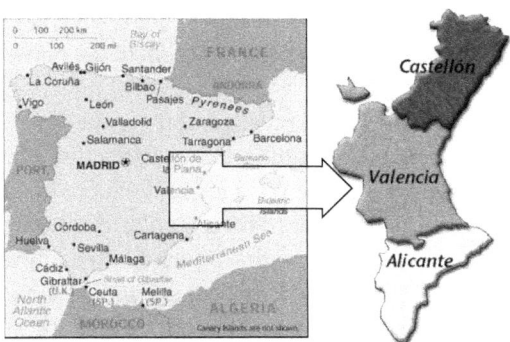

Figure 2: Spain and the Valencian Community. Source: Safont (2007: 91)

During the 90s and first years of the 21st century, bilingual immersion programs including Catalan as the language of instruction were very successful not only in the Valencian Community, but also in other Catalan-speaking parts of Spain, like Catalonia and the Balearic islands. The promotion of the minority language together with the social presence and status of the majority language enabled young learners to become bilingual speakers with equal and very often higher competence in Spanish than that of students in monolingual Spain. Our research also confirms this fact. We particularly refer to previous research on the pragmatic competence of three hundred adult learners of English as an L3 (Safont 2005). In the above mentioned study, adult learners were subdivided into two groups in line with the language program they had been engaged in during their school years, which could be either Catalan (n = 150) or Spanish-based (n = 155). The group who had received instruction within the Catalan-based program overcame those coming from the Spanish-based one as far as their pragmatic production and comprehension in English were concerned.

For the last ten years, reality has changed. The status of Catalan has decreased and its use tends to diminish as a result. A number of events seem to point to a backward movement towards old monolingual Spain. To name but a few, (i) access to Catalan TV Channel (TV3) from the Valencian Community is not possible, (ii) the only TV Channel including Catalan language , that is the Valencian autonomous public TV (Canal 9) is shut down now as agreed by the Autonomous Government, (iii) The new Law of Education affecting all areas in Spain (*LOMCE*) includes the compulsory teaching through Spanish, (iv) The New Decree for Plurilingual Education abolishes previous immersion bilingual programs (PEV and PIL) to incorporate instruction through Spanish in all schools. As a consequence, teaching through Catalan has dramatically decreased, and in many cases disappeared.

In fact, we may now refer to a monolingual turn in Valencian society. This has affected institutions like universities which were old precursors of the identity and culture of the region, and have now embraced the idea that equal percentage enables true multilingualism, and this has resulted in the promotion of the majority language, that is Spanish.

The country's economic situation and the social prestige of the English language are now used as excuses to eliminate any institution or social action that was born with a view to promote Catalan in the early stages of democracy. As a consequence, protests and demonstrations take place on a regular basis with little or no effect on political decisions. We believe that these sociopolitical facts might affect people's attitudes towards languages, as they develop within a specific political, cultural and ideological context (Cenoz 2009). For this reason, we have examined parents' attitudes towards English, Spanish and Catalan in a multilingual speech community.

1.2 Parental attitudes to languages in contact

Language attitudes are defined by Garrett (2010) as complex constructs including three main components, namely, cognition, behavior and affect. In short, cognition includes all those beliefs related to language use and acquisition; behavior refers to language choice and use; while affect has to do with those emotions whether positive (i.e. enthusiasm) or negative (i.e. dislike) that might be linked to a given language or languages. In line with Pavlenko and Blackledge (2004), we see language attitudes as integrated within a larger social, political, economic and historical context. In so doing, the study of attitudes cannot be carried out without considering their dynamic relationship with the wider context. Their relationship thus is best explained by referring to the Dynamic Model of Multilingualism (henceforth DMM) (Herdina and Jessner 2002), which sees affect as one of its main tenets. Additionally, the existing interaction among the multilinguals' languages and between those languages and the social context (see Jessner 2008), might not only promote a series of new abilities and capacities that multilinguals may display, but it may also foster new and more complex reactions and perceptions on individuals about their own multilingualism. Identity and ideology are linked to such complexity and to the inherent dynamism of multilingualism.

Ideology has been defined as "a process that organizes and enables all cultural beliefs and practices as well as power relations deriving from these" (Bucholtz and Hall 2004: 379). Bearing this view into account, identity may be seen from a different angle than that stating that language reflects one's own identity and culture. Instead, the view here is that identity is a cultural effect, and language is a fundamental resource for identity production. A view that is in line with the DMM as the cause may turn out to be the consequence and the reason the effect. Drawing on this idea, the language and/or languages present in education and promoted by social authorities do play a role in children's creation of identity, just as they do have an effect on their parents' attitudes. This view from linguistic anthropology may best explain the construction of identity in a changing multilingual world.

Garrett (2010) states that language attitudes are part of our lives as they are present at all levels of language. This author also states that language attitudes are not innate, but acquired early in the lifespan. They can be learned from the environment where children grow up. Hence, parents' prior experience and knowledge may shape children's attitudes to languages (Bartram 2006). In fact, the influence of parents may be a determining factor in their children's formation of language attitudes.

Yet, existing research on adults' attitudes towards languages has not considered parents' views. Instead, most studies have focused on the classroom or educational context. We find results from teachers, would-be teachers (Lasagabaster and Huguet 2007) and learners (Nightingale 2012; Portolés 2011) that call for the importance of promoting positive attitudes towards languages and language learning if the desired goal is to become multilingual. Lasagabaster and Huguet's volume (2007) includes a number of studies examining language attitudes of would-be teachers with a focus on three languages in contact, a majority, a minority and a foreign language. Results show that the linguistic model followed at school has an effect on the language attitudes of the participants. More specifically, the study conducted in the Valencian Community (Safont 2007) shows that those adult participants who had received instruction in the minority language (i.e. Catalan-based program PIL or PEV) during their school years (e.g. 6–12 years) have more positive attitudes towards all three languages in contact than those having studied within the framework of a Spanish-based program (PIP) during school. These last ones show favorable attitudes towards Spanish and English but not towards the minority language, that is, Catalan. Similarly, Portolés (2011) emphasizes the fact that adult learners who were taught through Catalan as children now show positive attitudes towards this minority language unlike those ones who were exclusively taught through Spanish during their school years.

As results from previous research show, the effect of the school linguistic policy on language attitudes is still present in adulthood. Moreover, according to Sears (1983) parents' attitudes influence their children's attitudes too, and these may remain for long. Taking these facts into account, we have examined parents' language attitudes from a dynamic perspective, that is, considering the current sociolinguistic situation and the extent to which their choice of school, as far as the linguistic program is concerned, may or not relate to those attitudes. We have also analysed whether there is a connection between the parents' degree of multilingualism and their beliefs on multilingual development. In so doing, we may illustrate those challenges they face in promoting their children's trilingualism. In addition to that, we have tried to describe their language choice when talking to their children in public space. In so doing, we try to focus not only on the cognitive but also on the behavioral subcomponent of the attitudinal construct. Following Mihaljevic-Djigunovic (2009: 199), the complexity and dynamism attributed to language attitudes needs to be considered not only through the interactions with the learning context but also through internal interactions among the cognitive, behavioral and affective subcomponents. As argued by Garrett (2010), this behavioral component is the most controversial one, as the assumed predictable behavior related to specific beliefs was not confirmed in a number of studies (La Piere 1934; Hanson 1980). Garrett points to the Theory of Reasoned Action (Ajzen and Fishbein 1980) as a way to establish the relationship between cognition and behavioral intentions. The principle underlying this theory states that behavior may be influenced by expected consequences and evaluations of such consequences.

Similarly, as argued by Liebscher and Dayley-O'Cain (2009), the attitudes may be constructed in interaction through negotiation with interactants in specific circumstances. Individuals construct language attitudes differently depending on which situational context and which communities they see themselves in. This approach allows for variability in results and it closely relates to the premises of the DMM. Furthermore, it bears a connection with the Theory of Reasoned Action (Ajzen and Fishbein 1980) as the intention of choosing a given language in a multilingual community may be influenced by predictable reactions depending on the specific situation in which that choice takes place.

Hence, the link between attitudes and behavior may be influenced by the complexity of the domains in which a language is used. We believe that such complexity will increase as more languages come into play with more options and contexts for using them. The issue becomes even more controversial when those languages do not share the same social prestige. In addition, such beliefs and actions may be somehow connected to parents' ideas on language acquisition and multilingual development as our data might illustrate.

2 Examining familial challenges and parents' attitudes towards multilingualism and multilingual education

As mentioned before, it is our aim to examine familial challenges in the promotion of multilingualism. In so doing, we have particularly focused on the analysis of parents' language attitudes in the Valencian Community. Taking into account previous research in this same sociolinguistic setting, we know that the school language program, that is, whether it is Catalan-based or Spanish-based, affects language attitudes in the long run (Safont 2007; Portolés 2011). Besides, parents' influence on their children's language attitudes may be crucial (Bartram 2006), as they are not innate but acquired across the lifespan (Garrett 2010). In our view, the complexity of this attitudinal construct might be linked to the dynamism and inherent complexity of multilingualism (Jessner 2008). The existing interaction between the subcomponents of the construct may be identified by examining the extent to which cognition and behavior relate.

In light of the above ideas, we have analysed parents' attitudes towards three languages in contact in the Valencian Community. In so doing, we have examined the extent to which those attitudes might be related to the language program adopted in the school chosen by these parents. In addition to that, we have tried to qualitatively analyse the attitudinal behavioral subcomponent by identifying parents' language choice when addressing their children in public space. A descriptive analysis of such practice considering the fact that attitudes may be constructed in interaction (Liebscher and Dayley-O'Cain 2009) is also presented.

Our study is thus guided by the following research questions.

RQ1: What are parents' attitudes towards Spanish, Catalan and English?

RQ2: Does school choice relate to favourable language attitudes towards a particular language?

RQ3: Are their beliefs on multilingual development related to parents' degree of bilingualism?

RQ4: What language/-s do parents use with their children in public space?

2.1 Participants

A hundred parents including mothers (n=53) and fathers (n=47) of preschool and primary education children took part in the study. According to the information obtained from the questionnaire employed in the study, seventy-five per cent are living in Castelló, one of the main cities in the Valencian Community with 280.000 inhabitants, and twenty-five per cent live in towns nearby with a population of 60.000 inhabitants.

According to our data, 45 % of participants are receptive bilinguals, that is, they understand both Catalan and Spanish, but only use Spanish; while 55% are productive bilinguals as they use both Catalan and Spanish. Only 5% state some knowledge of English and 2% mention its occasional use.

In line with Preston's arguments for the analysis of non-expert attitudes (2011), where the focus should go to different contexts, we have conducted this study in a non-educational setting that of a pediatric clinic in Castelló. This setting enabled us not only to distribute our questionnaire, but also to observe parent-child interactional behavior in public space.

2.2 Data collection procedure

Given the dynamic focus of the study, a unique method for examining language attitudes may present a partial account, while a combination of quantitative and qualitative data may provide us with more reliable information on the language attitudes of a group of subjects and their relationship with the sociocultural and educational setting. On that account, we have examined parents' attitudes towards languages by means of a direct quantitative method, that of a questionnaire, and an indirect qualitative one, that of discourse analysis and observation.

The particular situation we are interested in is that of father/mother-child interaction in public space, as it may show how carers' attempts to modify or guide children production illustrates their attitudes towards languages and might be perceived as such by children. This is particularly important if we are dealing with a multilingual group in a multilingual setting, like our own, where languages in contact present unequal sociolinguistic status.

For the purposes of our analysis, two sets of data were thus obtained. On the one hand, we were interested in identifying parents' beliefs about multilingualism and actions taken in its promotion. On the other, we observed their actual language practices in dyadic conversations. Data on beliefs and specific actions were collected by means of a questionnaire designed on the basis of Huguet and Lasagabaster's (2007) study. The questionnaire was distributed to 100 parents in a pediatric clinic in order to avoid wherever possible a direct link to the educational world, and get data from the general public (i.e. Wilton and Stegu 2011). Besides, the researcher observed and took notes on a number of dyadic conversations between mother or father and child in an attempt to present a qualitative analysis on language choice.

As our data were not normally distributed according to the Kolmogorov-Smirnov test ($z=4,478$; $p=0.000$), we made use of a MannWithney U, Wilcoxon, Friedman and Spearman correlation tests in our quantitative analysis of the data obtained from the questionnaire. Data from observation are qualitatively described afterwards.

3 Results and Discussion

3.1 Results related to the first research question

We first wondered about parents' attitudes towards the three languages in contact, namely those of Catalan, Spanish and English. In order to provide an informed answer to this first research question, we have analysed data from the questionnaire distributed by considering favourable attitudes.

As illustrated by figure 1 below, parents hold positive attitudes towards Spanish and English, and Catalan is ranked lower.

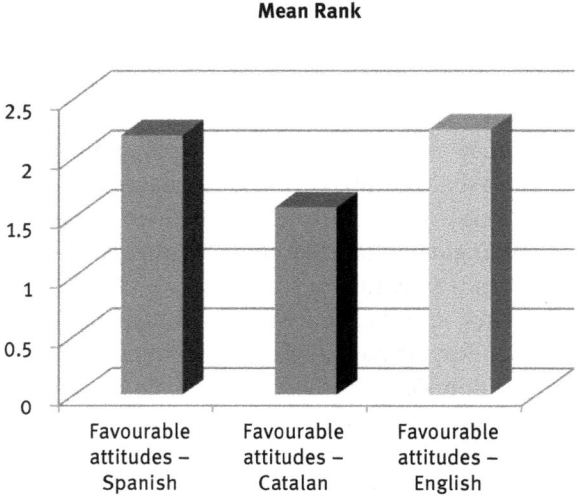

Figure 1: Parents attitudes towards Spanish, Catalan and English.

The existing difference between their attitudes towards the majority (Spanish), foreign (English) and the minority language (Catalan) has been examined by applying a Friedman Test to our data. Results from this test ($\chi^2 = 77.149$) show that the differences between their attitudes towards Catalan and the other two languages are statistically significant ($p = 0.000$).

These findings coincide with parents' comments in the questionnaire, as there are many cases in which they relate the use of Catalan with bad manners (i.e. item 11). Furthermore, 40% of parents agree with items 12 and 13 which refer to the fact that Catalan is not as useful as Spanish and English, and thus, it should not be included in education as a compulsory language. These results are worrying for a bilingual community with a majority and a minority language. Yet, we also believe that these findings illustrate the sociolinguistic situation of the three languages involved as the higher the social prestige of the language the more favourable the attitudes towards it are. In fact, English is ranked the highest, followed by the majority language, Spanish. Thirdly, Catalan is less valued coinciding with the current decrease in both use and social prestige. As argued in the introduction to this paper, facts like the lack of access to mass media in Catalan as well as a new Educational reform including more Spanish and eliminating bilingual education programs might relate to our findings. As argued by Wilton and Stegu (2011), policymakers influence the way in which a language is represented in a speech community. Policymakers in the Valencian Community decided to cancel any access to Catalan on TV or radio, while promoting the presence of Spanish under the excuse of a higher percentage of teaching in English. As our findings show, these decisions have resulted in most favourable attitudes towards Spanish and English and less favourable towards the Catalan language.

In an attempt to further examine the reason for the attitudes displayed, we wondered whether there would be a link between the attitudes shown here and the linguistic program chosen for their children's education.

3.2 Results related to research question 2

Our second research question addresses the relationship between school choice and attitudes towards languages. As has been previously mentioned, public schools follow a Catalan-based language policy (i.e. PEV/PIL program), while private schools teach through Spanish (i.e. PIP program) exclusively. At this stage, we wondered whether school choice, that is, private or public, would be linked to favourable attitudes towards a particular language. In order to provide an answer to this second research question, we have related data on parents' language attitudes to the type of school chosen, that is, a contrast has been drawn between parents selecting a bilingual immersion program (i.e. Catalan-based or public schools) and those whose children are involved in a traditional monolingual program (i.e. Spanish-based or private school).

As illustrated in figure 2 below, results partly coincide with previous findings. We see that parents selecting private, thus, monolingual-based schools, show higher scores for English and Spanish, and rank lower the Catalan language. On the contrary, attitudes towards Catalan are high on the part of parents who chose a public, thus, Catalan-based school language policy.

In order to find out whether that difference in attitudes towards Catalan from parents in the private and public sector is significant, we have applied a Mann Withney U test to our data. Results from the MannWithney U test (U = 97.500; z = −975) confirm that such difference is statistically significant (p = 0.000). We see that the main difference in parents' attitudes refers to the Catalan language as the mean rank is lower for private Spanish-based schools than for public Catalan-based programs. Hence, in replying to this second research question, we may state that school choice relates to favourable attitudes towards particular

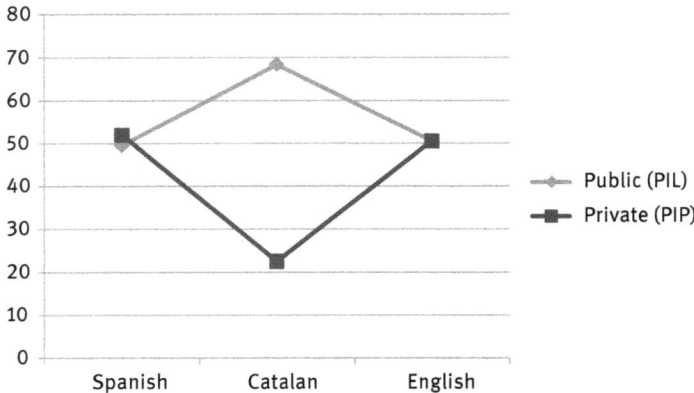

Figure 2: Mean ranks showing language attitudes related to school choice

languages as follows. Private schools relate favourably with English and Spanish over Catalan, while public schools relate favourably with Catalan over English and Spanish. Yet, it is worth mentioning here that attitudes towards English and Spanish are the same for the two parent subgroups (i.e. from private and public institutions). Therefore, while Catalan is highly valued in Catalan-based schools, Spanish and English are also ranked high. We may then state that bilingual immersion programs also relate to favourable attitudes towards the three languages in contact.

As mentioned before, social and political events relate to these findings, but there is something more. In line with Bucholtz and Hall's (2004) ideas, language may be a resource for identity production. The languages present in the school may have had an effect on parents' attitudes (Garrett 2010), which in turn may shape their children's attitudes (Bartram 2006) as well. These last ones may have an effect on their own language learning and multilingual development.

Previous research (Portolés 2011) showed that adults who had been instructed within the framework of a Catalan-based program displayed favourable attitudes toward that language later in life, and their attitudes towards all languages in contact were higher than those of adults being instructed in Spanish-based programs during childhood. We believe that parents from bilingual programs may have also chosen those bilingual programs for their children. These are the parents that now struggle to cope with their children's multilingualism. Familial challenges refer to this subgroup of parents whose children attend public schools that follow a Catalan-based language programs. Fostering a minority language in a community where use and exposure decreases dramatically is a difficult task. Moreover, if there is an interest for introducing a third language, the issue becomes even more complex, especially if it coincides with the promotion of a majority language as the status of a language may be crucial for its acquisition.

Hence, there seems to be a division in terms of attitudes, identity and beliefs which may not only reflect the current situation but may also contribute to it. Language is a resource for identity production; the overwhelming presence of the majority language is shaping children's identity, while influencing parents' beliefs and attitudes towards languages. Our results show that there seem to be two subgroups of parents with opposing attitudes towards the minority language.

In addition to paying attention to the above mentioned division, we are also interested in finding out if there is also a difference in those parents' beliefs about multilingual development. In this line, we formulated our third research question.

3.3 Results related to Research Question 3

We are particularly interested in ascertaining the extent to which parents' linguistic competence may influence the potential actions that they may take to foster their children's multilingual development. Hence, we wonder whether their degree of bilingual competence may be linked to their beliefs on language learning. In order to find that out, we asked parents whether they agreed or not with statements related to (i) the age of onset in learning English, (ii) the suitability of exposing children to TV in English versus attending private academies and (iii) the extent to which the school language policy might affect their emotional development (García and Sylvan 2011).

As illustrated in figure 3 below, we see that the two subgroups of parents present different beliefs. Interestingly, there is a coincidence between parents' perceived degree of bilingual competence and beliefs on multilingual development. On the one hand, we see that those receptive bilinguals believe that the sooner the better, and do not see any link between languages in the school and emotional development. On the other hand, productive bilinguals do not always agree with the early learning of English and see a link between the school language and the emotional development of children.

In order to identify whether the above-quoted difference between the two parents' subgroups is statistically significant we have resorted to a Mann Whitney U Test and Wilcoxon analysis. Results from the test show that the difference in ascertaining that age of onset in learning English ($U = 780$; $W = 2671$; $z = -4,102$) and the role of the school language in the emotional development ($U = 195$; $W = 975$; $z = -8,117$) is statistically significant ($p = 0.000$). From a dynamic perspective, the interaction among multilinguals' languages and between the lan-

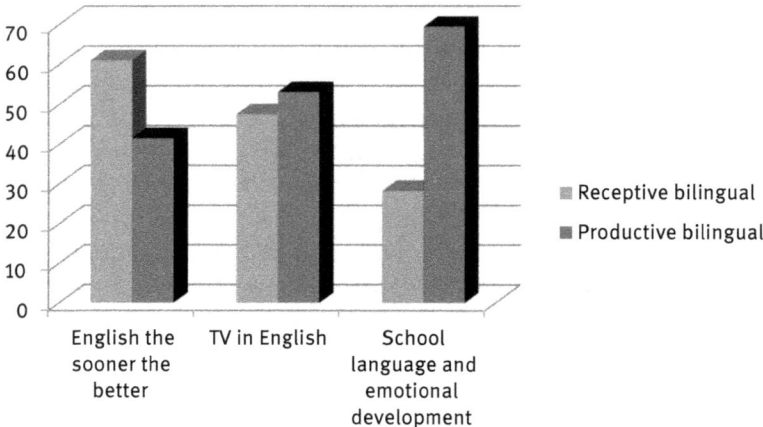

Figure 3: Self-perceived bilingualism and beliefs

guages and the social context might foster more complex reactions and perceptions about their own multilingualism. In this line, we believe that those parents with self-perceived bilingual competence and with previous language learning experiences do think and reflect upon their own and their children's multilingualism as they see how school affects their emotional development. These parents that are now struggling for promoting multilingual development (see also results from RQ2 above) also think that age of onset does not determine the acquisition of the English language. Their challenge in exposing their children to languages other than Spanish may be related to these findings. They see that it is not only English that needs to be socially promoted but also and more urgently Catalan. A language they use and which is not present in a number of activities addressing children like storytelling, arts and crafts, cinema, toys, and the like. On the other hand, receptive bilinguals that only use Spanish make an effort in exposing their kids to English and show a concern for its early acquisition. They focus on the foreign language, while the status, use and learning of Catalan is not regarded as a priority or part of their challenge.

Interestingly, we may say that parents' perceived degree of bilingual competence relates to peculiar views on ways to foster their children's multilingual development. In an attempt to further relate these findings to the school choice a Spearman correlation test has been applied to our data. Results from the Spearman test show that the degree of bilingual competence and school choice correlates (Rho = −0.866) and such correlation is statistically significant ($p = 0.000$). This finding may refer to the issue of ideology, as explained before, which links identity and the sociolinguistic situation. According to Bucholtz and Hall (2004) language is crucial for identity production. The languages present in education may affect parents' attitudes as our data shows. In our case, they also seem to have an effect on parents' beliefs related to the promotion of their children's multilingual development.

We believe that our results illustrate the complexity underlying multilingualism and the existing interaction between the subcomponents of the attitudinal construct. This interaction is further analysed in our research question number 4 which deals with parents' language choice.

3.4 Results related to Research Question 4

In the last research question of our study, we have wondered about the actual use parents make of their language/-s with their own children. We are interested in their use in front of other people as we think that it may illustrate how language use in a multilingual community is sometimes influenced by expectations of others and potential consequences. In order to provide an answer to this question, we observed 20 dyadic mother-child and father-child conversations in the waiting room of the pediatric clinic. As shown in figure 4 below, we see that in 35 % of cases the mother/father employ Catalan with the child and do not switch into Spanish if addressing another parent or child in the waiting room. However, this is not the case in over sixty per cent of the conversations observed. Parents in this last case use Spanish or Catalan with their kids but always change into Spanish when Spanish speakers are present. It is never the case that a mother or father changes from Spanish to Catalan when a Catalan speaker is present.

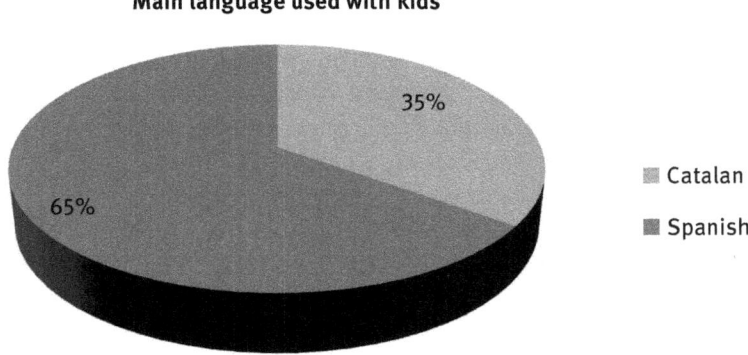

Figure 4: Language used with children in the Pediatrician's waiting room.

Interestingly, and as illustrated in Example 1 below, those children using Catalan with their parents address the other kids they meet in the play area of the waiting room in both Catalan (CAT) and Spanish (SPA).

Example (1)
Mother1 (CAT): *Vine...vols que llegim un conte?* (Come..shall we read a story?)
Child1 (CAT): *No..no..mira..vull jugar..*(No..no...look..I want to play..)
Mother 1 (CAT): *Vale..mira ...cuidao que la nena és xicoteta, eh?..*(OK..look.. watch out...it's a Little girl, ok?)
Child1 (CAT): *Nena? Vols això?* (Little girl? Would you like that?)
Mother1 (CAT): *Di-li Hola, soc X, com et dius?* (Say Hello to her, I am X, What's your name?)
Child2 (SPA): *La...la...mami..ta..*
Child1 (SPA): *Esto... quieres esto?* (This?... would you like this one?)
Mother2 (SPA): *sí cariño déjale el coche...déjale el coche...* (Love lend her the car...lend it to her..)
Child1 (CAT): I a qué jugue? (Then what shall I play with?)
Mother1 (CAT): *doncs juga a una altra cosa...tu eres major....*(Then play a different game...you're older..)

Example (2)
Mother 3 (CAT): *Ala... dus la jaqueta que no fa fred* (Take off your jacket. It's not cold)
Children 3 (SPA): *toma!...mira la casita! (Look a little house)*
Mother 4 (SPA): *(to her kid) ..quieres mirar los juguetes? No la muñeca la tiene el nene ahora...*(Would you like to see the toys? Not the doll, the little boy has it now)
Mother 3 (SPA): (to her kid) *déjale la muñeca, y coje le cocodrilo...va...*(Lend him the doll and take the crocodile instead..come on..)
(Mother 4 notices the two children wear the same school uniform and are probably the same age)
Mother 4 (SPA): *(to mother 3) a que maestra va a X?*(who is his teacher? Is it X?)
Mother 3 (SPA): *no es del otro grupo* (he is in the other group)
Mother 4 (SPA): *ah...*(hm)
Children 3 (SPA): (to children 4) *mira un camión brmm* (look a lorry brrrmm)

As illustrated by Figure 4 and Example 2 above, most parents (n=65%) use Spanish with their kids although they are Catalan speakers. Children in these cases use only Spanish while playing with other children in the play area. Following Liebscher and Dayley-O'Cain (2009), attitudes are negotiated through interaction. Thus, in our case, Catalan and Spanish speakers negotiate which language they will use. They may choose one language or the other because all parents in the study are bilingual. The difference seems to point to their use of the Catalan language. Besides, the use of one language or the other is connected to changing views on social bilingualism.

Great institutional efforts were made in the past to revive the presence of Catalan in society and raise people's awareness of the fact that they could use Catalan in all situations (i.e. addressing all speakers irrespective of their L1). The idea underlying those attempts was to try normalizing social bilingualism. Nevertheless, as previously mentioned, the situation has changed and now efforts seem to be made to undermine the presence of Catalan (e.g. banning TV in that language, restricting teaching hours, among others). As a result, the expected behavior now is using Spanish as default language when meeting a stranger. According to the Theory of Reasoned Action (Garrett, 2010), verbal behavior is influenced by expected consequences and evaluations of such consequences. In our study, most parents switch to Spanish whenever a Spanish speaker is present. In these cases, children observe how their parents change to Spanish if a Spanish interlocutor is present, but never how they switch to Catalan if a Catalan speaker appears on the scene. This is the case of Example 2 above, where the mother uses Catalan (line 1) and then changes into Spanish when the other interlocutor is present (lines 5 and 8). We believe that resorting to the majority language in public space may influence children's verbal behavior and attitudes towards the languages of a bilingual speech community. In fact, a recent study (Portolés, 2015) conducted in the Valencian Community shows how very young children (aged 4–5 years) have preferences for Spanish over Catalan, and how these preferences seem to match with their parents' linguistic behavior.

Our data shows that behavior and beliefs may not have a direct link in terms of language use. Although it seems that both Catalan and Spanish are valued as community languages, most parents resorted to Spanish in public space. The complexity of the relationship between attitudinal subcomponents may be best illustrated by dealing with a multilingual setting and multilingual subjects, as it is the case of our study. Nevertheless, a further analysis of the data dealing with other variables like that of the socioeconomic status, together with the possibility of video-recording the aforementioned dyadic conversations might provide us with useful information for understanding the existing attitudes towards languages in bilingual communities.

4 Conclusion

We have focused on parents' attitudes towards multilingualism and existing challenges that multilingualism presents for them. This paper aimed at examining parents' beliefs and behavior related to language choice and use in a multilingual community with three languages in contact: a majority (ie. Spanish), a minority (i.e. Catalan) and a foreign language (i.e. English). In order to meet our goal we have dealt with (i) parents' language attitudes, (ii) the extent to which school choice may relate to specific attitudes, and (iii) the relationship between bilingual competence and specific beliefs on multilingual development. In addition, we were interested (iv) in identifying the language that parents employed with their children in public space.

Our results show that Spanish and English are ranked higher than Catalan, and that difference is statistically significant according to Friedman Test index. Our study also shows that the linguistic policy adopted in the school chosen by parents has a clear effect on their attitudes towards Catalan, while there is not a difference in parents' attitudes towards Spanish and English. Parents choosing a Catalan-based (i.e. public) school display positive attitudes towards Catalan, Spanish and English, while those selecting a Spanish-based, thus, monolingual (i.e. private) school show positive attitudes towards Spanish and English, and not so much towards Catalan.

In addition to school choice and the linguistic program followed, parents' perceived degree of bilingualism also has an effect on their beliefs about multilingual development. Receptive bilingual parents (i.e. those who knew Spanish and Catalan but used only Spanish) argue for the early introduction of English and the lack of connection between school language and emotional development. On the contrary, productive bilinguals (i.e. parents using both Spanish and Catalan) do not see the urgency in early English learning and relate emotional development to school language. Both parents' subgroups see an advantage in exposing their kids to TV in English. An aspect that they think might be more beneficial than attending private language academies. We have attributed our findings to (i) the dynamism and interaction of attitudinal subcomponents, (ii) the sociolinguistic status of the three languages in contact in the Valencian Community, (iii) the relationship between the school linguistic program and language attitudes as well as to (iv) the effect of language on identity production.

From a descriptive perspective we have observed examples of language choice that also seem to be in line with the sociolinguistic situation in the Valencian Community. We have shown how Spanish seems to be widely accepted while there may be some reluctance to use Catalan with Spanish speakers. This fact together with the high prestige attributed to the English language and the desire to know it may be used as an excuse to undermine the importance of learning minority languages. Furthermore, identity and ideology are not necessarily linked to a particular language, they are constructed, and they may be the effect of language use, and language learning. The power of education for language practices is well-known among politicians, who constantly reform education laws. In addition to that, we cannot ignore the power of mass-media access to information which would actually illustrate the real interest of a given government in multilingualism if three and not only one language were present in the media. Interestingly, Spanish is now the only language used on TV channels and radio stations in the Valencian Community.

The study presented here is subject to a number of limitations. A longer version of the questionnaire complemented by an oral interview with respondents might have provided us with further data on their attitudes. As a suggestion, we believe that further research may consider a deeper analysis of parent-to-parent discourse within the framework of the DMM, as it would account for the dynamic nature of communication, the adaptations we make as we communicate and the attitudes that those adaptations show or promote. These adaptations as Garrett points out (2010) are signals of our own attitudes. This theory may be seen as the implementation of attitudes in discourse. In fact, attitudes are also components of our own communicative competence that "underpin our deployment of linguistic, non-verbal and discursive resources to achieve our communicative goals" (Garrett 2010: 120). These adaptations in multilingual discourse are worth a further analysis (Bourhis, El-Geledi, and Sachdev 2007). More specifically, it would be very interesting to see how multilingual discourse displays attitudinal changes in unstable diglossic communities and its effect on both parents' and children's language attitudes, and how they change and evolve over time.

Acknowledgments

This study is part of a research project funded by Fundació Universitat Jaume I and Caixa Castelló-Bancaixa (P1.1B2011–15) and by the Spanish Ministerio de Economia y Competitividad, co-funded by FEDER (FFI2012–38145). The author would like to thank the reviewers and the editors of this volume for their valuable comments on an earlier version of this chapter. Special thanks to Pediatrician Joaquin Mataix-Gil for his support and help during the data collection process.

References

Ajzen, Icek & Fishbein, Martin. 1980. *Understanding attitudes and predicting social Behavior*. Englewood Cliffs, NJ: Prentice Hall.
Bartram, Brendan. 2006. An examination of perceptions of parental influence on attitudes to language learning. *Educational Research*, 48: 211–221.
Bourhis, Richard El-Geledi, Shaha & Sachdev, Itesh. 2007. Language, ethnicity and intergroup relations. In Ann Weatherall, Bernardette Watson & Cindy Gallois (eds.) *Language, Discourse and Social Psychology* (pp.15–50) Basingstoke: Palgrave Macmillan.
Bucholtz, Mary & Hall, Kira. 2004. Language and identity. In Alessandro Duranti (ed.) *A Companion to Linguistic Anthropology*, 369–389. Malden: Blackwell Publishing.
Cenoz, Jasone. 2009. *Towards Multilingual Education*. Bristol: Multilingual Matters.
Cruz-Ferreira. Madalena. 2011. First language acquisition and teaching. *AILA Review*, 24: 78–87.
García, Ofelia & Sylvan, Claire. 2011. Pedagogies and practices in multilingual classrooms; singularities in pluralities. *The Modern Language Journal*, 95: 385–400.
Garrett, Peter. 2010. *Attitudes to Language*. Cambridge: Cambridge University Press.
Hanson, David.1980. Relationship between methods and findings in attitude behavior research. *Psychology 17*: 11–13.
Herdina, Philip & Jessner, Ulrike. 2002. *A Dynamic Model of Multilingualism*. Clevedon: Multilingual Matters.
Jessner, Ulrike. 2008. A DST Model of Multilingualism and the Role of Metalinguistic Awareness. *The Modern Language Journal*, 92: 270–283.
Lasagabaster, David & Huguet, Angel (eds.). 2007. *Multilingualism in European Bilingual Contexts*. Clevedon: Multilingual Matters.
La Piere, Richard. 1934. Attitudes versus actions. *Social Forces 13. 230–237*.
Liebscher Grit & Dayley-O'Cain Jennifer. 2009. Language Attitudes in Interaction. *Journal of Sociolinguistics* 13. 195–222.
Mihaljevic-Djigunovic, Jelena. 2009. Individual differences in early language programmes In Mariane Nikolov (ed.) *The Age Factor and Early Language Learning*, 199–225. Berlin: Mouton de Gruyter
Nightingale, Richard. 2012. *Bridging the Gap between the Internal and the External: The effect of sociocultural factors in adolescent learners' attitudes towards English*. Berlin: LAP Lambert Academic Publishing.
Pavlenko, Aneta & Blackledge, Adrian. 2004. *Negotiating Identities in Multilingual Contexts*. London: Cromwell press ltd.
Portolés Falomir, Laura. 2011. *A Multilingual Portrait of Language Attitudes in Higher Education*. Saarbrücken: VDM Verlag Dr Müller.
Portolés Falomir, Laura. 2015. *Multilingualism and Very Young Learners. An Analysis of Pragmatic Awareness and Language Attitudes*. Berlin, New York: De Gruyter Mouton.
Preston, Dennis. 2011. Method in (applied) folk linguistics. *AILA Review*, 24:15–39.
Safont, Jorda & Maria Pilar. 2005. *Third Language Learners. Pragmatic Production and Awareness*. Clevedon: Multilingual Matters.
Safont, Jordà & Maria Pilar. 2007. Language use and language attitudes in the Valencian community. In David Lasagabaster and Àngel Huguet (eds.) *Multilingualism in European Bilingual Contexts,* 90–116. Clevedon: Multilingual Matters.

Sears, David. 1983. The persistence of early political predisposition: the role of attitude object and life stage. In Ladd Wheeler & Philip Shaver (eds.) *Review of Personality and Social Psychology*, 251–278.
Wilton, Antje & Stegu, Martin. 2011. Bringing the folk into applied linguistics.(Special Issue) *AILA Review*, 24:1–115.

Part II: **Educational challenges**

William Heidenfeldt
3 Conflict in the second language classroom: a teacher of Spanish facing the complicated dimensions of multilingualism

> several of the kids wear these...tee shirts that say know your history you have to know your history to be free and and I part of me really believes that you should know your history
> (Interview with Dionne Simpson, 6/13)

Abstract: This chapter explores the linguistic and identity transformations of one multilingual teacher of secondary-level Spanish within the United States through her use of language and her selection of lesson material. I interrogate how this instructor of Spanish as a second language negotiates her many positionalities through her linguistic repertoire in the classroom. As teachers move among different linguistic varieties and registers in their classrooms, these teachers are positioned by their administrations, students, and themselves as representatives of the "Other." The second language classroom is thus a space with potentially competing beliefs about language learning, and what it means to be multilingual.

Through the analysis of one Spanish teacher's classroom lessons on language and history, this chapter proposes that, through her language use, this language teacher responds creatively to her shifting linguistic and professional landscapes. These shifting tensions around language learning allow for potential identity transformations that multilingual language users undergo as they operate among different languages and cultures. In these transformations, language users see language, themselves, and others in changed and potentially upsetting ways.

1 Introduction

It was the last period of the school day, and Señora Simpson, as her students called their Spanish teacher, ended her lesson with a cultural presentation[1]. This

---
[1] I use pseudonyms for both the high school and the focal teacher.

William Heidenfeldt, University of California, Berkeley, US, wheidenfeldt@berkeley.edu

second language class in Northern California had spent the period working on the different tenses of the Spanish subjunctive. Simpson was now addressing the cultural and historical content of the chapter in the textbook *Realidades*, which featured a simplified history of the initial European-Aztec contact. The cultural notes displayed images of Mexico City's tourist sites and fact-based summaries, presenting this first contact as a bloodless encounter and the inevitable adoption of Spanish as the civilizing language of the land.

Instead of using these cultural notes, Dionne Simpson presented an alternative history in Spanish through a self-designed lecture that focused solely on the pre-European history of central and southern Mexico. With a hand-drawn outline of Mexico and labels of its pre-European cities, she described the struggles between the Toltecs of central Mexico and the Chichimecas of northern Mexico. The students, mostly European-American and born in Northern California, followed their teacher's lecture intently, alternately watching her and taking notes. A few students offered responses when prompted. Because this indigenous, pre-Colombian legacy is seldom taught in US history classes, students in this Spanish classroom were encountering a new history in a potentially surprising context. In relating it, Simpson was giving voice to those silenced in other history classes, introducing an unofficial history. In concluding her lesson, Simpson asked what else the students knew about Mexico's history. After a few seconds of silence, one student responded, "Nada." The teacher asked with surprise, "¿Nada de la historia de México?" ["Nothing about Mexico's history?"]. Another student then declared, "It's not something you learn in school…until like now." As we shall see, the lesson in this second language classroom conflicted with the legitimized curriculum sanctioned by the textbook. This conflict indicates larger tensions around the multiple understandings of language and language learning, and in turn impacts language learning and teachers of second languages.

2 Competing Notions of Language, Language Learning, and the Role of Language Teachers

Second language teachers' personally motivated, creatively designed lessons and the legitimized, state-approved second language curriculum form two conflicting poles in the second language classroom. At one pole, Dionne Simpson's Spanish-language history lesson exemplifies her own pedagogical investment through her revision of a textbook lesson on the Spanish Conquest of Mexico. This unique lesson plan reflects the teacher's multilingual and multicultural interests, not expressly linked to formal learning expectations or student assessment. Although the content of the lesson itself is not opposed to state-approved curriculum, this teacher's goal in presenting it ("you have to know your history to be free") does not align neatly with the specific goals of the state's foreign language expectations.

At the other end of the spectrum, the state-approved and district-enforced California Foreign Language Framework legitimizes formalized academic goals for students of second and foreign languages, and directs the approved second language curricula that school districts and independent schools adopt. The Framework comes from a monolingual bias; in this context, within each second language classroom, there is one target language and culture to be learned. By first examining the rationale of the California Foreign Language Framework, we can uncover the larger discourse of language learning as primarily an economically beneficial skill achieved through the mastery of academic subject matter. As such, this discourse influences the official learning standards that focus on assessment of this mastery, not on development of deeper understandings of conflict and history as embedded in language and language learning.

2.1 Considering The California Foreign Language Framework

> If California students are to become world-class business leaders, they will require an education comparable to their overseas peers. (*Foreign Language Framework for California Public Schools, Kindergarten Through Grade Twelve*: 3)

The authors of the framework–administrators, teachers, corporate advisors, and professors from both private and public universities base the curriculum's rationale and content on three goals which appear as motifs throughout the publication:
- academic achievement
- educational reform
- leadership in the global economy (*Foreign Language Framework for California Public Schools, Kindergarten Through Grade Twelve*: 2–3)

The authors of the foreword situate these goals within the context of California's importance in the global economy (p. v). They link this importance to student proficiency in a language other than English. This proficiency develops students' intellectual skills and cultural understandings and, ultimately, "provides access to the world's marketplaces" (p. v). Language proficiency is thus an asset that, like a passport or bankcard, can help students succeed on the global playing field.

This framework lays out the plans for California schools' language programs, including suggestions for curriculum design, assessment tools, and professional development, all of which support student achievement and leadership in the global economy. Each district implements the foreign language program, and then monitors each school's performance through standardized test scores and submission of program materials that align with the framework. Second language teachers thus receive the structure of the framework and approved textbooks to guide their curriculum planning. Nonetheless, this framework and the approved curricula can conflict with teachers' professional beliefs and knowledge about language learning and use, with the classroom becoming a space of conflict between the state's expectations and teachers' beliefs and practices.

2.2 Language as Economic Commodity

The belief that language is a commodity, a skill that can be measured and evaluated, has influenced administrators', teachers', and learners' opinions about language education (Johnson and Golombek 2011: 37). This commodification of language is an understanding of language as comprising assessable skills, a commodity that can be acquired, improved, and then used publicly as a form of economic, social, or symbolic capital (Bourdieu 1979: 326, 331). Understanding language in this way enables it to be subject to rigorous assessment, with a set list of objective categories that assessors (administrators, teachers, and learners) can use to determine its usable value.

In this understanding, linguistic ability is a "value added" (Heining-Boynton and Redmond 2013: 53); that is, it represents additional social and linguistic capital that learners can exchange for economic gain in the global marketplace. This perspective on language and its use has altered administrative expectations for language education. Heining-Boynton and Redmond (2013) argue that "[t]he language education community must step up to the plate, primed to do its part to prepare productive global citizens" (p. 56).

As evidenced in the California Foreign Language Framework, this understanding of language as an economic commodity drives the creation of assessable, clearly defined learning outcomes at individual schools. To demonstrate how students achieve their school's student learning outcomes, administrators and faculty create formal checklists and narratives that summarize the relationship between student performance and the school's target outcomes. This type of assessment then shows the success to which schools achieve the expectations established by the Foreign Language Framework. This trickle-down approach (from California's Department of Education to individual school sites) reifies language as a set of skills that students need in order to have something additional to bring to the global marketplace.

2.3 Language as a Sociocultural Resource

In contrast to the ideas of language as a commodity and, consequently, language teachers as mere dispensers of a commodity, considering them as language users with multilingual repertoires presupposes an understanding of language itself as "comprising dynamic constellations of sociocultural resources" (Hall et al. 2005: 2). These resources inextricably link language users to the social, cultural, and historical contexts of the languages that they use at any given moment. From this perspective, language is not an assessable skill nor a fixed target but rather a cultural practice that is linked closely to users' lived experiences, daily activities, and group membership (Heller 2003: 474). In this light, language is a resource that members of a community of practice draw upon to make sense of themselves and others. The second language classroom is thus a space with competing beliefs about what language and culture are and what students should know about them. Language teachers guide student learning of language and culture within these competing beliefs.

We see this conflict in the classroom where the unofficial history of Mexico was presented in contrast to the textbook's "official" history. These tensions are caused by the potential "transformations of language and identity" (Heller 2003: 473) that multilingual language users undergo as they operate among different languages and cultures. Although the California Framework for Foreign Languages does not address the personal and professional transformations that language learning can cause, these transformations reveal the deeper processes of language learning, of language education, and of being a multilingual user of language. In these processes, language users see language, themselves, and others in changed and potentially upsetting ways. Engaging learners with other languages, traditions, and histories opens up spaces for both students' and teachers' own personal and academic transformations. These transformations are revealed particularly in second language teachers, who both move among different languages and linguistic registers in their classrooms and position themselves and are positioned by their administrations and students as expert representatives of the "Other," the target language and culture.

2.4 Positionings of Multilingual Language Teachers

Language teachers themselves possess multilingual repertoires as a result of ongoing and diverse experiences with the different languages in their lives. These multilingual repertoires are often the result of some combination of a multilingual family, of formal schooling, or of living abroad. In order to have this multilingual repertoire, language teachers must have, at the most basic level, the ability to operate among languages in order to think and then communicate with others.

Despite making language learning quantifiably valuable, the conceptualization of language as commodity has produced local resistance in language classrooms. In these spaces, teachers address specific, shifting contexts of the languages they teach, exhibiting their agency through their pedagogical decision-making. Their decisions include using both the official, state-mandated curriculum aligned with their language program's goals and the personally created, unofficial lessons and lived stories that they bring to their students. The teachers' subjectivities challenge the idea of language as only a commodified skill, in turn, making language a living, dynamic resource that is as personal as it is interactive. The interactions of these oppositions (i.e. language-as-commodity vs. language-as-personal-resource, language learning-as-objective vs. language learning-as-subjective, and teacher-as-information-provider vs. teacher-as-lived history) magnify the conflict in the goals of second language education. Added to the conflict between state-approved goals and teachers' pedagogical beliefs are local and national tensions surrounding language use and identity. These tensions situate the work of second and foreign language teachers in a context of potentially clashing ideologies about language and language learning.

3 The Spanish Classroom in Context

The San Francisco East Bay region provides a linguistically and culturally rich context in which language teachers perform their work. Spanish has a unique significance as both a commonly spoken immigrant language and as the most commonly studied world language in the high schools within the East Bay. Although casual observers may highlight a certain continuity in the everyday use and academic study of Spanish due to its prevalence in the region, teachers, students, and other users of Spanish sense a tension in the recognized prestige and power of Spanish in both local and global contexts. Approximately 28 percent of the population identify as immigrants (approximately 700,000 immigrants), of which 25 percent (approximately 175,000) have arrived from Mexico[2]. These residents speak a various languages in different contexts, of which English and Spanish are the most commonly and widely spoken. Additionally, many of the Mexican-born families speak an indigenous language (namely, Nahautl or a Mayan language) alongside or in place of Spanish.

---

[2] http://csii.usc.edu/documents/EASTBAY_web.pdf

We see emerging tensions for the Spanish teacher between language use and power distribution most clearly through how Spanish, Mexican indigenous languages, and English are positioned in both the official, text-based curriculum and in teachers' self-generated lessons. The state framework reflects the assumption of one nation-one language in addressing target languages studied in California classrooms, eliding the multilingual realities of many citizens of Latin America. Consequently, in their presentations of discrete Latin American countries, state-approved textbooks present each nation as monolingual, if not multicultural. Spanish teachers' own lived experiences often contradict this monolingual framework since their own experiences might connect them to a variety of monolingual and multilingual speakers of European and indigenous languages. The tension between a monolingual Spanish framework and a multilingual, culturally based framework challenges teachers to examine the shifting values of the many languages that could appear in their Spanish classrooms.

In this study, I turn to the reflections and activities of one teacher of high school-level Spanish to document how she responds to competing tensions within a profession invested in the cultural and linguistic study of California's second most widely spoken language. These tensions include the state's expectations for second language learning; immigration patterns of Spanish speakers into the East Bay; the teacher's personal value of Spanish; the academic Spanish that the teacher presents to students; the local varieties of familiar Spanish present in the classroom; the inclusion of indigenous, non-European Mexican languages; and the presence of English in the classroom. How does this teacher of Spanish in an English-medium public school construct her identity as a Spanish teacher within these conflicting goals and expectations? Which languages, histories, and legacies are privileged in the classroom by the textbook and by the teacher? How does she position herself and Spanish through her pedagogical decisions?

3.1 Methodology

The data come from an urban high school, East Bay Mechanical School, located in the region where I live and work. My proximity to the site and my familiarity with the local context and school district gained me access to the site. East Bay Mechanical School (EBMS) is an urban public high school in the San Francisco East Bay area, governed by the local school district. The school district established the school in 1914, and, from the beginning, it served a multilingual student population, primarily heritage speakers of Italian. At the time of the study, this particular school offered four years of instruction, organized within clustered academies on the campus. Students in tenth, eleventh, and twelfth grades registered in one of the school's seven academies, each of which promoted specific contexts for learning according to students' multiple abilities. Students who planned to pursue four-year higher education after high school were required to study a language other than English for a minimum of two years. The world language program, as the school calls it, thus crossed all the academies, complying with the schoolwide learning goal of offering a curriculum that meets the University of California entrance requirements.

I captured the subjective ways in which one high school teacher of Spanish, Dionne Simpson, understood her professional activities and relationships to language use, using ethnographic methods, focusing specifically on teacher narratives and activity. I collected data using van Lier's (1988) model of educational ethnography, seeking direct evidence of the interrelationships between the focal subject's personal and professional history and the local context within which she taught. Thus, the guiding activities for the data collection that I performed as researcher in the classroom were *asking* and *watching* (Erickson 1981 *via* van Lier 1988: 56) through interviews and classroom observations. Ritchie and Wilson (2000) call for narrative as a research methodology that captures the relationship between an individual's reflection and activities: "in forcing us to compose, articulate, and reinterpret our lives, [narrative] can move us toward action" (p. 21). Furthermore, consistent with Bahktin's notion of dialogism, narratives offer language teachers imagined spaces to embrace or resist outside positionings of what they should do (Reis 2011: 33), becoming "the intertextual ground for contesting others' voices, re-accentuating their utterances with new meaning, and re-interpreting the self through [dialogue with] another" (Hall et al. 2005: 156). Simpson's stories created a space in which, as researcher, I sought to contemplate "the multiple ideologies of schooling and personhood as they intersected" in her life (Ritchie & Wilson 2000: 12). The narratives of her linguistic history and her pedagogical beliefs provided Simpson with "opportunities to see [her] teacher identity as performative, as 'effects' or constructions rather than as natural, inevitable, or essential" (Ritchie & Wilson 2000: 14).

I conducted two audio-recorded interviews after school with Simpson in her classroom and nine classroom video-recordings, taking fieldnotes during each recorded activity. The interviews framed the classroom recordings: the first interview occurred three weeks before the first classroom recording, and the second interview took place three weeks after the final classroom recording. In the first interview, I asked six guiding questions focusing on a biographical and linguistic description of Simpson, her early encounters with Spanish, her motivation to become a teacher of Spanish, and her perceptions of students' motivations to study Spanish. During the video-recordings, I positioned myself as a nonparticipating observer behind the students' desks. In my fieldnotes, I specifically noted the time and utterances during her instruction that provided clear connections to this study's central questions or that illustrated ideas introduced by the teacher during the pre-observation interview.

After completing the classroom recordings, I edited short clips framing specific moments that I then played back to Simpson during the post-observation interview. During this final, audio-recorded interview, I triangulated the data from the classroom recordings, asking the teacher questions that focused alternately on specific pedagogical decision-making and on broader reflections of the profession and of her identity as a teacher of Spanish. These classroom moments and the teacher's reflections on them provided insight into how one teacher responded in a local context to the challenges of multilingualism and language learning within broader social and cultural contexts.

3.2 Focal Subject: "I've been a difficult personality all my life!"

"Señora" Dionne Simpson spent her workdays in a colorfully decorated classroom on EBMS's first floor. My preliminary meeting with her took place in spring 2013 after the last class of the day. Proverbs, moral sentences, and political-artistic images competed for space on her classroom walls with examples of student work. The images came from both indigenous and national communities of Latin America, providing linguistic and cultural nuances not apparent in the textbook curriculum. Some of the artifacts were Spanish-English bilingual, indicating the variety of linguistic communities to whom the information would be available (See Figure 1).

The purpose of this first meeting was to discuss her participation in the case study and then to schedule my visits to her classroom. Our conversation began with my self-introduction and my research interests in Romance linguistics and second language learning. She identified with my interests because she had earned a doctorate in Spanish at a public university in California, specializing in twentieth century Latin American literatures and cultures, and, like I, had taught at a variety of levels from pre-kindergarten through the undergraduate level. Through these professional and personal connections, Dionne Simpson positioned herself immediately as an experienced and sensitive interlocutor who had spent much reflective time in desks not unlike those of her students.

Previously a high school instructor of English literature and, more recently, a chair of the school's World Languages department[3], Simpson was presently

---

3 I use the term "world languages" in contexts in which the school administration and language teachers did. This term has replaced "foreign languages" in most state-created educational literature and departmental names since 2010.

Figure 1: Samples of posters in Dionne Simpson's classroom

teaching Spanish full-time. Her current teaching assignments included third and fourth year Spanish (Spanish 3 and 4), non-Honors electives for students. Additionally, she chose to be a teacher union representative, which required regular communication with both union and non-union teachers on staff. Until the prior school year, Simpson had served as the head of the school's Environmental Academy, a position that afforded her direct encounters with more students and more colleagues.

These professional responsibilities are linked to her self-professed "very political" identity. In these selections from the first interview, Simpson positions herself as a user of different languages in a specifically political context–here, solidarity meetings for the citizens of Nicaragua during the Revolución Popular Sandinista in the 1980s. Although a native speaker of English and an English-dominant language user, her use of Spanish in the context of these political meetings recalled in the following narrative indicate her own resistance to a label imposed by others:

> when I was very political...mid-eighties early- to mid-eighties um until I had to go back to working fulltime and {laugh} supporting the kids um which was really I think how **I honed my Spanish** uh um you know having political arguments with men who were **shocked** that I was as fluent as I was in Spanish because you're a **gringa** yes but...but I can argue speak

Spanish with you argue and speak Spanish and argue politics with you (Interview with Dionne Simpson, 5/1/13, speaker's emphasis)

Not only is she a "gringa...who can speak Spanish and argue politics," but also a speaker who can use language to defend herself. Simpson "hones" her use of the language through "political arguments with men" who are native speakers of Spanish. Spanish is a tool for her here, if not a potential weapon. Her use of the deictics "I" and "you," and her switch to direct speech suggest that her use of Spanish in this remembered event was more than just for communicative competence. Indeed, as a gringa, appropriating Spanish for political arguments with a group of Nicaraguan native speakers, and as a woman, gaining respect and legitimacy from Nicaraguan men, suggests a symbolic competence, an ability to understand the meaning-making potential and contexts of semiotic forms (Kramsch 2006: 251). Simpsons's switch to direct speech ("you're a gringa yes but I can argue speak Spanish with you"), in which she voices both sides of the dialogue, illustrates her response to precarious position she is in as a non-native woman speaker of Spanish. She points to both her national (i.e. U.S.) identity and her identity as a woman, which foreshadows some of the work observed in her classroom. Simpson understands the power of this language in this context spoken by these people, herself included, and this understanding provides a foundational memory of how she positions herself as a user of Spanish.

Simpson continues, exploiting her positionality as multilingual:

and one of them was being really obnoxious about Sartre and I said uh I read Sartre in French you know {whispering, barely audible} they couldn't stand it (Interview with Dionne Simpson, 5/1/13, speaker's emphasis)

Simpson's declaration of having read the philosopher Jean-Paul Sartre in French to a Spanish-speaking man who may not have been able to read French is revealing. Her whispered statement that "they couldn't stand it" points to a quiet, confrontational satisfaction that she can do something that these men do not expect of her. She matches them in this perceived multilingual power game. After having established herself as a competent user of Spanish in one particular domain (political discussions), she reveals more about her linguistic capability through her literacy in French. Not only can she read French, she can read philosophical texts in the language, the admission of which reportedly upsets the group of men. She is not the monolingual, US "gringa" that they were expecting to encounter. In this narrative, she establishes an oppositional multilingual identity, which she develops as she concludes the retelling of this memory, shifting frames from broadly political to specifically feminist and then personally evaluative:

we would have meetings in Spanish...think what I felt more about that was th-the sexism of the whole situation which is one part of the culture that I'm **not** comfortable with and so I have to defy it right I'm not usually that obnoxious to people I don't usually flaunt things but he was being {lowering voice} such an asshole {laugh}... I think...I've been a difficult personality all my life (Interview with Dionne Simpson, 5/1/13, speaker's emphasis)

She labels the context of these political meetings for Nicaragua ("the whole situation") as sexist and links that sexism to "one part of the culture." Although demonstrating a comfort level with the language and with an imagined community of speakers from Nicaragua, she perceives an uncomfortable embedding of sexism in Nicaraguan culture. A fundamental conflict arises between Simpson's desire to pass for enough of a native-like speaker so to be taken as an equal conversational partner and her not wanting to pass as a native woman speaker, with the sexism that that entails. This discomfort, personified by one man who questions her linguistic ability in Spanish, leads her to "flaunt things" like her multilingualism and her capability as a female language user. This behavior exemplifies Simpson's internal conflict, one that will also play out in her classroom.

Her multilingual competence is thus a tool for defiance against others' preconceived expectations of who she is and what she can do. Her tag of "all my life" is noteworthy because it brings the remembered story from thirty years ago in line with her contemporary self, the one who still uses Spanish, but now as a Spanish instructor in a high school classroom in Northern California. In the following classroom analysis, we catch a snapshot of a speaker who still uses Spanish to defy preconceived notions of what should be taught in the classroom and how Spanish itself should be presented.

In Bay Area classrooms, both native speakers and learners position the Spanish language within a continuum of conflicting statuses, ranging from highly valued as an academic language to its association as a first language for speakers of low socioeconomic status. As a Spanish teacher, Simpson links her self-described defiance to her classroom presentation of the target language and culture. Simpson consciously spotlights minority languages and cultures of the Spanish-speaking world in lesson plans that accompany the course textbook *Realidades*. These selections sometimes support the "official" textbook curriculum sanctioned by the California Foreign Language Framework, as is the case in her reviews of the chapter's grammar. Some self-designed lessons, however, go beyond the official curriculum. They legitimize languages and histories not readily endorsed by the school-supplied materials, as evidenced in Simpson's alternative presentation of Mexico's history.

Through her pedagogical choices, Simpson resists fixed ideas about language use in Latin America and Spain. For example, in a focused lesson on the divisive sixteenth-century figure La Malinche, a multilingual Nahua woman and Hernán de Cortés's translator and lover, Simpson asks her students to consider a question that already frames her subject and seemingly limits her students' possible understandings of this figure:

> pero la la pregunta es que si fue una mujer buena o una mujer mala
>
> [but the the question is whether or not she was a good woman or a bad woman]
>
> (Classroom Observation, 5/14/13)

This constitutes a turning point in this lesson, where the figure of La Malinche comes to symbolize more than simply a historical character associated with the Spanish Conquest of Mexico. As we shall see, Simpson problematizes certain ideas about a woman's ability to move with ease between languages and cultures (including those of both the dominant and the dominated peoples) and her potential worth in society.

4 Analysis and Findings

4.1 "La Maldición de Malinche"

The data set comes from Dionne Simpson's intermediate-level Spanish foreign language class. This part of the lesson occurred about during the last period of the school day. After the students had completed a grammar review, Simpson announced that the class would listen to "La maldicíon de Malinche" ("The Curse of Malinche"), a contemporary Mexican folk song that critiques the Spanish conquest of Mexico. In the song, nameless indigenous people observe the Spanish invasion. The Nahua companion of the Spanish conqueror Cortés, Malinche herself does not appear directly as a character, but the narrator roots the decimation of pre-European Mexico in her supposedly traitorous acts. The song does not limit its critique to the colonial period, but positions this conquest as ongoing, expanding the timeframe from the first Spanish colonizers to the contemporary Mexican citizens who "humiliate" and treat "as...foreigner[s] in [their] own land" the indigenous population[4]. Before listening to the song, Simpson distributed the lyrics and then began describing the historical subject Malinche.

---

4 *"Pero si llega cansado/un indio de andar la sierra/lo humillamos y lo vemos/como extraño por su tierra"* ["But if an Indian arrives tired/from walking the mountains/we humiliate him and we see him/as a stranger in his land"] (Palomares, "La Maldición de Malinche")

4.2 Women on the Edge: Dionne Simpson, Malinche, and "Excellent" Language Users

Dionne Simpson introduced her students to La Malinche through a self-designed narrative of the Nahua woman's adult life. Simpson's brief narrative begins with the arrival of Hernán Cortés in the present-day Yucatan Peninsula and ends with the birth of Cortés's and Malinche's son, Martín, considered the first child of mixed indigenous and Spanish heritage. The data that follow in this section all come from a continuous lecture that Simpson delivered as part of the larger lesson featuring "La maldición de Malinche."

DS1	entonces cuando llegó aquí!	so when he arrived here
DS2	encontré a Malinche como esclava	I met Malinche as a slave
DS3	y ella? pudiera hablar cuales idiomas?	and she was able to speak which languages
DS4	nahuatl sí eh el idioma azteca y: maya	Nahuatl yes eh the Aztec language and Maya
DS5	entonces ahora	so now
DS6	tenía el español para traducir español a	she had Spanish in order to translate Spanish to
DS7	maya	Maya
DS8	y luego maya a nahuatl	and then Maya to Nahuatl

(Classroom Observation, 5/14/13)

Simpson first describes Malinche as a slave whom Cortés meets, then emphasizes Malinche as a multilingual woman operating between languages, which becomes the frame for Simpson's narrative (l.3–8). Interestingly, Simpson's use of Spanish includes two morphological errors: in line 2, the first person "encontré" should be "encontró" to refer to Cortés, and in line 3, the imperfect subjunctive "pudiera" should be the indicative "podía." Although Simpson uses these grammatically incorrect verb forms, it diminishes neither the impact of her narrative nor her expertise as a user of Spanish. She is able to tell the story of Malinche in a clearly understood way.

Throughout the first part of the lesson, Simpson spotlights Malinche's capability to move between languages. Simpson positions Malinche as more than a language *speaker* here: she is a language *user*, able to translate from one code to another. She "had" these languages and was able to operate among them. But, as Simpson's classroom narrative details, Malinche's linguistic ability makes her exceptional:

DS15	pero Malinche! era **muy** inteligente	but Malinche was very smart
DS16	y aprendió el español	and she learned Spanish
DS17	y la otra cosa excelente que es que	and the other excellent thing that is that
DS18	ella sabía hablar nahuatl	she knew how to speak Nahuatl
DS19	hay dos registros de nahuatl	there are two registers of Nahuatl
DS20	en casa ah! *pialli*	at home ah! "hello" (tr. Nahuatl)
DS21	okay pero con el **señor**! con el em-	okay but with the lord with the em-
DS22	emperador	emperor
DS23	hay que hablar de una manera	you have to speak in a
DS24	completamente diferente	completely different way
DS25	hay que repetir cada cosa con tres	you have to repeat each thing with three
DS26	sinónimos	synonyms
DS27	hay que hablar co:n prefijos y sufijos	you have to speak with prefixes and suffixes
DS28	que que expresan reverencia	that that express reverence
DS29	es muy complicada	it's very complicated

(Classroom Observation, 5/14/13)

In this part of the description, Simpson does more than list the languages that Malinche uses: she judges Malinche as "muy inteligente" (l.15), stressing the degree to which Malinche is intelligent, and her ability to move between different Nahuatl registers as "excelente" (l.17). This evaluation positions Malinche as a language learner with an expanding linguistic repertoire, which differs from accounts of her that focus solely on the effects of her role as Cortés's courtesan (as discussed in Karttunen 1997, Cypess 1991, Candelaria 1980).

Simpson provides examples of Malinche's diaphasic variation in her native Nahuatl (l.25–28), a linguistic privilege ordinarily reserved to politically powerful Nahuatl men, to prove Malinche's power through her language knowledge and use. This is a contested power, though, because Cortés was able to use her translation ability and indigenous identity to be welcomed into Tenochtitlán at the same time that Malinche was able to use exactly the same features to interpret the ideas and desires of the Nahuatl speakers (Candelaria 1980).

Simpson is telling two stories in this slice of the narrative. On the surface, she details and comments on the life and linguistic power of a woman historically portrayed as divisive because of how she and others used her multilingual ability. Simultaneously, Simpson provides subtle insight to her students on her own linguistic and political journey. Simpson can describe and marvel at Malinche's abilities because she too possesses an understanding of variation within Nahuatl, alongside degrees of fluency in other languages.

After describing how Malinche operates between her languages, Simpson brings her students out of her Malinche narrative momentarily to mention the traitorous behavior that unnamed others have claimed about Malinche:

DS38	dicen que ella traicionó a su gente!	they say that she betrayed her people
DS39	y luego ella tuvo hijo?	and then she had a son
DS40	con Cortés y su hijo que se llamaba	with Cortés and her/their son whose name was
DS41	Martín! Cortés	Martín Cortés
DS42	bueno Cortés tenía dos hijos	all right Cortés had two sons
DS43	los dos se llamaban Martín Cortés	both of them were named Martín Cortés
DS44	uno con su esposa! legítima! en España	one with his legitimate wife in Spain
DS45	y otra otro con Malinche	and the other (f.) the other (m.) with Malinche

(Classroom Observation, 5/14/13)

She raises her tone at the end of line 38, emphasizing the significance of this statement. Simpson's statement acknowledges this popular, dominant understanding of la Malinche since Mexican independence from Spain in the early 19th century (Karttunen 1997). She then returns to the narrative, adding the fact that Cortés and Malinche had an illegitimate son together named Martín, recognized as the first *mestizo*:

DS46	y entonces el fue dicen el primer mestizo	and so he was they say the first mestizo
DS47	que:s mestizo	what is a mestizo
St48	it's a it's the it's r- the mix between two-	it's a it's the it's r- the mix between two-
DS49	-sí! la combinación de indígena y:	-yes the combination of native and
DS50	los españoles lo blanco	the Spanish the White

(Classroom Observation, 5/14/13)

She asks the class to identify the word "*mestizo*" (l.47), to which one student responds in English (l.48). Simpson switches the classroom discourse back to Spanish and recasts the student's answer (l.49–50). This switch back and forth between Spanish and English suggests that the primary work at this moment in the language classroom is not for students to practice forms in the target language; rather, it is primarily about verifying student understanding of a cultural lesson. Simpson insists on *her* own use of Spanish but not her students'. English and Spanish remain juxtaposed in this bit of classroom discourse, not blended in any one speaker's turns at talk. Additionally, in characterizing the mixed cultures, she adds on the descriptor "lo blanco" (l.50), which brings in the notion of a distinct race, previously absent from her linguistically focused lesson. In the end, she does not return to this idea, but its implication of racial mixing lingers as part of the lesson.

To expand Simpson's idea of mixture introduced in the story of Martín, she describes the naming of Malinche as a combination of both Spanish and Nahuatl linguistic and cultural processes, beginning with the Spaniards' baptizing her as "Marina." To illustrate the development of Malinche's name, Simpson writes on the whiteboard to show the students three linguistic processes at work: (1) the change in liquid consonants, from the trilled Spanish /r/ to the alveolar lateral approximant /l/ in Nahuatl; (2) the translation of the honorific Spanish title *Doña* to the Nahuatl honorific suffix –*tzin*; and (3) the palatalization of /tz/ in *Malintzin* to /tʃ/ in *Malinche*. To illustrate the last process, she vocally stresses those specific consonants. This explanation reinforces Simpson's expert linguistic knowledge as she explains, in simplified terms, multilingual phonological and morphological adaptations in the very name of her lesson's subject.

Figure 2: The linguistic changes in the name of Malinche (Classroom Observation, 5/14/13)

At this point, Simpson poses the critical central question of this lesson to her students:

> pero la la pregunta es que si fue una mujer buena o una mujer mala porque traicionó? Cortés no hubiera sido capaz de conquistar a México sin Malinche no?
>
> [but the the question is whether or not she was a good woman or a bad woman because she betrayed? Cortés would not have been able to conquer Mexico without Malinche no?]
>
> (Classroom Observation, 5/14/13)

Simpson points toward the written name of *Martin el primer mestizo* on the whiteboard while saying the causal clause "*porque traicionó*." Her raised tone at the end of that clause posits a rhetorical question to her students. This interrogative structure is echoed in her tag of "no" and a raised tone at the end of the following statement. Interestingly, the verb *traicionar* is a transitive verb, but, in Simpson's utterance, she supplies no direct object. This absence emphasizes the questioning of Malinche's acts as a traitor and avoids naming what or whom she betrayed.

The final parts of this lesson shift from a description of Malinche to a description of the instruments in the song "La maldición de Malinche." Simpson directs student attention to specific instruments: "*las guitarras las cuerdas...la los flautas y los tambores*" ["the guitars the strings the (f. sing.) the (m. pl.) flutes and the drums"]. As Simpson focuses student listening on particular instruments, she emphasizes their cultural origins. She categorizes them by the ones originating in Europe ("*instrumentos europeos*") and those originating in the Americas ("*instrumentos indígenas*"). The flutes and the drums are of indigenous origin and provide the foundation for the melody and rhythm of the song.

Simpson comments that the guitars are not just European but originally North African, bringing to light a longer timeline than the one proposed in the textbook chapter. These instruments have traveled from North Africa to Spain during the European Middle Ages, then to Mexico during the Spanish colonial period. Here, the guitars appear in a twentieth-century folk song that first juxtaposes, verse-by-verse, Moorish-European instruments with pre-Colombian ones, eventually putting them all together in the final verse and chorus. Simpson presents this "blend" or hybrid as "interesting" and worthy of students' attention. What begins as *either* European or indigenous American, both in the music and in her description, becomes *both*, resulting in a blend. This is, however, in contrast to the song's lyrics, which side with Mexico's indigenous peoples, even as the music becomes blended. Simpson's depiction essentially reframes the chapter's focus from the *contact* between the Spanish and the indigenous Mexicans to the *mixing* of several languages and cultures, first through her retelling of Malinche's life, then more emphatically, in her contextualization of the lesson's focal song. The teacher does not, however, ignore the unequal and shifting power present in this mixing of cultures, especially as she puts into question Malinche's role in the Conquest and the musical arrangement in "La maldición de Malinche."

4.3 "Speak in a completely different way"

Already perceived as an expert in Spanish in her classroom, Simpson in this narrative pushed the boundary of her own linguistic identity to demonstrate her ability to "speak in a completely different way" from what is expected of a language teacher. She resisted the notion that her work was only to provide textbook lessons in Spanish to her students so that they could pass tests and meet school requirements. Her resistance demonstrated a certain courage to teach both what she knew and what she believed to be right. Simpson provided her students (and herself) complicated examples of past and present subjects who speak in a variety of ways, often expanding the restricted views that larger power structures, such as entrenched gender roles and national and professional identities, place upon them. For Malinche, although remaining the subservient right arm of Cortés, she provided the voice that linked the Spanish to the Aztecs and, eventually, the colonizers to the colonized. Simpson goes beyond the curricular expectations for her teaching by using the language to craft her own historical narratives. Malinche and Simpson have different levels of power within different historical constraints, but they share the ability to operate between languages. Conversely, the students themselves did not speak often, and they used one language, English, as their preferred language, rarely moving between languages in speech.

Simpson brings to light other power structures, but not all, in her Spanish classroom, in addition to the textbook's construction of the unidimensional Mexican state. Different histories, languages, cultural memories, and overlapping timescales intersect each of these power structures. In reflecting on her teaching of alternative Mexican histories that spotlight indigenous histories alongside the official Conquest-centered history, Simpson claims

> it has to be in a context there's a long lo:ng history that's these kids are living in this place where a hundred and fifty years ago there was so little here and other people live in cultures where they **have** a sense of history where it goes back and it goes back. (Interview with Dionne Simpson, 6/13)

For her, teaching Spanish to residents of Northern California must be "in a context." This context does not emerge entirely from the textbook and the official curriculum nor does Simpson clearly delimit the context. Rather, Simpson wants her students to see the historicity of Spanish (indeed, of languages other than English) in the context of pre-modern, pre-national North American history. The lesson on Malinche addresses certain histories that the textbook ignores, although Simpson does not extend those histories to comparisons that might be fruitful for students in an increasingly multilingual California. Simpson does not acknowledge that "these kids are living in this place" once inhabited by dozens of indigenous tribes with diverse languages, then colonized by the Spanish and the Spanish language, then recognized briefly as its own brief, multilingual republic, before finally becoming a U.S. state. Simpson contrasts what these students do not know with unnamed "other people," who, in the context of this lesson and her positionality during the interviews, are likely the hybrid peoples of Mexico and Central America but not the ones in her students' immediate location.

This "long history," which Simpson emphasizes through the repetition of the word "long" and her elongation of its vowel, functions on a different timescale than that of the focus of this particular chapter, entitled "Encuentro entre culturas" ("Encounter between Cultures"), which highlights the Iberian cultural roots in its presentation of Latin America. These "other people" have a "sense of history" that exists on a different timescale, one not regulated solely by modern nation-building. The timescale of this history "goes back…and goes back," predating, running contemporaneously to, and intersecting with the chapter's sections on the arrival of the Spanish. As she brings Malinche, the Toltecs, Olmecs, Aztecs, and Mayans back to life in her classroom alongside the Spanish figures of the Conquest, Simpson contests the curriculum's dominant timeline that begins with Columbus's arrival in the Western Hemisphere and the subsequent arrival of Spanish colonizers.

She furthers her critique of this standardized timeline by extending its beginning point even farther than what the curriculum guidelines expect students to know:

> when I was teaching them the history of Spain the book starts with the Romans and I threw in before the Romans you know…it was Celtic before the Romans got there and then…the book goes the Romans the fall of the Romans the arrival of the Moors and I said…there's something between that you know like what happened in those four hundred years I mean four hundred years isn't the same as eight hundred years but it still counts (Interview with Dionne Simpson, 6/13)

Simpson positions the history of Spain similarly to her presentation of Mexican history: long histories with overlapping timescales of different peoples. In this excerpt, she claims that the book ignores the "four hundred years" between the fall of the Roman Empire and the apex of the Moorish rule in Spain. Additionally, she notes that the book leaves out the pre-Roman history of Iberia, allowing that these ignored histories might not be as long and thus as significant as the traditionally studied textbook histories of Spain. Nonetheless, she positions the book's perspective as limited and even adversarial to her own: "the book goes," but "I said." In this reflection, she wants to turn students' gaze towards those histories that are not captured in the official, legitimized history of the Spanish-speaking world, often occurring in times and spaces not recorded by empires. These alternative histories, and the people they contain, "still count."

5 Implications

The official, state-approved curriculum reinforces an ahistorical view of the target language and culture through its insistence on fact-based recall and standardized assessment, which reflects a narrow exchange or transaction model of activity.

In this model, students are rewarded for identifying, but not engaging with, linguistic and cultural facts, as presented in curriculum materials. The California Foreign Language Framework and the textbooks that build on it view language learning as mere skill-getting and ignore its historical dimensions (as seen in Heining-Boynton & Redmond 2013: 4–5). This view reduces language to a commodity on the market of economic exchanges. In "Encuentro entre Culturas" in *Realidades*, these facts are generalizations that imply one history from the colonizing perspective.

Students in the second language classroom who encounter, however, a variety of histories in the target culture have the opportunity to realize that, as Simpson related in her first interview, "there are two ways of seeing the world":

> even if the students are not completely fluent I want them to at least start...to think somewhat in Spanish and...because...you know it just embeds a different mindset and it's very important...in this world for people to know two languages so that they can be aware of how the language you were thinking in constricts your thoughts and just that there are two ways of seeing the world...well there might be two hundred ways of seeing the world (Interview with Dionne Simpson, 5/1/13)

Simpson wanted her students to reflect on their own languages and worldviews and then place them among the possibly "two hundred ways of seeing the world." Achieving fluency, one way of seeing language learning, as defined by official assessment tools, was not the ultimate goal of her teaching.

As her lesson plan and interviews reveal, Simpson was more interested in expanding students' constricted worldviews, using the languages and cultures of Mexico as the tool to do this. As using Spanish had once been a tool for her to "*defenderse*" against those who boxed her in as a *gringa* and as a woman, Simpson expected her students to take up the language, not for economic reasons, but for intellectual transformation and political awareness. Her student's admission that Simpson's alternative histories of Mexico are "not something you learn in school... until like now," reveals that, for at least this one student, he is now aware of other stories and other voices that gain legitimacy in this second language classroom.

The commodification of language and language learning flattens and oversimplifies who the language teacher is and what she does. In light of state-mandated expectations that purport to fulfill global economic goals, teachers become accountants of language learning, ostensibly making a checklist inventory of the official knowledge that students acquire. Such a broad economic view of language learning with its restricted focus on language as a value added asset may appear to simplify the process of language instruction, but it erases the multilingual possibilities that teachers encourage in their classrooms. Additionally, this view hides the personal and complicated histories and thought processes of the multilingual teachers who facilitate meaning negotiation among students, the curriculum, and themselves in the second language classroom.

After reflecting on their work, language teachers have the choice to respond (or not) in personally meaningful ways to the pressures and demands of their work as language educators. In the case of Dionne Simpson, in crafting her narratives during our interviews, she came to view the goals for herself and her students' learning of Spanish to extend beyond and to contest the official state framework's goals of "academic achievement," "educational reform," and "leadership in the global economy." For her, the study of Spanish linked her classroom to languages, cultures, and places that predated the European arrival in the Americas. Consequently, Simpson used these links to challenge the limited timescale of Spanish as presented in the state-approved textbook.

In showcasing Mexican Spanish and registers of Nahuatl, Simpson modeled not just a complex understanding of Mexico's languages and people but also her own linguistic repertoire. This presentation challenged the restricted goal of language learning for U.S. students to become only "world-class business leaders"; it offered them a way to think critically about how their language teacher and a historical figure used their various languages to both support dominant power structures and subvert them.

Language teachers who see themselves as "multilingual subjects, with memories, passions, interests, and ways of making sense of their own and their students' lives" have the power to "transmit what [they] know...through direct teaching and indirect modeling" (Kramsch 2009: 208). This power then shifts the work of the second language teacher and ultimately the goals of second language learning away from simply "provid[ing] access to the world's marketplaces" (*Foreign Language Framework for California Public Schools, Kindergarten Through Grade Twelve*, p. v) and closer to "the nexus of the wider, interdisciplinary study of language, discourse, and social interaction" (Firth & Wagner 1997: 296). It calls for all language teachers to situate student learning in a context both larger and more personal than the current economic goals of language learning in the United States.

6 Conclusion

In this study, I sought to understand how an instructor of Spanish as a second language oriented her classroom work within the tension between the acquisition of an ahistorical skill and the development of a "social and historical consciousness" (MLA Report 2007: 4). Specifically, I hoped to document how a teacher of

Spanish in California directed activities in response to curricular demands and to personal experiences and beliefs. Dionne Simpson used her classroom to present complicated histories to her students as well as to reflect on the shifts in her own journey as a multilingual teacher of Spanish. Through the performance of a complex identity comprised simultaneously of woman, teacher, multilingual, academic, parent, and US citizen, this teacher opened ways for her students to understand multilingualism and consider the complexity of their own study of a second language.

This Spanish classroom in California became the site of different, occasionally conflicting historical voices. These voices, emerging from densely layered historical timescales and personal trajectories, combined to reflect a complex understanding of language learning in the twenty-first century. This understanding challenges a flattened view of language learning that is closely linked to the globalized commodification of language. Rather, with a view of language learning as a social and historical process, second language teachers and students build connections in their local classrooms among past and present events that link the target languages and cultures to their own lived experiences.

References

Blommaert, Jan. 2005. *Discourse: a Critical Introduction*. Cambridge: CUP.
Bourdieu, Pierre. 1979. *La Distinction: Critique Sociale du Jugement*. Paris: Éditions de Minuit.
California Department of Education. 2003. *Foreign Language Framework for California Public Schools: Kindergarten through Grade Twelve*. Sacramento: California Department of Education.
Candelaria, Cordelia. 1980. La Malinche, Feminist Prototype. *Frontiers: A Journal of Women Studies*, 1–6.
Cypess, Sandra M. 1991. *La Malinche in Mexican Literature: from History to Myth*. University of Texas Press.
Firth, Alan and Johannes Wagner. 1997. On discourse, communication and (some) fundamental concepts in SLA Research. *The Modern Language Journal* 81(3). 285–300.
Hall, Joan Kelly, Gergana Vitanova & Ludmila A. Marchenkova (eds.). 2005. *Dialogue with Bakhtin on Second and Foreign Language Learning: New Perspectives*. New York: Routledge.
Heining-Boynton, Audrey L. and Mary Lynn Redmond. 2013. The Common Core framework and world languages: a wake up call for all. *The Language Educator*. 51–56.
Heller, Monica. 2003. Globalization, the new economy, and the commodification of language and identity. *Journal of Sociolinguistics* 7(4). 473–492.
Johnson, Karen and Paula Golombek. 2011. *Research on Second Language Teacher Education: a Sociocultural Perspective on Professional Development* (ESL & Applied Linguistics Professional Series). New York: Routledge.

Karttunen, Frances. 1997. Rethinking Malinche. *Indian Women of Early Mexico*, 291–312.
Kramsch, Claire. 2006. From communicative competence to symbolic competence. *The Modern Language Journal, 90*(2), 249–252.
Kramsch, Claire. 2009. *The Multilingual Subject*. Oxford: OUP.
Lipski, John M. 1994. *Latin American Spanish*. New York: Longman.
MLA Ad Hoc Committee on Foreign Languages. *Foreign Languages and Higher Education: New Structures for a Changed World*.
Reis, Davi. 2011. "I'm not alone": empowering non-native English-speaking teachers to challenge the native speaker myth. In Karen Johnson and Paula Golombek (eds.). *Research on Second Language Teacher Education: a Sociocultural Perspective on Professional Development* (ESL & Applied Linguistics Professional Series), 31–49. New York: Routledge.
Ritchie, Joy S. and David E. Wilson. 2000. *Teacher Narrative as Critical Inquiry: Rewriting the Script*. New York: Teachers College Press.
Van Lier, Leo. 1988. *The Classroom and the Language Learner: Ethnography and Second Language Classroom Research*. New York: Longman.
Vitanova, Gergana. 2005. Authoring the self in a non-native language: a dialogic approach to agency and subjectivity. In Joan Kelly Hall, Gergana Vitanova & Ludmila A. Marchenkova (eds.) *Dialogue with Bakhtin on Second and Foreign Language Learning: New Perspectives*, 138–159. New York: Routledge.

Claire Kramsch and Lihua Zhang
4 The legitimacy gap: multilingual language teachers in an era of globalization

Abstract: As institutions of higher learning are currently enjoined to redefine themselves within a global economy that values multilingualism and transnational diversity, the demand for native speaker instructors continues to grow. Yet these native speakers are expected to represent a monolingual national model of foreign language and culture, when they are in fact multilingual global citizens with much experience to share. In this paper, we report on a study we conducted with 43 foreign born native instructors of 17 different languages at the University of California to better understand the conditions under which multilingual teachers exercise their profession, the opportunities and the challenges they encounter, and the rich insights they can give their students who will be called upon to play a role in global transnational spaces.

In their introduction to their 2013 book *Language, Migration and Social Inequalities*, Duchêne, Moyer and Roberts write: "It is through language that the complex relationship between the material and symbolic capital of migrants is played out on a local scale, as power institutions of the nation-state interact with the globalized economic order." (p. 1) and they encourage us to "recast institutions and work in multilingual and transnational spaces" (p. 1). The situation of migrants to the United States who are called upon as native speakers to teach their native language in foreign language departments takes on another meaning in an era of globalization than just fueling the debate about the "native speaker" in SLA.

As the two authors of this chapter experienced themselves, the legitimacy of the foreign-born, native language instructor becomes an issue at academic institutions that value their authentic linguistic skills and their insider's cultural knowledge, but do not necessarily acknowledge their multilingual and multicultural experience. Lihua, who grew up in China, studied German in Germany and Canada, ended up with a degree in German from an American university, and now teaches Chinese, coordinating the Chinese language program at UC Berkeley. Claire, who grew up in France, studied German in France and Germany/Austria, ended up with a degree in German from a French university, and now teaches German and applied linguistics at UC Berkeley. Their and many others' multilingual life experiences are not considered to be relevant to the monolingual

---

Corresponding Author: Claire Kramsch, University of California, Berkeley, US, ckramsch@berkeley.edu

mission of their respective departments that expect native speakers to represent a national model of foreign language and culture. And yet institutions of higher learning are currently enjoined to redefine themselves within a global economy that values multilingualism and transnational diversity. After a brief review of the debate about authenticity and legitimacy in second language acquisition, we report on a study we conducted to better understand the conditions under which multilingual teachers exercise their profession, the opportunities and the challenges they encounter, and the rich insights they can give their students who will be called upon to play a role in global transnational spaces.

1 Authenticity vs. legitimacy: The native speaker instructor in an era of globalization

Despite 25 years of proclamations that the native speaker is dead (Paikeday 1985) or needs redefining (e.g., Davies 1991; Rampton 1990), and despite the current multilingual turn in applied linguistics (e.g., May 2014; Weber & Horner 2012; Pennycook 2010) that prizes hybrid identities and translanguaging practices (Canagarajah 2011, 2013; Garcia 2009: 385), native speakers still retain their symbolic authority as language teachers in the global economy. The MLA Job listings invariably advertise positions for candidates with "native or near-native ability in the foreign language" (MLA 2012). Pedagogic materials in textbooks and online are striving to approximate more and more authentic contexts of language use (Kramsch and Vinall 2015, Gray 2013, Thurlow & Jaworski 2010), and accent reduction programs for non-native speakers of English are doing well. At the same time as teachers of English are urged to embrace and have their students take ownership of a variety of locally spoken Englishes (Higgins 2015) or to "disinvent languages" (Makoni & Pennycook 2006), educational institutions seeking to hire teachers of languages other than English still take as their models native or near-native speakers of the standard national variety. In all cases, what is sought is authenticity: authentic standard language practices of the world's educated elites on the one hand, authentic hybrid language practices of the world's global youth on the other. However, to paraphrase Bourdieu, linguistic and cultural authenticity is never a guarantee of social acceptability. The question is not: who is the most authentic speaker, but who has the most legitimacy? Legitimacy is the blind spot of second language acquisition research.

The term legitimate, originally meant to characterize a thing, person or behavior that conforms to the law and is therefore authorized, and hence good, just, and proper, has come to be extended to persons and behaviors that have the sanction of the public and that conform to accepted social norms (Foucault 1977). To say that native speakers still have legitimacy in academia is to say that their natural linguistic endowment and their cultural authenticity are seen by the foreign language (FL) establishment as having a unique profit of distinction that makes them desirable on the job market. It also says that the source of their legitimacy is a language ideology that sees languages as neatly bounded by national grammars and vocabularies embodied in the monolingual habitus of monolingual nationals.

According to Bourdieu, legitimacy is based on "misrecognition", i.e., the belief that someone's authority is attributable to natural, biological qualities, not to institutional power (Bourdieu 1991: 23). Foreign-born, native speaker (NS) teachers enjoy a great deal of *de facto* symbolic capital. They are hired precisely because of their NSship and the contacts they maintain with the target country. However, in FL departments, they do not always have the same status as senate faculty if they only teach language. They are not seen as the scholars and professionals that many of them are, but as 'mere' native speakers. Their culture is often exoticized, their history is interpreted through the lens of the local media. Many aspects of that history have become untellable because they contradict the dominant interpretation of events, or are seen by teenage students as no longer relevant. Outside the university, these same instructors are likely to encounter prejudice of various kinds because of their foreign accent and foreign behavior (Lippi-Green 1997, Hill 1993).

This is not to say that native instructors don't enjoy teaching their native language. Even though they are at least bi- if not multilingual, with a multicultural perspective on their various cultures, they start playing the monolingual NS and draw singular pleasure from it. However, the fact that they are multilingual, cosmopolitan individuals, often with a high level of education, global connections, double vision, and with a deep understanding and tolerance of paradox, remains to a large extent unrecognized or undervalued.

It is time to revisit the notion of native speaker, not to discard it in favor of other forms of attachment – inheritance, affiliation, or identification (Rampton 1990), third places (Kramsch 2009), voice (Canagarajah 2012) or translanguaging practices (Garcia 2009: 385), but to redefine it in our era of global migrations and multilingual subject-positions (see Kramsch 2014), and within the context of the existing tensions between national pride and global profit (Heller & Duchêne 2012). This paper explores how native language teachers deal with feelings of legitimacy or lack of legitimacy as they teach their own language and culture at American colleges and universities and how they deal with the paradoxes of their (il)legitimate subject positions. Our study includes an on-line survey and follow-up interviews that we report on in the next two sections.

2 The study (survey)

In mid January 2013, assisted by the University of California Berkeley Language Center, we sent a survey to program coordinators at the eleven University of California campuses to be distributed to all native speaker instructors. The survey "Multilingual and multicultural teacher" consists of four groups of quantitative and qualitative questions: Q1–10, general background; Q11–14, professional background; Q15–23, general cultural experience; and Q24–32, Cultural misunderstandings in the classroom. The survey was conducted electronically using a web survey tool. By the end of March, 43 responses were received from nine UC campuses. We report here on the quantitative data and report on the qualitative data in section 3.

2.1 Personal background

Of the 43 respondents, 86% (37) are female and 14% (6) male; 21% (9) are in age group 20–39, 65% (28) are in age group 40–59, and 14% (6) are in age group 60–79. One respondent received a BA, 56% (24) received an MA, and 42% (18) received a PhD or Ed.D. Moreover, 33% (14) hold degrees in Language and/or Literature, 28% (12) in Second/Foreign Language Acquisition or Teaching, 21% (9) in Linguistics, and 19% (8) in Education, History, Journalism, and Film.

While 21% (9) of the respondents are now American, 23% (10) have dual nationalities, and 56% (24) are foreigners. Dual nationalities include American and Dutch/German/Italian/Kenyan/Spanish/Taiwanese. Foreign citizens include Canadian, Chinese, Filipino, Finnish, French, German, Irish, Italian, Japanese, Peruvian, Spanish, Taiwanese, and Vietnamese.

Moreover, 91% (39) of the respondents learned English in their native country before arriving in the US. In addition to English, 80% (34) knew more than two languages including Arabic, Basque, Chinese, Dutch, Farsi, French, German, Greek, Haka Dialect, Ilokano, Italian, Japanese, Kikuyu, Kisii, Latin, Pangasinan, Portuguese, Russian, Sicilian, Spanish, Swedish, Tagalog, and Thai. The respondents came to the US for various reasons: more than half of them came to study in the US, about one third came for employment opportunities (Table 1). They have lived in the US from about a year to 44 years. Some 95% (41) still have family in their native country and maintain contact in various ways with various degrees of frequency (Table 2). While most respondents keep in telephone contact with their native country, they also frequently keep in touch through "Skype", "blogs", and "Facebook", they read their native country's newspapers, follow political events and return to their country for frequent visits. Clearly, the respondents still live/

Table 1: Reasons for coming to the US

Reasons	Response percent out of 43
Opportunity to study	55.8% (24)
Professional opportunity	32.6% (14)
Marriage with an American	23.3% (10)
Love of the U.S.	16.3% (7)
Economic hardship	11.6% (5)
Family ties	11.6% (5)
War in home country	2.3% (1)
Transfer	2.3% (1)

Table 2: Ways and degrees of keeping in contact with native country

Ways of maintaining contact with native country	Never	Seldom/ occasionally	Frequently/ at regular intervals
Telephone family and friends	0	16.3% (7)	83.7% (36)
Read country's newspapers	0	23.3% (10)	76.7% (33)
Follow political events	2.3% (1)	20.9% (9)	76.7% (33)
Return to visit	4.7% (2)	23.3% (10)	72.1% (31)
Watch country's TV/films	0	32.6% (14)	67.4% (29)
Read latest publications	4.7% (2)	46.5% (20)	48.8% (21)
Have professional contacts there	18.6% (8)	55.8% (24)	25.6% (11)

relive/remember the language and culture they lived in their native country. They do this for personal satisfaction and to keep abreast of their profession.

2.2 Professional experience

The 43 respondents teach 17 languages. They taught their native language in their native country, the US, and other countries at the beginning, intermediate, and advanced levels for various numbers of years (Table 3). Several respondents taught their native language in their native country and in other countries. In the US, the respondents taught their native language from a beginning level to an advanced level from one year to over 20 years. In addition to teaching their native language, 35% (15) taught another language or more in their native country, in the US, or other countries. Among them, 73% (11) taught English as a foreign/second language. Languages other than English include French, German, Spanish, Fili-

Table 3: Years of teaching native language at three levels

Level	Country	1–5	5.5–10	10.5–15	15.5–20	20+	Responses out of 43
Beg	Native country	7	4	1	0	2	14
	US	12	11	5	5	8	41
	Other countries	2	1	0	0	0	3
Int	Native country	7	5	1	0	2	15
	US	13	7	5	4	8	37
	Other countries	2	1	0	0	0	3
Adv	Native our country	5	5	1	0	2	13
	US	16	7	4	3	3	33
	Other countries	1	1	0	0	0	2

pino, and American Sign Language. The respondents hold full time, permanent, but non-senate faculty positions: eleven are language program coordinators, 14 are post-6-year lecturers, 13 are pre-6 year lecturers, four are visiting lecturers and one is a teaching assistant.

2.3 General cultural experience

Respondents chose three adjectives to characterize how they viewed their native and American culture prior to coming to the US. In total, 102 adjectives were used to characterize native cultures and 93 adjectives to characterize American culture. The purpose of these questions was to find out what aspects of each society were likely to cause difficulties in cross-cultural understanding between teachers and students and for students learning the language.

The respondents' characterization of their native culture reveals views about their native country's history, economy, politics, religion and morality and their views on growing up and their own values, e.g., "ancestral", "underdeveloped", "liberal", "conservative", "sacred", "monolithic", "hierarchical", "vibrant", "hybrid", "orderly", "dynamic", "collaborative", "family-oriented", "hard-working", and "respectful". For perceptions of American culture prior to coming to the US, the adjectives chosen deal with American economic culture, the geography and physical beauty of the country, technological innovation, the political societal culture. Before coming to the U.S., respondents reported having varying views of Americans, ranging from "ambitious", "intelligent", "energetic", and "optimistic" to "arrogant", "close-minded", "flaky", and "self-centered". Table 4 displays the basis of respondents' personal experiences that shaped their cultural views. It shows that while respondents' views on their culture prior to coming to the US primarily came from living that culture in their native country, they learned about American culture mostly indirectly from the media and the movies.

Table 4: Personal experiences shaping cultural views

Personal experiences	For native culture (out of 41)	For American culture (out of 42)
Human contacts	97.6% (40)	61.9% (26)
School textbooks	65.9% (27)	40.5% (17)
Songs	41.5% (17)	54.8% (23)
Movies	51.2% (21)	90.5% (38)
Political speeches	34.1% (14)	26.2% (11)
Media	78% (32)	95.2% (40)

The survey shows that for 86% (37) of the respondents many aspects of American culture were, or are still, difficult to understand. They include: individualism, selfishness; shallowness and superficial nature of relationships; social rituals, habits, etiquette, and manners as well as American exceptionalism, patriotism, capitalism, and materialism; American communication and discourse; importance of religion; family values; media censorship; violence and personal gun use; and pop-culture. Also, 95% (41) of the respondents found the following aspects of their native culture difficult for Americans to understand: interpersonal communication; social rituals, manners, social values; friendship; lifestyle; history, politics, religion; nature of societal culture; and stereotypes.

2.4 Misconceptions against native language and culture

The respondents report having encountered misconceptions or prejudice against their language and culture, primarily in interpersonal encounters, but also in the media, and in public places. They take the form of inappropriate interpretations of events, subtle mockery, jokes, and historical allusions. (Tables 5 and 6).

Table 5: Where misconceptions or prejudice occur

Social contexts	Response percent out of 38
Interpersonal encounters	86.8% (33)
Media	78.9% (30)
Public places	63.2% (24)
Service encounters	44.7% (17)
School	42.1% (16)
Work	42.1% (16)

Table 6: Forms of misconceptions or prejudice

Forms	Response percent out of 35
Inappropriate interpretations of events	68.6% (24)
Subtle mockery	65.7% (23)
Jokes	62.9% (22)
Historical allusions	62.9% (22)
Inappropriate inferences	51.4% (18)
Derogatory comments	42.9% (15)
Innuendos	40.0% (14)
Word associations	37.1% (13)

2.5 Classroom cultural misunderstandings

Most respondents, being teachers, encountered misunderstandings about their culture on the part of their students in various contexts and forms (Tables 7 and 8). The major sources of misunderstanding include: taking the American version of historical events as universal, choosing inappropriate words, and misinterpreting the historical context of a text. Moreover, 58% (25) of the respondents described students' misunderstanding the target culture as stemming from the students' lack knowledge of the history, political geography, or cultural diversity of the target culture, their use of stereotypes, and their inappropriate understanding of value systems different from their own.

These misunderstandings correlate with the students' level of proficiency in the language. Among the 43 respondents, 95% (41) taught beginning classes, 86% (37) intermediate classes and 77% (33) advanced classes. More misunderstandings occur in beginning classes (63%, 26/41), less misunderstandings with intermediate classes (43%, 16/37) and even less so with advanced classes (30%, 10/33).

Table 7: Time and frequency of misunderstanding

Time and frequency of misunderstanding	Response percent out of 40
Talking to students during office hours	27.5% (11)
Written assignments	25.0% (10)
Misrecognizing irony	19.4% (7)
Never	15.0% (6)
Once or twice a week	15.0% (6)
During pair and group work	12.5% (5)
In every class	10.0% (4)

Table 8: Forms of misunderstandings

Forms	Response percent out of 36
Taking American versions of historical events as being universal	61.1% (22)
Choosing inappropriate words	52.8% (19)
Misinterpreting the historical context of a text	47.2% (17)
Misunderstanding a speaker/writer's intention	44.4% (16)
Misunderstanding para-verbal speech features (gestures, smiles, body posture)	44.4% (16)
Inappropriate statements	41.7% (15)
Stereotypical derogatory statements	41.7% (15)
Using American concepts such as "opportunities, challenges, choice, agency" not having ideological equivalents in respondent's language.	36.1% (13)

2.6 Dealing with misunderstandings

How do these instructors deal with misunderstandings in class? Respondents were asked to respond to twelve statements by checking from "strongly disagree" to "strongly agree" (see Tables 9–12).

Six statements are about recognizing misunderstandings, dealing with them, and the goal of learning a foreign language (see Table 9). While 50% of the respondents strongly agree that it is difficult to recognize a misunderstanding because it often looks like a grammatical or vocabulary mistake (S1), 88% (strongly) disagree that they should ignore fundamental misunderstandings in the classroom and only focus on language (S2). On the contrary, 71% (strongly) feel the best way is to point out the misunderstanding and bring it to the class's attention (S3) and 76% strongly agree that the teacher should use the incident as a "teaching moment" and construct an appropriate lesson unit around it (S5).

Table 9: Recognizing and dealing with misunderstanding

Statements	(Strongly) disagree	Neutral	(Strongly) agree
S1. The most difficult thing is to recognize that there is a misunderstanding and not just a grammatical or vocabulary mistake.	6 14.3%	15 35.7%	21 50%
S2. The best way to deal with fundamental misunderstandings in a worldview in the classroom is to ignore them and focus on the language.	37 88.1%	2 4.8%	3 7.1%
S3. The best way is to explicitly point out the misunderstanding and bring it to the attention of the whole class.	3 7.1%	9 21.4%	30 71.4%
S4. The best way to deal with it is to talk it over with other colleagues to get different viewpoints on the matter.	1 2.3%	18 42.9%	23 54.8%
S5. The best way is to use the incident as a "teaching moment" and to construct a lesson unit around it.	3 7.1%	7 16.7%	32 76.2%
S8. One of the main purposes of learning a foreign language is to see the world from another perspective.	2 4.8%	1 2.3%	39 92.9%

The highest frequency, 93 % of the respondents, believes one primary purpose of learning a foreign language is to see the world from another perspective (S8).

Statements 6, 7, 9, 10, 11, 12 all relate to Statement 8, but they focus on the role and status of language teachers and of native speaker teachers in particular. Statements 6 and 7 are general statements about a language teacher's role; they have similar meanings but are phrased differently. Statements 10 and 11 focus on the specific subject position of native speaker teachers in American academia. Statements 9 and 12 are more narrowly focused on dealing with cultural differences in the U.S.; they are phrased in opposite terms. A cross-statement analysis shows the following results with (S)D = (Strongly) disagree, (S)A = (Strongly) agree, N = neutral.

For Statements 6 and 7 (Table 10), 60% (25) of the respondents are consistent in their two statements. They believe they should change their students' worldviews and make them aware of the relationship between language and ideology. The remaining 40% (17) are highly inconsistent both individually and among themselves.

Statements 10 and 11 show how native speaker teachers perceive themselves dealing with cultural misunderstandings in an American classroom in the U.S. The results from a cross statement analysis (Table 11) show a low rate of consistency. While 34% (14) of the respondents see themselves eminently suited to open American students' minds to other worldviews (S10) and do not feel they are vulnerable doing so (S11), seven respondents (strongly) agree and two (strongly) disagree with both statements. Fifteen respondents remain neutral for one statement, but (strongly) agree or disagree with the other. Three respondents are neutral on both statements.

Statements 9 and 12 have opposing viewpoints on how native speaker teachers should deal with the cultural differences between themselves and their stu-

Table 10: Language teachers' role

Statements	Response distribution out of 42							
	25	1	2	2	6	2	2	2
S6. It is not our role as language teachers to change the worldviews of our students.	(S)D	(S)A	(S)A	(S)D	N		(S)A	(S)D N
S7. One of our roles as language teachers is to make students aware of the relation of language and ideology.	(S)A	(S)D	(S)A	(S)D	(S)A	N	N	N

Table 11: Native speaker's position

Statements	Response distribution out of 41						
	14	7	2	5	5	5	3
S10. Native speaker teachers are eminently suited to open American students' minds to other worldviews.	(S)A	(S)A	(S)D	(S)A	N	N	N
S11. Native speaker teachers in the U.S. are in a vulnerable position and should be careful not to offend the American sensibilities of their students.	(S)D	(S)A	(S)D	N	(S)A	(S)D	N

Table 12: Dealing with cultural differences between teacher and students

Statements	Response distribution out of 42							
	4	7	16	1	2	3	1	8
S9. Native speaker teachers should not try to minimize the cultural differences between themselves and their students.	(S)D	(S)A	(S)A	(S)D	(S)D	(S)A	N	N
S12. Native speaker teachers in the U.S. should strive to reduce the cultural gap between themselves and their students.	(S)A	(S)D	(S)A	(S)D	N	N	(S)A	N

dents in the U.S. The results from a cross-statement analysis (Table 12) show an even lower rate of consistency. Only 26% (11) of the respondents are consistent in their statements. Four of them believe native speaker teachers should make an effort to reduce the cultural gap between themselves and their students and seven believe the opposite. Unexpectedly, 41% (17) of the respondents have inconsistent statements, with sixteen (strongly) agreeing and one (strongly) disagreeing. Six respondents agree/disagree with one statement, but are neutral on the other, whereas eight take no position. Our results thus show an increasing disagreement on the subject position of the NS teacher as we move from general statements on the role of the language teacher, to more specific statements on the role of NS teachers vis à vis American students in the US, to most specific statements on NS teachers dealing with cultural differences in their classes.

In sum, what this quantitative analysis reveals is the following: Most native speakers teaching their native language at the University of California are highly educated, 35% of them have been trained to teach English or another language, they have kept in frequent contact with their native country, both with their family and with social, cultural and political events as seen through their country's media; they have a high sense of professional mission and an unexpected amount of idealism. However, they are conscious of their vulnerable position as 'foreigners' and are variably cautious about their role as representatives of a foreign state and a foreign culture. They have varying opinions about how much they may or may not address the cultural differences between them and their students, or how to deal with cultural misunderstandings. Most of them are aware of their own linguistic and cultural shortcomings regarding American culture and are able to identify the sources of their students' shortcomings regarding the world beyond U.S. borders. But the inconsistencies and contradictions in their responses regarding their role as NS teachers is symptomatic of the precarious subject position they occupy in an American academic system that, while it values the authenticity of the multilingual/multicultural teacher, does not value the paradoxes and the vulnerabilities of those who have actually experienced the displacements that accompany translingual/transcultural competence and who would be able to make of these displacements precious "teaching moments".

3 The study (interviews)

While this survey gives us a good sense of how NS instructors position themselves in the American cultural landscape and academic hierarchy, a series of one-hour individual interviews conducted with 18 of the 43 instructors over summer 2013 further completed our understanding of how they view their legitimacy as FL educators at American institutions. Our selection criteria included availability for personal face-to-face encounters, linguistic and cultural diversity, and diversity of campuses within the UC system. The instructors came from six different campuses (at Berkeley, San Diego, Santa Barbara, Los Angeles, Riverside and Merced) and taught thirteen different languages (Table 13). All interviews were conducted by both investigators in English, except for two French teachers who were interviewed by Claire Kramsch in French and one Chinese teacher who was interviewed by Claire Kramsch in English and Lihua Zhang in Chinese. The interviews built on the responses to the survey. We were particularly keen on finding out how each of these instructors dealt with the paradoxes of their situation.

Table 13: Participants in the interviews (some names are pseudonyms)

Name	L2 taught	Age Group	Degree	Field of study	Years in US
Amy	Korean	40–49	PhD	Linguistics	24
Camilla	Italian	20–29	MA	Italian Film	6
Caroline	German	50–59	PhD	German	20
Dong	Vietnamese	40–49	MA	Southeast Asian Studies	9
Edwin	Swahili	30–39	MA	Journalism	20
Elke	German	50–59	MA	TESL	28
Florence	French	40–49	MA	TEFL	17
Francoise	French	60–69	MA	English	20
Han-Hua	Chinese	50–59	PhD	Language Education	26
Inez	Dutch	40–49	PhD	English	19
Latifeh	Farsi	50–59	PhD	History	25
Laura	Spanish	30–39	PhD	Linguistics	13
Santoukht	Armenian	60–69	BA	Education, English	44
Shuliang	Chinese	40–49	MA	Teaching Chinese as S/F Language	12
Susanna	Finnish	60–69	MA	TESOL	30
Victor	Spanish	40–49	PhD	Romance Languages & Literatures	25
Weisi	Chinese	20–29	MA	Chinese Linguistics	3
Yoshiko	Japanese	30–39	MA	Linguistics	12

We asked four main questions of our participants that captured their four main subject positions as native speakers, as knowledge providers, as professional teachers, and as language educators (Table 14). The responses revealed a range of complex feelings of both professional pride and professional vulnerability, and a heightened awareness of the legitimacy gap between themselves as multilingual expatriates and their monolingual compatriots back home, between themselves as non-native English speakers and native speakers of English in the U.S., and between their decentered position as immigrants and the self-centeredness

Table 14: Questions posed in the semi-structured interviews

1. As a native speaker and foreign national, what stories do you tell your students about your own experiences both in your country of origin and in the United States?
2. As a knowledge provider, do you feel it is your responsibility 1) to change your students' worldviews? 2) to open your students' minds to other worldviews? Or 3) to help them see the world from another perspective?
3. As a professional teacher, have the changes caused by globalization in your native country make your teaching of culture easier or more difficult?
4. As a language educator, explain the metaphor you chose to characterize your role as teaching your native language in the United States.

of the American academic universe. The interviews gave insights into a range of resourceful strategies that these instructors use to come to terms with the paradox of legitimacy inherent in their national/global subject position. We consider this legitimacy here under four aspects: linguistic/cultural, epistemological, professional, and ideological, that correspond to the four subject positions these instructors occupy. Some of these positions overlap but in the following we have kept them separate for the sake of exposition.

3.1 Linguistic/cultural legitimacy as native speakers

3.1.1 Legitimacy as native speakers in relation to their own language & culture

None of the participants reports feeling a sense of pride or of linguistic/cultural legitimacy at being a native speaker. Instead, many regret not knowing English well enough, and not knowing the American academic system well enough to be seen as a legitimate player in the academic game. They are eager to familiarize their students with the world they come from but at the same time this world seems to be historically, socially and culturally out of their students' reach. Moreover, the longer they are in the U.S., the less their students and colleagues understand why they still call their native country "home", and, over the years, the greater the tension between the multilingual multicultural person that they have become and the imagined monolingual culture that they have to represent and are called upon to transmit.

For example, Susanna, a native speaker of Finnish, finds it difficult to make an American acquaintance understand that when she returns to Finland she is not only going because she wants to see her family.

> I said well yeah it's great but it's so much more. I get to um read the real newspaper and have a cup of coffee in a cafe in Helsinki. And she just had no idea. She looked at me like "huh? What's wrong with you? "And I realized that this is really difficult to uh share that with someone who uh hasn't experienced it. They have this narrative that America is the best place to live. So they can't imagine that you would be interested in reading foreign newspapers …and wanting to go home.

And Latifeh, of Bah'ai faith and a native speaker of Farsi, feels that after some 25 years in the U.S. she has a much more transcultural identity than the Iranian identity her students want to see in her.

3.1.2 Legitimacy as foreign professionals

Moreover, some often feel like guests in the host country in which they teach and hence feel bound by an obligation to adapt to the world of their students. They are eager to share their experience as they have lived the language and culture that they teach, but they fear having their stories misunderstood, commodified, worse, made into objects of curiosity. For instance, Victor, a Spanish teacher from Guatemala, says he never talks with his students about the "atrocities" he witnessed during the war, but instead tries to "be more objective in conducting literary or cultural analysis".

> I do so for the following reasons. Um…I don't want my students to view me as someone who is trying to force-feed something about US history and what the United States government has done in the past. Uh I prefer that that awareness comes to them uh differently. From a text, from a video, from a film, from whatever else we're looking at. And then we can engage with it uh critically. Because I feel that I may-if I'm not careful uh strain that relationship with the students given that I'm Latin American and they might feel personally attacked by my comments or my views. This may not be the case coming from uh a professor born and raised here. Uh so I I over the years I've learned that is the case.

Others, like Shuliang, a native Chinese speaker, deliberately leave their prior history and cultural biography at the door of the classroom. "To be honest I don't really uh like to share too much about my you know privacy". Why not?

> Well because [laughs] because it's my privacy so so sometimes I don't want even though they feel interested but sometimes it's not really uh doesn't really connect very closely to the text I don't really wanna uh spend too much time on… on… on my personal stuff because I… I feel I will… I… I probably will waste …waste time. I mean waste my students' time.

For others, their professional legitimacy is jeopardized by the historical prejudices prevalent in the media and among their students concerning their language and culture. Such is the case for Caroline, who teaches German in Southern California. The negative perceptions of Germans in the media and among the population, the constant remarks about how "useless" German is nowadays have made her feel so "downtrodden" that she admits: "you get to the point where you don't like your language you don't like your culture."

3.1.3 Legitimacy in one's sense of self

Coming to the U.S., many of these teachers struggle to reconcile their sense of self and the image that the surrounding culture imposes on them – as a foreigner, as a member of the national community, as an accomplice in a society that they perceive as fundamentally opposed to their ideas of social justice (Tables 5 and 6 above). For example, Elke, who teaches German and has a German accent in English, encounters hostile remarks in public places:

> Because you are not seen as having as much of a right to be there and-as uh-and you know being taken seriously. I have experienced that but not at the University because I actually love being at the university for that reason. Because my foreigness is an asset there. And at the university itself everyone has an accent. And people are interested at the university in other peoples' culture and their experiences. But in my private life I have had a few incidents where this... well... sort of took power away from me.

3.2 Epistemological legitimacy as knowledge providers

With the overwhelming majority (98%) of these native speakers holding an M.A. or a PhD, yet teaching in a non-tenure track position, it is not surprising that many of them try to negate the institutional hierarchy of American academia, and seek to place themselves outside the competition, so to speak, and to capitalize on the distance gained from being both an outsider and an insider at their institution. This is the legitimacy of the language expert (Weisi, Han-Hua), the textual critic (Santoukht), the storyteller (Inez, Amy), or the performer (Edwin). We consider each in turn.

3.2.1 Legitimacy of expert linguistic and cultural knowledge

Because most teachers of East Asian languages have been trained in a structuralist approach to language, they see themselves as responsible for teaching only the structures of the linguistic system and to use cultural knowledge merely as a context for the practice of those structures in communication. They are thus led to compartmentalize the teaching of language and the teaching of culture. Here, Weisi explains how, despite globalization and the presence of McDonald's in China, she keeps Chinese and American cultures separate, as she does the two languages:

> R: So is hamburger now a Chinese kind of food?
>
> Weisi: No it's American food in China.
>
> R: It's American food in China? So you keep you keep the...
>
> Weisi: we keep the terms separate. Like in America we can uh eat Chinese food, right? It is still Chinese food, but it's eaten in America. American food, Japanese food they are still American or Japanese food. Not Chinese food.
>
> R: I see. But when you teach Chinese culture in the U.S., which Chinese culture do you teach: the culture of chopsticks or the culture of McDonald's?
>
> Weisi: Uhhhh. I think uh it depends on how you define culture. When I teach Chinese culture it's the pure, the traditional Chinese culture
>
> R: The stereotypical
>
> Weisi: Uh yeah.

3.2.2 Legitimacy of textual knowledge

All our participants prefer to bring in various materials to teach potentially controversial events, rather than try and share directly with their students their own cultural experiences or memories. They thereby objectify the events and create a space to consider critically multiple perspectives without necessarily putting themselves on the line, so to speak. Here, as an example, Santoukht, who teaches Armenian, rather than tell the horrific tribulations of her own family at the time, brings in historians' accounts of the Armenian genocide for the students to read in English or in a bilingual edition and to discuss in class.

> [The Armenian genocide] is everywhere it comes up in poetry in literature in sometimes even grammar exercises it comes up. But I do not dwell on it. I tell them to take the history class uh to be uh to to educate themselves. Uh I try to stay factual and not I I know history but I don't want to be the source of their knowledge about history. I just try to put things in perspective.
>
> R: Have students ever asked you directly uh your opinion?
>
> Santoukht: Sometimes they do ask. When I'm asked about my opinion I try to uh explain to them my own situation. I look at this question or opinion from that aspect.

3.2.3 Legitimacy of narrative knowledge

One way our participants seem to favor conveying cultural knowledge is in the form of narratives. The familiar narrative genre helps to soften the shock of the students' encounter with a foreign culture and they as storytellers acquire the legitimacy of the narrative genre itself which has its own autonomous conventions that they abide by. They thus regain in symbolic autonomy what they might have lost in institutional recognition. The heteroglossic voices they insert in those narratives divert from them the responsibility of being exclusively a mouthpiece or a representative of any one culture, language, or country. Here Inez, a Dutch teacher, has found that the narrative genre provides a critical distance to controversial cultural phenomena:

> I tell this story which is a very dramatic story I... I still... it gives me the chills when I tell it but um I had a friend who f-found who was my age two young children uh. she was terminal. At b – it was one of those cancers that have a horrible sort of end. She didn't want to have that end. Decided that uh she wanted to pull the plug when she felt she was ready. So she gave this huge party invited all her friends and family. At this party her father was a GP, she wanted her father to do it. So she says middle of the party... party was still going great...she says to her dad: "dad I'm ready." And they go upstairs and they did it. And that is something that is also again it's a very pragmatic thing. Um...and it is uh a very dignified way to die. Um...now euthanasia is... is a very problematic uh uh uh thing to discuss in a country like the States that that is still I think very 19th century in terms of religious beliefs. And what I do is I present them with this story and tell them why euthanasia works for the Dutch. And I'm not telling them that they should accept that as you know their worldview...I am here to widen their horizon just a little bit so that they can see again sort of get... get outside of themselves and take sort of a critical look at themselves and say hey there are some people in the world that do it differently.

Amy tries to convey Korean values to her students through a popular fairytale, albeit with scant success:

there's a famous um fairytale in Korea that everyone knows and of course I learned it when I was young. So when I began to teach um upper third level I read it as official material. It's a story about um these um fairies who came to earth and went bathing in the pond because they didn't have enough water in heaven [laughs]. So they were like doing the bathing and then um a very nice woodcutter he was um hiding and he watched them. And the fairies they had these um kind of special costumes so that they can fly back to heaven. The woodcutter lived in the forest so he didn't have a chance to meet women. He was not married but he wanted to. So he picked one fairy's costume, so she couldn't go back to heaven. And she was the princess of the heaven. Something like that. So they got married and they lived happily ever after. But there was one uh thing that the woodpec-woodcutter had to be cautious about. Until the fairy got three children, he was not supposed to say "ok you know I hid your costume". Because with three children she wouldn't be able to go back you know. But she was so homesick that when they had two children, she said "oh honey I you know I still love you blah blah blah". I mean she loved him but still she really missed her father. [So the woodcutter gave her back her hidden clothing] and with her children in her arms she went back to heaven. Something like that. So I thought…what do you think? Isn't it just a fun story?

R: It's a very interesting story.

Amy: And yet even the heritage students were shocked. You know the woodcutter he's is a bad guy you know hiding and the naked women and then he stole it and then she got married and what about the stupid fairy. She was just naked and followed him and got married. Ridiculous. And I was really shocked. It was the gap between old and new perhaps. Or Eastern Western. But it's um kind of more than that and we talked about it. We decided not to teach the material, because it may be offensive, but still sometimes I think- without knowing this specific story I mean they may not know the basic Korean culture. So I try to bring it up and then discuss about it so then we can practice language.

R: it's almost your story when you have your students here and you are now in America. I mean how much do you…

Amy: I think that's the same thing. I live here but whenever I go to Korea I'm here but whenever I live here I miss Korea. Something like I'm in between.

3.2.4 Legitimacy of performing cultural knowledge

Finally some of our participants choose to perform in the classroom some of the cultural knowledge they want to convey to their students. Edwin, for example, a teacher of Swahili, seeks to build an African-style community spirit. He discovered that, because he has a lot of athletes in his classes, his students had a competitive spirit that was foreign to him.

R: You didn't experience that in schools in Kenya? This kind of competitive spirit?

Edwin: No high school sports are not as uh established as here. There's like no money in there. I don't even think there's like college you know intercollege games. They are not taken that seriously. So I didn't really understand when I came here that sports is huge in colleges and high schools.

R: But you're linking it up with the American spirit of competitiveness in general.

Edwin: yes yes. Because the spirit of competitiveness is not just in sports it's also in foreign policy and all kinds of things. . . We don't come from a place where people just beat their chest and say I am the best. People have humility; they are very humble. They will compete but not in your face kind of competition. So that's one difference that I see between American students and African students.

R: How do you know when you have reached your students and changed their outlook?

Edwin: Um um one of the most uh successful thing I taught them was about um how people relate to each other. Teaching my students in um the communal way of life where we look out for each other so the classroom becomes um the real no-child left behind class and I say we are not in competition here. So let's be Africans and hold each other accountable and I would put them in groups. Some students have written to me saying wow I feel um that we grew up together as a community of (.) a learning community the way in Africa like you would not just like lift yourself and you know like screw everybody else. And when you put them together there is a lot of opposition from those who I don't want to sit with the athletes and I would say: "just give it time give it time". And in the end I had a graduate student come to me and say: "I feel like we became friends with the footballers" [laughs].

3.3 Professional legitimacy as professional teachers

By focusing on their achievements as educators in the classroom, and by showing pride in the L2 community they are constructing there, these teachers negate the usual alienating individual assessment/ accountability constraints that American academia imposes on teachers and students. The following examples show how many of them have resignified their professional legitimacy as language teachers.

3.3.1 How they view their role/mission as NS teachers

As we saw in the survey data, opinions varied greatly about the role of the language teacher, particularly the native teacher, in "changing their students' worldviews". The wide diversity of responses shows the wide differences among instructors in the historical relation between their country and the United States, their personal biography, their social status and their personal preferences as a teacher. Here we see a deep difference of opinions between the French and the North Vietnamese instructors.

> R: Would you consider that the ultimate goals of teaching a foreign language is to uh change the way your students see the world?
>
> Francoise (French): No, not totally. Uh I would like it to happen, not necessarily toward my language but through a certain openness of spirit so that they see other things. I would like them to benefit from other perspectives on their own culture. (our trsl.)
>
> Dong (Vietnamese): It's definitely our role to change the worldviews of our students! Any teacher, not only a language teacher, has a role to change the students' worldview. Because as an educator I think from early on it's one of our educational roles to keep constructing, and changing is also a way to construct and reconstruct...if not then I have failed at my job. At the end of every course I would ask them ok after all those readings have you changed, has my course changed you or brought in any new ideas or um make you think differently about that issue. And they so far all of them agree 100%. It can be a stronger or a weaker change. But education is like you know the root word for education is Lat. *e-ducere*, to bring the inside out. Let's try and help them to change from the inside.

3.3.2 How they deal with their vulnerable position

The survey showed that there was strong divergence of views among instructors regarding their room for manoeuver between wanting to open their students' minds to other perspectives and protecting their own vulnerability as non-native speakers of English. This ambivalence is expressed particularly forcefully by two Spanish instructors, Laura from Spain and Victor from Guatemala. Laura admits having learned over the years what not to do or not to say in order not to "offend" the sensibilities of her American students. Victor feels that his beginning students are not "culturally literate", i.e., they are not "ready culturally" to "confront the hundred years of US-Latin American relations, especially the past ten years when you know American culture has been so susceptible to any type of criticism". But he adds: "At the advanced level, when I can engage with literary texts critically, I do feel the freedom to go into it uh without restraining uh myself".

3.3.3 How they find a third place

Finally how do these native instructors find a legitimate epistemological place for themselves that respects their students' position and safeguards their own integrity? We had not expected the wealth of resourcefulness that our interviews revealed. Through honest reflexion (Laura), creative writing (Susanna), or extensive travelling (Caroline), they managed to find for themselves a third place that restores their sense of legitimacy. Here three examples.

Laura (Spanish)

> Um in Spain we know much more about the rest of the world. We know-sometimes even more about the history of the United States than the people in the United States themselves. But we don't have this concept of culture as 'oh they do it like that in their culture'. For example when people from other countries are in Spain and they do things differently, people say 'oh she's so weird.' They don't have this notion that maybe it's their culture. And here in the US even though many times they don't know what their culture is and many times they misinterpret what your personal traits are and confuse the personal with the cultural, they still have this concept of cultural differences which in Spain...we don't have.

Susanna (Finnish)

> R: You said that when you teach your language um you feel like a skillful circus performer. Is there an element-when you tell your stories in the classroom is there an element of storytelling performance?
>
> Susanna: I write a lot. I... I do creative writing.
>
> R: You write short stories? And you publish them?
>
> Susanna: Yeah. I publish them yeah. So um I'm writing actually um I'm writing a lot now. I'm writing on grief, kind of. Yeah.

Caroline (German)

> That's why I need to go and have therapy every year (laughs). My therapy consists of traveling. I go and travel and when I go to Germany it's like slipping on the glove. It fits. And nobody questions where you're from and this and that. I don't have an accent when I speak German. So the whole thing gets changed and you realize how relative everything is. In Brazil they like Germans. They treat me like a queen. Argentina the same thing. So it's just you realize how arbitrary the whole thing is.

3.4 Ideological legitimacy as language educators

Table 15 shows the range of responses to the survey question: "Choose a metaphor that characterizes how you see yourself as a native speaker teaching your language in the U.S." By focusing on art and creative writing, or by repositioning themselves in a global context through travel and self-reflection , they negate the narrow legitimacy imposed by the job market and justified by the economic goals of American FL education, and place themselves on a higher, more timeless level of multilingual, cosmopolitan distinction. We report below what some of these metaphors meant for the teachers who chose them.

Table 15: "Teaching my language in the US is like…"

Focus on their role as binational immigrants
– Doing missionary work (Inez) – Being an ambassador of my language and culture (Françoise) – Being a cultural ambassador (Victor) – Being an ambassador from a small, poor African country (Edwin) – Bridging the two cultures as a language ambassador (Amy) – Bridging the past and the present (Dong) – Being a balanced tight-rope walker (Susanna) – Opening two windows: one with a view of another culture and one with a new window on one's own culture (Elke)
Focus on their role as FL educators
– Being a zen master (Han Hua) – Having to sail against the tide (Laura) – Taking American students to a culture adventure (Weisi) – Creating a piece of art (Yoshiko) – A coach training athletes for the Olympics (Latifeh) – Being a scuba diving instructor at a hotel swimming pool (Dong) – Working like an ox or a horse for my work (Shuliang) – Teaching how to deal with an exotic animal (Caroline) – Being my students' Plutarch (pointing them in the right direction) (Florence)
Focus on their identity as bilingual/bicultural subjects
– A ray of sunshine that connects me to the source; a rope that helps me access the well of language and culture deep within me (Santoukht) – Meeting an old friend at a party crowded with strangers and getting to know him/her all over again (Camilla)

Yoshiko (Japanese)

R: "creating a piece of art". Why did you choose that metaphor?

Yoshiko: teaching Japanese is like uh making some sculpture or like a (.) a molding (.) molding.

Florence (French)

R. Why "being my students' Plutarch"?

Florence: I don't like the phrase "opening a student's mind", I find it too active. I think it should come from them. I didn't open their minds. I think they are the ones who open their minds.

R: So you would be more in favor of "helping students see the world from another perspective"?

Florence: Yeah, right, and that's why I think of Montaigne who referred to Plutarch who advocated "showing the way with your faith" and he said that Plutarch had shown the way. I don't want to be presumptuous, so I prefer showing the students the way and that they make the journey. I think it is a personal journey so I don't think I can, if they don't want to. To accept another culture means putting your own into question. And some are not ready for that.

Camilla (Italian)

R: "meeting an old friend at a party crowded with strangers and getting to know him or her all over again". Who is the friend?

Camilla: The old friend is first of all my old- my language and my country (*her eyes become moist*) because I before moving here I just [laughs] thought this sounds good so it's correct. And by by learning to be humble about it. And to go back and myself read the grammar book and read why this works and why this doesn't work and why this is the rule and why this is not the rule has allowed me to get a very very in depth knowledge

R: of your own language and c...

Camilla: of my own language and appreciate it more.

Dong (Vietnamese)

Dong collects antique porcelain ceramics from Vietnam and ancient China. He considers that it is this experience as an art collector that has most shaped his pedagogy as a language teacher, for, as he says, "art is the connector between worlds: the contemporary world and the ancient world." And yet, the metaphor he chose for his teaching was "instructing a scuba diving course at a hotel swimming pool". So we wanted to know how he connected the two.

Dong: For me teaching language in a foreign environment is like going underwater. As well-equipped as a scuba diver is, he still needs to rely on you know some apparatus to keep him alive and functioning in a foreign environment.

R: Is scuba diving something that people do in Vietnam?

Dong: yeah, yeah

R: And they scuba dive for what? For oysters? For fish?

Dong: No just for sight seeing. Oh ...and they do... they collect the sunken treasures from ... antiques from sunken ships as well

R: Treasures from sunken ships...of course!

4 Discussion

If, according to Bourdieu, legitimacy is the fit between one's habitus and the market of symbolic exchanges, NS instructors have a particularly precarious legitimacy. They are experiencing precisely what poststructuralists like Norton (2000) have identified as the multiple, changing, and conflictual identity conundrum of immigrants in a global condition, but unlike Norton's informants, NS instructors have to deal with this conundrum day in day out in the classroom since they have to model for their students a monocultural native speaker that, with their translingual and transcultural experience, they no longer represent. Indeed, they have come to understand the contradictions of national and global subject positions and have had to grapple with these contradictions. Because of their religious faith, their artistic bent, their professional integrity, their sense of educational mission, their world travels, their personal and political maturity, and their sensitivity to the social and historical contingency of their students' worlds, they are able to provide much more than just authentic grammar and phonology.

All our participants are engaged in a struggle to regain symbolic legitimacy in the face of a loss of economic and institutional capital. They have to deal with the sometimes negative image that the American media present of their culture, with their institution's downplaying of their scholarly expertise, and with their own critical feelings vis-a-vis both their native culture and the American culture they now live in. We had not expected to find that 91% of them had learned English and one quarter of them had been trained in TESOL and had taught English before they came to the U.S. Nor had we anticipated to find that 95% of them would still have intensive and frequent contacts with their home country, despite having lived in the U.S. for many years. Their transnational lifestyle and their personal transcultural trajectories have made them into legitimate global citizens with a remarkable sense of educational mission.

Their testimonies echo some of the insights offered by postcolonial and postmodern writers that have conceptualized third places (Bhabha 1994; Kramsch 1993), double-voiced discourse (Bakhtin 1981) and dialogism (Holquist 1990). They show an acute awareness of the tension between the single-voiced discourse of standard language grammars/dictionaries and cultural stereotypes on the one hand, and, on the other hand, the double-voiced discourse of multilingual subjects (Kramsch 2009). As global citizens themselves they have acquired and are now opening their students' minds to new perspectives while acknowledging and protecting their own vulnerability. Rather than calling them 'native speakers' it would be therefore more appropriate to call them 'multilingual teachers', who are precisely positioned in the ambiguous third place between the opportunities afforded by the nation-state and those afforded by the global market. Their attemps to manage the translingual/transcultural contradictions of this position could be seen as attempts to develop what Kramsch has called "symbolic competence" (Kramsch 2009).

It is time to make better use of these multilingual teachers and to take them, not as ideal native speakers, but as models for the multilingual subjects that we want our students to become in an era of globalization. It is time to draw on their rich experiences as expatriates and to learn from their unconventional trajectories, their imagination and their resourcefulness. Ultimately, what they bring to foreign language education is a deep appreciation for the paradoxes of life and the multiple, changing and conflictual allegiances they require.

References

Bakhtin, Mikhail. 1981. *The Dialogic Imagination*. Austin, TX: U. of Texas.
Bhabha, Homi. 1994. *The Location of Culture*. London: Routledge.
Bourdieu, Pierre. 1991. *Language and symbolic power*. Ed. and Introduced by John B. Thompson. Cambridge: Cambridge U Press.
Canagarajah, Suresh. 2011. Codemeshing in academic writing: Identifying teachable strategies of translanguaging. *Modern Language Journal* 95:3, 401–417.
Canagarajah, Suresh (ed.). 2013. *Literacy as Translingual Practice. Between Communities and Classrooms*. London: Routledge.
Davies, Alan. 1991. *The Native Speaker in Applied Linguistics*. Edinburgh: Edinburgh UP.
Doerr, Neriko Musha (ed.). 2009. *The Native Speaker Concept*. Berlin: Mouton de Gruyter.
Duchêne Alexandre, Melissa Moyer & Celia Roberts (eds.). 2013. *Language, Migration and Social Inequalities*. Clevedon, UK: Multilingual Matters.
Foucault, Michel. 1977. *Discipline & Punish*. New York: Vintage.

Garcia, Ofelia. 2013. *Bilingual Education in the 21st Century. A Global Perspective*. Chichester: Wiley-Blackwell.

Gray, John (ed.). 2013. *Critical Perspectives on Language Teaching Materials*. Basingstoke: Palgrave Macmillan.

Heller, Monica & Duchêne, Alexandre. 2012. Pride and profit. Changing discourses of language, capital and nation-state. In Alexandre Duchêne & Monica Heller (eds.), *Language in Late Capitalism. Pride and Profit,* 1–21. London: Routledge.

Higgins, Christina. (2015). Intersecting scapes and new millennium identities in language learning. *Language Teaching*. March, 1–17.

Hill, Jane. 1993. Hasta La Vista, Baby: Anglo Spanish in the American Southwest. *Critique of Anthropology* 13 (2): 145–176.

Holquist, Michael. 1990. *Dialogism. Bakhtin and his world*. London: Routledge.

Kramsch, Claire. 1993. *Context and Culture in Language Teaching*. Oxford: OUP.

Kramsch Claire. 2009. Third culture and language education. In Vivian Cook & Li Wei (eds.) *Contemporary Applied Linguistics. Vol.1 Language Teaching and Learning,* 233–255. London: Continuum.

Kramsch, Claire. 2009. *The Multilingual Subject*. Oxford: OUP.

Kramsch, Claire. 2014. Teaching foreign languages in an era of globalization. Special Issue of *Modern Language Journal* 98:1, 296–311.

Kramsch, Claire & Kimberly, Vinall. 2015. The cultural politics of language textbooks in the era of globalization. In Xiao Lan Curdt-Christiansen & Csilla Weninger (eds.) *Language, Ideology and Education: The Politics of Textbooks in Language Education*. London: Routledge, pp.1–28.

Lippi-Green, Rosa. 1997. *English with an Accent. Language Ideology, and Discrimination in the United States*. London: Routledge.

Makoni, Sinfree & Alastair Pennycook (eds.). 2006. *Disinventing and Reconstituting Languages*. Clevedon, UK: Multilingual Matters.

May, Stephen (ed.). 2014. *The Multilingual Turn. Implications for SLA, TESOL and Bilingual Education*. London: Routledge.

MLA. 2012. *Job Information List 2012*. New York: Modern Language Association.

Pennycook, Alastair. 2007. *Global Englishes and Transcultural Flows*. London: Routledge.

Rampton, Ben. 1990. Displacing the 'native speaker'" expertise, affiliation and inheritance. *ELT Journal* 44:2, 97–101.

Thurlow, Crispin & Adam Jaworski. 2010. *Tourism Discourse. Language and Global Mobility*. London: Palgrave Macmillan

Weber, Jean-Jacques & Kristine Horner. 2012. *Introducing Multilingualism. A Social Approach*. London: Routledge

Patrick K. Osterkorn and Eva Vetter
5 « Le multilinguisme en question ? » – The case of minority language education in Brittany (France)

Abstract: In this article the interplay between multilingual subject and educational space by analysing how adolescents live their multilingualism in a particular Breton immersion school in Brittany (France) is investigated. Multilinguals are conceptualised as subjects who creatively draw upon multilingual resources, i.e. as "resourceful speakers" in line with Pennycook (2012). In this approach the subject is closely interrelated with space since subjects co-construct space and at the same time, following Blommaert et al. (2005), space enables or disables the multilingual subjects to use their communicative resources.

The qualitative ethnographic study reveals that pupils rarely question the school's Breton monolingualism, although it disables them to fully draw upon their linguistic resources. The discrepancy between the educational space on the one hand and the pupils' communicative demands on the other becomes particularly obvious with respect to the emotional side of language that is largely silenced at school. Hence, the pupils develop subversive practices in order to circumvent the institutional space and create new spaces, while at the same time co-construct the institutional frame. The executors of the language regime, on the other hand, seem to invest considerable time and effort in order to maintain "the said regime".

1 Introduction

This contribution deals with the discursive construction of space in immersion schooling in the Western part of France, i.e. Brittany, focusing on the pupils' multilingual agency within the educational space. The contribution draws upon data collected within a three-month-period of field work in a secondary school from September to November 2012 (Osterkorn 2013a) and discusses data that was not explored yet. The particular school where fieldwork has been carried out is run by the non-profit association of DIWAN, an association that has been establish-

Corresponding Author: Eva Vetter, University of Vienna, Austria, eva.vetter@univie.ac.at

ing immersion schooling in Brittany since 1977 (Gwegen 1983; Osterkorn 2013a, b; Vetter 2013).

The private minority school network of DIWAN (diwan is the Breton word for English "sprout", Hoare 2003, 28), founded as a reaction against monolingual language policy in France, was modelled on Canadian immersion schools, which first appeared in 1965 in Ontario, as well as on *Ikastolas* (Basque country) and Welsh language schools (Wales) (Kuter 1999). This school type has created a particular linguistic regime, ideologically founded in language revitalization, which guarantees a Breton-only space. Today, DIWAN's private immersion schools are known as one of the best practice examples of minority schooling in Europe (Vetter 2013).

In this article we want to investigate how the pupils negotiate and, hence, co-construct the discursive space at school. In doing so, our focus remains inductive since we ground our study in the data collected within ethnographic fieldwork in the above-mentioned school.

This article is divided into five main parts. First, we contextualise the research question from a sociolinguistic perspective by briefly characterising Brittany (see Section 1). Second, we consider the theoretical framework our study is based on, particularly the concept of space (see Section 2.1.) and our understanding of pupils as multilingual subjects (see Section 2.2.). Our qualitative approach to the data is grounded in triangulation (see Section 3). The results presented here refer to the description of the educational space (Section 4.1) and the positions taken by the pupils (Section 4.2). In the concluding remarks we attempt to identify the dark side of multilingualism in our specific case and to suggest a trajectory for the future (see Section 5).

2 Minority multilingualism in the French school system

The history of DIWAN schools is filled with events and experiences related to the multilingual challenge since the French school system consistently ignored the other languages of France for centuries, allowing only for French as language of schooling. In fact, minority multilingualism has been successfully silenced and excluded from educational contexts. At least for some parts of the 19th and 20th century, this kind of multilingualism has been overtly combated. There is some evidence that France is slowly modifying its "one nation – one language" approach. The European challenge of diversity (Rindler-Schjerve & Vetter 2012) has finally resulted in the signing of the *European Charter for Regional or Minority Languages*

(Charter RML 1992) in 1999 and, most recently, the ratification debate has become more concrete. The French Constitution, long considered the major barrier for ratification because of its Article 2 ("la langue de la République est le français"), has been amended by the clause "Regional languages are part of France's heritage" in Article 75 (Loi constitutionnelle n 2008–724 du 23 juillet 2008).

Nevertheless, the history of the DIWAN schools can be read as a narrative of the fight against the one-nation-one-language ideology. Until now and beyond DIWAN, education system in Brittany (and generally in France) has hesitated to provide a space for languages other than French, excepting foreign language teaching. Nevertheless, multilingualism is still unquestionably present in Brittany. Seen from a linguistic perspective, it includes at least diatopic, i.e. geographic (Coseriu 1973) variants of Breton and French[1], standardised Breton and French, as well as Britto-Roman (=Gallo) in the Eastern part of Brittany.

Historically linked to French language policy and the process of French becoming the central symbolic component of the Republic "une et indivisible" (Hagège 1996; Lafont 1968, 1971; Kremnitz 1997), the Breton context is very well known for the physical and emotional burden that multilingualism can represent. Unsurprisingly, multilingualism in Brittany has frequently been described from a minority language perspective (see the special issue of *ILSL* 2013 "Breton: the Postvernacular Challenge").

However, it is not this perspective on ignored and past multilingualism that the present contribution addresses. At the same time, we are also far from enthusiastically celebrating postmodern multilingualism and its benefits. Our focus is on how adolescents live their multilingualism in the particular educational space, i.e. that of an immersion school in Brittany. We attempt to show how the pupils position themselves and how they co-construct space when using language(s). In doing so, we want to reveal the immense and creative potential of multilingualism as well as discrepant, problematic and hazardous issues.

3 The theoretical framework

3.1 The space

Although we are interested in multilingualism, it is not language itself, but the concept of space that serves as our starting point in this contribution. Conceptu-

---

[1] Most frequently, the following four diatopic variants are distinguished: Kerne, Leon, Treger et Gwened (Cornouaille, Léon, Trégor et Vannetais in French) (Jones 1998: 12)

alising space has rather recently and mostly in relation to research into linguistic landscapes, developed into a prominent endeavour in multilingualism research.

This interest in space is linked to the "spatial turn" going on in social sciences in general since the 1980s, in which the discursive and social construction of space has been stressed (Lefèbvre 1991/2004; Jaworski and Thurlow 2009, for an overview see Purkarthofer 2014). Similarly, Bourdieu (1984) conceives of "espace" and "champs" as both constitutive of and constructed by the actors. Our approach draws on the spatial turn and we particularly elaborate on the co-construction of space, i.e. the dynamics between space and actors. More precisely, we draw upon Blommaert et al. (2005), who from a sociolinguistic perspective assume that space can be considered a part of the context, that it itself is an agentive and not a passive aspect of communication. Space "does something to people", since it is characterised by "expectations and norms about communicative behaviour" (p. 203). In our contribution we interpret communicative behaviour as using language(s) in different ways, i.e. particularly following norms that we characterise as either monoglossic – one language in a specific situation – or heteroglossic – combining resources from different languages.

In addition to this agentive character of space, we want to highlight the complex and dynamic interaction between micro and macro levels in relation to space. Here, we follow Blommaert et al. (2005: 213) in assuming that space generates scalar indexical meanings that go beyond traditional concepts such as "micro" and "macro". In this respect, Blommaert (2013: 613) calls for a perspective of complexity. For the purposes of our study, we begin with the assumptions that at our local site different scales, i.e. the regional, local and global scale, are simultaneously present and dynamically interrelated and that they articulate different linguistic norms and expectations.

A further pertinent point in recent research is that the concept of space has lost the quality of being tied to a concrete place (see e.g. Huffschmid and Wildner 2008) and is conceived of as a dynamic network of relationships or as a nexus of practice (Scollon and Scollon 2003). Although we begin at a concrete site, we do not attempt to understand local practice at or within this particular place, but rather understand how space is constructed by actors who are part of a particular nexus of practice and at the same time influenced by the multiscalar working of space.

Hence, in our understanding space is agentive, multiscalar and co-constructed in relationships. Moreover, we will adopt a particular conceptualisation of space, i.e. Lefèbvre's (1991/2004) tripartite construct, for our research since it corresponds to the general assumptions presented above and may provide a link between theoretical conceptualisation and methodological practice in our work. Lefèbvre (1991/2004) conceives of space as "spatial practice", "representations of space" and "spaces of representations": "[...] l'espace (social) est un produit (social)" (Lefèbvre 2004: 39).

In these terms, space as a social product is constituted by social practices that can be further differentiated into spatial practice (=day-to-day practice), representations of space (=academic discourses about space) and spaces of representations (=living space through pictures, symbols, memorials, etc.) (Lefèbvre 1991: 38–39 and 2004: 48–49). The first of which, i.e. "spatial practice", is defined by Lefèbvre as (not premeditated) linguistic day-to-day practices of individuals in space that contribute to the construction of this space. "Representations of space" are defined as discourses of science, urban planning and technocracy on the relationship between space and language, which take effect as "language-ideological frame of reference" (Busch 2013: 137). As Löw (2008: 28) has put it, it is this „ideological, cognitive aspect of space, its representation, mathematical and physical models and plans, which enable space to be read." Finally, Lefèbvre uses the term "spaces of representations" to highlight the presence of images, symbols, monuments, memorials and so forth in space as well as the way in which individuals experience and interpret it. He furthermore raises the question of how individuals position themselves under the (often hidden) influence of such images, symbols etc. in space. These practices, i.e. the perceived, conceived and lived, are closely interrelated and cannot be separated from one another (Lefèbvre 1991: 38–39 and 2004: 48–49).

In our qualitative and ethnographic approach we simultaneously analyse "spatial practice", the language-ideological frame and the spaces of representations. From a sociolinguistic perspective, it is not only the regulations on language use but also the speaker's habits with regard to these regulations that are pertinent (Kroskrity 2000; Coulmas 2005). Drawing on Luedtke's (1999) differentiation between "administrative" and "non-administrative language", we define administrative linguistic practice as regulated by the institution, whereas non-administrative language use is not approved by the institution and characterises informal situations. This differentiation is useful when combining spatial practice and representations of space as well as the actor's attitudes towards language regulations concerning the use of one or several language(s). The language-ideological frame influences language use mainly at the level of administrative and less at the level on non-administrative language.

In summary, our focus is on the language(s)-related aspects of space. Our understanding of space is inspired by Lefèbvre's tripartite conceptualisation of "espace" as day-to-day practice, discourses about space and living space through pictures, symbols, etc. Moreover, we do not conceive of space as a container, but rather as a network of relationships in which micro and macro components of context are simultaneously present. Finally, we see space as co-constructed by the actors and agentive since it "does something to people".

3.2 Actors and agents as multilingual subjects

The nexus of practice comprises multiple, differentiated actors: Teachers, pupils, administrative staff and other actors are part of the network of relationships and are, at any moment, simultaneously co-constructing the space. Among these actors, our focus is on pupils as multilingual subjects and not as members of a particular speech community. This is an important theory-driven decision with wide-reaching implications. Particularly in language minority settings, language users are usually analysed as members of a linguistic community, the minority or majority language community. For several reasons our approach differs from this common perspective and conceives of the observed and interviewed young Breton speakers as multilingual subjects acting in a linguistic space.

The common linguistic repertoire on which the notion of speech community is based has become highly controversial in a world that is increasingly described in terms of super-diversity (Vertovec 2007). This holds all the more for the Breton context: Beyond the diatopic variants of Breton, there is a discrepancy between the language used by the older native speakers of Breton, who do not always possess literacy skills, and the younger language users, who are not likely to interact in the same domains as their elders. A debate has emerged around this "communal split", sometimes even questioning intercomprehension among Breton speakers (Adkins 2013: 58). We do not wish to contribute to this discussion, but would like to approach language users from a quite different perspective.

A general point with respect to language users is that we conceive of multilinguals as resourceful speakers, which helps us to overcome the little fruitful native-speaker debate (for more details see Pennycook 2012: 80–86) and brings us closer to the idea of resources that language users can draw upon. Understanding language in terms of resources or repertoire connects us to the 'post-Fishmanian' turn (Blommaert 2013: 614) and research that questions the idea of languages as distinguishable entities. In this field, alternative and more flexible models have been developed under the labels of, e.g., polylingualism (Jørgensen et al. 2011), metrolingualism (Otsuji & Pennycook 2010), translanguaging (García 2009; Canagarajah 2013) or semiotic resources (Blommaert & Huang 2010). We do not subscribe to one particular theoretical move, but follow a broad definition of multilinguals that corresponds to the 'post-Fishmanian' concepts. In our study we understand multilinguals as subjects who use multilingual resources in the sense of "verbal repertoires consisting of more than one variety (whether language or dialect)" (Weber & Horner 2012: 4).

Two notions that this understanding is based upon need further clarification at this point, i.e. the notion of subject and that of multilingual language use. As to subject, we refer to Claire Kramsch in highlighting the process character of the subject. In her conceptualisation of "multilingual subjects" Kramsch (2009) refers to Julia Kristeva's "subject in process" (1977):

> This is something that you become. You are not born a subject. Language shapes who you are and you become a subject throughout your life in contact with various symbolic systems, including language. That is why Kristeva talks about the "subject in process." By putting the subject in there I was focusing on the subjectivity and the identity of the learner. (Kramsch & Gerhards 2012: 75)

With respect to multilingual language use, we refer to the continuum of multilingualism suggested by Blackledge and Creese that allows for characterising language use alongside the two poles of "integrated/flexible" on the one hand and "separated (bi-/)multilingualism" on the other (Blackledge & Creese 2010; 2011). "Integrated/flexible (bi-/)multilingualism" is described as the usage and mixture of languages in a setting. In this respect, the authors refer to Baily's "heteroglossia" (2012), who draws on Mikhail Bakhtin ("the simultaneous use of different kinds of forms and signs", p. 499). Blackledge and Creese show that integrated multilingualism means using resources from different languages and combining them dynamically. Languages, in the sense of historically and socially constructed codes, cannot be clearly separated. In contrast to the integrated/flexible type, "separated (bi-/)multilingualism" is considered to be the usage of one language after the other. Hence, several languages can indeed be used in one particular setting, but separately and thus without any mixing. Blackledge and Creese (2011) demonstrate that the separated type of their continuum of multilingualism is typical of institutions that aim to promote minority languages: "Separate bilingualism can be understood as constituting a response to anxiety about the potential loss of the community language, and the cultural knowledge it is considered to index." (p. 1206)

An approach to pupils as multilingual subjects in process who draw upon their linguistic resources in a continuum of separated and flexible multilingualism appears to be more appropriate for our contemporary, post-modern times. Complexity and – in Vertovec's terms mentioned above – super-diversity (Vertovec 2007) bring about fluidity, variability and rapid change. The dynamically conceptualised multilingual subject and the idea of resourceful speakers (Pennycook 2012) offer a more appropriate theoretical answer than the concept of group membership.

As to the interplay between the subject and the space, we draw on Blommaert et al. (2005) and posit that linguistic competence is not to be seen as characteristic of subjects, but rather as a question of in how far a particular space enables or disables actors to use their communicative resources (p. 198). This entails that our study is not interested in who speaks what language to what level of competence. Our precise research questions in the present study are: How do the pupils contribute to the construction of the space? In how far does the differentiation between administrative and non-administrative language apply to their day-to-day practice? How do they negotiate the language-ideological frame and the lived practice (symbols, signs, etc.) available?

4 Methodology: Context, fieldwork and data corpus

From the background of conceived practice in Lefèbvre's terms, i.e. the language-ideological frame, the schools of DIWAN have remained within the model of immersion revitalisation since the first school, a *maternelle* (> Engl. "kindergarten"), was founded in 1977 (Vetter 2013: 156). To follow from DIWAN's principles as enshrined in the Charter of DIWAN (*Charte des écoles DIWAN*[2]), schools provide for total immersion in Breton at the elementary level and the use of Breton and French as languages of education at the primary and secondary level. Their main linguistic aim is to establish symmetry with respect to the pupil's proficiency in and use of Breton and French (Vetter 2013). Hence, in order to balance the clear dominance of French in society, the schools adopt a monolingual policy in elementary education, while French is introduced in primary education (from 2 hours per week to 7 hours per week) and is, in fact, used by teachers only during French lessons. At secondary school foreign languages (English and German *or* Spanish) are introduced and, similar to French, are used only during foreign languages classes (Osterkorn 2013a, b).

The school at which we have carried out fieldwork is located in a Breton city that has consequently introduced bilingual signage over recent years. The conceived practice of the urban space is a bilingual one, although spatial practice, i.e. day-to-day practice in the city, is clearly French-dominated. Here, scalarity in Blommaert's terms influences space since the particular school is, hence, located

---

2 URL: http://www.diwanbreizh.org/sections.php4?op=viewarticle&artid=26 (accessed 24 January 2014).

in an urban context where Breton and French are present in the linguistic landscape. Bilingual signage also indicates the way to the specific school studied[3].

We will draw on previous work on the Breton context and minority language education policy (Vetter 1999; 2005; 2013) and particularly on the unique data collected during a three-month period of empirical fieldwork in a DIWAN-school documented in Osterkorn (2013a) that have not been analysed elsewhere. From September to November 2012, a wide range of empirical data were collected within a qualitative ethnographic approach: field notes gathered during IN SITU-observation (Lueders 2010; Moore & Sabatier 2010), data from linguistic landscaping (Landry & Bourhis 1997; Weber & Horner 2012), as well as language biographical data such as language portrayals (Gogolin & Neumann 1999; Krumm & Jenkins 2001; Busch 2013) and narrative interviews (Hopf 2010; Talmy 2010). In total, 76 learners aged 10 to 14 produced language portrayals and 14 narrative interviews with pupils (with a talk time from about five to 12 minutes depending on the interview) were conducted on the basis of these portrayals. The interviews were conducted in French since French was the language that both, the interviewer and the pupils, felt comfortable with. From the methodological perspective, the principle of triangulation guided data collection and analysis. The aim was to gain a more comprehensive, though not necessarily more valid picture of the phenomena under investigation (Fielding & Fielding 1986; Fielding & Schreier 2001; Kelle 2001; Bendassoli 2013).

In the present contribution we approach our data with respect to the co-construction of space and focus on the interviews. We use ethnographic field notes on the linguistic landscape to gain a first insight into the language-ideological frame. The narrative interviews allow us to show how the multilingual subjects position themselves linguistically in the space.

5 Results

5.1 Producing a monolingual space – representations of space and spaces of representations

As soon as one enters the school building, the cosmos of monolingual Breton makes itself felt. People unable to speak Breton cannot distinguish the signposts to the *collège* (> engl. "secondary school") from those to the kindergarten. One

---

[3] URL: http://www.geobreizh.com/breizh/fra/signaletique.asp (accessed 24 January 2014).

reads the Breton words "Skolaj" and "Skol" and has to decide which direction to take. Children's window decoration in the left building suggests that there is a kindergarten, hence the other direction is followed in order to enter the *collège*. While entering the gateway above which "Skolaj Diwan Jakez Riou" is indicated in colourful letters, it has become impossible not to perceive the dominant monolingual dogma.

Each and every sign in the entrance hall is formulated in Breton only (direction signposts to the head of the school or to the secretary, information on door mechanisms – such as "push" or "pull" – signs for hygiene in toilets, etc.). On the big white wall in the school playground, the imperative "BREZHONEG YEZH AR SKOLAJ!" is vividly flashing in black letters – a note to everyone "acting" (Blommaert et al. 2005) in this space that the Breton language is to be used. Furthermore, original French advertisements or information posters of the urban bus company are "bretonised" when, e.g., French signs are more or less obviously pasted over with Breton words. French only emerges when the use of Breton is restricted by technical issues. That is why the operating system of the computers in the school building is installed in French. However, the class register which was produced by a French company in French does not permit the French language on the book cover since the title, year and grade level have been pasted over with corresponding Breton words by the school staff. The content of the class book remains in French because of the company mentioned above.

With regard to the institution of the school, we are facing a space that is characterised by a language-ideological frame which demands at the institutional level, as part of the "administrative language" (Luedtke 1999), one language only. To put it in Gogolin's term, the school thus articulates a "monolingual habitus" (Gogolin 1994). This seems to be completely in line with the school's strategy of immersion revitalization that focuses upon Breton as the language of "total immersion" for all pupils (Christian 1996; Decke-Cornill & Küster 2010; Vetter 2013). The educational space is a Breton one that pursues a specific objective with respect to the pupils' linguistic resources: Breton shall develop into a life language of learners. With this aim, a certain pressure to enable the use of Breton and disable the use of other languages is applied by the institution. The institution uses its authority and hence the administrative framework in which the school space is defined to force the sole use of Breton. Ethnographic research reveals in how far teachers enforce this administrative language-ideological frame: Whenever teachers or guards perceive a word in another language (which is usually French, since it is the first language of many learners), pupils are insistently reminded that the Breton language must be used at school. Conversations with teachers on the matter showed that, according to the teachers, learners have to be obliged to use Breton since otherwise the targeted level of Breton, as well as the aim to establish Breton as the language of life, would not be achieved.

However, through the investigation in the research field and the accompanying ethnographic observation, it became obvious that at the level of "non-administrative language" (opposed to "administrative language", Luedtke 1999) learners do indeed draw upon resources from languages other than Breton. Yet this depends on an essential condition: learners must feel that they are being neither observed nor heard by those acting in the framework of the institution in the administrative language (i.e. teachers, guards and other school staff). In this sense, especially during informal moments or unobserved situations (for example on the school playground, in the corridors or in the classroom), learners create a space in which they whisper or even speak in French. Learners tell jokes in French in the dining room, provided that the table next to them is not taken by the teachers. Furthermore, learners make intuitive use of French for spontaneous reactions, for instance while doing sports during physical education or when they feel irritated and hence curse and swear. In the event that such behaviour is perceived by a teacher, learners are immediately admonished in Breton. This poses a particular paradox, since the acquisition of expressive words, such as profanities or spontaneous interjections, in Breton is not encouraged or even allowed in the educational context and hence an important part of the pupils' real life language necessarily remains ignored. There are, however, formal situations in which learners completely submit to the prevailing language-ideological frame (Woolard 1998, 3): Ethnographic observation reports on a pupil who, during the German lesson, promptly stood up to beat his fists against the wall, behind which pupils in the neighbouring classroom were singing Happy Birthday in French. With this action, the pupil wanted to remind them that Breton was the appropriate language for singing Happy Birthday in school.

Referring to Lefèbvre's triad (1991) of "the spatial practices", "the representation of space" and "the spaces of representation", we can observe a monolingual Breton language frame at the administrative level. At the non-administrative level, learners do indeed try to break this frame during informal moments. The entire school staff is aware of this and tries to enforce the desired language use also in informal moments with the aim to make Breton the "language of the learner" (Osterkorn 2013a). This artificially created space is a local one that contrasts strongly with the urban space as well as with the globalised multilingual world.

There are, however, spatial practices that, although rarely, question the artificially constructed monolingualism. Breton only shows its subtle delimitation, when, for instance, teachers or other members of the school staff also lapse into other languages in their discourse, especially into French (or rarely into English), in case there is no suitable word in the Breton lexis. When outsiders, such as parents or suppliers, enter the school, they try to acknowledge the prevailing language frame by articulating at least salutations in Breton. In connection with this, the school secretary reports that people from outside, either in person or on the phone, are sometimes quite surprised when she, in case of misunderstandings in Breton on the part of the parents, responds in French. As to the pupils, they have been observed during IN SITU-observation to promptly switch to another language (French, the language most of them feel comfortable with) when leaving the school building. Outside school, learners are no longer exposed to the artificially constructed monolingual space and do not feel compelled to use the Breton language.

In summary, ethnographic research has confirmed Breton monolingualism particularly with respect to monolingual representations of space and spaces of representations at school. These are only rarely questioned, subversive practices quite regularly relate to non-administrative language. In this case, the multilingual subjects use a wide range of different strategies that contest the representations of space as well as the spaces of representations.

5.2 The multilingual subjects' positions

When investigating how the pupils linguistically position themselves in the network of relationships at school, we draw particularly upon the data from the narrative interviews with the pupils. Here, four transversal key ideas result from our text analysis, indicating the pupils' agency in creating the space, i.e. the idea of "separate" multilingualism, the dominant language as refuge, the necessary promotion of Breton and the fun factor of flexible/integrated multilingualism.

5.2.1 Living a "separate" kind of multilingualism

All narrative interviews make it clear that the learners perceive and live the dominant language frame at school. When reporting on a typical day at school, entering the school building is commonly constructed as a (more or less strict) switch to Breton.

Similar to Example 1 below, pupils quite frequently report speaking French before they enter the school premises. As soon as they set foot in the school space, they switch to Breton, as it is prescribed by the language-ideological frame. To once again refer to the spatial triad described by Lefèbvre (1991), the language-ideological frame is a Breton one at the administrative level and appears not to be questioned as such by the pupils. From their perspective, a "school language"

[10]

| PKO [v] | Ouais. | Ouais. |
| E12 [v] | dans ma salle • • •, et puis, • • • donc souvent je dis "Bonjour" aux/aux copains, | |

[11]

| PKO [v] | |
| E12 [v] | des/en breton, des fois ... parce que voilà, et après ben je parle breton dans la classe |

[12]

6 [01:15.4]

| PKO [v] | | Ahum, et dans |
| E12 [v] | parce qu'il y a • les profs et puis il faut... on parle breton quoi. | |

Extract 1: (In 12_9–12, Osterkorn 2013a)
E12 [v] in my room ... we do stuff, so I often say "Bonjour" to my friends,
E12 [v] in Breton, because sometimes ... well, and after I speak Breton in class
PKO [v]   Ahem, and then
E12 [v] because there are teachers... and then you have to speak Breton

as opposed to "private language" emerges. In formal moments at which they feel observed by the institution (teachers, school staff), they claim to use Breton, which represents the language of the school ("school language").

With respect to space of representations and representations of space, the interviews confirm the results from ethnographic observation. The space, at least in its administrative dimension, allows for one language and this frame appears to be accepted even by those who apparently have communicative problems in fulfilling the linguistic needs at school.

While in the first extract the interviewed pupil resumed the switch to Breton at school in the general statement "on parle Breton quoi" (In 12_9–12 Osterkorn 2013a), Extract 2 contains a direct reference to the concrete place: "Parce que c'est quand-même la langue du college ((2s)), et il faut bien voir/faire des efforts à la parler"/"Because it's nevertheless the language of the school, and we have to see/make an effort to speak Breton" (In 3_19–20, Osterkorn 2013a). There is a direct link between the building and Breton, hence space is constructed as a container requiring a particular language use from all who are inside.

Consequently and as mentioned before, leaving school implies leaving the language-ideological frame, which has the reverse effect of entering school, as is shown in Extract 3: "After school, we are waiting for the bus, we speak French. (...) In French, because we say, we have left school". Here again, school is constructed as a specific place calling for particular linguistic practice.

[17]

	14 [01:34.1]
PKO [v]	préau.
E3 [v]	Ben ((1s)), je parle avec les autres ((2s)), ehh souvent j'avoue que le matin,

[18]

E3 [v]	donc la cloche n'a pas sonné, je parle un peu français, mais j'essaie quand-même de

[19]

	15 [01:46.1] 16 [01:46.5]
PKO [v]	Ahumm.
E3 [v]	faire beaucoup d'effort en breton Parce que c'est quand-même la langue

[20]

	17 [01:52.1]
PKO [v]	Ahum. Et le matin
E3 [v]	du collège • •, et il faut bien voir/faire des efforts à la parler

Extract 2: (In 3_17–20, Osterkorn 2013a)
PKO [v] yard.
E3 [v] Well, I talk with others, eh, I admit that often in the morning
E3 [v] while the bell has not rung, I speak a little French, but even so I try to do-I put
E3 [v] a lot of effort into Breton. Because it's nevertheless the language
E3 [v] of the school, and we have to see/make an effort to speak Breton
PKO [v]   Ahem. And in the morning

Subversion of the dominant language frame is restricted to informal moments such as the boarding rooms, the classroom when there is a lot of noise, or the rearmost corner of the schoolyard. In these moments pupils circumvent the rules of the space by drawing on the language which is easier to use and emotionally closest to them: most frequently, this is French.

Due to this discrepancy between the monolingual language regime at the administrative level and non-administrative language practice, pupils develop a type of multilingualism which we can relate to the notion of "separated multilingualism" (separate use of languages) described by Blackledge and Creese (2010). The interviews reveal that the multilingual learners know when and with whom they may, should or can use a particular language.

[25]

	26 [02:42.2]	27 [02:46.2]
PKO [v]	Ok, tu manges pas ici. Après l'école?	
E13 [v]	pas, je mange pas là.	Ben, après l'école fin qu'

[26]

	28 [02:52.3]	29 [02:54.3]
PKO [v]	Ouais.	Et après en bus?
E13 [v]	on est/qu'on attend le bus, on parle français.	En français, parce qu'

[27]

	30 [02:58.0]	
PKO [v]	Ouais.	D'accord, ça marche. • • Et une journée type
E13 [v]	on n'est/on se dit on est parti de l'école.	

Extract 3: (In 13_25–27, Osterkorn 2013a)
PKO [v] Ok, you don't eat it here. After school?
E13 [v] no, I don't eat here.   Well, after school
PKO [v] And after on the bus?
E13 [v] we/we are waiting for the bus, we speak French.   In French, because that
PKO [v]   Okay, that figures. And on a typical day
E13 [v] is/we say, we have left school.

[28]

PKO [v]	
E6 [v]	le cusinier, il parle pas breton • • • et ensuite, ça dépend sur quelle table on est, parce

[29]

PKO [v]	
E6 [v]	que si on est ((rire))/si on est proche des professeurs, on parle breton quoi.

[30]

	20 [02:56.3]	21 [03:02.6]
PKO [v]	Ok • • •, je vois, après/après l'école alors, Studi [les études]?	
E6 [v]		Ah moi, je/je vais pas

Extract 4: (In 6_28–30, Osterkorn 2013a)
E6 [v] the cook, he does not speak Breton and then it depends on which table you are at,
E6 [v] because if you are (laughter)/ if you are close to teachers, we speak Breton.
PKO [v] Ok, I see, after/after the school, then. "Studi" [time to study]?
E6 [v]   Ah, I/I will not

In line 29 and 30 the teachers' role becomes obvious: "if the teachers are present, we speak Breton." They are perceived as those who execute the spatial language order. Ethnographic observation has shown that in case the usage of French is perceived by school staff, pupils are often verbally warned to immediately use Breton. This is generally respected, although a pupil reports that they would then speak Breton, but after five minutes fall back into French (In 1_118, Osterkorn 2013a).

However, there is a small minority among the interviewed students who overtly questions the language policy: One student for instance suggests that the teachers should stop warning pupils when they hear a French word, since students would then lose courage and end up using Breton even more rarely (In 3_74, Osterkorn 2013a). Another student clearly claims that if they were not forced to speak Breton, it would in fact make the use of Breton more likely (In 8_43, Osterkorn 2013a). Finally, one student argues that learners understandably react to pressure with defiance due to their age (and to puberty) (In 11, Osterkorn 2013a).

The interviews reveal in how far the pupils co-construct and hence confirm the monolingual space. Moreover, it can be hypothesised that the language policy impacts on the emotions and well-being of individuals concerning the use of Breton. These findings correspond to conclusions drawn by Blackledge and Creese (2011), whose study on multilingualism in minority schools demonstrates that a sense of compulsion and thus learners' experience of separate multilingualism is to be considered prototypical for this particular type of school. The fear of the extinction of a language quickly turns into language compulsion. Total immersion (or rather subtle submersion?) is a frequent strategy underlying the language frame. As our study additionally shows at this point, the experience of multilingualism is thus nearly completely missed by learners. The investigated learners bow to the rules of the space, and draw upon a wider range of resources only in informal situations.

5.2.2 French as a place of emotional refuge

The space is perceived as quite challenging and structured by transparent rules. This is evident in Extract 5. At the same time this extract also articulates a key idea about French. Pupils frequently comment on "being tired" (see Extract 6 below) of speaking Breton. French then serves as a refuge.

In Extract 5, once again, the rules are made explicit. Language choice depends on the theme of the conversation, on the concrete location and on the others present. Another point is "si on n'a pas envie de faire l'effort"/"if we do not want to make an effort" (In 4_25–26, Osterkorn 2013a). Using Breton thus demands a particular effort and French consequently emerges especially when pupils feel tired or listless. Similarly, another pupil admits that she no longer "controls" herself when she is in the boarding room and automatically speaks French (In 3_46, Osterkorn 2013a). Especially when communication issues are about intimate, political or other everyday banalities, learners find it easier to use the "private language". Furthermore, as expressed by still another pupil, the Breton language does not have many words used by young people (i.e. cool or vulgar expressions) or that these expressions are hardly used in the context of teaching (In 11, Osterkorn 2013a). Therefore, learners find it difficult to use Breton, for example in arguments, and thus report to curse in French (In 2_45, Osterkorn 2013a). Again, this makes clear in how far the space disables pupils not only to draw upon their linguistic resources and hence to act as "resourceful speakers", but also to position themselves according to their communicative needs.

[23]

	21 [02:06.9]	22 [02:08.9]	
PKO [v]	Ça dépend de quoi ou?		
E4 [v]	dépend.	Ça dé	Ça dépend de quoi on parle, ça dépend où on se

[24]

PKO [v]	Ahm.
E4 [v]	trouve, s'il y a quelqu'un à côté, si on a disons la flemme de parler breton, si on a pas

[25]

PKO [v]	Ahum.
E4 [v]	envie de faire l'effort, on parlera en français, parfois s'il y a personne qui nous

[26]

		23 [02:23.8]	
PKO [v]		Okey. Ahmm pendant le repas de midi?	
E4 [v]	entend, on s'en fiche un peu ((rire))		Alors,

Extract 5 (In 4_23–26, Osterkorn 2013a)
PKO [v]   It depends on what?
E4 [v] depends.   It depends on what we're speaking, it depends on
E4 [v] where one is, if there is someone nearby, if we are too lazy to speak Breton,
E4 [v] if we do not want to make an effort, we'll speak French, sometimes if there is nobody who
PKO [v]   Okay. Ahm during lunch?
E4 [v] hears us, we do not care a bit (laughs)   Then,

5.2.3 Promoting Breton

The third idea allows us to understand why pupils rather confirm than transform the space, although its language-ideological frame is perceived as limiting individual possibilities. Pupils at DIWAN-schools seem, for whatever reason, to possess a particular awareness of the future of the Breton language.

[13]

	10 [01:17.9] 11 [01:18.5]	12 [01:19.0]
PKO [v] mère, tu parles pratiquement tout le temps en breton?	Tout le temps?	
E3 [v]	Oui!	

[14]

E3 [v]	Pratiquement tout le temps. Ça nous arrive quand on est fatigué de parler en

[15]

E3 [v]	français, mais j'essaie de parler de maximum en breton pour que • • • ça nous

[16]

Extract 6 (In 3_13–16, Osterkorn 2013a)
PKO [v] with your mother, you talk almost all the time in Breton?   All the time?
E3 [v]   Yes!
E3 [v]   Almost all the time. It happens to us when we are tired that we speak
E3 [v]   French, but I try to speak a maximum in Breton in order to ... this upgrades my Breton

In Extract 6 the use of French in case of being tired is reiterated, but the motivation for using Breton becomes obvious as well. There is an awareness about the effort that is needed in order to be competent in Breton and Breton competence is an unquestioned goal: "J'essaie de parler un maximum en Breton pour que... ça nous améliore ((2s)) la langue"/"I try to speak a maximum in Breton in order to... this upgrades my Breton" (In 3_15–16, Osterkorn 2013a). Since the pupils have decided or it has been decided for them to attend one of the Breton immersion schools, the use of Breton is reported as acceptable and is frequently conceived of as "normal". The aim behind the Breton-only strategy seems to be accepted, although it is very rarely made as explicit as in Extract 7:

[46]

PKO [v]	Ahum.		Ahum.
E12 [v]	•• ben parler breton, pour moi c'est naturel ici, c'est naturellement, il faut préserver		

[47]

		31 [04:50.9]
PKO [v]		Ok
E12 [v]	le breton, du coup quand on m'oblige de parler breton, ben je parle breton.	

[48]

Extract 7 (In 12_46–47, Osterkorn 2013a)
E12 [v]   well, speaking Breton, for me it is natural here, it comes naturally, Breton has to be
E12 [v]   preserved, when I am responsible for speaking Breton, well I speak Breton.

"Il faut preserver le Breton"/"Breton has to be preserved" and so the pupils themselves are prepared to make the effort needed. However, the way the strategy is executed, hence the working of the spatial language frame, is perceived as problematic also by pupils who are willing to support what they perceive of as "the Breton language", as already mentioned in Section 4.2.1.

5.2.4 Fun factor of flexible/integrated multilingualism

The last key idea that can be deduced from the narrative interviews is that of having fun with languages. It subverts the lived kind of separated multilingualism at school and allows for a more integrated language practice that deconstructs not only the language-ideological frame at school but partially also questions the idea it is based upon, i.e. that of whole languages.

"It happens that we mix/that we make sentences with words from several languages, between, for fun. For example, we start in Breton, finish with English words, with a little bit of French and sometimes it happens that we mix German, too".

In informal situations that are not regulated by the educational space, pupils creatively draw upon the resources available. The same pupil talks about her multilingual dreams, in which very strange speech mixtures occur (In 3_82, Osterkorn 2013a), which she in turn finds funny.

Another pupil speaks of the fact that knowing a language certainly makes learning another language easier: He draws conclusions from the English language when he learns German (In 11_63, Osterkorn 2013a). For another pupil, it seems almost natural to construct phrases with Breton and French words at home, as she has spoken and heard so much Breton at school (In 4_52, Osterkorn 2013a). In these examples the fun factor of a form of multilingualism, which we will define as "flexible/integrated multilingualism" (Blackledge and Creese 2010) becomes obvious.

Extract 9 pertains less to integrated multilingualism than to the fun factor reported by students. It is a well-known fact that codes can also be used in order to exclude those that should not understand. Extract 9 reports on the use of Breton as such a "secret" language in public space outside school. Here, Breton is situated on a different scalar level with respect to the local space at school. Breton

[26]

PKO [v]	Ahumm
E3 [v]	français entre nous, parce qu'on est en cours de français ((1s)), ça nous arrive de

[27]

	27 [02:30.9]
PKO [v]	Aha.
E3 [v]	mélanger/ fin de faire des phrases avec des mots de plusieurs langues

[28]

28 [02:31.4]	29 [02:33.4]	
PKO [v]	Par exemple?	
E3 [v]	entre, fin, pour rigoler.	Ben, par exemple on commence en breton et on finit avec

[29]

E3 [v]	des mots d'anglais et avec un petit peu de français et parfois ça nous arrive de

[30]

	30 [02:42.3]
PKO [v]	Aha, c'est interessant ça ((2s)) okey, ahm, après pendant
E3 [v]	mélanger l'allemand avec.

Extract 8 (In 3_26–30, Osterkorn 2013a)
E3 [v] French for us, because we are in French lesson, it sometimes happens that we
E3 [v] mix/that we make sentences with words from several languages,
PKO [v] For example?
E3 [v] between, for fun. Well, for example, we start in Breton, finish with
E3 [v] English words, with a little bit of French and sometimes it happens that we
E3 [v] mix in German, too.
PKO [v] Aha, that's interesting. Okay, ahm, after

at this level serves not for wider communication but, on the contrary, prevents communication and reinforces the local kind of scalarity.

What these examples have in common is the fun factor, "pour rigoler", and that the pupils creatively draw upon their linguistic resources available in a space that is not constrained by a monolingual frame.

[43]

PKO [v]	Ahum.
E4 [v]	sinon quand on veut parler sur la tête des/des autres ((rire)) quand il y a quelqu'un à

[44]

PKO [v]	Oui.
E4 [v]	côté, fin je sais pas imaginons que nous sommes dans la rue ou quelque part et

[45]

PKO [v]	
E4 [v]	quand on a une remarque à faire ((rire)) sur quelqu'un qui soit dans la rue, on

[46]

	31 [04:10.9]		32 [04:12.4]	
PKO [v]		Avec des parents tu veux dire? Ahum.		
E4 [v]	parlera en breton.		Ouais, voilà.	Avec mes parents

Extract 9 (In 4_43–46, Osterkorn 2013a)
E4 [v] except when we want to talk about the head of/someone else (laughter) if there is someone nearby,
E4 [v] I don't know, imagine that we are in our street, somewhere,
E4 [v] and when we make a remark (laughter) on anybody in the street, we'll speak
PKO [v]   With your parents you mean? Ahum.
E4 [v] in Breton.   Yes.   With my parents (inc)...

6 Concluding remarks

We began by conceptualising space as an agentive and multiscalar network of relationships that relates to a specific kind of linguistic practice. From our theoretical perspective it appeared of great interest to observe those who play an active part in this network and to ask in how far they co-construct space. Here, our focus was on the pupils. We considered them in terms of multilingual subjects who creatively draw upon the linguistic resources available to them. In our study on multilingual pupils in a minority immersion school we encountered space in terms of a network that enabled and disabled linguistic practice in a particular way. Against the background of school monolingualism, the multilingual subjects are disabled to fully draw upon their resources. They invent strategies in order to circumvent the institutional space and hence create new spaces while at the same time co-constructing the institutional frame.

It is the emotional side of language that we can identify as the problematic side of the regulations in the particular school under investigation. The focus on the space and the multilingual subjects has revealed a discrepancy between the space on the one hand and the pupils' communicative demands on the other. Pupils are allowed to position themselves in a very specific way. It is particularly the emotional and fun-related aspect that is silenced here. It comes as no surprise, then, that individuals have developed a range of strategies in order to escape this frame and that the executors of the language regime seem to invest considerable time and effort in order to keep the regime working in spite of this.

We want to conclude that the problematic side of this kind of multilingualism is the emotional disempowerment of the young speakers who cannot fully act as resourceful speakers at school. To indicate an alternative, it might be worth thinking about pursuing the idea of a "multilingual school" in the sense presented by Hélot and Young (2006), within which multilingual subjects may be able to find their place more successfully.

> We would define a multilingual school as a place where linguistic and cultural diversity is acknowledged and valued, where children can feel safe to use their home language alongside the school language [...] to learn and to communicate, where teachers are not afraid and do not feel threatened to hear languages they do not know, and where multilingualism and multilingual literacies are supported. In other words, a multilingual school is not just a place where pupils can learn two or more languages. It is also a place where the plurilingual repertoire of bilingual/multilingual pupils is recognised and viewed as a resource to be shared and built upon, rather than a problem. (Hélot and Young 2006: 69)

References

Adkins, Madeleine. 2013. Will the real Breton please stand up? Language revitalization and the problem of authentic language. *International Journal of the Sociology of Language* 223: 55–70.

Bailey, Benjamin. 2012. Heteroglossia. *The Routledge Handbook of Multilingualism*. 499–507. New York: Routledge.

Bendassolli, Pedro F. 2013. *Theory Building in Qualitative Research: Reconsidering the Problem of Induction [50 paragraphs]*. Forum Qualitative Sozialforschung/Forum: Qualitative Social Research 14(1). http://nbn-resolving.de/urn:nbn:de:0114-fqs1301258. (accessed 24 January 2014)

Blackledge, Adrian & Angela Creese. 2010. Multilingualism. *A Critical Perspective*. London: Continuum.

Blackledge, Adrian & Angela Creese. 2011. Separate and flexible bilingualism in complementary schools: Multiple language practices in interrelationship. *Journal of Pragmatics* 43. 1196–1208.

Blommaert, Jan, James Collins & Stef Slembrouch. 2005. Spaces of multilingualism. *Language & Communication* 25. 197–216.

Blommaert, Jan & April Huang. 2010. Semiotic and spatial scope: Towards a materialist semiotics. *Working Papers in Urban Language & Literacies 62*. 1–15.

Blommaert, Jan. 2013. Complexity, accent, and conviviality: Concluding comments. *A complexity perspective. Applied Linguistics* 34(5). 613–622.

Bourdieu, Pierre. 1984. Espace social et genèse des "classes". *Actes de la recherche en sciences sociales*, 52–53. 3–14.

Busch, Brigitta. 2013. *Mehrsprachigkeit*. Wien: Facultas.

Canagarajah, Suresh. 2013. Theorizing a competence for translingual practice at the contact zone. In Stephen May (ed.), *The Multilingual Turn. Implications for SLA, TESOL and Bilingual Education*, 78–102. New York and London: Routledge.

Charter RML. 1992. *European Charter for Regional or Minority Languages – Strasbourg*, 5.XI.1992. – Online Document: http://conventions.coe.int/Treaty/EN/Treaties/Html/148.htm (13.12.2014)

Christian, Donna. 1996. Two-way immersion education: students learning through two languages. *The Modern Language Journal* 80. 66–76.

Coulmas, Florian. 2005. Changing language regimes in globalizing environments. *International Journal of the Sociology of Languages* 175–176. 3–15.

Coseriu, Eugenio. 1973. *Probleme der strukturellen Semantik*. Tübingen: Narr.

Decke-Cornill, Helene & Lutz, Küster. 2010. *Fremdsprachendidaktik. Eine Einführung*. Tübingen: Narr.

Fielding, Nigel & Jane, Fielding. 1986. *Linking Data: The Articulation of Qualitative and Quantitative Methods in Social Research*. Beverly Hills and London: Sage.

Fielding, Nigel & Margrit Schreier. 2001. Introduction: On the Compatibility between Qualitative and Quantitative Research Methods. *Forum Qualitative Sozialforschung/Forum: Qualitative Social Research* 2(1). http://www.qualitative-research.net/fqs-texte/1-01/1-01hrsg-e.htm (accessed 21 January 2014)

García, Ofelia. 2009. *Bilingual Education in the 21st Century. A Global Perspective*. New York: Wiley-Blackwell.

Gogolin, Ingrid. 1994. *Der monolinguale Habitus der multilingualen Schule*. Münster & New York: Waxmann.

Gogolin, Ingrid & Ursula Neumann. 1999. Sprachliches Handeln in der Grundschule. *Die Grundschulzeitschrift* 43. 6–13.

Gwegen, Jori. 1983. "Diwan", or the strategy of the "fait accompli". In Cathal Ó Luain (ed.), For a Celtic future. A tribute to Alan Heusaff, 118–131. Dublin: The Celtic League.

Hagège, Claude. 1996. *Le Français, Histoire d'un Combat*. Boulogne-Billancourt: Editions Michel Hagège.

Hélot, Christine & Andrea Young. 2006. Imagining multilingual education in France: A language and cultural awareness project at primary level. In Ofelia García, Tove Skutnabb-Kangas & María Torres-Guzam (eds.), *Imagining Multilingual Schools. Languages in Education and Glocalization*, 69–90. Clevedon et al.: Multilingual Matters.

Hoaré, Rachel. 2002. *L'Identité Linguistique des Jeunes en Bretagne*. Brest: Brud Nevez.

Hopf, Christel. 2010. Qualitative Interviews – ein Überblick. In Uwe Flick, Ernst von Kardorff & Ines Steinke (eds.), *Qualitative Forschung. Ein Handbuch*, 8th edn. 349–360. Hamburg: Rowohlt Taschenbuch.

Huffschmid, Anne & Kathrin Wildner. 2009. Räume sprechen, Diskurse verorten? Überlegungen zu einer transdisziplinären Ethnografie. *Forum Qualitative Sozialforschung* 10(3).

Jaworski, Adam & Crispin Thurlow. 2009. Introducing semiotic landscapes. In IDEM. (eds.), *Semiotic Landscapes: Language, Image, Space*, 1–40. London: Continuum.

Jones, Mari C. 1998. *La Langue Bretonne Aujourd'hui à Plougastel-Daoulas*. Brest: Brud Nevez.

Jørgensen, J. Normann, Martha Sif Karrebæk, Lian Malai Madsen & Janus Spindler Møller. 2011. Polylanguaging in Superdiversity Diversities – An online journal published by UNESCO & MPIMMG 13 (2). http://unesdoc.unesco.org/images/0021/002147/214772e.pdf#214780 (accessed 6 december 2012).

Kelle, Udo. 2001. Sociological explanations between micro and macro and the integration of qualitative and quantitative methods. *Forum Qualitative Social Research* 1. http://www.qualitative-research.net/fqs-texte/1-01/1-01kelle-e.htm. (accessed 23 January 2014)

Kramsch, Claire. 2009. *The Multilingual Subject: What Foreign Language Learners Say About Their Experience and Why It Matters*. Oxford: Oxford University Press.

Kramsch, Claire & Sascha Gerhards. 2012. An interview with Claire Kramsch on the 'multilingual subject'. *Die Unterrichtspraxis/Teaching German* 45(1). 74–82.

Kremnitz, Georg. 1997. *Die Durchsetzung der Nationalsprachen in Europa*. Münster: Waxmann.

Kristeva, Julia. 1977. *Polylogue*. Paris: Seuil.

Kroskrity, Paul. 2000. Regimenting languages: language ideological perspectives. In IDEM (ed.), *Regimes of Language: Ideologies, Polities, and Identities*. 1–35. Oxford: James Currey.

Krumm, Hans-Jürgen & Eva-Maria Jenkins (eds.). 2001. *Kinder und ihre Sprachen-lebendige Mehrsprachigkeit*. Sprachenporträts – gesammelt und kommentiert von Hans-Jürgen Krumm. Wien: Eviva.

Kuter, Lois. 1999. The Diwan phenomenon: A catalyst for change in the schools of Brittany. In Philippe Blanchet, Roland Breton & Harold Schiffman (eds.), *Les langues régionales de France: un état des lieux à la veille du XXIe siècle*, 177–183, Louvain-la-Neuve: Peeters.

Lafont, Robert. 1968. *Sur la France*. Paris: Gallimard.

Lafont, Robert. 1971. *Décoloniser en France: les régions face à l'Europe*. Paris: Gallimard.

Landry, Rodrigue & Richard Y. Bourhis. 1997. Linguistic landscape and ethnolinguistic vitality: An empirical study. *Journal of Language and Social Psychology* 16. 23–49.

Lefèbvre, Henri. 1991/2004 [1974]. *The Production of Space*. Malden: Blackwell./La production de l'espace. Paris: Anthropos.

Löw, Martina. 2008. The constitution of space. The structuration of spaces through the simultaneity of effect and perception. *European Journal of Social Theory* 11/1. 25–49.

Lüders, Christian. 2010. Beobachten im Feld und Ethnographie. In Uwe Flick, Ernst Von Kardorff & Ines Steinke (eds.), *Qualitative Forschung. Ein Handbuch*. Hamburg: Rowohlts Enzyklopädie, 384–401.

Lüdtke, Helmut. 1999. *Sprache zwischen 'Chaos' und spontaner Ordnung*. In Thomas Stehl (ed.), *Dialektgenerationen, Dialektfunktionen, Sprachwandel*, 1–17. Tübingen: Narr.
Moore, Danièle & Cécile Sabatier. 2010. *Une Semaine en Classe en Immersion Française au Canada. Approche ethnographique pour la formation*. Grenoble: Presses Universitaires.
Osterkorn, Patrick K. 2013a. Vivre un multilinguisme dis joint? L'expérience du multilinguisme des collégiens dans une école minoritaire vivant en breton. Wien: Universität, Diploma thesis.
Osterkorn, Patrick K. 2013b (publication in press). *Separated multilingualism? The experience of students' multilingualism in minority language education in Brittany (France)*. SALi. *Studies of Applied Linguistics (Charles University of Prague)* 2.
Otsuji, Emi & Alastair Pennycook. 2010. Metrolingualism: Fixity, fluidity and language in flux. *International Journal of Multilingualism* 7 (3). 240–254.
Pennycook, Alastair. 2012. *Language and Mobility. Unexpected Places*. Bristol: Multilingual Matters.
Purkarthofer, Judith. 2014. Sprachort Schule. Zur Konstruktion von mehrsprachigen Räumen und Praktiken in einer zweisprachigen Volksschule. Wien: Universität, Dissertation (unpublished).
Rindler-Schjerve, Rosita & Eva Vetter. 2012. *European Multilingualism. Current Perspectives and Challenges*. Bristol: Multilingual Matters.
Scollon, Ron & Suzie Wong Scollon. 2003. *Discourses in Place: Language in the Material World*. London: Routledge.
Talmy, Steven. 2010. Qualitative interviews in applied linguistics: from research instrument to social practice. *Annual Review of Applied Linguistics* 30. 128–148.
Vertovec, Steve. 2007. Super – diversity and its implications. *Ethnic and Racial Studies* (29), 1024–1054.
Vetter, Eva. 1999. *Plus de Breton. Conflit Linguistique en Bretagne Rurale*. Brest: An Here.
Vetter, Eva. 2005. Wie viel Differenz ist zumutbar? Eine Diskursanalyse zum bretonisch-französischen Sprachkonflikt. In Verena Berger, Friedrich Frosch & Eva Vetter (eds.), *Zwischen Aneignung und Bruch. Studien zum Konfliktpotential von Kulturkontakten in der Romania*, 65–82. Wien: Löcker.
Vetter, Eva. 2013. Teaching languages for a multilingual Europe – minority schools as examples of best practice? The Breton experience of Diwan. *International Journal of the Sociology of Language* 223. 153–170.
Weber, Jean-Jacques & Kristine Horner. 2012. *Introducing Multilingualism: A social approach*. London: Routledge.
Woolard, Kathryn A. 1998. Introduction. Language ideology as a field of inquiry. In Bambi B. Schieffelin, Kathryn A. Woolard and Paul V. Kroskrity (eds.) *Language Ideologies. Practice and Theory* (pp.3–47). New York/Oxford: Oxford University Press.

URL: http://www.diwanbreizh.org/sections.php4?op=viewarticle&artid=26 (accessed 24 January 2014).
URL: http://www.geobreizh.com/breizh/fra/signaletique.asp (accessed 24 January 2014)

Part III: **Institutional challenges**

Brian Lennon
6 Challenges to monolingual national literatures

Abstract: Both social-existential and literary forms of multilingualism pose meaningful challenges to monolingual national literatures, but the reverse is also true. Claudio Guillén's typology of responses to the "latent" multilingualism of many societies distinguished between mere *Sprachmischung* and a more radical literary bilingualism, and was conscientiously attentive to the social dynamics of domination and subordination that guide the choice of a language of expression for multilingual or equilingual writers. And yet, like most who have written on this subject, Guillén had little to say about what I consider the primary *counter-challenge* posed by monolingual national literatures to the literary multilingualism that challenges *them*: the organization of the book and other print publication industries, which all too often block the publication of radically multilingual literature at the point of entry to the market or even at the creative source, barring access to the literary posterity of the library and archive or even dissuading multilingual writers from undertaking multilingual writing projects altogether.

1 Literature against publication

Both social-existential and literary forms of multilingualism pose meaningful challenges to monolingual national literatures, but the reverse is also true. In his typology of responses to what he called the "latent" multilingualism of many societies today, Claudio Guillén (1993; 1985) distinguished between mere *Sprachmischung* and a more radical literary bilingualism, and was conscientiously attentive to the social dynamics of domination and subordination that guide the choice of a language of expression for multilingual or equilingual writers. Guillén observed that "[i]n countless places and times, multilingualism is the characteristic feature of the society and consequently determines the posture of a writer toward that society. Multilingualism is also common among primitive peoples [...] But the advent of writing caused a rift and required a choice of language [...] diglossia is typical above all of countries in which the speech of common people is subjugated and devalued by another dominant language" (Guillén 1993, 265, quoted with omissions). Guillén faulted the late nineteenth century disciplinary formation of *littéra-*

Brian Lennon, Pennsylvania State University, US, blennon@psu.edu *ture comparée,* whose scholarly practitioners earned fame for the multilingualism of their erudition, for its neglect of *literary* multilingualism: the multilingualism of the artifact rather than of the scholar studying it. He suggested quite pointedly that for all the implicit resistance of comparative research methods to the Romantic and imperial nationalism of the age, its practitioners were more deeply bound by it than they may have believed (Guillén 1993: 260–261).

Guillén made several distinctions that are still useful in thinking about challenges to monolingual national literatures, even if they were finally rather impressionistic and left without elaboration. The first was a distinction between the "latent" multilingualism of a unilingual culture *or* work of literature, formed by the historically routine hegemony of one language over others, and what we might call the "manifest" multilingualism (Guillén's own word is "obvious") of authors like Ramón Llull, who insisted nevertheless on "expressing themselves in more than one language" in their written work and so deliberately maintaining the means of doing so. (For Llull, Guillén notes, this meant cultivating Catalan as a literary language along with Latin, Arabic, and Provençal.) "It is important," Guillén argued, "to distinguish between writers whose multilingualism – effective or not – is a personal destiny, results of avatars of their singular life story, like Joseph Conrad, and those who became multilingual in response to the peculiarities of their social surroundings and the particular historical moment handed them by fate. Great differences, both spatial and temporal, obtain between these innately polyglot circumstances, and the critic attempting to evaluate a bilingual writer should be acutely aware of these differences" (Guillén 1993: 268). What Guillén meant here remains typologically unclear, as he tended to defer rigorous exposition in favor of illustration through "a few examples" (Guillén 1993: 270). But he appears to have wanted to distinguish between 1) a kind of cultivated, even virtuosic multilingualism which, while certainly not socially and historically uncaused, remains idiosyncratically "artistic" in character; and 2) a less freely chosen, more externally determined multilingualism, leaving different traces in the different kind of literary artifact it produced.

Under the domination of something close to actual force, as in military conquest and colonization, Guillén noted, it is truly exceptional for a writer like Juan Wallparrimachi (1793–1814) to be able to "cling tenaciously" to a dominated language (in this case, Quechua). Equally rare was "the equal domination of two languages, or true equilingualism": most often, a writer who produces or even publishes in more than one language will favor one language, in one way or another, and "the patently polyglot writer will be neither equilingual nor equipoetical" (Guillén 1993: 270). A radical literary bilingualism, Guillén concluded, had "little to do with the so-called *Sprachmischung*, if by that we mean the transitory use of other languages inserted into the dominant language of the comedy, a novel, or poetry": such a mixture is basically a kind of seasoning of a text in a "native" language with the words of a "foreign" language (Guillén 1993: 272). It was both difficult and important, Guillén believed, to "determine whether or not these accidental mélanges reveal a true multilingualism, even a latent, genuine one": although Camilo José Cela, for example, had used more than three hundred Galician words in *Mazurca para dos mertos* (1983), Cela's prose, Guillén concluded, had not been transformed in any structurally significant way by the modification. Accordingly, Guillén concluded, Cela's "bilingualism does not go beyond a superficial and picturesque level" (Guillén 1993: 272–273).

Surprisingly perhaps, and yet very much like most who have written on this subject, Guillén had little to say about the primary *counter*-challenge posed by monolingual national literatures to the literary multilingualism that challenges *them*: the organization of the book and other print publication industries, which all too often block the publication of radically multilingual literature at the point of entry to the market or even at the creative source, barring access to the literary posterity of the library and archive or even dissuading multilingual writers from undertaking multilingual writing projects altogether. We might say that what little study of multilingual literary artifacts we do have, at all, has often been in thrall to structural or "systemic" approaches that, intentionally or unintentionally, devote themselves so fully to the pursuit of the legible extant artifact, and to the description of its literary relations, that they fail to consider what it means that so few radically multilingual works of literature ever come into being, to begin with.

2 The consolation of typology

To date, only one literary critic whose work is available in the English language has attempted a rigorous narratological analysis of national-language code-switching in printed works of literature, as distinct from a simultaneously more generalized and more exclusively internal national heteroglossia. That critic is Meir Sternberg, whose probing and suggestive reflections on literary polylingualism are grounded first and foremost in a methodological segregation of the terms and objects of professional sociolinguistic discourse from those of literary criticism and scholarship. Literary works, Sternberg insists as a kind of condition for making use of his work, are in strictly textual terms "unilingual" and "polylingual," whereas "monolingualism" and "multilingualism" "are sociolinguistic terms for speakers and communities," useful in characterizing the range of a speaker or a community of speakers but not the diversity (or lack of diversity) of a literary text. A literary text, Sternberg observes, has the capacity to represent a unilingual reality even where the individual speakers or communities of speakers thus represented are multilingual speakers or communities of speakers; and it also has the capacity to represent a polylingual reality even where the individual speakers or communities of speakers thus represented are monolingual speakers or communities of speakers (Sternberg 1981: 222).

Attacking what he called the "reproductive fallacy" presuming that literary dialogue is meant to represent speech (Sternberg 1981, 237), Sternberg insisted that the putative realism of literary polylingualism has meaning only within the reality-model of the fictive world presented by a work of literature. This swift, expedient segregation of the literariness of representation from the broader politics of representation with which it is so often entwined, in the official culture of the nation state, the school curriculum, and the book and other cultural markets, enabled Sternberg to build up an armature of typological concepts and terms whose considerable descriptive virtue must be weighed against its deferral of other modes of critical thought. Sternberg's insistence that "[i]n literary art [...] the realism of polylingual discourse – like the realism of discourse in general and of all nonverbal objects within the represented framework – cannot be understood apart from the text's overall referential strategy, of which it is both a miniature and a part or means" (Sternberg 1981: 233) subordinated the context of literary production to the internal structure of the produced artifact, understood as a miniature "world" bordering or containing other such miniature worlds. Relating such fictive structures to the putatively real world in which we produce, exchange, and consume them is a sensitive business indeed, fraught with all manner of methodological hazards, on warning us of which Sternberg expended considerable energy. Thus "to classify (or even worse, condemn) a work as unrealistic for failing to resort to translational forms that are in fact historically inaccessible or functionally irrelevant (if not detrimental) to it would be as absurd as the common practice of raising the stick of 'realism' against a work whose whole sin actually consists in leaving out certain areas of reality that are beneath its notice, outside its existential ken or beyond its artistic bounds" (Sternberg 1981: 233).

In some ways this could not be further from the spirit of Guillén's distinction between "mere" *Sprachmischung* and a more "radical" literary bilingualism, in so far as that distinction licensed reasonable critical evaluation of the cultural-political choices made, very much for better or for worse, by working writers in the process of producing their works. While where scholarly discipline is desired, at least, Sternberg's scholarly discipline is to be preferred to Guillén's fickler critical impressionism, it must be said that Sternberg's quasi-structuralism suffered the most typical liability of that kind of approach. In insisting so strongly on the demystification of an imagined "necessary correspondence between mimetic form and mimetic function" (Sternberg 1981: 234), it risked obscuring the historical specificity of any instance where such terms might correlate or even converge, with political consequences outside the domain of the artifact itself – or where there are simply other, potentially more urgent questions at hand. Thus to Sternberg's postulate that "[w]hat is artistically more crucial than linguistic reality is the model(s) of that reality as internally patterned or invoked by the individual work and/or conventionally fashioned by the literary tradition and/or conceived of by the reader within the given cultural framework" (Sternberg 1981: 235), it is too easy to reply: But what if "artistic" importance is not what is important at all? The impoverishment of such a discourse is perhaps plainest in Sternberg's remarks on "Ian Fleming's representation of Negro dialect in the James Bond saga," which conclude that "[t]o dismiss his rendering as grossly inaccurate is to miss the whole point, and not simply because we have to do here with a genre of popular literature. To Fleming, such foreign speech is not a dialectological problem but a rhetorical tool – a possible source of local color and picturesque effect" (Sternberg 1981: 236).

Nevertheless, it is worth reviewing Sternberg's schema. At its core is the argument that the "interlingual tension" between (1) language as something represented in a work of literature and (2) language as a – rather, *the* – means of such representation itself, is best imagined as a mimetic tension, rather than as a communicative tension: that is, as a structural challenge for the descriptive literary critic, rather than an ostensibly external question of interpretation. "Literary art," Sternberg observes, "finds itself confronted by a formidable mimetic challenge: how to represent the reality of polylingual discourse through a communicative medium which is normally unilingual" (Sternberg 1981: 222). Sternberg identified three main "procedures" for either meeting, or avoiding this challenge. The first, "referential restriction," directly negates the conflicts it presents, "confining the scope of the represented world to the limits of a single, linguistically uniform community whose speech-patterns correspond to those of the implied audience, sometimes to the point of excluding interdialectical as well as interlingual tensions, as in the novels of Jane Austen" (Sternberg 1981: 223). The second, "vehicular matching," accepts such conflicts "as a matter of course, as a fact of life and a factor of communication"; we find this commonly in scholarly writing itself, Sternberg notes, but also in "different varieties of polyglot art, whether Jean Renoir's bilingual film *La grande illusion* or G. B. Shaw's polydialectical *Pygmalion*" (Sternberg 1981: 223). A third, "homogenizing convention," represents a kind of strategic, rather than naive reduction of polylingual extraverbal reality to textual uniformity: in *Antony and Cleopatra*, Sternberg argues, "the development of the most complex figurative patterns known to literary art hinges on the antihistorical Englishing of the polylingual discourse held in the world of Romans and Egyptians" (Sternberg 1981: 224). This third procedure is opposed, Sternberg suggests, not to vehicular matching so much as to an ancillary fourth procedure, the "vehicular promiscuity" that Sternberg finds "typical of macaronic writing – from the medieval *muwaššah* to Joyce's *Finnegans Wake* – where shifts of medium are mimetically gratuitous and polylingual means are often flagrantly summoned to represent a unilingual reality of discourse" (Sternberg 1981: 224).

Each of these three procedures, Sternberg observes, aims in its own way to eliminate the mimetic challenge of representing heterolingual discourse. In actual practice, this challenge can only be met by what Sternberg called "mimetic compromise," as various mimetic elements and strategies are tried and combined (Sternberg 1981: 225). Still, such compromise is defined by two extremes of polylingual representation. At one extreme, the one more commonly observed in extant literary artifacts, polylingual representation is effectively submerged in the unilingual representation of an extraverbal reality, or suppressed altogether. At the other extreme, the representation of an extraverbal reality is subordinated to "polylingual play." This second approach, Sternberg notes, "is not so common on a large scale – certainly not in drama and the novel, for fairly obvious generic reasons" (Sternberg 1981: 236).

Along the continuum defined by these two extremes, Sternberg located four types of the negotiation he termed "translational mimesis." The first, "selective reproduction," in which a heterolingual discourse is quoted intermittently, serves "as a kind of mimetic synechdoche" by which a standardized unilingual discourse is re-authorized, indexically acknowledging the historical polylingualism from which it emerged: for example, the shift from Hebrew to Aramaic in the "Persian" documents embedded in the Hebrew narrative of the Book of Ezra, Tolstoy's insertion of reported Francophone speech in *War and Peace*, Nabokov's insertion of Russian in *Pnin*, or Mann's insertion of Latin, French, and English in *Der Erwählte (The Holy Sinner)* (Sternberg 1981: 226). "Minimal units" of such selective reproduction include the "mimetic cliche" of such expressive interjections as "Damn!," "Parbleu!," "Donnerwetter!," or other mannneristic, low information density tag phrases as are commonly used in popular culture and mass media, and which tend not to presume or demand multilingual reader competence (Sternberg 1981: 226). But "selective reproduction" can also describe the more challenging, indeed "uncompromising demands of unique dialogue and esoteric quotation (especially prevalent in minority culture and/or canonical literature)" (Sternberg 1981: 227), and it can include deliberately distorted or otherwise manipulated forms of "deviant allusion and internal misquotation," as well (Sternberg 1981: 227).

Two of the remaining three modes tend to make greater demands on reader competence. The second, "verbal transposition," is an overtly stylized and "mimetically oblique" mode, describing the interlingual tension and interference of code mixing or superimposition, as in the literal translation of Spanish idiom in Hemingway's *For Whom the Bell Tolls* (Sternberg 1981: 228). The third, "conceptual reflection," is marked not by the verbal forms of another language or languages so much as by its semantic and other referential ranges (Sternberg 1981: 230). A fourth mode, "explicit attribution," directly identifies an instance of discourse as having been spoken or written in another language (for example, "He spoke French"). Because it so directly asserts the reality of a heterolingual discourse, Sternberg suggested that explicit attribution was the most radical of the four modes, while noting that it could be difficult to distinguish from selective reproduction, in so far as textually, it too resolved to "the uncontested unilingualism of the representational medium" (Sternberg 1981: 232).

3 Does a bell toll in a (particular) language?

As Sternberg provides fewer examples of either "conceptual reflection" or "explicit attribution" than of "selective reproduction" or "verbal transposition," we will look more closely at the linguistic texture of one work he cites in connection with the latter. The pages of Hemingway's *For Whom the Bell Tolls* (1940), the most suffused with Spanish of his works of fiction, are studded with Spanish words and phrases that might be said to localize both political and cultural (including linguistic) conflict in the mind of the character Robert Jordan, a U.S. volunteer for the International Brigades in the Spanish Civil War.

Though the linguistic texture of *For Whom the Bell Tolls* arguably generates many both centripetal and centrifugal interlinguistic effects, scholarship focused on the novel has always, often polemically, noted its limits as a form of tokenization, which one might certainly choose to read at odds with the cultural internationalism of the cause it supports. Josephs (1983) catalogued over sixty unique Spanish-language errors in the 1940 edition of *For Whom the Bell Tolls* that went uncorrected in subsequent editions. While admitting that such errors were mainly orthographic and typographic, Josephs argued that collectively, they destroyed the "credibility" of both Robert Jordan as a fictional character (an ostensibly fluent speaker of Spanish and professor of Spanish language and culture) and of Hemingway himself. This was, perhaps, too ready a claim, too deeply grounded in the kind of unexamined criteria of authenticity and believability that Sternberg's structural world/modeling approach very productively lets us leave behind. A plausible argument could certainly be made that such inconsistency serves in itself, irrespective of authorial intention and integrity, to question the ideal of native-level fluency, and that value obtains from reading it rhetorically in any case. That is to say that the novel's narrator, as a construction of perfect linguistic cosmopolitanism – a Robert Jordan who, we are told, is "understanding the language completely and speaking it idiomatically" – moves us in one direction, while the novel's linguistic texture, riven with archaism, awkward translation, and error, moves in another.

A generation earlier, Edward Fenimore had observed that the Spanish in *For Whom the Bell Tolls* "serves [...] as a justification for breaking down the forms of a colloquial English, thus opening the way for a kind of reconstruction in which, although the Spanish is never wholly forgotten, the essential is the recapture of the varying tones inherent in a more or less unfamiliar, frequently artificial, but also vigorously poetic English" (Fenimore 1943: 83). Still, this "vigorously poetic English" might also, as Josephs prefers, be received as the textual expression of the ethnocentrism of an internationally celebrated Anglophone author who, taking for granted a monolingual audience, clumsily and monolingually appropriated the language of Spain the way he traded for his own gain on the cultural capital of an exoticized version of its social culture. This is the position taken by Milton M. Azevedo:

> Hemingway seems to rely, whether consciously or not, on our not having a knowledge of the language, on our having rather a linguistic ingenuousness which will allow us to accept, or at least not to question, what Hemingway presents as Spanish [...] *For Whom the Bell Tolls* was not written for anyone who reads Spanish [...] the novel had been written for an American public and a public ignorant of Spain and Spanish [...] What *For Whom the Bell Tolls* is, then, is not at all the novel of the Spanish Civil War written by a "citizen of the world"; it is, rather, a novel about the Spanish Civil War written by an American. (Azevedo 2000: 217–218; Azevedo 2000: 219, quoted with omissions)

In his own way, and despite partly refusing its implications, Fenimore saw this quite well:

> When Spanish *mucho* [...] is used in a manner conflicting with the proper use of English "much" the echo in an ear still objectively conscious of Spanish will hold something of the primitive [...] in such cases [...] knowledge of that language is immaterial to the important thing – the tacit assumption that it is Spanish, and, based upon this assumption, our acceptance of a non-colloquial English [...] we feel it "Spanish" [...] for it carries out what might be termed the essentially unilinear psychology of the speakers, a concentration upon the solitary fact which is completely harmonius [sic] with the primitive tone. It is Spanish in the sense that as readers we tacitly assume the primitive, in common with all the unfamiliar, to be necessarily Spanish. (Fenimore 1943: 73–75; Fenimore 1943: 78; Fenimore 1943: 85, quoted with omissions)

In the postwar "postmodern" period, U.S. novelists writing for a majority Anglophone readership wrought variations on the interwar modernism bequeathed them by Hemingway and his contemporaries. The "border culture" novels of Cormac McCarthy, comprising *Blood Meridian or the Evening Redness in the West* (1992a), *All the Pretty Horses* (1992b), *The Crossing* (1994), and *Cities of the Plain* (1998) are one prominent instance, each novel incorporating greater quantities of Spanish phrasing and dialogue than the previous, in a manner that took greater and greater risks with the encoding or concealment of content in the de facto second national language of the United States.[1] McCarthy's novels were written for a North American readership closer to the end of the twentieth century than to its middle, and they demanded at least a rudimentary knowledge of North American borderlands Spanish – understood here as the language of those on the losing end of the U.S. invasion of Mexico, not merely victims themselves but the co-sponsors of indigenous genocide. McCarthy's Satanic "judge," the indestructible force roving *Blood Meridian*'s apocalyptic frontier landscape, is a figure of multilingualism as evil, able to acquire and manipulate any "Indian lingo" with ease (Masters 1998: 27). Unlike Hemingway's Robert Jordan, who in his ability to move easily through Spanish linguistic and cultural landscapes and to serve as a love object for a Spanish national (the character Maria, standing for Spain itself in her portrayal as a victim of rape) embodies a benevolent cosmopolitan fantasy of mobility and transparency, McCarthy's judge is a malevolent trickster who speaks not only Spanish, French, and Dutch, but any given indigenous language he encounters, and who seems to acquire detailed and accurate ethnographic and geographic knowledge of indigenous culture upon first contact. The judge's totalizing appropriation of the frontier, indeed his ambition to subsume within his ever-present "notebook" the cultures of the entire planet, is a harbinger of apocalypse, and the permission the narrative voice of *Blood Meridian* gives to untranslated Spanish asks us to identify with the terror of his monolingual counterpart, the character known only as "the kid."

---

[1] *Blood Meridian* contained 125 interpolated Spanish words, phrases, or short dialogue passages of 1–10 words each, on 44 of 337 pages, with the longest continuous passage of Spanish being four consecutive dialogue sentences of four, one, five, and eight words each; *All the Pretty Horses*, 205 words, phrases or dialogue passages on 77 of 301 pages, with the longest continuous passage of Spanish five sentences of five, four, nine, six, and seventeen words each, and as many as eighteen dialogue passages in Spanish on a single page; *Cities of the Plain*, 268 words, phrases or dialogue passages on 80 of 291 pages; *The Crossing*, 453 words, phrases or dialogue passages on 155 of 425 pages. This progressive intensification of Spanish in McCarthy's novels came to an end with the more homogeneously Anglophone *No Country for Old Men* (2005).

4 The refusal to translate...

Of what he called "large-scale vehicular matching," Sternberg observed that it was often "so inconsistent with the normal conditions of communication" as to "be thought to divert attention from more important matters and to require too much polyglot expertise on the part of the author and his reading-public" (Sternberg 1981: 225). For a sense of what is elided in the deployment of such apparently natural categories as "normal," "communication," "expertise," "author," and "reading public," we must turn to less methodologically segregated or segmented approaches to literary multilingualism, approaches freer from a dependence on the consolation of typology. Of the refusal of the U.S. Latina writer Susana Chávez-Silverman to "translate her multilingual life into just one language," Ania Spyra concludes that it "creates a text interstitial in both language and genre" (Spyra 2011: 199). Such interstitiality is not merely a problem of description for the literary critic, recapturable through the addition of another term and concept to a typological schema; in marking additionally, perhaps ultimately the cultural-political context for the *production* of works of literature, rather than only their reception, it reaches into the disorderly translation zone that scholarly discipline so often attempts to hold at bay. "Writers who mix languages at the level of syntax, as Chávez-Silverman does," Spyra suggests, "respond to globalisation with a radical politics of language that refuses to admit monolingualism even at the level of subjectivity, let alone of a national literature" (Spyra 2011: 199).

When they circulate in North American translation, works of literature published in national variations of Spanish spoken and written *outside* North America pose yet another set of problems. Where the Spanish interpolated into *For Whom the Bell Tolls* or *Blood Meridian* necessarily "vanishes" when its base language, English, is translated for a Spanish edition, English phrasing and dialogue in Spanish-language works such as Julio Cortázar's *Rayuela* (1963) and Juan Goytisolo's *Makbara* (1980) is correspondingly lost in translation for English editions. The exuberantly improvisational, encyclopedist trilingual and quadrilingual chains of literary and musical association spun by Horacio Oliveira in the alcohol and nicotine-fueled amities of *Rayuela*'s Paris settle a specific weight on the English-language lyrics of U.S. ragtime, blues, and jazz song, with the paradoxical result that the privilege the novel's world grants to the iconic specificity of North American Anglophone popular cultural production literally cannot be "seen" in the novel's translation for a North American monolingual Anglophone reader.

Much has been made of the structural device Cortázar prepared to invite two different readings of the novel: one linear, made by turning the pages in order, and one non-linear, beginning with the seventy-third chapter and following numbered "links" provided at the close of each chapter (or following the table Cortázar included up front). Less often remarked is the contrast between the exuberant national plurilingualism of the novel's first section, taking place in a bohemian and cosmopolitan Paris "del lado de allá," and the comparative monolingualism of the novel's second section, which takes place "del lado de acá," in Oliveira's native Buenos Aires. Its own linguistic and complex symbolic containments (of possibilities for social solidarity across gender and class lines) notwithstanding, *Rayuela* also contains passages of strong plurilingualism, which countermand those containments as well. In high modernist style, the novel bristles with citations: titles and quotations from real and imagined literary works, but also titles and lyrics from U.S. and U.S.-influenced popular music. The novel's interpolated English phrasing is very seldom glossed or translated, and is often counterposed to French treated in much the same way:

> Desvalida, se le ocurrían pensamientos sublimes, citas de poemas que se apropiaba para sentirse en el corazón mismo de la alcachofa, por un lado *I ain't got nobody, and nobody cares for me*, que no era cierto ya que por lo menos dos de los presentes estaban malhumorados por causa de ella, y al mismo tiempo un verso de Perse, algo así como *Tu es là, mon amour, et je n'ai lieu qu'en toi*, donde la Maga se refugiaba apretándose contral el sonido de *lieu*, de *Tu est là, mon amour* [...] y que la música de Hines coincidiera con manchas rojas y azules que bailaban por dentro de sus párpados y se llamaban, no se sabía por qué, Volaná y Valené, a la izquierda Volaná (*and nobody cares for me*) girando enloquecidamente, arriba Valené, suspendida como una estrella de un azul pierodellafrancesca, *et je n'ai lieu qu'en toi*, Volaná y Velené, Ronald no podría tocar jamás el piano como Earl Hines, en realidad Horacio y ella deberían tener ese disco y escucharlo de noche en la oscuridad, aprender a amarse con esas frases, esas largas caricias nerviosas, *I ain't got nobody* en la espalda, en los hombros, los dedos detrás del cuello, entrando las uñas en el pelo y retirándolas poco a poco, un torbellino final y Valené se fundía con Volaná, *tu es là, mon amour and nobody cares for me*, Horacio estaba ahí pero nadie se ocupaba de ella... (Cortázar 1980: 62)

> Helpless, she thought sublime thoughts, quotations from poems which made her feel that she was in the very heart of the artichoke, on one side "I ain't got nobody, and nobody cares for me," which was not entirely true, because at least two people were present who were in a bad mood over her, and at the same time a line from Perse, something like "*Tu es là, mon amour, et je n'ai lieu qu'en toi*, where La Maga took refuge snuggling up to the sound of *lieu*, of *Tu es là, mon amour* [...] while Hines's music matched the red and blue spots which danced around behind her eyelids, which for some reason were called Volaná and Valené, Volaná on the left ("and nobody cares for me") spinning madly, Valené on top, hanging like a star in a pierodellafrancesca blue, *et je n'ai lieu qu'en toi*, Volaná and Valené, Ronald would never be able to play the piano like Earl Hines, Horacio and she should really own that record to listen to at night in the dark, to learn how to make love to the phrasing, those long, nervous caresses, "I ain't got nobody" on the back, on the shoulders, fingers behind the neck, nails working in and out of the hair, one last whirlwind and Valené merges with Volaná, *tu est là, mon amour* and nobody cares for me, Horacio was there but nobody bothered with her... (Cortázar 1966: 65)

In Rabassa's English translation, untranslated French continues to be marked with italics, as it is in the Spanish original; no such preservation is possible with the original English phrasing, which fades into the target language. Either Rabassa, or one of his editors, resorts to quotation marks to mark the first three instances of what would otherwise be invisibly untranslated English, but relinquishes them in the fourth instance. To be sure, in the original, this passage provides (here, "jazzy") structures of repetition, which serve in part to neutralize the opacity of non-Spanish phrases for a reader lacking English (or French), by integrating them into a kind of lyric supplement to the narrative (a record playing, the character La Maga listening and thinking) that is only fully marked in the Spanish original. Furthermore, such phrases are quotations, and as such, might be said to be sacrificed without enormous loss, since the information value of a quotation is mostly illustrative. "*I ain't got nobody, and nobody cares for me, que no era cierto…,*" on the other hand, does seem to request comprehension of the English phrase, since the quotation is not supplementing a statement but making one, one the truth content of which the next clause in Spanish qualifies. We might say that such "invisible difference" centrifugally constitutes a linguistic particularity anchoring the text to a specific interlinguistic context, and at the same time – in its prediction, indeed in its generation of that difference, in configurations that vary for each potential translation and circulation situation – a centripetal excess of that particularity.[2]

By the same token, the English dialogue spoken by U.S. tourists on the pages of Goytisolo's *Makbara,* in the scenes set in a Marrakech tannery pit, or the entire paragraphs culled from a Pittsburgh municipal visitor's guide (itself part of a sequence mercilessly lampooning the professional conduct of U.S. academic postcolonial studies, at an unnamed Pittsburgh university's "Cathedral of Learning") and interpolated in their original English, remain untranslatably linguistically specific in their determining function as untranslated markers of the mediality of U.S. Anglophone discourse.[3] The Moroccan Darija that Goytisolo also interpolates onto the pages of *Makbara,* meanwhile, serves to triangulate this reversible incommensurability, in a third language incomprehensible to the novel's spectatorial subject positions as marked by any of its hegemonic languages. (*Makbara* is dedicated "A quienes la inspiraron y no leerán": To those who inspired it and will not read it.) Like the passage in Darija followed by six Arabic lines from sura 109 of the Quran that closes an earlier novel, *Juan sin Tierra,* this is meant quite

---

2 See Sorensen (1999). On the global market economics of the Latin American Boom, beyond my purview in this essay yet essential to the broader cultural context here, see in particular Herrero-Olaizola (2000), Levinson (2001), and Cohn (2006).
3 See Goytisolo (1980), Goytisolo and Lane (1993).

straightforwardly to estrange and exclude a typical (even typically multilingual) Euro–U.S. reader.⁴ Goytisolo quite deliberately presumes unfamiliarity with Arabic in his Hispanophone readership: "El breve texto en árabe lo introduje para crear un efecto de ruptura [...] Gracias a ello lograba que el mensaje final resultara incomprehensible y el lector se sintiera excluido, como si le hubieran dado con la puerta en las narices" ("I introduced the brief text in Arabic to create an effect of rupture [...] Thanks to it, the final message was incomprehensible and the reader felt excluded, as if the door had been slammed in his face").⁵

5 ...and its mediation

It is in this spirit, perhaps, that Spyra echoes Guillén's indictment of the discipline of comparative literature in its merely professional multilingualism, dependent as it is on "comparisons between literatures conceived as national and linguistic monoliths" (Spyra 2011: 199). To this restrictive cultural cosmopolitanism, she counterposes the notion of a cosmopolitan poetics, or "cosmopoetics," that "refuses the monolingualism of translation" and pits the linguistic diversity of what Sternberg would call "extraverbal reality" against "the monolingual norms of nations," especially the "homogenizing claims of global English" (Spyra 2011: 199).

So far, we see that what takes shape in these different critical perspectives is a conflict between critical claims made for literature's capacity to represent or otherwise to mediate the world, on the one hand, and the world itself, on the other: that "extraverbal reality" that the critic often imagines – or must pretend to imagine – as inert, but which the writer, especially the writer of multilingual literature, may experience as profoundly dynamic, often disturbingly or even disablingly so. In some ways, multilingual literature merely accents a structural tension found in all the relations of art production to the verbal criticism in which it is described, but which is peculiarly intense in the domain of literature, in so far as unlike music, the plastic arts and even theatre, works of literature are created, preserved, and consumed more or less exclusively in language as the very same "medium" in which literary criticism itself is created, preserved, and consumed.

---

4 See Goytisolo (1978), Goytisolo (1977).
5 Qtd. in Kunz (1993: 245). See also Goytisolo (1984: 118): "The 'meteco' [of *Makbara*] is [...] not just any North African émigré. He also shortens, in condensed and caricaturesque form, the Occidental phantasmagoria concerning Islam and the Arabs: strange, opaque, soundless (sordo = deaf) by virtue of his earless condition; converting it to the logical and 'rational' discourse of Europeans, he expresses himself in a language incomprehensible to them."

Not infrequently, the pressure this convergence exerts on the division of labor segregating the literary artist from the literary critic erupts in a new form of contemporary writing that destabilizes the generic distinctions on which that division of labor rests, as much as on standardized, even unitary linguistic codes. To call these works critical "memoirs" of multilingualism is, while not unuseful, to resort to expedient shorthand for a phenomenon that is anything but settled.

Ariel Dorfman's *Heading South, Looking North: A Bilingual Journey* is a structurally and psychically labyrinthine narrative of oscillation between the renunciation and embrace of two world languages which are also national languages: Argentine and Chilean Spanish, on the one hand, U.S. English on the other. Dorfman's narrative is structured by epochal transitions back and forth between these two languages, both of them hegemonic and yet asymmetric in their own relation. Appropriately, perhaps, from the very start these transitions back and forth between Spanish and English are imagined simultaneously as a fall from origin and as as kind of originary doubling, repetition, or iteration. Born in Buenos Aires, the book's child-narrator is hospitalized in New York after his parent's emigration following the Argentine coup of 1943. Reflecting on his repudiation of Spanish during and after this trauma of clinical and cultural isolation, the book's adult narrator later likens it to suicide, a killing of one's "other person" in the name of a new, substitute myth of origin (Dorfman 1998: 43).

But the oscillation this narrative enacts is also an enactment of the dynamism of national monolingualism and multinational multilingualism, themselves. These two social and political forms, one particularistic, one generalizable, are joined in a cultural analysis that confronts the incompatible yet mutually absorptive ideals of U.S. monoculturalism and Latin American hybrid culture. Here, the child narrator understands multilingualism as a natural condition, purposefully disavowing it in the name of the cultural condition of monolingualism. That the "fall" from multilingualism is imagined as a forgetting of origins is only the first swing of the pendulum that subsequently sections the adult narrator's life: try as he might, he tells us, the adult narrator cannot remember being the infant whose native language was Spanish: "the stone of my past became smoother and more enigmatic the more I fingered it" (Dorfman 1998, 48). Subsequent "falls" into the other language – first Spanish again, then English again, then Spanish again, as the narrative of *Heading South, Looking North* moves at once forward and around the adult narrator's life – might seem to serve as points of attachment and revival for a myth of primordial presence; but in truth they are additional, chained displacements, what the adult narrator calls "fallings again," repetitions of the child narrator's first entry into language (Dorfman 1998: 45).

As it turns out, the child narrator of *Heading South, Looking North* owes his very conception to the Spanish language not as a native, but as an acquired language, his Romanian-born, Yiddish-speaking mother and his Ukrainian polygot, but not Yiddish-speaking father meeting as émigrés to Buenos Aires. For the adult narrator, this is a genetic analogue, as it were, for the fundamental ambivalence of the imperialism of imperial languages (both Spanish and English): violently translative and absorptive on the one hand, and serving as a shelter from some of life's *other* violences, on the other. The narrator's lifelong relationship with the United States and its language, culture, and society is constantly fissured by this ambivalence, for which the narrative of *Heading South, Looking North* offers a sociopolitical analogue in both biography and autobiography: persecuted as a leftist by Argentine fascists, the narrator's father visits the United States on a Guggenheim fellowship, then moves to a Rockefeller-funded State Department position, dependent thereafter on the largesse of U.S. liberal capitalism; meanwhile the narrator himself, in the course of his adult life, will leave Chile behind on two separate occasions for academic opportunities in the United States.

This "madness of being double" (Dorfman 1998: 42) is constantly reimagined as sanity, the sanity of being *one* reverting to "true" madness. Aggressively, if often also squeamishly unapologetic when it comes to exploiting his social mobility, the adult narrator accepts his native-level English proficiency as cultural capital, "a way of making a living, an advantage in the marketing of myself" (Dorfman 1998: 190). It is a pragmatism that accrues its own costs and benefits. On the plus side of this political balance sheet, there is deep insight into the reductions of partisan ideological conflict, particularly in a long history of United States interference in Chile, for which the narrator himself, as a cultural and media advisor in Allende's government, pays the price of a second exile (at first, in a kind of abyssal birth-echo, to Argentina "again"). There is a real cosmopolitanism, as well, relinquishing the home/away binary of exile and nostalgia, seeing the possibility of love as a counter-desire in the seductions of U.S. capitalist charisma, and finally extricating the English language from its possibly provincial identification with the United States (Dorfman 1998: 130). Finally, there is real insight into the world-historical specificity of a Latin American modernity as hybrid, monstrous, unclassifiable, a "fantastic composite" (Dorfman 1998: 193), neither Latin nor Hispanic and not even strictly speaking the global South (Dorfman 1998: 193).

On the minus side, there are innumerable discomforts of representation: being taken for a representative of the global North, on the one hand; on the other, having contributed (in the adult narrator's view) to Allende's misfortunes, by alienating moderate allies through a radicalism violently disavowing such *méconnaissance*. In the register of international relations, the compromise of these two language-selves and sociopolitical identities is imagined, by the adult narrator, as a truce. In the register of the family, meanwhile, he imagines it as a (an unlawful) marriage: in his own words, the adult narrator becomes a bigamist of language, "marrying" both Spanish and English – always heading North, while at the same time always looking South (Dorfman 1998: 270). The most powerful passages of *Heading North, Looking South* offer the adult narrator's reflections on this antinomy of home, which takes the form, as he puts it, of two irreducible and irreconcilable myths. One, that there *is*, indeed can ever be a "home" for anyone, imagined as a paradise of belonging, to be expelled from which is falling and death, to return to which is redemption. Another, that every such home was founded by a wanderer, an exile, someone for whom paradise was and is lost (Dorfman 1998: 275–276).

6 Conclusion: literature and its "outside"

Still, the truth is that in constituting new literary artifacts themselves, such works are testimonies of survival, and of the survival represented by publication itself, above all else. Beyond the question of the survival of works of literature there is the question of the survival of the human beings who create or – in perhaps fewer or perhaps many more cases – are never afforded the opportunity to create them in the first place. Here, we must look to literary-critical approaches that have directly and deeply integrated the history of political violence and warfare into the analysis of literary artifacts, or, where no such approaches can be found, past them altogether. Vicente L. Rafael's descriptions of a renewed "weaponization of language" by the post-2001 U.S. security state are apposite here. Of the "theater-specific" Arabic, Pashto, or Dari acquired by U.S. combat personnel and contractors in Afghanistan and Iraq, Rafael has observed the "powerful fantasies" enacted and embodied in such necessarily expedient U.S. military language instruction. "[L]earning a foreign language," Rafael reminds us, "especially one with the degree of difficulty of Arabic or lesser-taught languages like Dari and Pashto, takes a very long time, far longer than the time of invasions and occupations whose temporal horizons usually contract from one national election to another [...] Designed to be a weapon, the Language Enabled Soldier thus becomes obsolete even as he or she is being trained" (Rafael 2012: 59–60). For the most part, despite continued if relatively modest investments, electronically automated translation systems such as the DARPA-sponsored Phraselator (Rafael 2012: 62) have failed to take up the slack as hoped, leaving the multilingual discursive textures of intercultural military operations on the ground, structured by both strategic tokenization and unwelcome failure to translate, evoking nothing so much as the multilingual literary textualities analyzed with such care and precision by Sternberg, in a scholarly zone cordoned off from the non-literary world. The question then, perhaps, is just what to make of the world's irruption into it.

References

Azevedo, Milton M. 2000. "Shadows of a literary dialect: for whom the bell tolls in five romance languages." *The Hemingway Review* 20 (1): 30–48.
Cohn, Deborah N. 2006. "A Tale of Two Translation Programs: Politics, the Market, and Rockefeller Funding for Latin American Literature in the United States During the 1960s and 1970s." *Latin American Research Review* 41 (2): 139–164.
Cortázar, Julio. 1966. *Hopscotch*. Translated by Gregory Rabassa. New York: Pantheon.
Cortázar, Julio. 1980. *Rayuela*. Caracas: Biblioteca Ayacucho.
Dorfman, Ariel. 1998. *Heading South, Looking North: a Bilingual Journey*. New York: Farrar, Straus & Giroux.
Fenimore, Edward. 1943. "English and Spanish in for Whom the Bell Tolls." *ELH* 10 (1) (March): 73–86. doi:10.2307/2871541. http://www.jstor.org/stable/2871541.
Goytisolo, Juan. 1977. *Juan the Landless*. New York: Viking.
Goytisolo, Juan. 1978. *Juan Sin Tierra*. Barcelona: Seix Barral.
Goytisolo, Juan. 1980. *Makbara*. Barcelona: Seix Barral.
Goytisolo, Juan. 1984. "From Count Julian to Makbara: a Possible Orientalist Reading." *Review of Contemporary Fiction* 4 (2).
Goytisolo, Juan, and Helen R. Lane. 1993. *Makbara*. London, New York: Serpent's Tail.
Guillén, Claudio. 1985. *Entre Lo Uno Y Lo Diverso: Introducción a La Literatura Comparada*. Barcelona: Editorial Crítica.
Guillén, Claudio. 1993. *The Challenge of Comparative Literature*. Translated by Cola Franzen. Cambridge, MA: Harvard Univ. Press.
Hemingway, Ernest. 1940. *For Whom the Bell Tolls*. New York: Charles Scribner's Sons.
Herrero-Olaizola, Alejandro. 2000. "Consuming Aesthetics: Seix Barral and Jose Donoso in the Field of Latin American Literary Production." *MLN MLN* 115 (2): 323–339.
Josephs, F. Allen. 1983. "Hemingway's Poor Spanish: Chauvinism and Loss of Credibility in for Whom the Bell Tolls." In *Hemingway, a Revaluation*, Donald R. Noble (ed.), 205–223. Troy, N.Y.: Whitston.
Kunz, Marco. 1993. "El Final Bilingüe De 'Juan sin tierra'." In *Literatura Y Bilingüismo: Homenaje a Pere Ramírez*, Elvezio Canonica and Ernst Rudin (eds.). Kassel: Reichenberger.
Levinson, Brett. 2001. *The Ends of Literature: the Latin American "Boom" in the Neoliberal Marketplace*. Stanford, CA: Stanford University Press.
Masters, Joshua J. 1998. "'Witness to the uttermost edge of the world': Judge Holden's Textual Enterprise in Cormac McCarthy's Blood Meridian." *Critique: Studies in Contemporary Fiction* 40 (1): 25–37.
McCarthy, Cormac. 1992a. *Blood Meridian, Or, the Evening Redness in the West*. New York: Vintage.
McCarthy, Cormac. 1992b. *All the Pretty Horses*. New York: Knopf.
McCarthy, Cormac. 1994. *The Crossing*. New York: Knopf.
McCarthy, Cormac. 1998. *Cities of the Plain*. New York: Knopf.

Rafael, Vicente L. 2012. "Targeting Translation: Counterinsurgency and the Weaponization of Language." *Social Text* 30 (4 113): 55–80. doi:10.1215/01642472-1725793. http://socialtext.dukejournals.org/cgi/doi/10.1215/01642472-1725793.

Sorensen, Diana. 1999. "From Diaspora to Agora: Cortazar's Reconfiguration of Exile." *MLN* 114 (2): 357–388.

Spyra, Ania. 2011. "Language, Geography, Globalisation: Susana Chávez-Silverman's Rejection of Translation in Killer Crónicas: Bilingual Memories." In *Literature, Geography, Translation: Studies in World Writing*, Cecilia Alvstad, Stefan Helgesson, and David Watson (eds.), 198–208. Newcastle upon Tyne: Cambridge Scholars.

Sternberg, Meir. 1981. "Polylingualism as Reality and Translation as Mimesis." *Poetics Today* 2 (4): 221–239. doi:10.2307/1772500. http://www.jstor.org/stable/10.2307/1772500.

David Gramling
7 Multilingual and intercultural competence on the threshold of the Third Reich

Abstract: This article surveys primary sources from the 1910s to 1940s in Germany that show how phenomena of interculturality and multilingualism were institutionalized and envisioned in the advent of National Socialism in Europe. The presumptive image of the Third Reich as a monocultural, monolingual landscape tends to erase the vast and complex web of communities, institutions, and disciplinary initiatives that were researching and developing programming in multiple languages deep into the period of National Socialist dominion. Importantly, however, many progressive German theorists of the World War I era had seen Germany's "special path" into geopolitical modernity as offering a more just approach to cultural diversity than the Leninist, French, English, and US American capitalist approaches that had been developing alongside them since the mid-1900s. Out of this progressive conviction grew an ambitious tradition of thought spearheaded primarily by the historian Karl Lamprecht, one that was neither fascist-totalitarian nor nationalist-ethnocentric in its visions, but also one that Nazi political operatives ultimately found easy to functionalize for its genocidal purposes. This context thus provides ample evidence that multilingualism and intercultural exchange are not always liberatory or enriching for the parties involved, and that 21st-century research in multilingualism and intercultural competence has a great deal to gain, empirically and conceptually, from a sustained (re-)engagement with the darker hours of political modernity.

> If it isn't a German you haven't invited this year [to address you], but me instead, this has something to do with the fact that you perhaps do not consider me a stranger, a foreigner. And, doubtlessly, somehow you are right in this.
>
> – Jorge Semprún, Spanish-born, French-writing author and former prisoner at Buchenwald (1943–45), in a speech to the German Parliament, January 27, 2001

Looking back at Nazi-occupied Europe from an intercultural and Second Language Studies perspective reveals a course of events that is as astonishing on its own terms as it is invisible in the predominating narratives about the years 1918–1945. Let us begin by considering one such moment in May 1942. To her colleagues at the *Deutsche Akademie* conference in Munich, the managing editor of the leading German-as-a-Foreign-Language textbook *Gesprochenes Deutsch* (*Spoken German*)

Gramling David, University of Arizona, US, dgl@email.arizona.edu

Magda Gerken raised a concern of newly pressing urgency: she was increasingly noticing that the representative literary texts used most in German-as-a-Foreign-Language classrooms were prohibitively difficult for the new generation of beginning-intermediate learners (Michels 2005: 178). Though Gerken and her co-editor Wolfhart Klee were already hard at work on a new edition of the text book, which they were planning to call *Lebendiges Deutsch* (*German Alive*), the manuscript would ultimately not be ready for Munich's summer intensive language programs in 1943, during which 373 learners from 17 countries would arrive for various levels of German-language learning. (In the end, a paper shortage in 1944 scuttled the project entirely.) Meanwhile however, in 1942–43, preparations were underway for a small companion volume for *Gesprochenes Deutsch* called "Deutsch lernen leicht gemacht"/ "Learning German Made Easy", specifically designed for heritage learners throughout Europe. A second companion volume was also in press for nonnative-speaker volunteers in the *Waffen-SS*, which included the annotated texts of the Horst-Wessel Song, the oath of allegiance, some key geographical and historical facts about Germany, as well as a few extra thematic chapters: one on "family" and one on "honor" (177). Committed as it was to the "direct method" of language instruction – which prioritized oral communication and practical, relevant input over the literature-for-literature's-sake hauteur of the 19th-century's New Humanism – *Gesprochenes Deutsch* was by most contemporary accounts a modern, methodologically innovative teaching text, and indeed one that reached a circulation of 30,000 copies in 34 separate print runs between 1939 and 1945 (89). Such were just a few of the late-stage fruits of an institutional culture in National Socialist Germany that saw intercultural engagement as a task worthy of state investment, and a global challenge for various disciplines and their scholars to live up to.

Told in these terms, this tableau does not correspond well with what we tend to know of the Third Reich as a monocultural, monolingual machine of terror, murder, and standardization. Indeed, even invoking intercultural and multilingual lines of thought in this context may seem little more than one revisionist bridge too far. My contribution to the current volume seeks however to make exactly this wager: namely, that a complex constellation of efforts and counter-efforts to think ambitiously about multilingualism and interculturality were afoot in the very midst, design, and margins of the Third Reich. Furthermore, I will show how a liberal-cosmopolitan view of language learning and intercultural understanding that flowered in the years before World War I comingled with the nationalist-reactionary strains of political thought in the late 1920s, and that these two approaches to teaching for multilingualism became increasingly intertwined and indistinguishable for practitioners in the 1930s and 1940s. Rather than projecting a grand battle between the nationalists and the internationalists in their views on German as a global language, I will attempt to show how the slogans, rhetorics, and ideas about language learning were easily transposable from one end of the ideological spectrum to the other. This mutation of concepts from 1910 to 1945 was abetted by the fact that – in contrast to other domains of cultural programming like film, literature, political science, etc. – it was often the case that the same people were making foreign-language education programming decisions in 1925 as were in 1940. Only very few of them were dismissed over the course of the 1930s on political, personal, or methodological grounds; institutionally sanctioned developers of intercultural and multilingual programming and learning outcomes indeed seem to have benefitted from a kind of salutary neglect amid the otherwise merciless, career-and-life-ending expulsions of *Gleichschaltung,* or standardization.

Of course, beyond the National Socialist-sponsored institutions in which Magda Gerken and her colleagues were employed, other domains of mass multicultural practice and intercultural exchange were emerging. These ever-widening contact zones of language and culture, which easily dwarfed the Deutsche Akademie's academic agenda, arose out of the continent-wide spatial machinery of human trafficking, displacement, occupation, and genocide between 1933–1950 and beyond. This landscape required unprecedented forms and densities of compulsory multilingual interaction, where German was often only one source of symbolic capital among many. Extending beyond this ad hoc socio-institutional realm of camps and transports in the Third Reich was an even wider sphere of activity: the daily labors of symbolic survival practiced by tens of millions of occupied European, Asian, American, Australian, and North African citizens, for whom translingual engagement with National Socialism grew from obtuse specter in 1933 to daily necessity after 1940 (Klemperer 2006, Levi 1987). The Spanish-born author and Buchenwald-prisoner Jorge Semprún's thought that opens this essay indicates how two generations of Europeans had to become, in various ways, German – a form and experience of multilingual and intercultural competencing that 21st-century applications of these terms only rarely acknowledge.

Despite the sheer mass and diversity of multilingual and intercultural experience characterizing the fascist period in Europe, Semprún's speech before the German parliament in 2001 epitomizes how post-Nazi Europe's acute intercultural relationship with its former occupier is still ambivalently tangled in qualifiers like "if", "somehow", and "perhaps". To a great extent Semprún's tentative stance corresponds to disciplinary constraints on the ways we are willing to know things about the Third Reich and other dark hours of political modernity. Indeed, the concentric realms of transculturation in Nazi Europe have escaped most disciplines' accounts of National Socialism, in which the Third Reich stands as the epitome of all that multilingual, interdisciplinary, and intercultural inquiry might hope to prevent.

Perhaps behind this opposition lies a more complex historical constellation. For one, the European Union's Common European Framework of Reference (CEFR) for Languages CEFR and its vision of a fully multilingual European populace are unthinkable without the specter of National Socialism, upon whose ruins the spirit of the European Coal and Steel Community was forged in 1950. The mass refugee resettlement and repatriation apparatus that set to work after 1945 – and continues, arguably, today – demonstrates that the Third Reich induced almost as much de facto intercultural competence and multilingualism on the continent as it destroyed. Yet, in the absence of a cogent multilingual and intercultural research mandate vis-à-vis the period of Nazi dominion throughout Europe, we are left with 1) undertheorized notions about cultural and linguistic heterogeneity in totalitarian contexts, as well as 2) an overly affirmative impression of what multilingual and intercultural endeavors have actually looked like over the course of European and colonial modernity. Through a survey of primary theoretical sources leading up to fascist dictatorship in Germany, this article hopes to shore up these two related problematics.

1 Multilingual Trouble, in and after the Third Reich

Despite an emergent scholarly discussion about the multilingual landscape of the concentration camp system (Taterka 1995, Oschlies 1996, Aschenberg 2002, Gramling 2012), scholars seldom use the affirmative lexicon of multilingualism or interculturality to describe anything within the Third Reich's sphere of operations. It makes a certain sense that discourses on multilingualism and intercultural competence focus on phenomena inimical to violently propagandistic or otherwise ideologically normative contexts, and that the critical terms of these discourses have rarely been of use in dealing with totalitarian and fascist societies. What is nonetheless surprising is how infrequently Nazi-occupied Europe is even described *factually* as a multilingual, intercultural, transnational, even globalizing space – and indeed one characterized by unprecedented disruptive magnitudes of each. Beyond the concentration camp system that forced millions of speakers – of scores of languages – to survive or die together in unimaginably bleak conditions, non-German speakers also became increasingly a feature of the expanding 'domestic' German landscape over the course of the War – with 1,000,000 French POWs working as forced laborers in German cities and towns, and over 3,000,000 foreign workers in total (Herbert 1997: 124). By 1940–41, nearly 25% of all penal sentences for political crimes in Germany were related to the offense of "prohibited contact with foreigners and prisoners of war", and by 1942 such contact with foreigners was as common a crime as "political opposition". Also embedded in this landscape, each concentration camp held speakers of 30 languages on average (Oschlies 1996: 98), speakers whose sociolinguistic practices were transformed so acutely over the course of their internment that, after the war:

> Polish editors came to an impasse with this unique KZ-language. Uncomprehending, they sat over manuscripts of former KZ-inmates depicting the world of the KZ, who again and again fell back into the lexicon and "tone" of their time in captivity; the editors struck whatever did not seem to them appropriate under normative language standards. The "soul" of the manuscripts was consequently removed.
>
> [An dieser unikalen KZ-Sprache scheiterten damals auch polnische Verlagslektoren. Verständnislos saßen sie über Manuscripten ehemaliger KZ-Häftlinge, in denen diese die Welt der KZ schilderten und dabei immer wieder in Lexik und "Tonfall" ihrer Haftzeit zurückfielen; die dadurch überforderten Lektoren strichen, was ihnen unter normativem Sprachaspekt als unangemessen erschien. Damit war den Manuskripten die "Seele" genommen.] (Oschlies 99, translations mine unless otherwise noted)

Such confrontations between editors (representing pre-Nazi Europe's national languages) and the newly translingual subjectivities of returning camp-inmates in the 1940s and 1950s were common, and the impasse that ensued between them became a structural feature of post-War publishing. Cumulatively, this structural bias against translingual phenomena like 'camp language' has made it difficult for contemporary scholarship to empirically re-engage the extensive though liminal pluralities of culture and language characterizing this period – or what Frantz Fanon considered the popular "zone(s) of occult instability" that tend to escape research altogether (1967: 168). In his book-length study of Nazi occupation newspapers in the Netherlands, Christoph Sauer notes this structural elision with potent regret:

> The silence of others on the question of these occupation newspapers and in general on the textual formation of National Socialism as an occupying power should not be understood as a "keeping silent"; the necessary dimension of intent is too lacking for that to be the case. It can be understood rather under the rubric of the forgotten, the unknown, and the uninteresting. As the garbage of the war, and the refuse of occupation, German occupation newspapers have sat in the dust of archives and libraries. To be sure, they are still readily accessible, but reading them takes energy, soils one's clothing and hands, and demoralizes the souls of today's reader, who has cast off the eternal trivia and banal quotidian reality inscribed in these texts. But the chattiness of the flow of words has yet another effect: it is just plain uncomfortable to wade through it; nothing spectacular is to be hoped for; the basic structures seem familiar and are preserved in an almost unmanageable heap of publications, especially if one considers everything that was published in the formerly occupied

countries. It seems the "always-the-same", as Adorno puts it, has had a rather laming effect on scholarly curiosity.

> Das Schweigen der anderen zu diesen Besatzungszeitungen und zur textuellen Gestalt des Nationalsozialismus als Besatzungsmacht überhaupt sollte nicht als ein *Verschweigen* aufgefasst werden, es fehlt die dazu doch nötige Dimension der Bewusstheit. Eher rangiert es unter der Rubrik des Vergessenseins, der Unbekanntheit und des Desinteresses Als Abfall des Krieges und Besatzungsmüll verstauben die deutschen Besatzungszeitungen in den Archiven und Bibliotheken. Zwar sind sie ohne weiteres zugänglich, doch kostet ihre Lektüre Mühe, sie beschmutzen Kleidung und Hände und zermürben die Seele des heutigen Lesers, der sich dem ewigen Kleinkram und der alltagsbanalen Realität aussetzt, die diesen Texten inskribiert ist. Die Geschwätzigkeit der Wörterflut tut ein übriges: Es ist schlicht unbequem, sich da hindurchzuwühlen. Spektakuläres ist nicht zu erwarten, die Grundstrukturen scheinen bekannt und sind in einer nahezu unüberschaubaren Menge von Publikationen festgehalten, vor allem, wenn man die Veröffentlichungen in den ehemals besetzten Ländern mit einrechnet. Es hat den Anschein, als ob sich das 'Immergleiche', mit Adorno zu sprechen, eher lähmend auf die wissenschaftliche Neugierde ausgewirkt hätte. (1998: 13)

Indeed Arendt (1948) had already made a claim similar to Sauer's, just two years after the collapse of Hitler's regime. Though she did not address multilingualism as such, Arendt suggested – just three years into the post-Shoah period – that the primary narrative records about life under Nazi internment were often not only being ignored but actively suppressed by readers and publishers alike: "There are numerous such reports by survivors; only a few have been published because, quite understandably, the world wants to hear no more of these things, but also because they all leave the reader cold, that is, as apathetic and baffled as the writer himself, and fail to inspire those passions of outrage and sympathy through which men have always been mobilized for justice, for" – and here Arendt cites a recently published concentration camp memoir from the Frenchman David Rousset – "'Misery that goes too deep arouses not compassion but repugnance and hatred'." (743)

Instead of sifting through the confounding and banal translingual data that might ground an applied linguistics of the Third Reich, scholarly and lay discourses alike tend to posit that fascism as a form and National Socialist totalitarianism as an instance were, in their very logic and essence, unidirectional hydraulic pumps of monoculturality and monolingualism. It is then easy to extend this presupposition to a further one: that there is something patently dangerous and pathological about monolingual sociality and monocultural statecraft (Ellis 2006, Oller 1997). As an easy corollary, multilingual institutions and communities are often imagined to be tendentially resistant to totalitarian instrumentalization (Skutnabb-Kangas 2000). The evidence I present below, suggests that National Socialism was impossible without the historical backing of intercultural thinking and multilingual training – both of the progressive-transnational and the racist-reactionary sort. Though "multilingual" and "intercultural" were not the concepts in currency in the 1920s, a robust, progressive, and yet often opportunistic discourse of *zwischenvölkische[m] Verständnis*, or "understanding between peoples", greased the wheels of totalitarian consolidation from 1925–1942, rendering major aspects of the Nazi civic vision palatable for centrist scholars at German, European, and American universities along the way.

At stake in the current analysis is a clearer understanding of the ways in which certain lines of thinking about translation, interculturality, multilingualism and "understanding the other" may always have the *potential* to abet institutions and practices that coercively expropriate meaning and annihilate livelihoods in the process. I approach the Third Reich as one of the first modern purveyors of anti-universalist globalization, founded as it was upon discourses of cultural particularism and linguistic diversity – in an anti-American, anti-Bolshevik, and anti-French vein. A separate and methodologically important claim is that early intercultural and multilingual theorizing in turn-of-the-century Germany was in no way fated for a telos in fascist implementation. Indeed much of the academic "foreign cultural politics" of the Wilhelmine period, to which I now turn, demonstrates a vision very much in consonance with twenty-first century research on similar questions.

2 Propaganda, or the Arrested Development of Interpopular Democracy

The category of practices and products now understood, almost without exception pejoratively, as *propaganda* – metonymically linked as it is now with Joseph Goebbels' Imperial Ministry for Propaganda and Popular Enlightenment in the Third Reich – first gained its negative, coercive meaning only around World War I. Up until that point, propaganda had been looked to as a potentially neutral and even democratizing means toward the informative "propagation" of popular values and qualities. The word had first been used widely in the work of the Counter-Reformation Catholic order of the *Sacra Congregatio christiano nomini propagando* under Pope Gregory XV in 1622. In particular, the *Academia polygotta* of this Congregation of the Propagation of the Faith recruited young believers from around the world to recite poems in their native languages for the Feast of Epiphany (Jackall 1985: 9). This means that the proper genealogical context for what we now call "propaganda" was multilingual and intercultural by design: a highly organized assembly of practitioners designed to espouse, celebrate, translate, and disseminate their particular experiences of the faith.

Secular and church-critical forms of propaganda emerged later in coffee houses, salons, lending libraries, and reading societies in the course of the 18th and 19th centuries. By the post-1848 period, during which multiple popular nationalist movements were beginning to outpace the mandate and credibility of aristocratic regimes, propaganda bore an at least neutral, if not positive connotation as a means of representing the needs and realities of a *people* to other *peoples*, as opposed to guarding the vested interests of the exclusively aristocratic diplomatic corps, who had up until that shift held sole responsibility for "intercultural" representation. (Rühlmann 1919: 4, Döscher 1987: 19). In his 1919 treatise on "cultural propaganda" in the wake of the disastrous Versailles Treaty, the German historian and government minister Paul Rühlmann lamented how

> It is not coincidental that our diplomats are so often mistaken about the truly popular characteristics of foreign territories, given that the many imponderables of the foreign popular soul only became known to the German people's representatives abroad very late. The whole apparatus was just not set up for that, the embassy atmosphere simply didn't let popular tones in.
>
> Es ist daher bei diesem System durchaus nicht zufällig, dass sich unsere Diplomatie über die rein volksmäßigen Qualitäten des Auslandes so oft in Irrtum befunden hat, dass alle Imponderabilien der fremden Volksseele den deutschen Volksvertretern draußen gewöhnlich sehr spät bekannt wurden. Der ganze Apparat war ja eben nicht hierfür eingestellt, die Botschaftsatmosphäre ließ volksmäßige Töne einfach nicht durch. (Rühlmann 5–6)

Here Rühlmann diagnosed his vanquished Germany not with ethnocentric hubris, but with a class paternalism in its diplomatic institutions that entirely prevented true "intercultural being" from unfolding (Phipps & Gonzalez 2004, Levine 2014). This powerful thought, from 1919, reminds us that the structural exclusion from public relevance of vernacular, non-expert forms of intercultural competence has had disastrous consequences. Twenty-first-century visions of intercultural competence that presume that propaganda and other historical forms of ideological communication across cultural frontiers have always been at their core coercive and ethnocentric, miss a key progressive aspect of early 20th century models of cultural exchange: namely, that they were designed to wrest the prerogative to voice popular values away from aristocrats who were not only oblivious to them, but who had also nonetheless been the sole, consecrated representatives of those popular cultures abroad since the dawn of political modernity. Yet a prevailing habit of thought in endeavors at intercultural competence often holds that any institutions or individuals who seek to propagate ideas across cultural frontiers are anathema to its values still holds sway, in much the same way as a rigid antiprescriptivism has done in modern linguistics (see Cameron 1995). The work of intercultural theorists such as Karl Lamprecht, Kurt Riezler, and Max Weber in the early German twentieth century cast some doubt on the validity of this dehistoricized opposition between propaganda and intercultural exchange.

3 The Dream of a Foreign Cultural Politics

Even before the outbreak of World War I, theorists in Germany were becoming aware that the aristocratic-diplomatic system of international understanding was a costly and tone-deaf failure, and academic historians like Karl Lamprecht (University of Leipzig) were ambitiously searching for alternatives. What came of this shift was a stream of theorization at the beginning of the 20th century that was truly hopeful about the philosophical potential and practical procedures of 'interpopular' [zwischenvölkischem] exchange, freed from aristocratic patronage. Many prominent industrial speculators in Germany, particularly the bourgeois merchants of the Hanseatic cities, came to believe that the increasing traffic among once distant sectors of the global economy would render conventional warfare superfluous. In an era when geographic, communicative, and war-tactical distances were perceived as shrinking, "foreign cultural politics" [*Auswärtige Kulturpolitik*] emerged as a profitable and practical alternative to territorial and military "power politics."

Lamprecht's 1913 article "On Foreign Cultural Politics" in the *Frankfurter Zeitung* conveys his ambitious sensibility about intercultural study, which he advocated at the highest levels of German governance:

> Like all historical research on culture, it requires a deeper penetration of the sources than that which is necessary for the normal pursuit of political history; this is because it almost always depends on not just establishing a mere chain of events, but on forging into the entire spirit of the sources. And in practice this quickly reveals that such an intensive engagement with the sources is impossible without recourse to the assistance of scholars who belong to the culture under investigation.

> Wie alle kulturgeschichtlichen Studien, so verlangt es auch seinerseits eine intensivere Penetration der Quellen, als sie für den herkömmlichen Betrieb der politischen Geschichte notwendig ist; denn es kommt fast ständig darauf an, nicht bloß Ereignisreihen festzustellen, sondern in den Gesamtgeist der Quellen hinzudringen. Und hier zeigt sich nun in der Praxis sehr bald, dass eine so verschärfte Behandlung der Quellen ohne Zuhilfenahme der Tätigkeit von Gelehrten, die der untersuchten Kultur angehören, nicht möglich ist. (Lamprecht 1913)

This 1913 text, first delivered in Leipzig as a public lecture, is an important benchmark in what intercultural theory had been before it became Republican geopolitics in the 1920s and then fascist power-mongering in the 1930s. Throughout, Lamprecht promotes no "German" nor commercial interests whatsoever: the goal of his theorization is the possibility of intercultural understanding itself in the service of a "universal history", free from manipulation by states or markets. In Lamprecht we see a vision of interpopular inquiry that is concerned with the complexities of mutual perception and the possibility of a more accurate, less egocentric-nationalistic or market-pragmatic view of the world. I choose the term "interpopular" as distinct from "international" or "transnational" because Lamprecht's historicist essentialism seeks a "zwischenvölkische Verständigung" – an understanding between peoples – rather than the sort of international relations that presumes diplomatic outreach via organized, elite political or business delegations. Lamprecht's view was much more expansive than this, envisioning a mode of particularist exchange between popular communities characterized by historically specific dispositions in their current moment of becoming – all in the service of a universal, but not a universalist picture of world cultures.

In the text, Lamprecht promotes several ideas that still seem close to the cutting edge of critical multilingualism studies in the 21st century. He distinguishes between classroom-based language learning and learning in informal contexts, ruminates on the possibilities and the costs of translingual being and identification, advocates contrastive and critical methodologies, and admits that advanced learning of foreign languages and cultures often requires intensive research partnership and apprenticeship in the target L/C2. Further, he is interested in what it means to 'feel' in another language, not out of mere exoticism or curiosity, but as a methodological affordance for researching multilingually. Lamprecht tells his audience in Leipzig, and his readers in Frankfurt:

> Certainly it is possible for the European to have command of the languages of these [Japanese and Chinese] cultures and their historical transmission to the extent that he can correctly and grammatically understand their meanings as such. It would however be an error to believe that the historical sense of this transmission has thereby been also disclosed to him as well. If one pursues this and then checks the result against the judgment of an educated Japanese or Chinese, it will almost always turn out that their tradition diverges from the European so greatly that the outcome will be one that differs from that he has found. But there will indeed be Europeans who can teach themselves to think and feel Chinese or Japanese.

> Gewiss ist es dem Europäer möglich, die Sprachen dieser Kulturen und ihrer geschichtlichen Überlieferung so weit zu beherrschen, dass er deren Sinn an sich und grammatikalisch richtig versteht. Es wäre aber ein Irrtum, zu glauben, dass sich ihm damit auch der historische Sinn der Überlieferung eröffnet hätte. Sucht man ihn und kontrolliert man dies

Ergebnis durch das Urteil eines unterrichteten Chinesen oder Japaners, so wird sich fast stets ergeben, dass diese in der Auffassung so von der europäischen abweichen, dass ein von dem gefundenen abweichendes Resultat gewonnen wird. Nun werden sich allerdings Europäer wohl auch so schulen können, dass sie schliesslich chinesisch oder japanisch denken und fühlen. (Lamprecht 1912: x)

By 1900, Lamprecht and his contemporaries had already been hearing about or witnessing aggressive campaigns of English and American missionaries in Japanese schools, French exports of art, craft, and literature in Southeastern Europe and the Ottoman Empire, and the building of an American University in China. He did not seem to sense any contradiction between his appeal for a just and nuanced universal intercultural history on the one hand, and a strong role for Germany amongst this accelerating geopolitical game of peaceful competition: "We Germans cannot fall behind: for fear that the world be apportioned once again without the contribution of the German poets and thinkers." ["Da dürfen wir Deutschen nicht zurückbleiben, soll anders die Welt nicht einmal wieder vergeben sein, ehe der germanische Dichter und Denker auf dem Plane erscheint."] Yet he remains critical of how other Western European nations have in part abused foreign cultural political operations in the service of geo-political jockeying, and calls for a systematic, scientific, and speculative form of foreign cultural politics in which commercial interests derive from philosophical ones, and not vice-versa, and legitimate political influence abroad obtains only when this order of priorities is observed.

Other nations, notes Lamprecht, pursue their external cultural politics based on the weak philosophical resources of the present, while a German intercultural approach will seek a deeper foundation, one based in the universal history of culture as such. Here, Lamprecht is advocating for his model not only over French and capitalist-US forms of cultural nationalism, but also those 19th-century models indebted to an international political understanding of world history as guided by great and terrible men and their great and terrible decisions. His vision, instead, requires a subtle and modest differential and syncretic engagement with the various progressive developments of the world's peoples, though no clear telos or ranked assessment of various peoples' cultural maturation is proposed. A more diffuse principle is afoot: the weak progressive axiom that all popular communities seek improvement and excellence according to their own historically, organically cultivated strengths. As such, Lamprecht's major philosophical foe is the crude ahistoricism of power-brokering through commercial holdings, a criterion according to which Imperial Germans would clearly rank behind their Dutch, French, British, and American peers.

Nor was Lamprecht's intervention a purely academic affair. No lesser than the Imperial Chancellor Theobald von Bethmann-Hollweg was deeply interested in Lamprecht's promise of a "decisive foreign cultural politics," and he declared as much in an open letter to Lamprecht in the *Vossische Zeitung* on Dec. 12, 1913. But the Chancellor regrets that the people itself is not quite ready to live up to Lamprecht's vision, a paternalistic dismissal the likes of which theorists like Paul Rühlmann would later admonish as symptomatic of the diplomatic core's negligence vis-à-vis popular culture. Chancellor von Bethmann-Hollweg writes ruefully to Lamprecht in his open letter:

> We're not that far along. We aren't sure and aware enough of our own culture, our inner essence, our national ideal. This likely has to do with a quirk of our rather individualistic and not-quite-stabilized culture, that it doesn't have the same suggestive power as the British and the French, and that not every German abroad represents his homeland within him, as the Frenchman does Paris and the Englishman the British Isle.

> "Wir sind noch nicht soweit. Wir sind unserer Kultur, unseres inneren Wesens, unseres nationalen Ideals nicht sicher und bewußt genug. Es liegt wohl in der Eigenart unserer doch wohl individualistischen und noch nicht ausgeglichenen Kultur, daß sie nicht die gleiche suggestive Kraft hat wie die britische und französische, dass nicht jeder Deutsche im Auslande seine Heimat in sich abbildet, wie der Franzose Paris und der Engländer die britische Insel. (Kloosterkuis 1994: 3)

A fascinating admission from a head of government, Bethmann-Hollweg's letter here endorses Lamprecht's scientific endeavor for intercultural study, but insists that cultural self-awareness must first be cultivated among its people before the Lamprechtian ideal can be operationalized in governance. Faced with the opportunity to replace a broken system of diplomatic cultural exchange among out-of-touch aristocrats with a methodologically rich and critical mode of interpopular engagement, the Chancellor chooses not to trust "the people" with the prospect of thinking and feeling in another language and culture.

4 Republican Geopolitics

In the lugubrious aftermath of the Versailles Treaty in 1919, Lamprecht's intercultural vision looked both disingenuous and naive at once. And yet, war-weathered post-War theorists like Paul Rühlmann saw something prescient within it:

> The state-form of the twentieth century was for [Lamprecht] the „tentacle state". Like a giant octopus, it stretches its tentacles – that is, its touching, singing, and catching arms – far beyond its actual state-body into the global sphere. In seemingly inextricable plaits, these

arms move through, over, and against one another, in order to provide nourishment for its central state core, which it governs in a unified way. The more finely and richly the tentacular character of a state is developed, the better it approximates the state-form of the future.

Der Staatstyp des zwanzigsten Jahrhunderts ist ihm der "Tentakelstaat". Einem riesigen Polypen gleichend, streckt er weit über seinen eigentlichen Staatskörper hinaus in die Weltsphäre seine Tentakeln, seine Tast, Sang- und Fangarme. In scheinbar unlöslichen Verschlingungen bewegen sich diese durch-, über- und gegeneinander, um schließlich doch dem zentralen Staatskern, der sie einheitlich leitet, Nahrung zuzuführen. Je reicher und feiner der Tentakelcharakter eines Staates entwickelt ist, umso mehr nähert er sich dem Staatstype der Zukunft. (Rühlmann 1919: 1)

There is a certain ecstasy here in Rühlmann's retrospective gloss of the Lamprechtian ideal of foreign cultural politics, to which he adds the following sobering observation:

In Wilhelmine Germany, one could already observe efforts toward the tentacular formation of the state. [...] Unfortunately, as we must now painfully conclude, these were all singing and catching arms rather than touching and feeling ones. Our prestige in the world was too one-sidedly focused on economic and military power development. What was completely lacking was our spiritual and cultural sphere of influence and thus our mutual exploration of individual cultures, the finer relationships between individual peoples, an "ultimate cultural osmosis".

Auch beim wilhelminischen Deutschland konnte man Ansätze zur Tentakelstaatsbildung beobachten. [...] Nur waren es leider, wie wir heute mit dumpfem Schmerz feststellen müssen, wohl Sang- und Fangarme, nicht aber Tast- und Fühlarme. Unsere Weltgeltung war zu einseitig auf wirtschaftlich und militärische Machtentfaltung gestellt. Es fehlten fast vollständig die geistigen, die kulturellen Ausstrahlungen und somit das gegenseitige Abtasten der einzelnen Kulturen, die feineren Kontaktbeziehungen zwischen den einzelnen Völkern, die "kulturelle Endosmose". (Rühlmann, 1919: 1)

In the 1920s, Germans across the political spectrum became aware of the violent persecution that ethnic Germans outside of the Reich's shrunken territory had sustained during wartime, and the rhetoric of interpopularity grew from a Lamprechtian critical method to a pragmatics of almost ecstatic consolidation. The idea of "foreign cultural politics" after the Great War thus was transformed to promote two symbiotic cultural desiderata: supporting ethnic German communities throughout Europe's eastern regions while developing potential trade and cultural exchange partners in those areas. (Michels 2005: 22) This dual logic enhanced the appeal of an aggressive foreign cultural politics, increasingly referred to as "geopolitics", across the political spectrum of the early Weimar Republic.

Cosmopolitan Social Democrats, academic pacifists, and monarchist Pan-Germanists [*Alldeutsche*] alike strategized to promote German culture and language around the globe. In contrast to the territorial empires of France and Great Britain, politicians and intellectuals in Weimar Germany tended to view this "peaceful imperialism" (Kloosterhuis 1994) as the *de facto* cultural logic of the new Europe, the intellectual resource that would accomplish what conventional warfare had heretofore failed to do for Germany. It was in this context that the economist Arthur Dix coined the now cliché metonym "global village" [Das Dörfchen Erde] in 1929:

> I have [...] coined the phrase "The Global Village," in which everyone can look in his neighbor's window. We live – I cannot neglect the opportunity to repeat – on the threshold of a new epoch, or are already in a new age.... Earlier [we saw] the promotion of transmission of thought from person to person through the entire people: Gutenberg with his printing – today transmission of thought over the entire earth in seconds by broadcasting, by radio, by wireless telegraphy and telephone and transmission of thought in a propagandistic sense, also by the cinema.... As once the world seas were conquered and all five continents converged in the further course of navigation, so today the decisive step has been taken to convergence, to the further shrinking of the globe by airship travel and the airplane through the conquest of the air ocean. " (Dix in Murphy 1997: 94–95)

Lamprecht had espoused no such global visions as this, and his method of interpopular speculation would have bristled at the heuristic crudeness of a concept like "the global village." Yet Dix's pragmatic futurism and fetishization of spatial proximity would characterize the stance of most intercultural program developers in the 1930s and 1940s, at the expense of Lamprecht and Rühlmann's efforts.

5 Spracharbeit: Language Work

The first President of the young *Deutsche Akademie* (DA)'s newly formed Practical Division in 1925 was the geopolitical theorist Karl Haushofer, a professor at the University of Munich and mentor of Hitler's eventual spokesperson in the Nazi Party, Rudolf Hess. In 1923, Haushofer began lecturing on his concept of "geopolitics" [*Geopolitik*], which held that non-military and non-territorial means should be preferred in maintaining control of political regions beyond German borders. His concept of living-space [*Lebensraum*] was not precisely a territorial principle, but a cultural one, based in the notion of facilitating receptiveness toward Germanness abroad. By 1926, the more nationalistic supporters of the DA, such as Karl Christian von Loesch, suggested that journalists from southeastern Europe could be influenced most effectively if the DA were to offer more language courses throughout the Balkans and southern Europe. As this focus on German-language teaching increased, program directors and funders at the DA strategized to saturate untapped landscapes in the European foreign language market. This was fundamentally a struggle against the French influence in these regions. Since France had long held a monopoly on second language learning in eastern and southern European capitals, the *Deutsche Akademie* began to establish language schools in the provincial cities and countryside.

Until the late 1930s, the DA's expansion plans focused on cities where less French linguistic competition existed and where inhabitants were demonstrably motivated – for economic, cultural, or political reasons – to learn German. (Michels 2005: 90) This practice allowed the DA to champion the rural ethnic-German communities who had suffered persecution during and after World War I, while simultaneously laying claim to the linguistic devotion of villagers and townspeople throughout the European countryside (ibid. 111). Though DA administrators considered Yugoslavia to be the key to cultural preeminence throughout the Balkans, French enjoyed a firm foothold as the obligatory first foreign language at Yugoslavian universities. Bulgaria, on the other hand, remained relatively uncommitted in its second-language policies, and therefore the DA planners opened more language schools [*Lektorate*] in Sofia and other provincial Bulgarian cities. Promoting the German language internationally grew in political urgency throughout the 1930s, and the notion that German could become Europe's primary language of commerce and communication quickly transformed itself from a chimerical improbability to an administrative necessity. By 1932, as the DA began to accrue significant financial power, its General Secretary Franz Thierfelder advised his program coordinators that they should "methodically, step by step, wrestle for intellectual influence throughout the region, in which the general developments of an openness for German cultural work has been established." (ibid, 110)

Spracharbeit im Ausland, or language work abroad, enjoyed a peculiar independence from the National Socialist governmentality during this period. In exchange, the National Socialist government enjoyed the benefits of an international German language-teaching apparatus that was not perceived as a deputy institution of the new Hitler regime, which had consolidated most other social and cultural organizations after February 1933. The Nazi government had resisted the temptation to streamline the DA and *Deutscher Akademischer Austauschdienst* (German Academic Exchange Service) into its other domestic cultural conglomerates. In the spring of 1935, the Bureau of Foreign Affairs [*Auswärtiges Amt*] rejected a plan to consolidate all of the foreign relations and language teaching organizations into one umbrella apparatus called the "German Cultural Exchange." (108) Equally noteworthy is the fact that the *Deutsche Akademie* teaching staff underwent no major personnel changes between 1933 and 1938 (113). In contrast to other cultural spheres – visual art, domestic higher education, elementary education, youth groups – language teachers abroad were allowed remarkably free rein in their curricular choices. In a letter to Karl Haushofer in 1933, General Secretary Thierfelder foresaw the prudence of maintaining an independent language-teaching profession around the world during the political transformations afoot in Germany: "We can only successfully continue and strengthen our cultural promotion work abroad, if the scholarly cloak of our organization does not become threadbare." (108) The ambiguity in Thierfelder's forewarning – between the necessity to 'be rigorous researchers" of second language acquisition and to 'look like rigorous researchers' of it – epitomizes the ongoing predicament of these highly trained academicians over two decades of rapid political mutation in their midst.

By the late 1930s, language program coordinators at the Foreign Bureau were assessing the results of five years of National Socialist governance on German cultural policy abroad. Foreign language education planners began to foresee new dilemmas for the future linguistic management of Europe. Wilhelm Burmeister, Director of the DAAD in 1937, expressed concern about what he perceived as Germany's growing cultural isolation – even from such allied states as Italy. According to Burmeister, this challenge of interpopular understanding [*zwischenvölkisches Verständnis*] could be remedied by a more sensitive approach to teaching the language and culture of the New Germany. From such scholars as Burmeister, we notice a reaching back to the slogans or concepts of earlier generations of researchers such as Lamprecht and Rühlmann, in a bid to both save and legitimize their own profession.

6 A Lingua Germana

Ultimately, Franz Thierfelder's 1938 treatise *German as a World Language* [*Deutsch als Weltsprache*] is conscious that a sober intercultural engagement must take the place of the halcyon expansionism of early National Socialist cultural policy. He stressed that Nazi language policy must assist foreigners in overcoming the difficulties endemic in the German language itself – such as the inconsistencies in its "two-script" system (Thierfelder 1938: 47). The rapid changes in the living language of German since the end of the 19th century have made it increasingly difficult even for "America-Germans" to understand the language of the "New Germany." In charting a course for a foreigner-friendly language method, Thierfelder steers clear of both crass utilitarianism and philological purism; for him, impurity and mutation in the language are the price that German must pay to become a language of global importance [*Kaufpreis für Weltgeltung*]. If German was to become a language of "use between peoples" [*zwischenvölkischen Gebrauchs*], Nazi language policy could not afford to purify German of French and Latin influences, and Thierfelder opposed policies that would outlaw "foreign words" in the German language. It would have been a grave mistake, for instance, to create a German medical vocabulary to replace the existing physiological lexicon of Latinate derivation, as this would exacerbate Germany's potential isolation on the world stage. Organizations interested in a revitalization of the German language, he contended, should concentrate on removing lifeless ornamentation and "paper-bound style," rather than ferreting out foreign words, which had earned "guest rights" [*Gastrecht*] and offered much-needed assistance to second language learners.

Nor could German language teachers abroad afford to demand perfection from their learners. (52) Thierfelder reasoned that since teaching German abroad had become a matter of "public service" in the National Socialist age, the DAAD had to employ only the most "humane" pedagogues, regardless of their academic credentials. By this, he meant to promote the hiring of instructors who would gladly stray from the philological and grammatical dreariness of the lesson plan to build inroads into the "heart" of the foreigner. (59) The National Socialist language teacher was entirely capable of overcoming these intercultural problems, he argued, because "Germans are most capable and prepared to understand the foreign nation in its innermost being and to recognize its special value." (59) Gaining access to the hearts of his foreign students required that the teacher know the political relationships between the German people and the host country. The teacher must resist the temptation to remain isolated in the monolingual company of his German contemporaries. He or she must learn the language of his guest country, regardless of its ranking or currency among world languages, if only out of a commitment to "human duty." Since "the personal, internal gain achieved from the learning of any language is beyond doubt," the National Socialist teacher can return to Germany with "a piece of the world," ensure that Germany will not become isolated from that world again, and lay the groundwork for the revitalization of Europe through German stewardship and dominion. (60)

For Thierfelder, if these cosmopolitan provisions for a global German were consistently embodied among German-as-a-Foreign-Language teaching professionals, each teacher would ultimately succeed in his or her task. Still, each teacher needs to understand that "The imperial German language teacher [*Reichsdeutscher Sprachlehrer*] would step into the circle of his pupils often as the first representative of his people, and from the outset he will be greeted with an implacable and uninterrupted critique." Some foreign students, claims Thierfelder, will be for example disappointed to find their German teacher is not blond, and thus doesn't correspond to the students' expectations. Here Thierfelder is clearly more concerned with how the teacher insinuates himself into a harmonic relationship with German learners, rather than with how rigidly that teacher conveys the dictates of the Nazi state. It is thus the first responsibility of the language teacher to be patient about his or her students' expectations, particularly their tendency to conflate the medieval German archetype, the Wilhelmine German, the Republican German, and the National Socialist German. The teacher must therefore be "a son of his time" [*Sohn seiner Zeit*], demonstrating to his pupils the commonalities between the National Socialist and Germans of bygone ages, and when necessary, making his "otherness" [*Anderssein*] understood. (58) Since the prejudices of peoples toward one another are stronger than a mere logical or factual refutation could counter, the language teacher must be a living counter-example to the vices ascribed to Germans over the ages: self-righteousness, heavy drinking, a predilection for physical altercations and sentimentality, lack of grace, tactlessness, and brutality. Yet Thierfelder was certain that "in general, the openness to the German essence will overcome any deep-seated rejection." (58) The work of counteracting these stereotypes among foreign learners, he claimed, required that the German teacher demonstrate good taste, physical fitness, and cleanliness in the maintenance of his person, home, and effects. Thierfelder insisted that the German language must not shy away from expressing those qualities – masculinity, complexity, and organicity – that allow it to "stride forth respectably, like a German." The intractable shapelessness of the German sentence is deceptive; it veils a strict yet supple capacity to imitate the actual "process of living speech" [*lebendigen Sprechvorgangs*], while English and French remain stranded at the level of "abstract thought process" [*abstrakten Denkvorgangs*]. (54) Teaching these life-affirming features of the German language, even though they present consistent difficulty to second-language learners – setting the bar high, he reasons – will prepare the foreign language student for the great challenge of engaging with the German *Volk*.

In Thierfelder we see embodied an empire that has learned to send its *least* ideologically doctrinaire representatives to the frontier of intercultural exchange, so as to establish relationships that will facilitate students' harmonious integration in to the civic polity of German as a Global Language. His approach leads with "openness," "patience," and an ability to defy and negotiate expectations in the nitty-gritty of classroom-based and informal intercultural encounter. For 21st-century teachers of foreign languages and intercultural competence, it is disturbing to discover the extent to which the *Deutsche Akademie's* staff during the Third Reich felt indeed that they were not just talking the talk, but walking the walk of modern, self-critical transcultural engagement.

Meanwhile, the training of translators in Germany had skyrocketed, with the Institut für Sprachenkunde und Dolmetscherwesen der *Deutschen Auslandswissenschaftlichen Fakultät* (DAWF) in Berlin graduating 4000 translators between 1940–1943 (Winter 2012: 24). Along with similar Institutes in Leipzig, Königsberg, Vienna and Heidelberg, this institute taught the broadest spectrum of languages – including Rumanian, Russian, Dutch, and Asian and African languages. One of the brochures for the Translators' Institute in Vienna, founded in 1943, recommended its curriculum on the basis that "Given the future tasks of the German Empire in Europe and in the colonies, the translation and interpretation profession offers advantageous prospects for employment options. (Winter 2012: 24) "Im Hinblick auf die künftigen Aufgaben des Deutschen Reiches in Europa und in Kolonien bietet der Beruf des Übersetzers und Dolmetschers günstige Aussichten für Einsatzmöglichkeiten, allerdings nur für wirklich tüchtige Kräfte" (A glance at the course offerings at this institute indicates that forming a translation curriculum seems to have been an opportunistic decision, heavily reliant on philosophy and literature, without very much in the way of practical training for interpreters and translators in the field.) For its part, the armed forces proctored no fewer than 50,000 tests for "Wehrmachtssprachmittler", or military language mediators up until 1941, and a communiqué from the Imperial Branch for Translation in 1941 summarized its role as follows: "The challenges of the war effort, as well as the employment of many million foreign workers of the most diverse ethnicities in the territory of Empire, – place interpreting and translation services in one of the most important and war-critical key positions." "Die Erfordernisse der Kriegsführung aber ebenso sehr auch der Einsatz von vielen Millionen ausländischer Arbeiter verschiedenster Volkszugehörigkeit im Reichsgebiet, – stellen heute das Dolmetschen und Übersetzen in eine der wichtigsten und kriegsentscheidenden Schlüsselstellungen." (Winter 2012: 29)

For the state-appointed Director of Languages Services (*Sprachendienst*) in Berlin, the Romance-languages scholar Paul Gauthier, this meant a new commitment to advanced language learning as a form of "total mobilization": He writes:

> Even in peacetime, a partial solution to the problem of language specialists would not be sufficient. But now with the war, in which the ideological struggle is being pursued with unspeakable acrimony, it is now a matter of winning over an entire army of qualified language personnel as essential and irreplaceable comrades in the fight. This can only occur when linguistic labor is no longer carried out secondarily and in arbitrary form, but rather is elevated through regulation, safeguarding, and valorization to that which it is and always was – a most important link in the chain of activities that will help Germany toward its victory.

> Schon für die Friedenzeit wäre eine Teillösung des Problems der Sprachtätigen unzulänglich gewesen. Jetzt im Kriege, wo der geistige Kampf mit unsäglicher Schärfe geführt wird, gilt es, die ganze Armee der geeigneten Sprachkräfte als unerlässliche und unersetzliche Mitkämpfer zu gewinnen. Das kann nur geschehen, wenn die sprachliche Tätigkeit nicht mehr nur nebenbei und in willkürlicher Form ausgeübt wird, sondern durch Regelung, Schutz, und Wertung zu dem erhoben wird, was sie in Wirklichkeit immer war und ist – ein wichtigstes Glied in der Kette der Tätigkeiten, die Deutschland zum Siege verhelfen sollen.
> (Winter 35)

Gauthier, as his colleague Thierfelder had done, is adept at blending the liberal universalism of his own early twentieth-century training with the slogans of the war machine. Language studies and language learning, in their most rigorous forms, are exalted to a central position within the political project of German futurity in the world, not only in wartime, but for the peace that is to follow.

7 Further Methodological Constraints

> Before the Nazis, in short, geopolitics meant many things to many people. After 1933, it meant one thing, the use of a certain kind of political-geographic rhetoric to justify the racial policies of national socialism.
> (Murphy 23)

Even Murphy's foreclosure above truncates the diversity of approaches, perspectives, and investments that characterized intercultural and multilingual thinking in the Third Reich, deep into the 1930s and 1940s, where practitioners and researchers trained in the philologies struggled to reconcile their old conceptual commitments with the new slogans. There are accordingly a handful of problems facing the project of researching multilinguality and documenting interculturality in this context and period, problems that are primarily discursive and/or terminological in nature. One methodological commitment of this study has been to conceive the "margins" of the Third Reich as a temporally and spatially dynamic domain. There was always more time, space and human experience involved in the process of "becoming" or "becoming occupied by" the Third Reich, than of "belonging to" it, and those domains of becoming (and of divesting) touched the lives of far more people, cultures, and languages than did the strictly territorial claims of the Nazi state. Before, after, around, and neighboring National Socialism were and are domains of experience and practice that still suffer various forms of methodological and structural exclusion from scholarship. For one, Christopher Hutton (1999) points out that decades of intellectual and institutional historians have felt compelled to determine, for example, what was "Nazi linguistics" and what wasn't, who was a "Nazi linguist" and who wasn't. Hutton explains the accumulated effect this moral triage has had on what we actually know and think about the study of language in the midst of fascist totalitarianism. Hutton suggests that

> it is important to define National Socialist linguistics as simply the linguistics carried out by German scholars in Germany or under German rule after the purge of civil servants in 1933 until 1945. While this does not offer precision, I believe it offers a much better starting-point than polemical attempts to isolate the 'Nazi core'. Any attempt at a definition would also have to deal with the question of the émigré linguistics of the victims of the Nazis, which on a theoretical level cannot be neatly separated from the linguistics of Nazi Germany. (23)

In general, the container 1933–1945 and its constitutive historiographic cesurae make it very difficult to think about the cultural and linguistic liminalities that made National Socialism succeed, and that allowed other things to subsist other things work contemporaneously and intersectionally amid National Socialism. Often this pursuit gets reduced to a resistance/collaboration model, which often brings with it a prejudicial crudeness toward the intricacies of social practice and moral intention that has long since been considered inadmissible in the study of contact-linguistic settings in other domains of colonization and survival. The persistence of this *jurisprudential* model of Holocaust Studies research leaves us with an astonishing array of categorically unstudied areas.

Meanwhile, it is clear that what began as a philosophically democratic theory of intercultural awareness and multilingual exchange in the 1910s and 1920s was gradually repurposed throughout the 1920s and 1930s for pragmatic-geopolitical and then fascist ends. In many cases, the same professionals, using the same terminology, remained in the state's employ throughout the Third Reich, and were then reengaged in the post-War period to form the post-Nazi institutions of German-as-a-Foreign-Language via the newly founded Goethe Institut (see Michels 2005). This continuity posed a structural and ideological challenge to post-War curriculum developers and teachers at Goethe Institute branches around the world who went to great lengths to reconcile their profession with recent German history, and to restore the intellectual legitimacy of German-as-a-Foreign-Language teaching for the late 20th century. Indeed, since then, the Goethe Institut has grown into one of the world's most ambitious and admirable promoters of pro-immigration, multicultural programming and learning.

It has been the purpose of this article to shed light on the continuity, ambiguity, contingency, and ideological flexibility of these theoretical approaches and their representatives over a fifty-year period, and to offer this historical context as a cautionary reminder for twenty-first century intercultural and multilingual discourses, currently in their course of development. It also serves as a reminder that the contemporary threat of what Barbara Schmenk calls the "sloganization" of language studies, the topic of a recent conference at the Humboldt University in Berlin, bears an intricate hundred-year history with it – a history offering endless case studies for twenty-first century theorists interested in interculturality, multilingualism, and the rhetorical uptake of these discourses in eras of acute political transformation.

References

Arendt, Hannah. 1948. "The Concentration Camps." *Partisan Review* 15.7: 743–763.
Aschenberg, Heidi. 2002. "Sprachterror. Kommunikation im nationalsozialistischen Konzentrationslager." *Zeitschrift für romanische Philologie* 118.4: 529–572.
Cameron, Deborah. 1995. *Verbal Hygiene*. London: Routledge.
Döscher, Hans-Jürgen. 1987. *Das Auswärtige Amt im Dritten Reich*. Berlin: Siedler Verlag.
Ellis, Elizabeth. 2006. "Monolingualism: The Unmarked Case." *Estudios de Sociolingüística* 7(2). 173–196.
Fanon Frantz. 1967. *The Wretched of the Earth*. London: Penguin, Harmondsworth.
Gramling, David. 2012. *An Other Unspeakability: Levi and Lagerszpracha. New German Critique* 39.3: 165–187.
Herbert, Ulrich. 1997. *Hitler's Foreign Workers: Enforced Foreign Labor in Germany under the Third Reich*. William Templer, trans. Cambridge: Cambridge University Press.
Hutton, Christopher. 1999. *Linguistics in the Third Reich*. London: Routledge.
Jackall, Robert. 1985. *Propaganda*. New York University Press.
Klemperer, Viktor. 2006. *Language of the Third Reich*. Translated by Martin Brady. London: Bloomsbury.
Kloosterhuis, Jürgen. 1994. *Friedliche Imperialisten: Deutsche Auslandsvereine und auswärtige Kulturpolitik, 1906–1918*. Frankfurt am Main: Peter Lang.
Lamprecht, Karl. 1913. *Über auswärtige Kulturpolitik*. http://archive.org/stream/uberauswartigeku00lamp/uberauswartigeku00lamp_djvu.txt
Levi, Primo. 1987. *If this is a Man, and, The Truce*. Trans. Stuart Woolf. London: Abacus.
Levine, Glenn. 2014. "From Performance To Multilingual Being In Foreign Language Pedagogy: Lessons From L2 Students Abroad". *Critical Multilingualism Studies*. 2(1). 74–105.
Michels, Eckard. 2005. *Von der Deutschen Akademie zum Goethe-Institut. Sprach- und auswärtige Kulturpolitik 1923–1960*. Munich: R. Oldenbourg Verlag.
Murphy, David Thomas. 1997. *The Heroic Earth: Geopolitical Thought in Weimar Germany, 1918–1933*. Kent, Ohio: The Kent State University Press.
Oller, John W. 1997. "Monoglottosis: What's Wrong with the Idea of the IQ Meritocracy and its Racy Cousins?". *Applied Linguistics* 18(4), 467–507.
Oschlies, Wolf. 1996. "Lagerszpracha: Soziolinguistische Bemerkungen zu KZ-Sprachkonventionen". *Muttersprache* (96). 98–109.

Phipps, Alison and Mike Gonzalez. 2004. *Modern Languages: Learning and Teaching in an Intercultural Field*. Sage Publications.
Rühlman, Paul M. 1919. *Kulturpropaganda: Grundsätzliche Darlegungen und Auslandsbeobachtungen*. Berlin: Deutsche Verlagsgesellschaft für Politik und Geschichte.
Sauer, Christoph. 1998. *Der aufdringliche Text: Sprachpolitik und NS-Ideologie in der "Deutschen Zeitungen in den Niederlanden."* Wiesbaden: Deutscher Universitäts-Verlag.
Skutnabb-Kangas, T. 2000. *Linguistic Genocide in Education, or Worldwide Diversity and Human Rights?* Mahwah N.J.: Lawrence Erlbaum.
Taterka, Thomas. 1995. "Zur Sprachsituation im deutschen Konzentrationslager." *Juni. Magazin für Literatur & Politik* 21: 37–54.
Thierfelder, Franz. 1938. *Deutsch als Weltsprache*. Berlin: Verlag für Volkstum, Wehr und Wirtschaft.
Winter, Miriam. 2012. *Das Dolmetscherwesen im Dritten Reich*. Frankfurt am Main: Peter Lang.

Fabienne Baider and Marilena Kariolemou

8 Linguistic *Unheimlichkeit*: the Armenian and Arab communities of Cyprus

Abstract: Using ethnic narratives, this chapter explores the linguistic (and social) *Unheimlichkeit* felt by the members of minorities speaking heritage languages in Cyprus: the Armenian community living in the Republic of Cyprus and the isolated Cypriot Arabs (also called Maronites) enclaved in the village of Kormakitis in the northern part of Cyprus. *Unheimlichkeit* is here to be taken in its psychoanalytic sense of "strangeness" or "estrangement" and in its more metaphoric sense to describe the feeling of being in a familiar yet alien place at the same time. Indeed, national linguistic minorities speaking different languages and with a different history than the one articulated and promoted by the State are caught between the global and the local languages, cultures and values, within a same nation. Moreover within an ethnic conflict setting, a dominant language such as Greek in the Republic of Cyprus will construct (and 'estrange') the other competitive tongues. The narratives from speakers of both communities testify, discuss and analyse in which ways this double bind or 'social and linguistic strangeness/ estrangement' is emotionally constituted in both, the excluder and the excluded as well as linguistically negotiated.

1 Introduction

> FL educators seem to be confronted with the tasks of having to teach two kinds of culture: a global culture of communication for the sake of communication and local cultures of shared values (Kramsch 2014: 302).

Heritage language minorities speaking different languages and with a different history than the State are caught as well between the global and the local cultures and values, within the same nation. On the one hand, they (may) practice at home the minority language which stands for their community's shared values; on the other, they have to learn the State language for the sake of communicating in the broader society and in order to have access to the cultural – and other more tangible – capital attached to the dominant language. In the process they may learn to put aside, disregard or even despise the shared values of their community. The goal of this paper is to examine in which ways this double bind or 'social

Corresponding Author: Fabienne Baider, University of Cyprus, Cyprus, fabienne@ucy.ac.cy

and linguistic strangeness/estrangement' is emotionally constituted in both, the excluder and the excluded (Pavlenko & Blackledge 2004) as well as linguistically negotiated.

A dominant language within an ethnic conflict setting will construct (and 'estrange') the other competitive tongues as part of the national struggle. Indeed, most studies, which explore the relationship between identity construction and language within the Cypriot society (Charalambous 2012; Spyrou 2006), tackle language learning in Cyprus from the 'Cyprus problem' perspective (i.e. the *de facto* division of the island since 1974). Learning the language of the Other is therefore thought of as Greek Cypriots learning Turkish (Charalambous & Rampton 2011, Zembylas 2010, 2012) and to a much lesser degree as Turkish Cypriots learning Greek[1]. However, the 'Us' and the 'Other' can be defined by different criteria in the multilingual and multi-ethnic Cypriot society. As a matter of fact, if many studies framed within a post-modern stance have emphasized the shifts in identities in the speakers (Kramsch 2009: 16–17), this shift is also true for the Other, a fluid identity constructed and deconstructed in everyday interactions, emerging locally from verbal and social interactions in historically contingent contexts (Kramsch 2012: 119).

For the purpose of our study focusing on the Armenian community in the Republic of Cyprus and the isolated Arab Cypriots (also called Maronites) in the northern part of Cyprus, we will be using ethnic narratives to describe the relation of members of small minorities to their respective languages. These narratives will refer to testimonies from Armenian and Arab Cypriots. Through collected data and interviews, we inquire how ideology – defined here as a set of dominant or subaltern ideas, discourses, and signifying practices used to acquire or maintain linguistic power (Woolard 1998: 7) – shapes the acceptance or the reluctance of speakers to learn, hear or speak the dominant language and the way they live their sameness/strangeness and estrangement. The discussion will be framed within identity politics theory (Ahmed 2004, Zembylas 2012), both groups having been constructed as marginal or inexistent in mainstream discourse and research.

---

[1] Usually Cypriot Greek refers to the language and the word Greek Cypriot to the community. We kept that difference for referring to each community: Arab Cypriot, Armenian Cypriot, Turkish Cypriot without implying that they feel first their ethnical background and then Cypriot.

2 Theoretical framework

Very few studies have looked into the emotional trauma of other communities living in Cyprus who may have to (un)learn the language spoken by an historical enemy or a contemporary nationalist neighbour. If the notion of citizenship reflects how a state understands its unity and collective identity (Kymlicka 2001), on the Cypriot territory this identity is basically Greek Cypriot and sometimes Turkish Cypriot (Constantinou 2007). In recent years, many researchers have pointed to the difficulties encountered by indigenous linguistic minorities in a society that, since the end of the 19th century, has been characterized by a bipolarity (Greek Cypriot and Turkish Cypriot) inscribed in its very Constitution. (Mavrides & Maranda 1999; Constantinou 2007, 2009). Constantinou (2007) in particular underlines the impossible challenge of individuals or groups who have intersected the religious, ethnic and language barriers that formed the quintessence of ethnic division set as follows: Greek-speaking Orthodox Greek vs (Ottoman) Turkish-speaking Muslim Turk. This positioning fits what Pavlenko (2003) described as a site where learning languages may become linked to the history of emotional trauma in the context of ethnic conflicts and postcolonial societies. Language policies are power relations and ideologies working at the crossroads of theories common to gender/class/ethnicity issues. In particular, our study examines the importance of the dominant languages, here Greek/Cypriot Greek/English, and for the enclaved Arab Cypriots who leave isolated in the occupied part of Cyprus, Turkish/Cypriot Turkish, as indicators of power, affluence and influence in this local context. According to previous studies, the two communities under investigation, the Armenian and the Maronite communities, have constructed their identities in opposition to the dominant ethos whether Greek Cypriot or Turkish Cypriot, language and religion.

Our contribution, focused on language use, language attitudes, and beliefs, testifies to the fluidity of what is said as regards who is an Arab Cypriot and who is an Armenian Cypriot and in relation to who is the Other within each of the communities. Indeed, identity narratives emerging through language are "fragmented, decentered, and shifting" narratives (Pavlenko & Blackledge 2004: 18), resulting from the complexities of multilingual and socially diverse contexts. Speakers may be positioned or position themselves in a variety of social contexts, because of their choice of language or their belonging to a linguistic minority. Moreover, their positioning varies according to the degree of 'closeness' they feel about the languages they speak, including their avowed mother tongue or at least the language that defines their belonging to their indigenous community. However, during our investigation regarding the meaning of being 'multilingual', we often encountered the question of who is an authentic 'patriot', in the literal sense of the word (*Am I Cypriot first or Armenian? Are Armenians really Cypriot?*) and who is a legitimate speaker (*They were born here, they should speak Cypriot-Greek*)[2]. Indeed, even though Armenian Cypriots and Arab Cypriots have access to symbolic and material resources, they do seem to hover between feeling 'in' and feeling 'out' of their community as well as 'in' and 'out' of the broader Cypriot society, their linguistic and ethnic loyalty being continuously tested when choosing their political camp, their schools or even their life partner. As a matter of fact, even though they share the same political community and geographical space as the dominant groups, when political and structural tensions arise, the divide along language lines occurs, shifts or deepens, and sometimes very brutally so as the history has shown in Cyprus repeatedly. The notion of verbal hygiene – signaling the symbolic attempt to impose order on the social world by regulating language and here languages from above – comes to mind when nationalist discourses erase minority languages from the linguistic landscape or the minority language speakers themselves censor the public presence of their mother tongue, interiorizing their linguistic oblivion in the socio-mediated environment.

3 Social and historical frames

Historically, the strategic position of Cyprus in the easternmost part of the Mediterranean made it a vulnerable spot for conquest; each interference left its mark on the social, political and linguistic landscape (Baider & Hadjipavlou 2008; Karyolemou 2005; Hadjipavlou 2007). The co-existence of many communities is at the origin of the current multi-ethnic character of the island. The Greek presence dates back to the second millennium BC and the Turkish-Ottoman were established on the island with the Ottoman Empire (from the 16th century onwards).[3] However, Cyprus includes minorities such as Maronites (Arab Christian religion of Syriac and Lebanese origin), Armenians (Orthodox religion for most although the Catholic Armenian were first on the island), Latins (Catholic) and Roma (Muslim) or Kurbet people, all present in the island since the 12th century,[4] at least, and together representing the often forgotten 2% of the population.

---

[2] Cf. Kramsch (2012: 110) for authenticity and legitimacy regarding the speakers.
[3] Because of the focus of the notions of the present study on autochthonous linguistic minorities, we do not tackle the huge and pressing task to work with the non-historical linguistic communities whose numbers have increased exponentially.
[4] The presence of Armenians and Arabs on the island dates back to the 6th – 7th century A. D.

Throughout history, colonizing powers had been politicizing differences between ethnic groups to better serve their interests in the Middle East (Pollis, 1973, 1996). During the 50s, the struggle against the British crystalized ethnic division, each dominant community wanting to be attached to Greece and Turkey respectively. In 1960, the independence of the Republic of Cyprus was organized by outside powers (Greece, Turkey and Britain). In 1963, the constitutional crises alternated with violent communal clashes perpetrated by militias on both sides. When, ten years later, in 1974, the north of the island was occupied by the Turkish troops, the small communities were caught in the struggle, leaving behind, each time, their shop, their home, their neighbourhood: "We have been victims three times: first in 1915 then in the 60's and then in 1974. Every time lives and life hood had been lost" recalled bitterly the young Arevig[5]; Arab Cypriots had to leave their villages situated in the northwest uppermost coast of the island (Karyolemou 2012), only a few of them remaining in the enclaved village of Kormakitis. Since then, in the two divided parts of the island, an endogenous nationalism has been an effective tool to promote homogeneity and national values that readily obscure intra-dissensions whether they are linguistic or cultural.

At the same time, in the South, the emphasis on the military conflict overshadows any other social problem and favors the erasure of any 'other presence' than the presence of the two dominant linguistic communities, the Greek-speaking and Turkish-speaking communities. The presence and the role of religion in this divisive atmosphere are not to be neglected, whether they be the weight of Orthodox prelates in the Greek Cypriot community, imams in the Turkish Cypriot community, or the religious authorities in the Arab Cypriot and the Armenian Cypriot communities.

4 The Armenian and Arab Cypriot communities: a brief history

Armenian – the mother tongue of the vast majority of Armenians in Cyprus – and Cypriot Arabic – a unique variety of Arabic spoken solely in Cyprus – were recognized as minority languages of Cyprus as of 1st of December 2002 and 5th of November 2008, respectively[6].

---

5 All personal names used in this paper are fictitious in order to preserve informant identities.
6 At the opposite of Armenian, Cypriot Arabic was reluctantly recognized by the Cypriot government, admittedly, after persistent external pressure. See on this issue C. Constantinou (2008).

The small number of Armenians living in Cyprus have been part of the Cypriot community since the Middle Ages and for some families as early as the 6th century the connections between Cyprus and the Armenian Kingdom of Cilicia are well-known. However, according to available information, Armenians in Cyprus are mainly refugees from the 19th century and early 20th century massacres which happened in Turkey. It is after the genocide in 1915 that the biggest wave of immigrants arrived in Cyprus. A large number of these (Armenians) immigrated to the United Kingdom in 1955–1959 during the inter-communal violence. Traditionally Armenian Cypriots speak the Western Armenian language, common to other communities who came from Anatolia. As for the language, Western Armenian is a diasporic language facing extinction since the native speakers have been relocating from Anatolia all over the world, adopting the language of the host country. Recently the Eastern Armenian language has been spoken on the island because of a wave of immigrants from the Republic of Armenia and Georgia.

The Arab Cypriot community has also been established on the island of Cyprus since at least Medieval times (Hourani 1998, 2009). Initially a quite dynamic and wealthy community, the Arab Cypriot community spread in tens of villages all over the island, but was gradually reduced and since the beginning of the 20th century it was confined to four villages –Asomatos, Agia Marina, Karpasha, Kormakitis– now under Turkish administration. In 1974, most Arab Cypriots were displaced from their villages as a result of the Turkish invasion and are now living scattered around the island; only a handful of mostly elderly people have remained enclaved in their homes under Turkish administration[7]. The community holds an exceptional place within the realm of Arab communities, being at the periphery of the Arabic-speaking world, isolated and in contact with the Greek and Turkish languages. The question of the origins of the community has long been debated and is not yet definitively settled. They are usually considered to be of Lebanese origin (Boustany 1954), but this is also disputed (Borg 1985, 2004).

As for the Armenian Cypriots, fluency in Armenian grew tremendously since the refugees from the 1915 genocide arrived in Cyprus. Since they would not all be talking Armenian but more likely Turkish, the importance of learning the Armenian language to create the community on the island was tremendous (Pattie 1997: 96). Family ties, home, church and school helped to spread and maintain the Armenian language. Maybe this importance given to the Armenian language

---

"The Indeterminate Status of Cypriot Maronite Arabic". http://news.maronitedaily.com/index.php/component/k2/item/525-the-indeterminate-status-of-cypriot-maronite-Arabic <15/02/2014>
[7] 103 persons according to the lists provided by the Department responsible for citizens enclaved in the Turkish occupied area at the Ministry of Interior, Cyprus (October 2012).

could also be interpreted as the attempt by Armenian Cypriots to distance themselves from the Turkish language after the 1915 genocide or to explore the freedom to speak and learn their mother tongue, the foundation for the preservation of their national and cultural heritage: "Armenians consciously identify with Armenian, their mother tongue (...) A feeling of being special and part of a community and the larger Armenian family." (Pattie 1997: 212). Moreover since Cyprus independence in 1960, Armenian Cypriots, Arab Cypriots and Latins have been recognized as "religious groups" by the Constitution[8]. A constitutional provision, according to which ethnic groups or individuals of a different ethnic background living in Cyprus at the moment of independence had to be affiliated to a larger ethnic group (Cyprus Constitution, Article 2§3), obliged them to choose between the Greek Cypriot or the Turkish Cypriot community. They opted to belong to the co-religious Greek Cypriot community (as expected), something which consequently defined their political options in the game of inter-communal controversy. More importantly, this choice affected, as well, their relations with the Turkish Cypriots: whereas in the 60's populations were living together in mixed neighbourhoods, this political choice turned against the linguistic minorities which were seen thereafter as an extension of the Greek Cypriot political choices. When the Armenian quarter of Nicosia had to be left behind by the non-Turkish Cypriot population, a very vibrant, multiethnic and multilingual community, home not only to Armenians but to many Turkish and Greek Cypriots, Arab Cypriots and Latins,[9] disappeared with this relocation. Consequently in 1974, 100 Armenian families and almost the totality of the Arab Cypriot population had to relocate as a result of the Turkish invasion and, along with thousands of Greek Cypriots, they became refugees.

5 Socio-linguistic minorities

Currently, Armenians maintain a presence of about 2,900 on the island (including about 1,500 non-Armenian Cypriots, mainly from Armenia, Georgia, Lebanon,

---

[8] Appendix E of the *Treaty of establishment* between the United Kingdom, Greece, Turkey and the Republic of Cyprus: *The Rights of Smaller Religious Groups in Cyprus*. 1960.
[9] The departure of Armenian Cypriots during the insurgency (1955–1959), the migration movement of Diaspora Armenians to Soviet Armenia, reduced the Armenian Cypriot community to half of what it was after 1917. However a reverse trend, Armenians from Armenia coming to Cyprus, may give hope for a future revival. Our interviews are only within the Armenian community originally from the Middle-East and from Cyprus. We had no respondents from the Eastern European block recently arrived in Cyprus.

etc.)[10]. The increased number of marriages outside the community (more than half of the young interviewees – under 35 – were married to non-Armenian speakers) as well as the arrival of thousands of Armenians from neighbouring countries have changed the Armenian Cypriot community: insecurity and fear for the survival of their language and culture were very strong in the interviews we conducted (Hadjipavlou 2007, our data). While today over 95% of the Armenian population speak Armenian and are Armenian Orthodox (Gregorian), this percentage could drop dramatically in the next twenty years.

Arab Cypriots, on the other hand, have maintained Sanna and transmitted it orally through the centuries (Roth 1986, 2000, 2004); only recently has the language been given a writing system. Since the end of the 19th century, Sanna is spoken solely by people originating from the village of Kormakitis. Currently, it has barely any competent speakers under the age of 30. According to estimations (Karyolemou 2012), the number of Arabic-speaking Cypriot Maronites does not predictably exceed one fifth of the total Arab Cypriot population[11]: although estimations vary from 1000 to 1300, a number close to 900 speakers, all degrees of competence considered (active, passive, semi- and terminal- speakers), seems more realistic (Karyolemou 2012). The fact that Sanna is minoritized both vis-a-vis the dominant Greek (and Cypriot Greek) variety and vis-à-vis Classical Arabic and other prestigious forms of Arabic (e.g., Lebanese) renders its position extremely fragile.

The Armenian and Arab Cypriot linguistic communities are minorities in all respects but above all in relation to power, status and entitlement (May 2006: 255). Religion for example may be used to amplify ethnic differences and create hierarchy among ethnicities: previous research had stressed religious discrimination (Hadjipavlou 2004: 148). Armenian Cypriots regret, as well, the absence of substantial reference to their community in the history books on Cyprus used by the Greek Cypriot schools (Hadjipavlou 2004: 150; Sanam, Yervan, our informants). However, this minority status imposed somehow by social infrastructures does not mean a reciprocal feeling of being a community of lesser value. On the contrary, many of the stories told during the interviews showed pride for the culture, history and the language of the two communities. What could be felt though in some informants was either a frustrated nostalgia regarding the Great Armenia or the hope in the new state of Armenia. In the same way, claiming an Armenian or an Arab Cypriot identity does not simultaneously mean a claim against being Cypriot. Most of the Armenian and Arab Cypriots would call them-

---

10 Number was drawn from the 2011 census.
11 Estimated at approximately 5000 persons or 0,7% of the total population of Cyprus according to the *Demographic report* of 2010/2011.

selves as much Cypriot as Armenians or Maronites (our data, Hadjipavlou 2004); none of them, however, would see how they could be called Greek. In our data, Armenian Cypriots claim that Cyprus is their home, hence, they are Cypriots, but Armenian is their culture and language, hence, they identify themselves as Armenians. Many Armenians born in Lebanon and many Arab Cypriots show an attachment to Lebanon, which they consider to be their place of origin, some of them having visited it as much as 15 times. However, they do not consider themselves Lebanese, claiming a genuine Cypriot identity (our informants). Multilingualism including the Turkish language was practiced by many Cypriots on the island, on a daily basis, and even more so for the minorities until 1974.

Identity in Cyprus is then often *linguistically* negotiated in the political struggle that is still with the island in 2015. By examining the linguistic choices Armenian and Arab Cypriots make when they speak, and the social meanings such choices produce, this study explores how identities are negotiated through language shifts, as well as the complex interrelationship of choosing to use a language and choosing not to use or to hear another.

6 Methodology and data

Our work relies extensively on personal interviews and conversations with research participants. As mentioned by Ganat (2003), this technique "allows the researcher access to emic levels of explanation normally untapped in sociolinguistic analysis concerned with power and identity". On the other hand, we are also aware of the role taken by the participants while enjoying the conversation and how many of the informants' identity narratives could be affected by our questions and presence. There is always the question of the distance between how the participants actually report perceiving an issue and feeling about it and how they ideally perceive themselves as perceiving the issue and feeling about it. In the case of the Arab Cypriots, we included questions that elicited the reported responses. In the case of the Armenians, some of the opinions expressed were elicited during everyday conversations and were later on integrated in the field notes.

For Arab Cypriots we have used: (a) previous sociolinguistic and ethnolinguistic work including the results of interviews conducted with native speakers who are members of the community, (b) sociopolitical research dealing with the history of the community or of other minority communities living in Cyprus more generally (Mavratsas 1998, Varnava et *al.* 2009). Finally, ethnographic work in the form of semi-structured interviews with three native speakers of Cypriot Arabic living in the village of Kormakitis: Ioannis (74 years), Nino (62 years) and Sharpel (35 years). Interviews were in Cypriot Greek by a Greek Cypriot interviewer. The speakers were bilingual in Cypriot Arabic and Cypriot Greek. All of them were enclaved, often living away from their children and grandchildren. One of them (Sharpel) is an exceptional case of a native speaker under 35 years married to a Turkish Cypriot woman. All of them had their primary level education in Kormakitis: one of them (Nino) went to a private bilingual secondary religious school in Nicosia for three years, whereas Ioannis studied in a private English medium college in the northern part of Nicosia.

For Armenian Cypriots we have used interviews and conversations that were conducted in English. Most of the Armenian Cypriots interviewed were trilingual (Armenian, English and Greek), and English, not Greek, would be the second language of those who had been educated in English-speaking high schools, had lived in England or had completed their tertiary education in an English-speaking country. They also have families – close or extended – in England or the United States whom they visit on a regular basis. English was not the mother tongue of the interviewer but she was bilingual. We believe that being a foreigner to the Armenian community (but acquainted with the community) helped, since nothing was at stake with the revelations which sometimes were controversial; anonymity was also more surely preserved. Being a foreigner to the Greek Cypriot community was also an advantage given the ambiguous feelings we will see later in this paper regarding the Greek Cypriot community and its language for some of the informants. The data come from a dozen semi-structured interviews whose length varied from half an hour to four hours; data come as well from regular contacts with the Armenian Cypriots who are neighbours, gym fellows, students, acquaintances. They took place, then, in the gallery of an Armenian painter, at the gym, in a coffee shop, the university office, etc. The informants were all based in Nicosia where most Armenians live (names have been changed): Samson (45), Adrine (around 60), Aharon (around 65), Kohar (30), Sanam (70), Arevig (21), Siran (40), Yervant (45), Takouhi (35).

7 Linguistic practices of the Arab Cypriot community

7.1 An invisible and silent minority

Arab Cypriots have been an invisible and silent minority (Karyolemou 2009). Their invisibility resulted not only from their geo-demographic isolation but also from the political circumstances of their coexistence with their fellow Greek and Turkish Cypriots, and dramatically so, from the consequences of the political conflict between the two aforementioned communities.

The concealment of one's identity is a strategy that contributes to one's own invisibility while, at the same time, aims at protecting oneself from discrimination or indiscretion (Varnava et al. 2009). Our younger informant, Sharpel, who has a first name that could be easily identified as Christian Arabic, said that he used his father's name, Joseph (Josifis), which bears no mark of his ethno-religious origin, whenever he wanted to avoid questions about his identity (Interview 3/31:00–34:20).

Like many other small ethnic minorities Arab Cypriots are multilingual. In the course of time, however, most of them ceased to speak *Sanna* (or *Arapika*), their native Arabic variety, gradually shifting to either (Cypriot) Greek or Turkish. Reverting to Cypriot Greek (Romeika) has been a somehow expected outcome of the political decision of Arab Cypriots to become part of the Greek Cypriot community. Yet, it has not been an unproblematic and smooth process[12]. Two of our older informants remember the communication gap between children and their Greek Cypriot teachers who ignored everything about the community and its language. Even so, all our informants express their fidelity to the Greek language by stating that they would rather keep Greek and not Cypriot Arabic, if they were asked to choose. It is not uncommon for members of the community to unconsciously adopt the dominant point of view, even when by doing so they contradict their own reality and experience. At times, this may be confusing. Consider the following excerpt from our 62 year old informant, a farmer living in Kormakitis, where he recounts how, at the age of 15, he was taken out of school to work as a car engineer apprentice to a Greek Cypriot living in Nicosia. Note more specifically lines 5–8 where a misunderstanding occurs as regards the interpretation of the expression "foreign language".

---

[12] For what speakers say about "Arapika" and "Romeika" cf. Kermia Ztite at http://www.youtube.com/watch?v=ODysXq1fS6Q

Interview 2 [2:40/3:35][13]
LS = interviewer   *N* = Informant

1-LS: Did you know Greek?
2-N: We knew some. We went to primary school.
3-LS: You were learning Greek in primary school, didn't you?
4-N: Yes, yes, yes ...
5-LS: Was Greek like a *foreign language* to you, or did you hear Greek around here?
6-N: No, we have been raised in Greek. The *foreign language* that you heard talk about is Arabic, is the Arabic [variety] of the village.
7-LS: (perplex) Just a minute, just a minute, I am confused. When you were born ... What language did your parents talk to you [as a child]?
8-N: Arabic too, Arabic most of the times. We learned Greek, at school.

From the point of view of the interviewer – a young Greek Cypriot woman – "foreign language" alludes here to the Greek learnt by Arab Cypriot children at school. It is obvious that the informant misleadingly takes "foreign" to refer to the Cypriot Arabic vernacular, indeed a foreign language for any Greek Cypriot, but a native language to him, seemingly adopting an external point of view. We can also note the ambiguous wording of the interviewee as to his learning of Greek which results in a confusion confessed by the interviewer: "we were raised in Greek", but his parents were talking "Arabic, most of the times", then the final admission: "we learned Greek at school".

From the point of view of ethnic identification, all our informants clearly distinguish themselves from Greek Cypriots living in the 'Greek domain'. They declare that they are Cypriots or Maronites of Cyprus and all of them acknowledge their relation to the Maronites of Lebanon, even though they sometimes question the veracity of their Lebanese ascendance.

If Greek was learnt at school, Turkish, on the contrary, was learnt on the spot, through personal contact and face-to-face[14] interactions. Although Arab Cypriots were generally on good terms with Turkish Cypriots living in the surrounding villages, they did not feel it necessary to learn Turkish because Cypriot Greek served as a lingua franca to all of them. The need for a more systematic learning of the Turkish language was an outcome of Arab Cypriots administrative and economic dependence from Turkish Cypriot authorities and workforce after 1974 (Vassili

---

13 For reasons of commodity and clarity, the interventions of a third person have been omitted.
14 As far as I know, there are no studies treating the question of the relation between Cypriot Turkish and Cypriot Arabic, in a comprehensive manner.

2010: 29). Almost all Arab Cypriots who remained in Kormakitis were or became farmers and many used to employ Turkish Cypriot employees to help them in the fields. Our informants repeat, time and again, that they learnt Turkish in order to understand their co-workers or employees (Nino), Turkish administration and officials (Ioannis), the members of their family (mixed marriages – Sharpel). All of them report, however, that they still have difficulty in understanding specific uses of Turkish, e.g. the lyrics of songs, thus admitting the utilitarian function and partial learning of the language.

It seems, therefore, that Arab Cypriots living under Turkish administration have adjusted to their Turkish-speaking environment. None of our interviewees has expressed any negative feelings or views as regards the Turkish language. They all state that they "got used to it [the language]" because they hear it day after day. Consider the following extract from Ioannis' interview:

Interview 1 23:01/24:35]
LS = interviewer   *I* = Informant

1-LS: When you hear someone speak Turkish, how do you feel?
2-I: Look, Turkish, let's say, Turkish Cypriots have their own language [...] and when they ta..., of course, let's say, we don't understand, but we cannot accuse them because it's their language.
3-LS: Yes, yes, I agree but there are some languages where you say this one, I don't know... When I hear French, it is a language for lovers, it's like sweet. So when you hear Cypriot Turkish or Turkish, I don't know, what words would you use, let's say, for this language?
4-I: Look, because Turkish Cypriots are ..., because we hear them often, let's say, and they speak the language, let's say, Turkish, let's say, because it has been a long time, if it is good or it is not good, we digested it, we say it is good, what would we say?
5-LS: No, no what would we say, we don't need to say anything to anybody ... (laughter). How do you feel? I mean m ... yes, do you feel anything special?
6-I: Just, I don't feel neither good nor bad, because, let's say, it's their language [inaudible] they speak whatever they want. What would we say?
7-LS: You could say that it is ugly, I don't know...
8-I: *No, we don't say that, no, we don't say their language is ugly.*
9-LS: Is it a pleasant language, is it an unpleasant language?
10-I: We say, let's say, it's their language, let's say, however they talk, let's say, it's their language, it's pleasant, for us ok it's pleasant, what, what would we say?

The interviewer tries hard to elucidate the speaker's feelings as regards the Turkish language; the latter does not seem willing to provide a clear answer. In turns 2 and 4, avoidance strategies are used: he states the obvious – "Cypriots have their own language and nobody can blame them for using it" – and provides an answer with no informative value. At the beginning of turn 4, the speaker finally introduces an element of answer: "because we hear it often", "because it has been a long time", suggesting that liking the language is not a matter of personal appreciation but a matter of habit. In turn 6, he finally provides an answer, not without taking his distance vis-à-vis the Turkish language "I have neither good nor bad feelings about it". Could this be a covert way to state his indifference or even apprehension towards Turkish or does he try to please his Greek Cypriot interlocutor by showing that he doesn't really like the language? Both explanations could be valid. An element that corroborates the latter interpretation is the way the sequence is concluded:

Interview 1 25:16/25:34]
LS = interviewer   I = Informant

11-I: Look here, a language that you hear for the f..., when you hear for the first time a language that they speak, it seems strange. Whereas, if it's a language that you hear every day, you get used to it {LS "yes"}, and you say, their language is good [inaudible], you get used to it.
12-LS: Yes. Good. So, when you hear Turkish you like it?
13-I: We got used to them and, their language is good, we like it, what would we say?
14-LS: Hm. You like it?
15-I: No, we don't like it, we got used to it, be it good or bad, we got used to it.

It is worth noting in turn 8, his reaction to the interviewer's suggestion that the Turkish language might seem ugly to somebody: *No, we don't say that, no, we do not say their language is ugly.* It is also important to note here that the first "no" is in Cypriot Greek [oi], whereas the second in Standard Greek [oçi]. This switch enforces both the categorical nature of his statement "no" = "absolutely not" and gives his statement a character of reprimand towards his interviewer.

It seems, therefore, that Arab Cypriot speakers do not hold negative opinions as regards the Turkish language and are respectful of its place and function as the majority language of the area they live in, even though it seems that language acceptance depends upon personal circumstances and experiences. Sharpel, for instance, who is married to a Turkish Cypriot woman shows a greater degree of attachment to the language, declares he knows Turkish very well and, in the course of the conversation, reveals that he performs Turkish music at various events.

7.2 Identity construction and the multiple Other

As a minority, Arab Cypriots had to adjust and sometimes transform their linguistic repertoire in the course of historical events, to 'better fit' into different political and social settings. In recent times, this meant adopting the Greek language and, for those who remained in their villages under occupation, adjusting to Turkish as a majority language. In both cases, Sanna conserves its character as a minority language.

The fluid and seemingly natural way accommodation takes place leaves no doubt about the Arab Cypriots' capacity to adapt themselves to new conditions and circumstances, projecting each time a different image of themselves. Multilingual competence is seen as a way to accommodate to a world of changes and, potentially, of threat. Multiplicity is an innate part of the way ACs construct their identity by comparison, contrast or opposition to a "multiple Other". Each of these identifications makes appeal to a part of their inner self and helps them construct a multiple membership, which shows the true measure and complexity of their unique identity. Indigenized after more than ten centuries, the community is part of a political majority but still minoritised. Affiliated by faith to Western Christianity and by language to the Middle Eastern and Central Asian Christian Arab world, the community looks towards its mythic place of origin, Lebanon, but still constitutes a unique community because of the influence exerted by the Greek language and culture. Arab Cypriots have strategically been using their multiple membership to negotiate social benefits. Much in the same way, they have been using multilingualism to empower themselves in a society that relegates them to the historical and social background. Their ability to strategically position themselves is well expressed by Sharpel who declares, with a somehow utilitarian comment, that the best part of it [his identity] is the fact that he is neither Greek nor Turk, "because you are better treated by both communities" (= Greek Cypriot and Turkish Cypriot communities).

8 Linguistic practices within the Armenian community

8.1 Armenian, the mother tongue, the tongue of the mother

Contrary to the Cypriot Arabic language, the Armenian language knows a sustained domestic vitality since the Armenian Cypriot community is one of the few diasporic communities speaking Armenian. On the other hand, the language suffers a real public inertia: the linguistic landscape of Cyprus ignores the Armenian writing and is rarely heard or used in the media, except in specific programs. The latent dominance felt in these decisions could be explained by the need of the Nation state to achieve cohesion among different social groups against the other side of the Green line (Constantinou 2007, Joannidou 2012). Even in the 60's when the Armenian quarter was still vibrant, the Armenian writing was not displayed, recalled Adrine. This tension between the public and the private has repercussions on the linguistic identity of Armenians in Cyprus and the survival of the language of the community.

"My mother died and since then my first language is English; I used it all the time with my colleagues at work, my friends, the foreigners" said Samson. Indeed, the Armenian language tends strongly to be the tongue of the mother and the Armenian community in Cyprus is one of the few in the diaspora to speak Western Armenian. Armenian women feel and are made to feel responsible for the language to be learnt or spoken and are often expected to marry in their community since this is seen as a means to maintain the language, the homogeneity and thus the strength of their ethnic group. However, helping at the Armenian Church, Samson witnesses many mixed marriages within the Armenian community, with Greek Cypriots firstly and with other communities. Among our interviewees, four out of five couples under 40 years old were mixed marriages, i.e. with a Greek Cypriot, American, British, etc. several female informants expressed their deep concerns regarding the cultural future of the community and their linguistic survival against dominant languages, such as Greek or English. One family whom we know testifies to a matriarchal linguistic lineage and the struggle for survival in this multilingual world: Yervant is a British-Armenian and learnt his Armenian from his mother in London; since his return to Cyprus, his wife being a Greek Cypriot, he speaks English to his children, Badrig and Samuel, and his wife speaks Cypriot Greek to them. They learn Armenian willy-nilly from the grand-mother when she comes to visit, whereas at school they are taught in standard Greek.

The Armenian language is not only the imprint of one's mother tongue. It is also the result of a specific choice in education, as many Armenians choose to send their children to the Armenian primary school (called Nareg), which reinforces the social ties within the community: during the interviews, when the researcher was referring to one Armenian person, the response was often "*oh yes he/she was my class-mate*". A feeling of pride in one's heritage and a will to survive through the (revived) mother tongue were the strongest motivations to learn and speak the language:

1-LS.: So which language do you use on a daily basis?
2-I.: OK, we speak Armenian at home and with our Armenian friends, relatives. (pause) English, Greek with other friends, depends.
3-LS.: Would you say that Armenian is like a 'private' language, a language for intimates?
4-I.: (looking concerned) No, no, no, it is not like that! I participate to all the cultural activities organized by our associations, I watch movies in Armenian, I speak Armenian outside my home!

Indeed, a visit to Armenia was for instance felt and described by one 23 year old as the dream place where no linguistic division and no more fragmentation of the self was possible: the feeling of being surrounded by her own language and culture was so strong or maybe her desire to belong so dire, that she described her mother country to be Armenia as much as Cyprus, although she went only once to Armenia:

1-LS.: Have you visited Armenia?
2-I.: Yes, ... in the year 2000 (big smile)
3-LS.: So did you like it?
4-I.: It was like a dream, everything, ... everywhere was in Armenian (beaming)

One informant having done her Master degree in Armenia, reacted the same way:

1-I.: We were surrounded by the Armenian spirit, we were breathing Armenian.

Even though another informant mentioned the problems of poverty in Armenia hence his reluctance to move there, he also remembered fondly his trip to Armenia.
  Speaking Armenian may therefore embody for these informants the desire to escape the perceived 'strangeness/estrangement' when speaking a language not related to one's historical identity and social community.

However being visible can be as important for minority languages as being heard (Marten et al. 2011: 1). Cultural and social activities, as mentioned in the first interview, highlight the struggle and resistance of the Armenian speakers against structural disadvantages. They reinforce cohesion and empower the members of the community, at the most personal level, as well as helping with the survival of the language (Marten et al. 2011: 2). Samson was proud to mention that watching football gives him the opportunity to play with his linguistic repertoires, which empowers him against the State's forced choice of Greek as the official language (and its speakers who blame him for not speaking 'good' Greek): he could choose between the Armenian club to speak Armenian; the pub to speak English and the gym to speak Greek.

Multilingualism as well as a feeling of 'estrangement' are not new to the Armenian Cypriot community: already their forefathers experienced both when arriving in Cyprus as the following interviews with the older generation show.

8.2 The Turkish language: the language of the friendly neighbor/of the hostile Other

Indeed, the grandparents of Armenian Cypriots in their twenties nowadays were Turkish-speaking or bilingual Turkish-Armenian. Turkish was used at home and was not yet taboo for the survivors of the Armenian genocide who constituted the bulk of immigrants. Aharon's grandparents for instance were only Turkish speaking since in Turkey at that time it was discouraged to use Armenian; therefore good memories are evoked when hearing a Turkish song.

1-LS.: What are your feelings when hearing the Turkish language?
2-I.: I speak Turkish, I use it every time I go in the North. I am not the same as others, I am different, not like other Armenians, I do not feel the same. Turkish is the language of the songs my mother was singing when she was giving me a bath, it's like it has a sentimental value.

Armenian Cypriots had co-existed peacefully with the Turkish Cypriots until the 1960's events. This coexistence is very prominent in the answers recorded in our interviews and conversations with the generation born in the 40's. An elderly Armenian Cypriot would remember his mother singing in Turkish while bathing him; Turkish was not lived as the language of the Other but as the language of friends and neighbours. Adrine and Sanam learnt their excellent Turkish when living in the North (the occupied zone) in a mixed neighbourhood, from friends or friendly neighbours; and because of their fluency in Turkish, they could work for the Turkish programme on the national radio (CYBC). Proud to know the *language*, they are enthusiastic. Aharon himself speaks fluently five languages including Greek, Turkish and Arabic. The grandfather of a young student, who lost his shop and his home in 1974, knew Turkish as well because of the intermixing in his neighbourhood: being an Armenian speaker, he would also speak Turkish and Greek every day with his customers and other shopkeepers. She mentioned this when mentioning her being ill at ease when hearing Turkish:

1-LS.: Turkish can be learnt at the University, will you take it as elective?
2-I.: Maybe, it's always good to learn another language. I don't know ...
3-LS.: You are not sure? Something is bothering you?
4-I.: (hesitating) My grandfather spoke Turkish, with his shop he had customers, everyday they spoke Greek, they spoke Armenian, they spoke Turkish. But we lost the shop, twice, because of the Turks, you know. (she seemed tense)
5-LS.: So you don't feel, ... you feel as you do not want to learn Turkish?
6-I.: I don't like the sounds of the language. In my car I change the radio station when I hear Turkish.

She then mentioned her anger and sadness when thinking of the past: the more distance, physical and psychological, can be taken, the better, she concluded. Indeed when referring to parents who left for the USA, some informants mentioned that they fled away for their 'safety', the proximity of Turkey being lived as an imminent danger. Talking Turkish does not mean either that Turkish culture or people would be embraced or not felt as foreign. When asked whether they would be happy to have a Turkish neighbour, even the elderly generation who knew Turkish was reluctant to accept that idea. For the new generations, learning the language may be good for a future job but this should be preferably without contact with the culture or the history, a challenge on the pedagogical level as Charalambous & Rampton (2012) have pointed out, referring to Greek Cypriots learning Turkish.

8.3 Greek/Greek Cypriot: le sujet en procès/the subject in process

However, a more imminent linguistic danger than Turkish is 'Greek assimilation'. One's origin (the Middle East, the former Eastern European block or Cyprus), one's spouse as well as the political party to which one belongs would partly define allegiance or not to the dominant Greek language. To the question 'Do you feel first Cypriot or first Armenian?' answers differed drastically.

Some informants feel being part of the community because nobody mentions explicitly they are different: "I am first Cypriot and then Armenian". However, the issue of power relationships between the communities translates in many informants into a feeling of estrangement, a feeling of a latent (self)-marginalization and (auto)-exclusion:

1-LS.: Do you feel first Cypriot or first Armenian?
2-I.: (laughs) I am first Armenian and then Cypriot. Of course! You know, they will always consider us as foreigners; (...) because of the language first, also we will never belong to their community.
3-LS: What do you mean when you say they consider you as foreigners?
4-I.: Do you know that at football matches they would shout 'boukarmenos', they also say that we are stingy
5-LS.: Yes I heard about the stinginess[15] but what is 'boukarmenos', what does that mean? I never heard of it...
6-I.: It means 'shitty Armenian'!

Marginalization leads then to the common stereotyping of what and who is seen as different. Many of the interviewees referred to Them (Greek Cypriots) vs. Us (Armenian Cypriots), and complained that although brought up in Cyprus they 'do not belong', expressing the feeling of *Unheimlichkeit*, typical of a place being familiar and alien at the same time. This uncanniness is felt by the other party as well: "I remember it was a strange name" mentioned a Greek Cypriot bank employee when recalling the Armenian name of my neighbor.

As a matter of fact, Samson recalled that at the English-speaking school he attended, the schoolmaster upon seeing his name put him in the 'floater' category (i.e. in the group of students whose mother tongue was not Greek) so that he did not have to take the lessons in Greek provided in the school. The feeling of being a 'floater' of staying on the surface and not settling 'in' the society, still prevails among some Armenian Cypriots. It actually emphasizes their own feeling of being at once citizens of Cyprus *and* members of a large international Armenian community.

The Greek language became Samson's Achilles' heel and, if one speaks of the language of the 'other', for him it is Greek, not Turkish (which he does not speak at all), nor English which he knows well. For that particular speaker, speaking English or Armenian became an act of resistance to assimilation and a way to circumscribe the Greek hegemony because of what he describes as "the wall

---

[15] This stereotypical comment was witnessed within the Greek Cypriot community.

between the Armenian Cypriots and the Greek Cypriots". Indeed, strange/foreign are labels some Greek Cypriots would give to Armenian Cypriots and to the Armenian language as we have noted previously, ignorance and lack of visibility not helping to mutual understanding: sometimes the Armenian and the Turkish languages were assimilated by Greek Cypriots as the same language, as well due to the fact that the Turkish language was associated with an Armenian identity.

This eerie feeling of being a foreigner in one's own country is built as well by comments made regarding Armenian Cypriots' level of proficiency in the Greek language, a level which could be evaluated negatively by some interviewees ("my Greek is not good enough") and by some Greek Cypriots themselves ("They were born here, they should be speaking better Greek"!). It is not clear whether complaints about the level of Greek relates to Cypriot-Greek or to Standard Modern Greek (SMG)[16]. The feeling of exclusion from the Cypriot linguistic community can be explained as well by the use of the Cypriot vernacular in the mainstream society, while at school Armenians would learn SMG and some would not know well the vernacular. Since this is a problem encountered by the foreigners who learn the language 'academically' and not *in vivo*, the linguistic difference accentuates the estrangement of this indigenous community: like the 'true' foreigners, some Armenian Cypriots have difficulty with the language of intimacy for the Greek Cypriots.

Other comments revealed great contentment with the coexistence of languages and cultures and would, indeed, interpret the diversity of languages as a wealth, without mentioning any power relations. A prominent Armenian figure, fluent in Greek and English, thanked his hosts in English (the lingua franca of the multilingual community in presence) during a commemoration of his work that a well-known firm had organized. There was not a word of Armenian either in his speech, or on his brochure, although his ethnicity was put forward many times in the documentary made in his honour. As the fact was mentioned to him, he regretted not to have expressed his feelings of gratitude with a few words in his mother tongue. The public landscape in Cyprus, omitting any reference to the linguistic minorities on billboards or signs[17], seems to have influenced in turn one's individual linguistic choices: Armenian would not appear even when celebrating the achievement of a lifetime and the mother tongue became the estranged language at that specific time.

---

16 Indeed we could witness the very same people labelled 'non Greek speakers' speak fluently with their Greek Cypriot friends.
17 However signs in Chinese and Russian are seen for real estate advertising for instance.

9 Conclusion

Multilingualism or multiculturalism appears then to help to construct one's own social reality through small acts of discourse in everyday life (Kramsch 2009), resisting linguistic/cultural hegemony for some of the minorities' members. These small communities have indeed a dynamically evolving multilingual repertoire and the capacity to adjust linguistically to historical and social changes, learning and leaving languages over generations as they go. Because members of the two communities participate as well in a set of multiple identifications (linguistic, religious, social, political, ethnic), the notion of the "Other" is, in turn, multiple and fluid. Framing the issues of multilingualism and minorities within identity politics and the fragmented self, helps to understand how ethnic and linguistic identities are contested and contingent both pre- and post-independence, both pre- and post- the *de facto* partitioning of the island.

Further, the lack of understanding and empathy from the dominant communities may also encourage a desire for an *imagined community* in younger generations. On the one hand, Armenia has embodied, for some of the interviewees, a desire for belonging. Upon seeing the beaming face of some informants when evoking this country, we could only feel the affective power, as gateways to collective politics and social alliances, able to create a new national identity: it illustrates how much emotions can be 'material rhetoric' (Ahmed 2004). Learning, practicing one's own mother tongue allows the freedom of evasion, of building another self as much as discovering oneself, a phenomenon known to characterize foreign language learning (Kramsch 2003). On the other hand, Arab Cypriots' attachment to their Cypriot land is taking the form of a ceremonial return: "The language will survive if the people are allowed to come back", says one of the older speakers in the video "Kormakitis Language, point O",[18] referring to a possible solution of the Cyprus problem. But they, also, demonstrate a need to be part of a community elsewhere, in order to legitimate their feeling of being different from all the other Cypriots, thus, their attachment to Lebanon.

Identity politics articulate the important role of language in maintaining identity in the context of power relations at all levels in society. As assimilation of linguistic and cultural communities in Cyprus gains momentum, concepts of power and identity are reshaped and the role of language changes. However, if empowerment of minor languages (i.e. support from the Government to linguistic literacy for instance) is real, it has not been extended to *speakers* of minority lan-

---

18 Cf. (https://www.youtube.com/watch?v=ODysXq1fS6Q and https://www.youtube.com/watch?v=2OWF51-PVM) <30/10/2014>

guages in Cyprus as the principle of polarisation continues to remain central to language policy and to politics in Cyprus.

References

Ahmed, Sarah. 2004. *Cultural Politics of Emotion*. New York: Routledge.

Baider, Fabienne and Hadjipavlou Maria. 2008. « Stéréotypes inter-ethniques, communautés divisées: sources de conflits, d'unité et de résistance ». *Nouvelles Questions Féministes* 27 (3): 72–88.

Borg, Alexander. 1985. *Arab Cypriotic: A Historical and Comparative Investigation into the Phonology and Morphology of the Arabic Vernacular Spoken by the Maronites of Kormakiti Village in the Kyrenia District of North-Western Cyprus*. [Marburg]: [Deutsche Morgenländische Gesellschaft]. Stuttgart: Kommissionsverlag Steiner Wiesbaden.

Borg, Alexander. 2004. *Comparative Glossary of Cypriot Maronite Arabic (Arabic-English)*. Leipzig/Boston: Bril. Handbook of Oriental Studies, Section 1, Near and Middle East, vol. 70. pp. xxviii + 486.

Boustany, Fouad Ephrem. 1954. Un dialecte libanais conservé à Chypre depuis des siècles. *Proceedings of the 22nd Congress of Orientalists (Istanbul 1951)*. Leiden. 522–526.

Census of population 2011, Nicosia: Statistical service/Republic of Cyprus http://www.cystat.gov.cy/mof/cystat/statistics.nsf/populationcondition_22main_en/populationcondition_22main_en?OpenForm&sub=2&sel=2

Charalambous Constadina. 2012. "Learning the language of 'The Other' in conflict-ridden Cyprus: exploring barriers and possibilities. In Hillary A.Footit, & Michael Kelly (eds.). *Languages and the Military: Alliances, Occupation and Peace Building* (Palgrave Studies in Languages at War). London: Palgrave.

Charalambous Constadina and Rampton Ben. 2012. "Other-language learning and intercultural communication in contexts of conflict". In Jane Jackson (ed.) *The Routledge Handbook of Language and Intercultural Communication*. 195–210. London: Routledge.

Constantinou, Costas. 2007. "Aporias of identity: Bicommunalism, hybridity and the 'Cyprus Problem'". *Cooperation and Conflict* 42 (3): 247–270.

Constantinou, Costas. 2009. "The protection and revival of Cypriot Maronite Arabic", *Policy Brief* 1. PRIO Cyprus Centre. 4 pages.

Ganat George L. Book Review [of Pavlenko, Aneta and Adrian Blackledge (eds.). 2004. *Negotiation of Identities in Multilingual Contexts*. Clevendon, England: Multilingual Matters], *Working papers in TESOL & Applied Linguistics* 4 (1).

Hadjipavlou, Maria. 2004. *The women of Cyprus*. Nicosia: PrintWays.

Hadjipavlou, Maria. 2007. "Multiple realities and the role of peace education in deep-rooted conflicts. The case of Cyprus". In Zvi Bekerman and Claire AcGlynn (eds.). *Addressing ethnic conflict through peace education*. 35–49. Palgrave Mcmillan.

Hourani, Guita. 1998. "A Reading in the history of the Maronites of Cyprus from the eighth century to the beginning of British rule". *Journal of Maronite Studies*, http://www.kormakitis.net/modules.php?name=Forums&file=viewtopic&t=780 <30/10/2014>

Hourani, Guita. 2009. "The Maronites of Cyprus under Ottoman rule: Demise or eclipse.". In Andrekos Varnava, Nicholas Coureas and Marina Elia (eds.). *The minorities of Cyprus:*

Development patterns and the identity of the internal – exclusion. 111–135. Cambridge: Cambridge Scholars.
Joannidou, Thomael. 2012. "Identity in conflict: An exploration of gender across ethnicity in Cyprus". *Cyprus Review* 24(2) 109–124.
Karyolemou, Marilena. 2005. "An island, some languages and a dialect". In Johannes Deckers, Marie-Elisabeth Mitsou & Sabine Rogge (eds.). *Beiträge zur Kulturgeschichte Zyperns von der Spätantike bis zur Neuzeit.* 149–162. Munich: Waxmann.
Karyolemou, Marilena. 2009. "Minorities and minority languages in Cyprus". In Andrekos Varnava, Nicholas Coureas, Marina Elia (eds.) *The minorities of Cyprus: Development patterns and the identity of the internal – exclusion).* 316–336. Cambridge, Cambridge Scholars Publishing.
Karyolemou, Marilena. 2012. "Aspectes d'identitat a la comunitat àrab de Xipre". In Joan Argenter (ed.). *Identitat, Europa, Mediterrània. Dinàmiques identitàries a la Mediterrània.* 117–132. Βαρκελόνη: Càtedra UNESCO de Llengües i Educació & Institut d'Estudis Catalans.
Kramsch, Claire. 2003. "The multilingual subject". In Ines Florio-Hansen and Adelheid Hu (eds.) *Plurilingualitaet und Identitaet,* 107–124.Tuebingen: Stauffenburg Verlag.
Kramsch, Claire. 2009. *The multilingual subject.* Oxford: Oxford Applied Linguistics.
Kramsch, Claire. 2012. "Authenticity and legitimacy in multilingual SLA". *Critical Multilingualism Studies* 1 (1): 107–128.
Kramsch, Claire. 2014. "Teaching foreign languages in an era of globalization: Introduction". *The Modern Language Journal* 98 (1): 296–311.
Kymlicka, Will. 2001. *Politics in the vernacular: Nationalism, multiculturalism, citizenship.* Oxford: Oxford University Press.
Marten Heiko F., Luk van Mensel and Durk Gorter. 2011. "Studying minority languages in the linguistic landscape". In *Minority languages in the linguistic landscape.* Palgrave Studies in Minority Languages and Communities. 1–16.
Mavratsas, Ceasar. 1998. *Aspects of the Greek Nationalism in Cyprus* [in Greek]. Nicosia: Katarti
Mavrides Marios and Maranda Michael. 1999. "The Maronites of Cyprus: A community in crisis". *Journal of Business and Society* 12 (1): 78–94. Nicosia: Cyprus College.
May, Stephen 2006. "Language policy and minority rights". In Thomas Ricento (ed.). *An introduction to language policy: Theory and methodology.* 225–272. Oxford: Blackwell.
Pavlenko, Aneta. 2003. "Language of the enemy": Foreign language education and national identity. *International Journal of Bilingual Education and Bilingualism* 6 (5): 313–331.
Pavlenko, Aneta and Blackledge Adrian (eds.). 2004. *Negotiation of identities in multilingual contexts.* Clevedon: Multilingual Matters
Pattie Paul Susan. 1997. *Faith in history: Armenians rebuilding community.* Washington: Smithsonian Institution Press.
Pollis, Adamantia. 1973. "Intergroup conflict and British colonial policy: The case of Cyprus." *Comparative Politics* 5 (4): 575–599.
Pollis, Adamantia. 1996. "The social construction of ethnicity and nationality: The case of Cyprus." *Nationalism and Ethnic Politics* 2 (1): 67–90.
Roth, Arlette. 1986. "Langue dominée, langue dominante: à propos de deux scénarios d'extinction ou d'expansion de l'Arabe." *Hérodote* 42: 65–74.
Roth, Arlette. 2000. "Un usage linguistique en voie d'éviction. Observations sur la "réduction" syntaxique et stylistique dans le parler Arabe de Kormakiti (Chypre)." *Travaux de la Maison de l'Orient Méditerranéen* 31 (Chypre et la Méditerranée Orientale). 127–137.

Roth, Arlette. 2004. "Le parler arabe maronite de Chypre. Observations à propos d'un contact linguistique pluriséculaire." *International Journal of the Sociology of Language* 168: 55–76.

Spyrou, Andrea. 2006. "Constructing 'the Turk' as an Enemy: The Complexity of Stereotypes in Children's Everyday Worlds". In Dimitrios Theodossopoulos (ed.) *When Greeks think about Turks: The View from Anthropology.* 95–110. London & New York: Routledge.

Varnava, Andrekos, Coureas, Nicholas, and Elia, Marina. 2009. *The minorities of Cyprus: Development patterns and the identity of the internal – exclusion,* Cambridge. Cambridge Scholars. 337–336.

Vassili, Marios. 2010. *Code switching and language contact in the Arabic dialect of the Maronites of Kormakitis village* [in Greek]. Unpublished Master Dissertation. Dept. of Turkish and Middle Eastern Studies. University of Cyprus. Nicosia.

Woolard, Kathryn A. 1998. "Introduction: Language ideology as a field of inquiry". *Language Ideologies: Practice and Theory.* In Schieffelin, Bambi B., Kathryn A Woolard and Paul Kroskrity (eds.). 3–47. Oxford: Oxford University Press.

Zembylas, Michalinos. 2010. "Racialization/Ethnicization of School Emotional Spaces: The Politics of Resentment". *Race, Ethnicity and Education* 3 (2), 253–270.

Zembylas, Michalinos. 2012. "Citizenship education and human rights in sites of ethnic conflict: Toward critical pedagogies of compassion and shared fate." *Studies in Philosophy and Education* 31 (6): 553–567.

Part IV: **Scientific challenges**

Georges Lüdi
9 Monolingualism and multilingualism in the construction and dissemination of scientific knowledge

Abstract: This contribution stems from the European research project *Language Dynamics and Management of Diversity* (DYLAN).[1] It examined at close range how the very diverse linguistic repertoires of speakers operating in increasingly multilingual environments develop and how actors make the best use of their repertoires and adapt them skilfully to different objectives and conditions. Careful observation of actors' multilingual practices revealed finely tuned communication strategies drawing on a wide range of different languages, including national languages, minority languages and *lingue franche*. Understanding these practices, both their implications and meaning, helps to show in what way and under what conditions they are not merely just a response to a problem but an asset in business, political, educational, scientific and economic contexts. In the following paper we will try to apply these results to language use in academic settings and argue in favour of more multilingualism in science.

1 The 'doxa' concerning English as an international language of sciences and a shift towards the acknowledgement of higher creativity in multilingual teams

A widespread social representation claims that English is the language best appropriated for scientific publications and for university teaching. The arguments in favour of English are well known and numerous, one focus being effi-

---

[1] This was an integrated project from the European Union's Sixth Framework Program, Priority 7, "Citizens and governance in a knowledge-based society". 19 partners from 12 countries addressed the core issue of whether, and, if so how, a European, knowledge-based society designed to ensure economic competitiveness and social cohesion can be created despite the fact that, following enlargement, the European Union is linguistically more diverse than ever before. (cf. http://www.dylan-project.org for an overview and Berthoud, Lüdi & Grin 2013 for detailed results).

Georges Lüdi, University of Basel, Switzerland, georges.luedi@unibas.ch

ciency, the other equality of opportunity to participate in a community of global, scientific discourse (cf. Kekulé 2010). The assessment of individual scientists, but also of research groups and whole universities, is increasingly based on citation indexes and on the journal impact factor. Both privilege publications in English. Thus, many non-English-speaking researchers decide to publish their results in peer-reviewed, Anglo-American journals in order to be noticed worldwide. Simultaneously, more and more institutions of higher education offer English medium education (e.g. Coleman 2006, Doiz *et al.* 2012). They also do it in order to prepare their students for reading literature, writing research proposals, team discussion, publishing the results, etc. in English. Wright's (2011) argument that fostering 'deliberative democracy' in Europe depends "on the competence of the audience to evaluate evidence and draw conclusions from it" can be applied to science and favours the "building [of] a community of communication" through the promotion of an agreed single *lingua franca*, i. e. "English in its second language international form".

In fact, this *doxa* is grounded on a monolingual ideology as it developed in Europe since the Renaissance and in particular since the end of the 18th century. It claims that linguistic diversity is a problem and that the use of one single language can solve the world's communicative problems without negative effects. But there are also disadvantages. We will try to show here that the side effects of a "monolingual" language policy and ideology are important and that the price for an "English-only" strategy is very high, including a possible lack of creativity, losses of information, a malaise connected with not being able to use one's own language and the appearance of break lines between science and society. Instead of placing an emphasis on an eventual clash between national languages and English, however, we will look for possibilities to create a balance between both, based on examples of good practice. This means, for example, drawing on the chance offered by "plurilanguaging" in the research team and choosing a dissemination policy that includes the local community without renouncing the chance to publish original papers in English where there is a worldwide audience.

Our considerations stand on the context of a slow shift in research towards a revalorisation of bi- and plurilingualism respectively.

The first advantage here involves learning further languages (e.g. Bono & Stratilaki 2009). Della Rosa *et al.* (2013) explain this finding by suggesting

> that [the] left lower parietal region structural plasticity traced in early childhood is the result of dynamic functional requirements (i.e., attention, memory and phonological categorization functions) that are necessary for developing high levels of multilingual competence with the effect of enhancing attention functions deployed in order to monitor and control the different languages being spoken.

A recent research survey goes even further and claims that there is a link between individuals' plurilingualism and creativity, that multi- or plurilingualism respectively broaden access to information, offer alternative ways of organising thoughts and of perceiving the surrounding world and that adding a new language to one's repertoire increases the potential for creative thought (Compendium 1 2009: 19; see also Furlong 2009).

This cognitive advantage is not only exploitable at an individual level by plurilingual people, but also by agglomerations of several plurilingual individuals. The steady increase in the numbers of migrants, expats, exchange of scientists, etc. and the globalisation of communication through electronic media entail many forms of social multilingualism at the workplace, i.e. people with very different linguistic and cultural background are brought to work together in *mixed teams*.

This challenge has a double face. On the one hand, communication problems may arise and slow down the working processes. On the other hand, the heterogeneity of members of scientific teams can be conceived as a chance. Indeed, in mixed teams or research groups the clash of different perspectives, modes of interpretation or prediction (Page 2007), and different forms of language use in "conceptual spaces" (Boden 1996), more precisely in "in-between spaces" (Bhabha 1994) between cultures, results in cognitive creativity (cf. Mitchell & Nicholas 2006: 72).

The innovation concerns among others the way in which actors organise their meetings, structure their collaborative practices, set up rules, negotiate or even impose general attitudes concerning the use of languages – and finally the knowledge that is itself constructed (Berthoud *et al*. 2012: 2013).

It is not unreasonable to compare this process of construction of knowledge in mixed groups with decision-making in a context of cognitive diversity in top management teams as analysed by Olson *et al.* (2007) where cognitive diversity "should generate multiple perspectives, engender well thought out alternatives, and ultimately lead to better decisions." (2007: 200)[2]

Mitchell and Nicholas claim – given that the existence of different viewpoints is necessary for new knowledge to emerge – that: "open-mindedness norms are likely to impact on the creativity of outcomes" (2006, 72). The aim of interaction being deep and shared understanding, it incorporates boundary-spanning (Isaacs, 1993), i.e. taking into account "the understanding that members with different backgrounds operate from different perspectives underpinned by distinct

---

[2] See also Hong and Page (2001, 2004) and Page (2007) and Landemore (2013) who argues that "in groups of problem-solvers it is often more important to maximize cognitive diversity – i.e., a diversity of seeing and interpreting the world – rather than individual competence."

cognitive structures (...) [and that] effective interaction relies on (...) the ability to interact across the cognitive boundaries" (Mitchell & Nicholas 2006: 68).

2 Between plurilingualism and monolingualism: coping with linguistic diversity in scientific interaction

It is rare that all members of a mixed group share the same plurilingual repertoire and understand all others' preferred languages. Nonetheless, the choice of a *lingua franca* – mostly English – might be a suboptimal procedure when it comes to creating and transmitting scientific knowledge and can, in fact, entail severe drawbacks:
- Speaking the same language levels out differences and might create the illusion of shared values and representations. Different languages carry a different epistemic potential (Fetscher 2013) the perception of which could be part of boundary-spanning.
- The perception of one's lack of competence in the *lingua franca* is reflected in more insecurity.
- Communication in a *lingua franca* learned as a foreign language may be accompanied by a lack of emotional involvement (Fine 1996: 494).
- Speaking a FL may lead to less precise formulation and thus to a loss of information.

> Ich rede in meiner Sprache anders, freier, offener, selbstbewusster, sicherer. (...) Da gehen also wirklich viele Ideen eigentlich verloren, wenn man sich einfach für das Englische entscheidet in einer solchen Situation, weil dann nicht alle gleich, sich gleich wohl fühlen. (Maurice M., Agro A)

But speaking only English is not always the inevitable outcome. Several DYLAN teams carried out a fine-grained observation and analysis of interactional practices in research laboratories and institutions of higher education. The aim was to understand which communicative strategies are used in settings with several languages that are not all spoken equally well by all the individuals concerned.

One of the results of this research was the disproval of the common assumption that everyone speaks English. Participants adopt a wide range of strategies, and they do so in an extremely variable and dynamic way, constantly reassessing the solutions chosen. These strategies can be positioned on two axes. One axis contrasts "monolingual" strategies ("one language only" [OLON] and "one language at a time" [OLAT]) with "multilingual" ones ("all the languages at the same time" [ALAST], sometimes called "all languages at all time" [ALAT]), and the other one links the "exolingual" pole (greatly asymmetrical repertoires) with the "endolingual" one (participants share the same repertoire).

Analysing various plurilingual solutions emically elaborated in international professional meetings, the team around Lorenza Mondada showed that the participants orient to a double principle:

> on the one hand, they orient to the progressivity of the interaction, adopting all the possible resources that enable them to go on within the current activity; on the other hand, they orient to the intersubjectivity of the interaction, treating, preventing and repairing possible troubles and problems of understanding. (Markaki *et al.* 2013: 4)

In the framework of current representations of plurilingualism, the ALAST-strategies are most puzzling. They are not in line with traditional concepts, based on standardisation processes in national languages that have to be mastered as fully as possible, and on a conception of languages as idealised, timeless and decontextualised "objects", each neatly separated from the other, with language preceding language use, where a plurilingual person corresponds, in a sense, to the addition of several monolinguals. It is on this basis that forms of institutional multilingualism are chosen and that translators perform their crucial work as mediators between people and institutions speaking different languages. It allows stakeholders to stick to one language. Such an additive view of multilingualism reflects a fundamentally monolingual concept of communication. It can even lead to subtractive forms of multilingualism where a language is disregarded or simply has to be selected to the disadvantage of others.

In contrast, ALAST-strategies correspond with a 'rough-and-ready' notion of languages and multilingualism. In this case, "languaging" precedes language and "plurilanguaging" multicompetence. Grounded in the view that grammar emerges (Hopper 1998; Larsen-Freeman & Cameron 2008) from "doing being a speaker of a language" (Mondada 2004), the use of plurilingual resources can be very heterogeneous; in extreme examples, even the borders between languages disappear as in the following short interaction intertwining German, French, Spanish, Italian and Portuguese:

Customer =< duos passagem para Freiburg deutsch>.
 Two tickets to Freiburg german
Employee Freiburg Deutschland jä okey. (22) voilà. si vous
 Freiburg Germany yeah ok (22) here could you
 faire la carte à la machine? oui. (3) va bene. (5)

>
> put the credit card into the machine? yes (3) good (5)
> c'est sans une code. vous fais ((sic)) la signature
> *it is without code. you sign*
> après. (2) non non il va revenir.
> *Afterwards. (2) no no it will come back*
> ((client holds credit card instead of letting it go))
> Si vous fais votre signature pour cinquante huit ?
> *can you sign for fifty eight?*
> Customer ((signs)) (13)
> ((....))
> Employee voilà. il prossimo treno (.) binario cinco hm?
> *That's good. the next train (.) track five yes?*
> Dodici diciotto.
> *at eighteen past twelve*
> Customer (3) merci. [obrigado].
> *(3) Thank you ((in French)) thank you ((in Portuguese))*
> Employee [bitteschön]. Service
> *you're welcome ((German)) you're welcome ((French))*
> Customer obrigado (h)
> *thank you ((in Portuguese))*
> Employee molto grazio

In monolingual settings, where one language only is appropriated or possible, participants try to stick, as far as they can, to rules and elements perceived to belong to one "variety". In contrast, they freely exploit the whole range of their resources in a multilingual setting (Grosjean 2001), and juggle with all the elements needed for achieving the purpose of the communication (Lüdi & Py 2009; Lüdi 2011). The speakers do not resort to pre-existing varieties, but move creatively around in an open and variable space of linguistic resources, and take risks, in our example in speaking a kind of Pan-Romance plurilingual speech (Lüdi & Py [1986] [4]2012; Lüdi et al. 2013). Plurilanguaging thus challenges the notions of "language" and "language boundaries" in the sense that "hybrid words" (words still belonging to one language and already belonging to another) (e.g. Croft 2000; Cook & Wei 2009; Greco et al. 2013) emerge as production strategies at language boundaries. Notice that plurilingual speech is often dismissed as chaotic "bad usage". However, we agree with Jessner (2008a, 2008b) that multilingual settings are not characterised by the absence of norms, but by proper "multilingual norms". More precisely, they are the locus of "emergent multilingual grammars" comprising techniques of interaction such as code-switching (see Myers Scotton [2]1997 for a "grammar of code-switching"), spontaneous translations, or ways of using *lingue franche*. Adapting a statement of Larsen-Freeman (2003), one could speak of "the fixing or sedimentation of forms that are understood to constitute grammar", "grammar" being taken here in a broad sense.

In other words, there are intermediate solutions between OLON ("one language – here English – only") and interaction in the OLAT ("one language at a time") mode where those of the participants who do not understand the language chosen at a given moment are excluded, i.e. conferred the status of bystanders.

3 Plurilingual practices in the DYLAN project

One of the assumptions of the DYLAN project was that the use of multilingual repertoires as a resource for the construction/transmission of knowledge brings its own advantages. Consequently, we gave substance to one of the project's core ideas and took linguistic diversity seriously. Therefore, in May 2007, the Consortium adopted an internal language regime pertaining to the official languages of the DYLAN project, and the choice of languages for communications between teams, for the exchange of scientific documents between teams, for reporting to the European Commission and for public relations about the project.[3]

– Firstly, the languages of all the project partners were recognised as official languages of the DYLAN project. The core idea was to opt for a decidedly multilingual strategy that reflected the scope of actual language use among the partners.
– Secondly, in all "common" or "cross-project" communications (that is, communication destined for *all* partners), the partner should use at least one of the languages out of a group of three (English, French and German). Thus, the Consortium avoided a form of communication in which only one hegemonic language would be legitimised maintaining the co-legitimacy – in German *Gleichwertigkeit* (or "same-value-ness") – of more than one language. Partners who had a hard time reading the working language used were compelled to ask the sender to resend the message in one of the other two languages (or in any other language agreed upon bilaterally; for example, they might settle on Catalan, if both partners concerned speak it). The same principle was used for papers to be circulated among the partners of one of the workpackages or among all members of the Consortium. In practice, this meant that papers were drafted in English, French or German, or in two of these languages, or

---

[3] The following paragraphs rephrase a proposal of the project management team dated May 17, 2007.

in all three. Clearly, this regime drew on the principle of "intercomprehension" – that is, that authors draft a paper in the language in which they feel most comfortable, assuming other partners (or some of their members) can read this language.
- Of course, bilateral communication (or, trilateral, quadrilateral, etc.) between mutually consenting partners occurred, thirdly, in any language. Generally, a wide use of the resources of the partners' plurilingual repertoires was advocated, which implied that a message and its reply were often drafted in different languages.
- The fourth principle stipulated that oral presentations at DYLAN consortium or other plenary project meetings ought to combine two different languages, one for the written support (e.g. Powerpoint presentation, hand-out, etc.) and the other for the oral presentation itself. The languages chosen had to be German, English or French. Because of the possibility that a participant understood only one of these three languages and that the speaker used precisely the other two, the Project Advisory Board suggested having a person speaking at least two of the three languages to provide whispered interpretation ("chuchotage") of the presentation into the one language that the participant concerned understood.
- Scientific deliverables destined for the European Commission were drafted in German, English or French following an agreement with the EU officers who followed the DYLAN project; in contrast, English only had to be used for administrative reports, the European Commission, despite protestations to the contrary, still operating predominantly in English.
- Research teams have published and continue to publish research results in the form of books, chapters of edited volumes, articles in scientific journals, on-line materials, etc. in a wide possible range of languages[4] in order to contribute to the relevance of all these languages as legitimate vehicles of scientific activity.

The detailed mechanics of these language management strategies can be illustrated by the analysis of one workshop (among many others) that was videorecorded at the Consortium meeting in Lyon on Friday, April 18th, 2008. It was the first of three parallel transversal workshops attended by teams from different workpackages. The theme of this workshop was the impact of language policies and strategies: How to observe the impact of language policies and strategies?

---

4 Up to 2012, 42 % of the more than 430 titles recorded in the DYLAN-database were English, 34% French, 12% German, 6% Italian, 2% Swedish, 1% Catalan and 10% in various languages (Slovene, Finnish, Polish, Dutch, Spanish and Danish).

What "traces" of their implementation can be observed? How can these be documented? Short presentations by six teams (10 min), each followed by a short discussion (10 min) were expected to implement the plurilingual language regime mentioned. In fact, only English and French appeared except for the German Powerpoint presentation of the Helsinki team.

The video-recording reveals the following course of actions:

Introduction by the chair (0:00:31–0:03:27)	Start in French, reformulation (not literal translation) in English; scheme repeated twice
Negotiation of the technical details (0:03:27–0:06:39)	Bilingual French/English
Presentation by the Glasgow team (0:06:40–0:14:44)	Powerpoint slides in French, oral presentation in English
Discussion (0:14:50–0:21:19)	English
Transition by the chair and the next speaker (0:21:20–0:23:57)	French
Presentation by the Basel team (0:23:58–0:39:37)	Powerpoint slides in French, oral presentation: first sentences in French, reformulation and rest in English
Discussion (0:39:38–0:48:52)	English
Transition by the chair and the next speaker (0:48:53–0:49:45)	English by the moderator, French by the next speaker who then switches to English
Presentation by the Ljubljana team (0:49:46–0:58:36)	No Powerpoint slides, oral presentation in English only, except the two last sentences in French
Discussion (0:58:40–1:04:19)	English
Transition by the chair, the next speaker and the technical team (1:04:20–1:07:05)	English
Presentation by the Helsinki team (1:07:30–1:18:22)	Powerpoint slides in German (with many English lexical code-switchings), oral presentation in English
Discussion (1:18:25–1:27:00)	English
Coffee break	
Introduction of the second part by the chair (00:04:23–00:05:44)	After the technical problems have been solved, the chair makes an announcement in English, then reformulates it in French; he then turns to the next speaker in French saying that he assumes she will present in French, which she confirms
Presentation by the Cluj team (00:05:53–0:16:58)	Powerpoint slides *and* oral presentation in French

Discussion (0:17:00–0:31:20)	The chair expresses thanks in French, applause, then the chair comments in English on the notion CLIL; short negotiation of the language, then first question in English, switch to French; answer in French first, then in English (by another member of the Cluj team), discussion continues in English
Presentation by the Brussels team (0:32:00–0:41:32)	No Powerpoint presentation, oral presentation in English
Discussion (0:41:35–0:45:15)	English
Transition by the chair and the next speaker (0:45:22–0:47:05)	English by the chair, French by the speaker
Presentation by the Geneva team (0:45:10–0:57:30)	Powerpoint slides in French, oral presentation: first sentences in French, rest in English
Discussion (0:57:40–1:04:15)	English (with very few words in French at the beginning and in the intervention of a French discussant
Final conversation between the chair (who already stood up) and the last speaker (1:04:15–1:04:41)	French
Lunch break	

4 A strong orientation towards intersubjectivity in plurilingual practices in the DYLAN project

As became evident, the rule of bilingual presentations (written support in one language, oral presentation in another) was not followed by all teams. In addition, while the Glasgow teams presented in their L1, all the others did it in a L2. Introduction and transitions by the chair were bilingual i.e. English/French, with a clear dominance of the former, but an evident orientation towards the next speakers' preferred language. What is most striking, however, is the effect of language choice (bilingual vs. monolingual and French vs. English) on the participation in the discussion: in the bilingual discussion following the French only presentation of the Cluj team, participation calculated in number of participants was twice as important as in each of the English only discussions which followed the English presentations.

The result concerning participation in the discussion may be explained by a stronger orientation towards intersubjectivity in this interaction than in other discussions, i.e. towards treating, preventing and repairing possible issues and problems of understanding, in order to prevent an exclusion of the actual presenter due to her presumed approximate knowledge of English.

This can be illustrated with a short excerpt from this discussion:

1	Chair:	...It is a matter of debate (.) if teaching at a university level (.) a class
2		in a foreign language/ whether that can be called CLIL\ (.) right\ (.)
3		and CLIL specialits/ (.) I claim to be one (.) we think (.) no\ right (.)
4		it is not really CLIL\ but it is used more and more and in the DYLAN
5		context now everybody adopts CLIL happily adopts CLIL\ there is also
6		a French acronym/ it's called EMILE (.) enseignement (.) euh par inté-
7		gration ((looks to the ceiling)) enseignement [((shakes his head))
8	GL	[d'une matière [XXX]
9	Chair:	((points to GL))[d'une matière] par l'intégration d'une langue
10		étrangère (.) inventé par mon cher collègue Hugo Baetens Beardsmore
11		il y a quelques années\ there is one in Dutch even but XXXX\ ((louder))
12		anyway (.) reactions to the Cluj thing (...) Georges/
13	GL:	euh a couple of comments or questions\ the first one euh (...) is it okay
14		in English/ (.) ou est-ce que vous préférez en français\
15	LP:	ça va\ y a mon collègue qui est anglophone
16	Chair:	on peut peut-être parler français/
17	GL:	moi moi je préfère le français en fait\ j'ai simplement j'ai suivi (...) euh
18		j'ai suivi euh Piet euh I think the first question concerns the (...) ques-
19		tion of CLIL\ (.) in a way
20		((104 seconds are skipped))
21		CLIL could be used as a tool for monolingual English education/
22	Chair:	((low voice)) tu as tout compris là/
23	LP:	oui oui
24	GL:	alors I think this is my main concern with this CLIL approach ((much
25		faster)) c'est la raison pourquoi j'aimerais bien voir d'AUtres manières
26		de (.) et vous l'avez montré d'ailleurs tout à l'heure (.) d'autres manières
27		de mesurer l'impact des politiques linguistiques/par exemple combien
28		d'étudiants (.).suivent des cours (.) mais des cours de langue/combien
29		d'étudiants font des diplômes/en langues
30		((90 seconds are skipped))
31		je pense que l'implémentation d'une politique européenne (ne se
32		limite pas) à CLIL, c'est beaucoup plus large\
33	LP:	justement nous nous sommes occupés nous avons choisi pas CLIL au
34		début...

It starts with an example of collaborative formulation. The chair tries to explain to the audience what CLIL is. He does this in English, and adds then that there is also a French acronym: EMILE. But he also makes publicly available the problems in spelling the French acronym out loud (l. 6–7) by using several multimodal means (gazing at the ceiling, repeating a word, shaking his head, hesitation markers). GL immediately reacts to these indicators with a repair sequence offering the next word: *matière* (l. 8) which is taken up by the chair. Thus he not only allows the chair to complete his phrase successfully (*enseignement d'une matière par l'intégration d'une langue étrangère*) (l. 9), but also to add a side sequence, still in French, attributing the acronym to a well known colleague (l. 10–11).

A second moment of intersubjectivity concerns the negotiation of the language (l. 14ff.). The floor had been opened in English (l. 11–12) and GL begins his comments in the same language, thus aligning his choice to the chair. He then addresses the speaker directly in a participant-related code-switching to French. In the next exchanges, in French, a bilingual interaction space is opened in cooperation between the chair, GL and LP, but without a clear choice being made. In fact, GL continues in English, but in an exolingual mode, with a slow articulation, short sentences while distinguishing clearly each segment. At the beginning of a third moment of intersubjectivity, the negotiation of the participation framework, the chair asks her in a low voice whether she understood everything (l. 22). LP confirms in the same "private" mode that she did understand. Nevertheless, GL carries out another participant-related code-switching to her preferred language – speaking immediately faster, taking the risk of excluding other members in the audience that are less competent in French – and thus makes manifest her status as the main addressee (Goffman 1981), a status which she acknowledges by answering the comment (l. 33).

As Markaki *et al.* (2013: 4) put it:

> Specific multilingual solutions can be adopted to keep this difficult balance between progressivity and intersubjectivity; they vary according to the settings, the competences at hand, the linguistic and embodied resources locally defined by the participants as publicly available, the multilingual resources treated as totally or partially shared, as transparent or opaque, and as needing repair or not.

What we are focused on here is the impact of a flexible language choice on the quality of DYLAN meetings. This analysis of a somehow anecdotal case study is fully confirmed by much broader research in various academic terrains. So, the Barcelona team led by Luci Nussbaum showed that students' participation was favoured by plurilingual interaction formats, where hybridity is associated with multimodality, and where code-switching contributes to an orientation of participants towards more intersubjectivity, which is said to constitute the basis for the process of construction of knowledge (Borras Ribas 2013). Much earlier, a research team at the University of Basel led by Lorenza Mondada had already shown how participants elaborate results in multilingual research teams (in medicine and various human sciences) drawing on plurilingual resources:

> Autrement dit, les participants collaborent ensemble au choix d'une formulation, en exhibant à la fois une orientation vers les différences entre les deux langues utilisées (où «sozialer» ne se confond pas avec «social») tout en ne les traitant pas comme des univers clos et imperméables (au contraire le travail collectif sur la formulation permet une allée et venue entre l'allemand «bürgerlich artistokratisch» et le français «civique artistocratique»). De cette manière on peut dire que le travail collaboratif s'appuie à la fois sur la communauté et sur la différence entre les langues en présence. (Exposé du Colloque à huis clos «Langues et images de la science» du Conseil des Académies scientifiques suisses» le 28 fevrier 2003 à Thoune)

These findings were replicated and confirmed by the DYLAN team from Lausanne. They recorded several seminars at the Faculty of Law of Zurich about decisions of the Federal Court in Lausanne published in French. The teacher (PW) is bilingual, two students have German as L1 (MB and LS) and another French (JR). The particular interest lies in the fact that the conceptual construction is mediated through both languages, French and German:

MB:	il n'est pas n'importe QUI il [(est) le défendeur\
	he is not anybody, he is the defendant
PW:	[il est le dé/
	he is the de/
MB:	défendeur\
	defendant
PW:	pas tout à fait\ mais presque\
	not exactly . but almost
MB:	der verteidiger\
	((in German)) the defensor
PW:	oui/ . (le) défendeur c'est quoi/ (1.5)
	yes . (the) defendant what does this mean/
((...))	
PW:	was ist das auf deutsch\
	what is the German equivalent
LS:	le défens:eur\
	the defensor ((does not answer this question but gives the correct French term for 'Verteidiger'))

PW:	oui le déf:enseur n'est-ce pas\&
	yes the defensor isn't it
MB:	&(aha)
((...))	
PW:	voilà\ donc le défendeur c'est c'est quoi\ c'est qui\
	so\ who is the defendant
(5.4)	
PW:	c'est que celui qui se DEFEND/ .. contre . une accusation par exemple\
	it is the one who defends himself/-- against - an accusation for example
(2.4)	
PW:	ou contre une plainte\
	or against a complaint
(1.9)	
MB:	der beklagte\
	the defendant
PW:	JA genau nicht wahr\
	yes exactly isn't it
(4.9)	((PW writes on the blackboard))
PW:	der beklagte\ .. et celui qui . porte . plainte/ .. ou qui qui . qui (ec-) qui euh:: qui élève une prétention/ . on l'appelle comment\ parce que ça
	the defendant\ .. and the one who . charges or who who . ehm:: files a claim/ . how do you call him\ because this
	c'est plutôt en droit civil qu'on (a) parle de défendre\ ..
	is more in civil law that you talk about defending\ ..
	et&et le: le: . le CO-contractant/ . celui qui: . qui agit/ .. on l'appelle comment\
	the one who: . who acts/ .. how do you call him
(2.0)	
PW:	le pendant du défendeur c'est le quoi\
	the counterpart of the defendant is the what
((...))	
LS:	euh le accusateur\ ((mumbles))
	ehm the accuser
PW:	ça ça serait . de nouveau . euh::: plutôt du droit pénal\
	that that would be . again - ehm::: more in penal law
	mais en droit civil\ . der klaeger\ . wie nennt man den\
	but in civil law\ . the claimant\ how do you call him
	vous vous rappelez/ ((...)) c'est quoi en français\
	do you remember/ what is it in French

JR: c'est euh:: ...
it's ehm:: ...
MB: le demandeur\
the demander
PW: VOILA\

In this sequence, the participants are looking for the term to designate the person conducting the case on behalf of the party being accused or sued in a lawsuit. At the beginning, MB mentions an incorrect term, "défendeur" (*defendant*), whose form is very similar to the one they are looking for. The correct term, "défenseur" (*defender*), is subsequently mentioned by LS and by the teacher. The difference between the two terms initiates a negotiation. As the French terms can hardly be distinguished by an allophone, their German equivalents, "Verteidiger" and "Beklagte", are used to fix the respective meanings in German and in French. As Gajo *et al.* (2013) put it:

> Such an explicit work on the existing plurilingual resources benefits the linguistic processing of the content far beyond the scope of translating a subject-specific terminology from one language to another. In so doing, knowledge has been *mediated* and constructed in both languages via the negotiation of the linguistic opacity and its conceptual density. (...) The class so establishes a conceptual framework in two languages.

The confrontation forces a closer look at words and a deeper reflection on the linguistic substance of concepts residing in French and German that are situated and contrasted in their respective lexical fields, thus deepening and "fine-tuning" students' conceptual understanding even if their mother tongue is French.

In a study in the context of European Institutions, Joxerramon Bengoetxea (2011) similarly analysed the processes of legal reasoning at the European Court of Justice and the consequences of the use of a single common working language, French, in the context of a system where all the official languages of the Member States are official languages of the Court. The author showed that the Court is a reasonably well operating multilingual institution, receiving input and delivering its outputs in all the official languages, but that it relies on huge translation work instead of approaching EU law multilingually, i. e. "[the Court] does not reason multilingually by constantly and systematically contrasting language versions" (2011: 120f.). Subsequently, the author blames the preference for the single, common working language, i. e. for a monolingual solution, as a factor which impedes "the collective and cooperative development of a genuinely multilingual form of legal reasoning" (2011: 123).

Multilingual reasoning – that turns the coexistence of several language versions into an asset for the management of European law – was also in the centre of the argumentation in a paper by Michal Bobek, this time with the perspective on national courts. The author underlined the importance of multilingual interpretation because it allows the court to examine "whether the wording of the national language version represents the true meaning of the provision in question" and thus resolve divergent meanings by using other languages (2011: 161).

Multilingual reasoning is, of course, not limited to law, but can also be found in an English medium class in a technical university; the subject is the use of different techniques for the tanning of leather, and the switching to Catalan helps in deepening the understanding – here of the shades of the colours – by the students (Borras 2013):

FAT	a:nd\ (0.4) what's asking you is\ what colour is the: leather\ (0.2)
LAI	[hm:\]
AHM	[brown\] (0.4) i:n vegetable tannage/ [brown]\ yellow\
FAT	[which means XX\]
LAI	yeaha:/ (.) (val)\ (0.1) yellow/ no:\ no:/
AHM	vegetable\ (0.15)
LAI	+vègetal+/ (.) [yellow/] no:\ (.) +màrron+/ my: tsk (0.2)
FAT	[it's a:h changing with-]
AHM	[sometimes sometimes\ white\]
LAI	[brown/ brown\]
FAT	[brown\ brown\]
AHM	[brown\ brown\]
FAT	[yes\]
LAI	[brown] bro:wn/ not [brown\] hm: =
FAT	[brown\] ((moves fingers))
AHM	=brown\=
LAI	((to the teacher)) =color cre- color crema/ com és color crema/ o color clar/
CAT	a::h\ (0.2) on [t'es]
LAI	[it] depends de extract\ (0.3) color [depend de extract\]
FAT	it depends of the exTRACT\ (0.1) on the [extract\ yes\]
AHM	[exactly\] (0.2)
LAI	for example i:f the extract is +sintetik+ the colour is (0.6) m:ore intensive\ (0.2) ((to the teacher)) more/ no\ [more és més intensiu no/]
FAT	[bu:t for example vegetable\] if you are using mimosa and if you are using chestnut they are different colours [but a:l]most brown
LAI	[(right\?)] (2.2)

AHM =brown yeah\=
FAT =yeah\ (0.51) dark brown\ [light brown]
AHM [xxx] (0.4)
LAI a:h okay\ s./ yes yes/

The common element in all these studies is that plurilingual interaction – or "multilingual reasoning" – not only helps conceptual understanding but offers, in addition, insights into the different perspectives contained in academic discourse using different languages. These insights would remain hidden if one operated in one language only. In this sense – and proving that languages are not just transparent – the use of several languages in a multilingual mode in academic contexts is a real asset and represents a significant added value for the work of the scientists concerned.

5 English as a *lingua franca*: a borderline case of plurilanguaging

The preceding considerations draw upon a functional conception of multilingualism (CECR 2001). A set of skills in different languages, from near native to very partial, is seen as an integrated whole which is more than the sum total of its parts. Such a "multicompetence" (Cook 2008) or plurilingual "repertoire" (Gumperz 1982; Gal 1986; Lüdi 2006; Moore & Castellotti 2008; Lüdi & Py 2009, etc.) was defined as a set of "resources" – both verbal (registers, dialects and languages) and non-verbal (e.g. mime and gestural expression) – that are shared and jointly mobilised by the actors in order to find local solutions to practical problems (Mondada 2001; Pekarek Doehler 2005).

We have already observed that where one language only is appropriated or possible participants try to stick as much as possible to this choice. This is the case, for example, when English appears to be the only common means of communication in a mixed group. Nonetheless, the Vienna specialists in *lingua franca* speak of a "multilingual mode":

> When language users are in an ELF mode, the range of resources and possibilities available to them is not limited to English however. Even though English is apparent on the surface, all of the speakers' linguistic resources are concurrently available for use. They are not automatically switched off only because a non-L1 is chosen as means of spoken communication (Hülmbauer & Seidlhofer 2013)

As a matter of fact, the ways of using the *lingua franca* depend heavily on the speakers' levels of competence, ranging from a monolingual-endolingual mode (among speakers with a mastery of the *lingua franca* at a very high level) to a monolingual-exolingual one (where a barely mastered language is chosen for communication) or a multilingual-exolingual mode. The findings are very similar from all the DYLAN teams who have worked on this particular subject. The *lingua franca* is not a variety, but "actually constituted by very heterogeneous and multilingual varieties" (Markaki *et al.* 2013: 26), a kind of open, variational space. "Like any lingua franca, ELF emerges in multilingual settings. It is not only realised within, but also through linguistic diversity" (Hülmbauer & Seidlhofer 2013). The more exolingual the setting is and the broader the interlocutors' repertoire, the more the speakers will draw occasionally on other linguistic resources. Speech in *lingua franca* is "interwoven with speakers' overall linguistic repertoires" (Hülmbauer & Seidlhofer 2013: 387). Thus, English as *lingua franca* appears "to be a multilingual mode" and the linguistic means used correspond to the "kind of hybrid, "rough-and-ready" version of the language" mentioned above (Lüdi *et al.* 2013). In other words, the use of a *lingua franca* does not differ categorically from plurilanguaging, but constitutes a borderline case of the latter.

This result was confirmed by numerous conversations analysed in DYLAN, for example the following sequence of a meeting of the top managers of the European branches of a big multinational company based in France. The shared company culture requires the adoption of English as a *lingua franca*. However, mispronunciations occur. At first, they can be simply corrected in a repair sequence (line 12) that can, however, generate a lack of understanding (lines 13, 17, 23). The problem is manifested by a translinguistic formulation (*qu'est-ce que ça veut dire sinking?* [l. 17]) and is resolved by a code-switching to French (*couler* [l 19]) that has to be performed twice (l. 26) in order to secure complete understanding. Manifestly, the use of translation secures intersubjectivity, but slows down the progressivity of the activity mentioned above:

1	RIC	and then: the conclusion/ the final
2		[conclusion is this:/
		((RIC finishes his PowerPoint presentation with a slide that shows a duckling surrounded by grass, with a speech bubble attributing to him a critique about excessive workload))
3	XXX	[.hh hh (0.4)
5	RIC	eh::\ a:- a vAlue of the company is act quickly/
6		it's very important/ (.) be creative i think we
7		should do that/ h:: and NEVER give Up/ (0.3)
8		0and0 Even [if you think that you]&

9	CLA	[ffff:::]
10	RIC	&Are\ (.) thinking\
11	XXX	hf:
12	CLA	hh[: S [inking\]
13	VER?	[0xxxxx0
14	RIC	[thank you\] eHE/ he he/
15	MAR?	mhm/
16	RIC	[he he eh hh
17	REB	[qu'est-ce que ça veut dire sinking/
		[what does that mean sinking/
18	ROM	(no\)
19	MAR	COUler\
		SInk
20	REB?	[ah
21	ARI	[*<xx [(the overview)* ((to VER))>
22	CLA	[thAnk yOU\]
23	VER	[si- what does] it mean/[sinking/
24	ARI	[sink*ing is:/*
25	(.)	
26	REB?	[couler\]
		[sink\]
27	CLA	[+euh::][::::\
28	RIC	[COULER/
		[SINK/

6 "Thick standardisation"

In their 2013 contribution to the DYLAN book concerning English as a *lingua franca* Hülmbauer and Seidlhofer restrict the range of their findings to spoken language because it is "less constrained by the standardising forces associated with writing." (Hülmbauer & Seidlhofer 2013: 392). But what could it mean for the debate about language(s) for publication? We will try to approach this question starting with a virtual constellation that is, however, very near to real situations observed in various research contexts such as, for example, a research laboratory in bioinformatics at a famous American University (personal communication), in English medium courses at a European University (cf. Nussbaum *et al.* 2013, Borras 2013) and in research laboratories in a multinational pharmaceutical company based in Switzerland (Lüdi 2010, Lüdi *et al.* 2013).

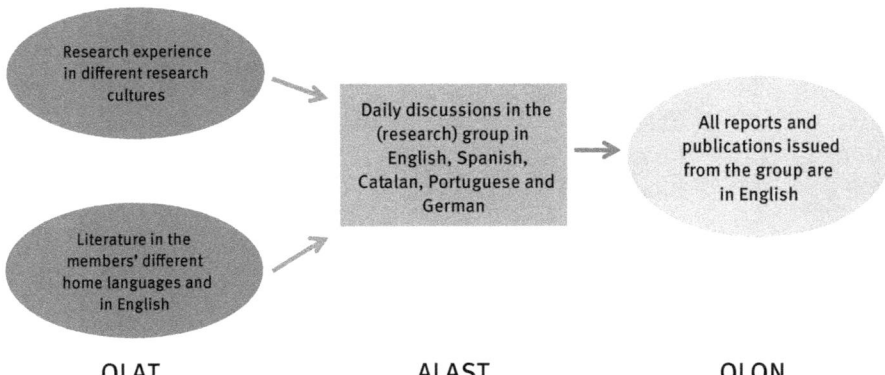

OLAT　　　　　　　　　ALAST　　　　　　　　　OLON

In all these cases teams are linguistically mixed, team members are plurilingual to different degrees, bring along reading and research experiences in different scientific cultures in their "educational suitcase" – and are facing the task of producing texts in English solely as an academic and corporate language. We start from the premise that the asset that should be exploited for major innovation is reflected by the content of the members' respective suitcases.

In our flow chart we suggest that English might, in fact, be the language of publication but that all of the speakers' linguistic resources might have been concurrently used during the process of elaboration of knowledge. In other words, even scientific discourse produced in academic English (i. e. eventually corrected by native proofreaders) "may only be superficially monolingual, in the sense that beneath the outward expression of this discourse, the many mental stages of its elaboration have taken place in another, or possibly many other languages"; thus, discourse in one given language "draws on a stratification embodying other linguistic inputs." The internal discussions correspond to the ALAST mode, be it more in English as *lingua franca* or in a more "mixed" plurilingual speech. Indeed, we have seen that, more and more, the view is taking hold that plurilanguaging and the use of a *lingua franca* are not contradictory *per se* but represent complementary strategies for exploiting plurilingual repertoires (Berthoud *et al.* 2013).

This leads to one of the important conclusions of DYLAN:

> This superposition of layers probably has particular relevance for scientific and academic discourse because the elaboration of analytical thought embodied in written or oral productions can proceed differently depending on the linguistic resources exploited in the process. (Berthoud *et al.* 2013: 451).

The (re)discovery of the layers beneath the surface may then be compared with an exercise in "thick description" – a notion proposed by Usunier (2010) in the continuity of Geertz's (1973) approach to the interpretation of cultures. "Thick standardisation" focuses on the complex dynamics between diversity and standardisation, the presence of the "different" within the homogeneous, and the diversity which exists within uniqueness. From the outset, the use of a standardised form, reflecting the desire to reach a certain threshold of mutual comprehensibility in the broadest sense, must be understood in full awareness of the potentially deceptive character of standardisation that may sometimes lead to a failure to understand even when you think you do. In other words, the use of a single language (whether English or any other) can create a false impression of shared meaning when, in fact, actual meanings may differ and reflect deeper linguistic layers. Here again, one implication is that communication will be more reliable if allowance is made for these complex, intrinsically multilingual processes. This is probably also the meaning of "multilingual reasoning" in the legal domain mentioned above.

7 Conclusions

The conclusions we may draw from this argumentation which represent a major outcome of the DYLAN project are manifold:

Firstly, there are very good reasons to promote languages other than English as academic languages, not only and even not mainly for reasons of equity (cf. the political discussion on the role of German, French, etc. as academic languages [e.g. Lamesh ed., 1987; Goethe-Institut ed., 2013]), but in order to take profit of the cognitive assets of plurilingualism hidden in mixed and multilingual teams.

One should therefore insist, whenever possible, that team members use their own languages bringing in their own perspective but also with the function of monitoring the processes involved in the construction of knowledge in order to avoid a loss of information.

This also means contrasting, whenever possible, the conceptual networks of different languages in the sense of "multilingual reasoning".

When it comes to publication, the drawbacks of standardisation must be compensated, among others by bridging the increasing gap between a globalised, monolingual ivory tower and the local communities. This can be done in several ways:

- by avoiding the deletion of all traces of hidden language layers (e.g. by leaving the quotations in the original language, with a translation in footnotes only if it is absolutely necessary);
- by publishing in different languages: (a) mixing different languages in the same book or journal (as it is the case, for example, for some of the major journals and handbooks in Romance languages), (b) using different languages to publish original results, (c) publishing abstracts in one or two languages other than the language of the paper (e.g. *Vox Romanica, Bulletin suisse de linguistique appliquée*). (d) publishing additional material in other languages (e.g. *Language Teaching*), etc.

Contrary to frequently uttered beliefs, (scientific) languages are not transparent. Through an exaggerated standardisation creativity is blocked and information gets lost. The respect for linguistic diversity is, therefore, a *conditio sine qua non* for meeting the increasing challenges of the world's superdiversity. The responsibility for this cannot be delegated but should be shared by researchers, publishers and academic institutions, including funding organisations.

References

Bengoetxea, Joxerramon. 2011. "Multilingual and multicultural legal reasoning: The European Court of Justice", in Kjaer, Anne L. & Adamo, Silvia (eds.): *Linguistic Diversity and European Democracy*. Burlington VT, Ashgate, 97–122.

Berthoud, Anne-Claude, Grin, François & Lüdi, Georges. 2012. *The DYLAN Project Booklet. DYLAN Project Main Findings*. Lausanne, SCIPROM.

Berthoud, Anne-Claude, Grin, François & Lüdi, Georges. 2013. "Conclusion", in Berthoud, Anne-Claude, Grin, François & Lüdi, Georges (eds.): *Exploring the Dynamics of Multilingualism. Results from the DYLAN Project*. Amsterdam, John Benjamins, 441–456.

Berthoud, Anne-Claude, Grin, François & Lüdi, Georges eds. 2013. *Exploring the Dynamics of Multilingualism. Results from the DYLAN Project*. Amsterdam, John Benjamins.

Bhabha, Homi K. 1994. *The Location of Culture*. New York, Routledge.

Bobek, Michal. 2011. "The multilingualism of the European Union law in the national courts: Beyond the textbooks", in Kjaer, Anne Lise & Adamo, Silvia (eds.): *Linguistic Diversity and European Democracy*. Burlington VT, Ashgate, 122–143.

Boden, Margaret A. 1996. "What is creativity?", In Margaret A. Boden (ed.): *Dimensions of Creativity*. Cambridge, MA, MIT, 5–117.

Bono, Mariana & Stratilaki, Sofia. 2009. The M-factor, a bilingual asset for plurilinguals? Learners' representations, discourse strategies and third language acquisition in institutional contexts. In *International Journal of Multilingualism* 6(2). 207–227.

Borras Ribas, Eulàlia. 2013. *La gestió del plurilingüisme a l'aula en l'educació superior. Estudi de cas: introducció de classes en anglès a l'Escola d'Enginyeria B*. PhD thesis, Universitat Autònoma Barcelona,
Council of Europe [CECR]. 2001. *Common European Framework of Reference for Languages: Learning, Teaching, Assessment*. Cambridge, Cambridge University Press.
Coleman, James A. 2006. 'English-medium Teaching in European Higher Education', Language Teaching, 39(1): 1–14.
Compendium. 2009. *Study on the Contribution of Multilingualism to Creativity. Compendium Part One: Multilingualism and Creativity: Towards an Evidence-base*. Brussels: European Commission. Last retrieved February, 12th 2012: http://eacea.ec.europa.eu/llp/studies/documents/study_on_the_contribution_of_multilingualism_to_creativity/compendium_part_1_en.pdf.
Cook, Vivian. 2008. *Second Language Learning and Language Teaching*. London, Arnold.
Cook, Vivian & Wei, Li (eds.). 2009. *Contemporary Applied Linguistics*, Vols 1 & 2. London, Continuum.
Croft, William. 2000. *Explaining Language Change: an Evolutionary Approach*. Longman, Harlow
Della Rosa, Pasquale A., Videsott, Gerda, Borsa, Virginia M., Canini, Matteo, Weekes, Brendan S., Franceschini, Rita & Abutalebi, Jubin. 2013. A neural interactive location for multilingual talent, *Cortex 49*, 605–608.
Doiz, Aintzane, Lasagabaster, David & Sierra, Juan M. (eds.). 2013. *English-medium Instruction at Universities: Global Challenges*. Bristol, Multilingual Matters.
Drubin, David G. & Kellogg, Douglas R. 2012. "English as the universal language of science: opportunities and challenges", *Mol. Biol. Cell 23:8*, 1399 *[doi:10.1091/mbc.E12–02–0108]*
Fetscher, Justus. 2013. „Das epistemische Potenzial der deutschen Sprache", In *Deutsch in den Wissenschaften. Beiträge zu Status und Perspektiven der Wissenschaftssprache Deutsch*. München, Klett-Langenscheidt GmbH, München
Fine, Marlene G. 1996. "Cultural diversity in the workplace: the state of the field", *Journal of Business Communication 33* (4), 485–502.
Furlong, Aine. 2009. "The relation of plurilingualism/culturalism to creativity: a matter of perception", *International Journal of Multilingualism 6/4*, 343 – 368.
Gajo, Laurent, Grobet, Anne, Müller, Gabriele, Serra, Cecilia, Steffen, Gabriela & Berthoud, Anne-Claude. 2013. "Plurilingualism and knowledge construction in higher education", In Anne-Claude Berthoud, François Grin & Georges Lüdi (eds.): *Exploring the Dynamics of Multilingualism*. Amsterdam, John Benjamins, 279–298.
Gal, Susan. 1986. "Linguistic repertoire". In Ulrich Ammon, Norbert Dittmar, Klaus J. Mattheier & Peter Trudgill (eds.). *Sociolinguistics: An International Handbook of the Science of Language and Society*. Berlin, Walter de Gruyter, 286 –292.
García, Ofelia. 2008. *Bilingual Education in the 21st Century: A Global Perspective*. Oxford, Wiley-Blackwell.
Geertz, Clifford. 1973. "Thick description. toward an interpretative theory of cultures", In *The Interpretation of Cultures. Selected Essays*. New York, Basic Books.
Goethe-Institut et al. (ed. 2013): *Deutsch in den Wissenschaften. Beiträge zu Status und Perspektiven der Wissenschaftssprache Deutsch*. München, Klett-Langenscheidt.
Goffman, Erving. 1981. *Façons de parler*. Paris, Minuit.
Greco,Luca, Renaud, Patrick & Taquechel, Roxana. 2013. "The practical processing of plurilingualism as a resource in professional activities: '*Border-crossing'* and '*languaging*' in

multilingual workplaces", In Anne-Claude Berthoud, François Grin & Georges Lüdi (eds.), *Exploring the Dynamics of Multilingualism. Results from the DYLAN Project.* Amsterdam, John Benjamins, 33–58.

Grosjean, Francois. 2001. "The bilingual's language modes", In Janet L. Nicol (ed.): *Language Processing in the Bilingual.* Oxford, Blackwell, 1– 25.

Gumperz, John. 1982. *Discourse Strategies.* Cambridge, Cambridge University Press.

Hall, Stuart & Paul Du Gay. 1996. *Questions of Cultural Identity.* London, Sage Publications.

Hong, Lu & Page, Scott. 2001. "Solving by heterogeneous agents", *Journal of Economic Theory* 97, 123–163.

Hong, Lu & Page, Scott. 2004. "Groups of diverse problem solvers can outperform groups of high-ability problem solvers", *PNAS* 101/46, 16385–16389 [www.pnas.org – doi 10.1073 pnas.0403723101]

Hopper, Paul. 1998. "Emergent Grammar", In M. Tomasello (ed.). *The new Psychology of Language.* Mahwah, NJ, Lawrence Erlbaum, 155–175.

Hülmbauer, Cornelia & Seidlhofer, Barbera. 2013. "English as a lingua franca in European multilingualism", In Anne-Claude Berthoud, François Grin & Georges Lüdi (eds.): *Exploring the Dynamics of Multilingualism. Results from the DYLAN Project.* Amsterdam, John Benjamins, 387–406.

Isaacs, William. 1993. "Taking flight: dialogue, collective thinking and organizational learning", *Organizational Dynamics,* 22/2, 24–49.

Jessner, Ulrike. 2008a. "Teaching third languages: findings, trends and challenges. State-of-the-Art Article", *Language Teaching* 41/1, 15–56.

Jessner, Ulrike. 2008b. "Multicompetence approaches to language proficiency development in multilingual education". In J. Cummins & N. H. Hornberger (eds.). *Encyclopedia of Language and Education* (pp.91–103). New York, Springer.

Kekulé, Alexander. 2010. "Soll Deutsch als Wissenschaftssprache überleben? Contra: Der Zug ist abgefahren", *Zeit* Online (http://www.zeit.de/wissen/2010-04/deutsch-forschungssprache/seite-2)

Landemore, Helene. 2013. "Deliberation, cognitive diversity, and democratic inclusiveness: an epistemic argument for the random selection of representatives", *Synthese* 190 (7), 1209–1231.

Larsen-Freeman, Diane. 2003. *Teaching Language: From Grammar to Grammaring.* Boston, Heinle/Cengage.

Larsen-Freeman, Diane & Cameron, L. 2008. *Complex Systems and Applied Linguistics.* Oxford, Oxford University Press.

Lévi-Strauss, Claude. 1962. *La pensée sauvage.* Paris, Plon.

Lüdi, Georges. 2006. Multilingual repertoires and the consequences for linguistic theory. In Kristin Bührig, & Jan D. ten Thije (eds.). *Beyond Misunderstanding. Linguistic analyses of Intercultural Communication.* (pp. 11–42). Amsterdam, John Benjamins.

Lüdi, Georges. 2011. «Vers de nouvelles approches théoriques du langage et du plurilinguisme», in: Petitjean, C. (ed.): *De la sociolinguistique dans les sciences du langage aux sciences du langage en sociolinguistique. Questions de transdisciplinarité. Travaux Neuchâtelois de Linguistique* 53, 47–64.

Lüdi, Georges. 2014. «Communicative and cognitive dimensions of pluricentric practices in French», in Soares da Silva, Augusto (ed.): *Pluricentricity. Language Variation and Socio-cognitive Dimensions.* Berlin/Boston, Mouton de Gruyter, 49–82.

Lüdi, Georges (ed.). 2010. *Le plurilinguisme au travail entre la philosophie de l'entreprise, les représentations des acteurs et les pratiques quotidiennes*. Basel, Institut für Französische Sprach- und Literaturwissenschaft (=Acta Romanica Basiliensia [ARBA] 22).

Lüdi, Georges, Barth, Lukas A., Höchle, Katharina & Yanaprasart, Patchareerat. 2009. «La gestion du plurilinguisme au travail entre la «philosophie» de l'entreprise et les pratiques spontanées», *Sociolinguistica 23*, 32–52.

Lüdi, Georges, Höchle, Katharina & Yanaprasart, Patchareerat. 2013. "Multilingualism and diversity management in companies in the Upper Rhine Region", in Anne-Claude Berthoud, François Grin & Georges Lüdi (eds.), *Exploring the Dynamics of Multilingualism. Results from the DYLAN Project.*. Amsterdam, John Benjamins, 59–82.

Lüdi, Georges & Py, Bernard. [1986] ^{4}2012. *Etre bilingue*. 4e éd. revue, avec une postface. Berne/Francfort, Lang.

Lüdi, Georges & Py, Bernard. 2009. "To be or not to be … a plurilingual speaker", *International Journal of Multilingualism*, 6/2, 154–167.

Markaki, Vassiliki, Merlino, Sara, Mondada, Lorenza, Oloff, Florence & Traverso, Veronique. 2013. "Multilingual practices in professional settings: keeping the delicate balance between progressivity and intersubjectivity", In Anne-Claude Berthoud, François Grin & Georges Lüdi (eds.), *Exploring the Dynamics of Multilingualism. Results from the DYLAN Project*. Amsterdam, John Benjamins, 3–32.

Mitchell, Rebecca & Nicholas, Stephen. 2006. "Knowledge creation in groups: the value of cognitive diversity, transactive memory, and open-mindedness norms" *The Electronic Journal of Knowledge Management* Volume 4 Issue 1, pp 67–74, available online at www.ejkm.com

Mondada, Lorenza. 2001. "Pour une linguistique interactionnelle", *Marges Linguistiques* 1, 142–162.

Mondada, Lorenza. 2004. "Ways of 'Doing Being Plurilingual' In International Work Meetings". In Rod Gardner & Johannes Wagner (eds.). *Second Language Conversations*. London, Continuum, 27–60.

Mondada, Lorenza. 2007. "Le code-switching pour l'organisation de la parole-en-interaction", *Journal of Language Contact*, 168–198. Last retrieved: February, 12th 2012 at http: www.jlc-journal.org.

Moore, Danièle & Castellotti, Véronique (eds.). 2008. *La compétence plurilingue: regards francophones*. Berne et al., Peter Lang.

Myers-Scotton, Carol. ^{2}1997. *Duelling Languages: Grammatical Structure in Codeswitching*. Oxford, Clarendon Press.

Nussbaum, Luci, Moore, Emilee & Borras, Eulalia. 2013. "Accomplishing multilingualism through plurilingual activities", in Anne-Claude Berthoud, François Grin & Georges Lüdi (eds.), *Exploring the Dynamics of Multilingualism. Results from the DYLAN Project.*. Amsterdam, John Benjamins, 229–252.

Olson, Bradley, Parayitam, Satyanarayana & Bao, Yongjian. 2007. "Strategic decision-making: the effects of cognitive diversity, conflict, and trust on decision outcomes", *Journal of Management* 33/2, 196–222 [doi: 10.1177/0149206306298657]

Page, Scott E. 2007. *The Difference: How the Power of Diversity Creates Better Groups, Firms, Schools and Societies*. Princeton, NJ, Princeton University Press.

Pekarek Doehler, Simona. 2005. De la nature située des compétences en langue. In Jean-Paul Bronckart, Bulea, Ecaterina & Puoliot, Michèle (eds.). *Repenser l'enseignement des langues: comment identifier et exploiter les compétences?* (pp. 41–68).Villeneuve d'Ascq, Presses universitaires du Septentrion.

Usunier, Jean-Claude. 2010. «Un plurilinguisme pragmatique face au mythe de l'anglais lingua franca de l'enseignement supérieur», In *Les enjeux du plurilinguisme pour la construction et la circulation des savoirs*. Bern, Schweizerische Akademie der Geistes- und Sozialwissenschaften.

Wright, Sue. 2011. "Democracy, Communities of Communication and the European Union", In Kjaer, Anne Lise & Adamo, Silvia (eds.): *Linguistic Diversity and European Democracy*. Burlington VT, Ashgate, 35–56.

Geneviève Zarate, Aline Gohard-Radenkovic and Fu Rong

10 Le *Précis du plurilinguisme et du pluriculturalisme* : une recherche internationale, face aux défis d'une conception plurilingue et d'une traduction en anglais et en chinois

At the risk of excluding non-francophone readers, we have decided to retain this chapter in its original language, for it illustrates in dramatic fashion the challenges encountered by an international team of multilingual researchers in applied linguistics. However, because Claire Kramsch was a member of that team, in addition to being the co-editor of the present volume, we decided that Claire would write a synopsis in English for non-francophone readers. This synopsis can be found at the end of the chapter. *The editors.*

Abstract: Ce chapitre témoigne des résistances intellectuelles possibles face aux règles d'un marché mondialisé et standardisé du savoir, notamment quand l'anglais est adopté sans questionnements épistémologiques comme langue de circulation du savoir en sciences humaines et sociales. Il analyse sous une forme réflexive les péripéties disciplinaires, translinguistiques, éditoriales issues de la conception collective d'un ouvrage rassemblant 90 enseignants-chercheurs, initié en français sous le titre *Précis du plurilinguisme et du pluriculturalisme* (2008), et traduit désormais en anglais (2011) et en chinois (2014). En explorant les interstices, généralement occultés ou lissés dans les publications, d'une conception qui assume sa polyphonie, l'article décortique les prises de risque qui ont jalonné cette expérience collective, d'abord dans les méandres des séances de travail du groupe de travail fondateur, puis dans ceux de la traduction en anglais et, ici, tout particulièrement en chinois. En donnant à voir « l'atelier » de la science en train de se faire, ce chapitre décrit les stratégies pragmatiquement développées pour contourner les standards unilingues et faire d'une recherche sur le plurilinguisme un objet plurilingue et pluriculturel.

This chapter documents the possibilities of intellectual resistance to the rules of a global standardized knowledge market that does not question the epistemological consequences of adopting English as the lingua franca for the circu-

---

Corresponding Author: Geneviève Zarate, L'institut national des langues et civilisations orientales (INALCO), Paris, France, GeneZarate@aol.com

lation of knowledge in the human and social sciences. It analyzes and reflects on the disciplinary, translinguistic and editorial challenges encountered during the construction of a joint project that brought together 90 researchers, titled in French *Précis du plurilinguisme et du pluriculturalisme* (2008) and that was subsequently translated into English (2011) and Chinese (2014). As it explores the interstices of this polyphonic project, generally made invisible or glossed over in the monolingual publications that resulted, the article teases out the risks taken during this collective experience, first in the lengthy discussions of the founding research group, then in the work on the English, and now here on the Chinese translations. By giving a glimpse into the workings of a scientific project in the make, this chapter describes the pragmatic strategies that were developed to circumvent the monolingual publication standards and to make research on multilingualism itself a multilingual and multicultural object of research.

1 Pourquoi le *Précis/Handbook* peut-il être défini comme un projet de recherche alternatif?

Dans un contexte universitaire et économique qui adopte les règles d'un marché mondialisé du savoir, l'ouvrage le *Précis du plurilinguisme et du pluriculturalisme* (coordination : Zarate G., Lévy, D., Kramsch C. ; Paris, Editions des archives contemporaines, 2008 ; voir aussi le site http://precis.berkeley.edu/index.php/Main_Page) qui s'inscrit dans une démarche alternative, est l'exemple d'un produit paradoxal de recherche. Il montre que des marges de manœuvre sont possibles alors que des règles standardisées imposent une définition de la recherche dite « d'excellence »[1] dans un espace universitaire où domine la polarisation anglophone. L'ouvrage a ensuite été traduit en anglais sous le titre *Handbook of Multilingualism and Multiculturalism* (Editions des archives contemporaines, 2011). Il est en cours de traduction en chinois par une équipe de chercheurs juniors et seniors de l'Université des Langues étrangères de Pékin, dirigée par le Professeur Fu Rong. Une proposition de traduction en arabe est actuellement à l'étude. C'est le débat autour de la traduction en chinois que cet article relate avec précision.

---

[1] Le terme d'« excellence » a été utilisé par le Ministère français de l'Enseignement supérieur et de la recherche, sous la Présidence de Nicolas Sarkozy, pour étalonner les laboratoires (dits Labex), les Initiatives d'excellence (dites Idex).

1.1 Une aventure intellectuelle fondée sur une solidarité scientifique

En quoi le *Précis du plurilinguisme et du pluriculturalisme* peut-il revendiquer le statut de projet alternatif ? Les conditions de sa mise en œuvre et les choix qui ont présidé à sa conception et publication témoignent de son originalité, de sa créativité et de la solidarité scientifique que le projet a progressivement cristallisées. Au cours des cinq années du projet (2003-2008), le noyau initial fondateur s'est progressivement élargi. Des séminaires, journées d'études tenus en France, Italie, Suisse, deux colloques internationaux (*Teaching Languages in Multilingual Multicultural Environments*, Berkeley, 2005 ; *Grandes et petites langues et didactique du plurilinguisme et du pluriculturalisme : modèles et expériences*, Paris, La Sorbonne (3-5 juillet 2006), le partenariat avec deux associations de chercheurs (le DORIF-Università, Italie ; la Société Internationale pour l'Histoire du Français Langue Etrangère ou Seconde (SIHFLES)) ont offert un cadre régulier de rencontres centrées sur le projet, mais aussi articulées autour de ces événements. Le projet, qui était défini comme une « aventure intellectuelle », à partager ou non, ne reposait donc pas sur un projet formellement et initialement décrit, un calendrier et des sources de financement identifiées dès sa création, mais sur des adhésions universitaires de chercheurs, puis de recherche, ensuite concrétisées par un bricolage administratif et financier. S'il fallait quantifier l'audace théorique, le feuilletage des financements, à charge de chaque participant coordinateur, en serait un garant. Aucun budget centralisé n'a donc garanti le financement des rencontres successives[2], même si l'appui financier et politique du fonds France-Berkeley a pu être invoqué pendant une partie du projet.

---

[2] Rencontres préparatoires de 2001 à 2003 dans le cadre du Séminaire « Frontières culturelles et diffusion des langues » (dirigé par G.Zarate) : état des lieux des dictionnaires existants dans le domaine des langues et cultures sur les marchés éditoriaux, dont la présentation du *Dictionnaire khazar* de Milorad Pavic proposant des entrées multiples et contradictoires sur une même histoire, qui a préfiguré le futur *Précis*. Mars 2004, séminaire organisé conjointement avec le *Berkeley Language Center de l'University of California at Berkeley (États-Unis)* et la formation doctorale *Politica, educazione, formazione linguistico-culturali* de l'Université de Macerata (Italie) ; Journées d'études en partie ouvertes au public de la Sorbonne Nouvelle, dans le cadre du soutien accordé par un financement du Fonds France/Berkeley (2004-2005). Février 2005, réunion suivant le colloque international *Teaching Languages in Multilingual, Multicultural Environments*. L'architecture d'ensemble de l'ouvrage y a été définitivement adoptée. Mai 2005, la Société Internationale pour l'Histoire du Français Langue Etrangère ou Seconde (SIHFLES) a rejoint le projet lors d'une journée d'études tenue à l'INALCO. Juillet 2006, à la suite du colloque international,« *Grandes* » *et* « *petites* » *langues et didactique du plurilinguisme et du pluriculturalisme : modèles et expériences*, qui s'est tenu à la Sorbonne, un groupe élargi, comprenant tous les coordinateurs de chapitres, s'est réuni en juillet 2006 sous les auspices de l'Université

Les solidarités théoriques entre participants étaient soudées autour de la critique d'une vision monolingue de l'enseignement des langues où la pluralité linguistique est majoritairement abordée dans sa forme minimale – une addition de langues – s'appuyant sur des postulats plus singuliers que communs. La suprématie anglophone était une évidence qu'il fallait interroger avec des anglophones. Les conditions d'enseignement des langues, produits de la mondialisation, étaient un défi qui devait être incarné dans des situations concrètes. La tradition nationale de cet enseignement, héritage des XIXème et XXème siècles européen et occidental était un cadre à dépasser. Le déficit de réflexion scientifique sur les « langues du monde », « grandes » et « petites », un objet à construire. La didactique des langues était un espace à reconstruire d'abord conceptuellement, plutôt que sous forme de « bonnes pratiques », selon l'usage dominant qui veut qu'elle s'incarne en préceptes, manuels, exercices.

1.2 La prise de risque de chaque chercheur pour un projet international hétérodoxe

Ces défis étaient donc à percevoir comme une stimulation et une prise de risque constitutives de la condition de chercheur. L'acceptation de cette prise de risque était un préalable qui mobilisait ou rebutait des chercheurs, faisant appel à un *habitus* scientifique, inégalement distribué selon l'âge, la position dans l'espace national ou international de la recherche. Au fur et à mesure que ce credo prenait une forme collective, les rencontres, bi-annuelles, devaient devenir des « rendez-vous », qui, pour être fédérateurs, devaient faire du projet une des priorités de l'agenda du chercheur. Le groupe a du donc prendre progressivement conscience de l'originalité de son fonctionnement, se définir comme une « parole d'autorité » collective qui pouvait se positionner comme un contrepoids généralement reconnu à une instance scientifique nationale ou transnationale[3]. Elle supposait

---

de Macerata et a adopté le cadre éditorial définitif. Février 2007, un dernier séminaire, dans le cadre d'un colloque international intitulé : *Plurilinguismes et pluriculturalismes : conceptions politiques, interprétations des institutions et stratégies des individus*, organisé par l'Université de Fribourg (Suisse) et son Centre d'Enseignement et de Recherche en Langues Etrangères, a permis une évaluation collective des propositions reçues.

3 La légitimité d'une recherche française ou européenne se construit sur des bases précises qui n'autorisent aucune auto-légitimation. Outre les projets financés par appels d'offre de l'Union européenne, la mise en place d'instances nationales gradue différents niveaux de légitimités scientifiques. Créée en France en 2005, l'Agence nationale de la recherche (ANR) fixe et finance des thèmes prioritaires de recherche. Créée en 2007, l'Agence pour l'Evaluation de la Recherche dans l'Enseignement Supérieur (AERES) se réfère au processus de Bologne et revendique son

donc que chaque chercheur accepte que le projet, certes paré de l'intérêt d'une recherche internationale, fonctionne dans un cadre hétérodoxe, mal et imparfaitement identifié dans chaque cadre national. Sans cadre juridique institutionnalisé comme le sont les contrats signés pour les projets européens ou nationaux actuels, on notera combien il est facile pour le chercheur déçu de quitter un projet qui ne porte pas les fruits espérés et d'en signaler urbi et orbi la mauvaise fortune.

Pour assumer cette prise de risque sous forme de pari intellectuel, il faut donc mobiliser un *habitus* capable de puiser dans un capital personnel de terrains de recherche, de réseaux, de concepts et d'expérience, sans penser à une rentabilité scientifique immédiate (par exemple une publication qui fait dériver un projet sur cinq ans vers un bénéfice immédiat) et d'accorder une valeur ajoutée prioritaire à l'indépendance intellectuelle.

2 « *Researching Multilingually and Multiculturally* » : penser et écrire collectivement et en plusieurs langues et traditions scientifiques

2.1 La construction d'un credo scientifique commun aux prises avec les traditions anglo- et francophones

Le déroulement du projet n'a donc pas été d'une paisible linéarité, découlant de l'harmonie générale, même si la coopération des chercheurs participants a été une règle tacite et effective. Bien que le projet ne passe pas par le dépôt d'une demande de financement explicite et pluriannuelle, il restait « sérieux », si les chercheurs non-européens intégraient le fait que la structure de la recherche en Europe et dans le monde anglo-saxon ne fonctionne pas sur le même modèle. Les équipes de recherche européenne sont validées à niveau local et national et avec des jurys internationaux pour un programme quadriennal ou quinquennal. Elles ont ainsi gagné une liberté – de durée limitée – dans le choix de leurs priorités de recherche.

---

inscription au registre *EQAR* (*EuropeanQuality Assurance Register for Higher Education*), signant ainsi son adhésion aux normes européennes. Si une recherche décidée collectivement dans une équipe de recherche est toujours possible dans les faits, elle souffre donc de la concurrence de projets validés de façon externe, et est donc susceptible de dévaluation.

Le projet est aussi constitué des impasses vers lesquelles débouchent parfois les échanges plus ou moins formels, les choix radicaux qui doivent faire l'objet d'un accord collectif sous peine de dislocation du projet, les flous terminologiques déstabilisants qui émergent d'un débat et mettent les convictions du chercheur à l'épreuve de la crudité d'un savoir en train de se construire. Il faut partager un credo commun qui veut que ce sont ces déséquilibres vécus qui font le sel d'une recherche collective, et non la ratification par plusieurs d'une position personnelle. Les participants au projet ont donc progressivement découvert une dimension imprévue, musclant sa difficulté. Les débats sur les termes de *agency*, *hybridity*, « représentations » par exemple, un moment testés comme des mots clefs capables de structurer le *Précis/Handbook*, ont été mémorables : ils ont mis au jour combien le débat anglophone et francophone sur les langues s'articulait sur des concepts invisibles pour l'autre partie. Il a fallu à une étape du projet renoncer à un angle indépendant d'une langue et d'un contexte donnés. Le contexte francophone/européen, dynamisé par la publication du *Cadre européen commun de référence pour les langues* (Conseil de l'Europe, 2001) a finalement emporté le morceau quand les discussions s'enlisaient entre priorités européennes et anglo-saxonnes.

2.2 Des débats internes sur le plurilinguisme qui deviennent timidement plurilingues

Mais dans les convictions théoriques qui rassemblaient les participants, un socle conceptuel commun ambitieux, en cohérence avec l'objet même de la recherche, s'est établi autour du plurilinguisme et pluriculturalisme : ne privilégier aucune langue ; garder un angle ouvert sur le monde, tout en réfutant la tentation encyclopédique ; ne pas viser le seul panorama des propositions existantes et se doter d'un regard ouvert sur l'avenir (c'est le sens incarné par les *Contrepoints* en fin de chapitres) ; donner à voir le champ du plurilinguisme comme un champ spécifique qui n'est pas seulement le prolongement ou l'amplification des travaux sur le bilinguisme.

Le ralliement progressif des chercheurs, devenus ensuite coordinateurs de chapitres, s'est fait sans plan initial concerté, mais progressivement, avec le souci de l'ouverture théorique et géographique et celui de la complémentarité des compétences déjà rassemblées. Si le français est la langue de travail initiale, l'anglais est devenu la seconde langue. Les débats se sont donc faits au croisement de ces deux langues, inégalement partagées par tous. Au fil des réunions et des rencontres qui, de la France, se sont déplacées aux Etats-Unis, en Italie, en Suisse, les compétences linguistiques de participants se sont modelées. La timide francophonie des uns s'est révélée et affermie, la pratique rustique de l'anglais des autres a pris d'audacieuses envolées, les liens construits autour de l'italien langue d'immigration se sont mis au service des débats, la pratique de l'espagnol s'est immiscée dans les échanges. Les échanges amicaux hors séances de travail ont parfois été nourris des récits de langues savoureux des uns et des autres. Comme Jacques Demorgon l'avait déjà noté à travers sa pratique d'observateur des échanges franco-allemands[4], la mise en place d'échanges bi- ou plurilingues dans un groupe constitué requiert une temporalité spécifique. Si un groupe monolingue poursuit un objectif commun en ayant le souci d'une optimisation du temps, le groupe plurilingue doit sans cesse composer avec la pluralité qui le compose, en adoptant une économie spécifique qui laisse sa place à l'intercompréhension, aux traductions de voisinage informelles, aux demandes d'éclaircissements, aux récapitulations collectives, aux schémas visuels, aux comptes rendus écrits de réunions. En travaillant sur la pluralité des langues, un consensus s'est établi pour mettre concrètement en pratique un mode de communication lui-même lié à son objet, qu'une vision étroitement productive aurait ruiné.

2.3 Les conditions qui ont incité à la mise en chantier de la traduction du *Précis* en anglais

Le basculement vers une traduction en anglais s'est décidé après l'achèvement de la version française et n'était en rien initialement prémédité. La lourdeur du premier projet n'y était en effet pas pour rien. Le conseil d'un collègue anglais évaluant notre équipe a souligné le risque d'un pillage de l'ouvrage par des lecteurs opportunistes publiant en anglais. Remettre en chantier une seconde version, après une mobilisation pluriannuelle, sans financements spécifiques, dans le rapport inégal que l'équipe de coordination entretenait avec l'anglais – une seule anglophone, Claire Kramsch – pouvait invalider le premier projet et apparaître comme une redite médiocre. La demande des collègues travaillant en contexte anglophone, désireux de faire valoir ce qui était singulier dans cette entreprise, a prévalu sur la conscience des écueils possibles. Dans le contexte français, il était aussi clair, dès 2010, que la valorisation de la recherche devait passer par une diffusion en anglais. Une équipe de recherche reconnue par le Ministère de l'Enseignement supérieur et de la recherche français s'était créée sur le socle du *Précis* à l'INALCO – l'équipe d'accueil EA 4514 PLIDAM. Un doctorat italien – *Politica, Educazione, Formazione Linguistico-Culturali*, abrité par l'Université de Macerata

---

4 Demorgon J., Will E., Carpentier N., *Guide interculturel pour l'animation de réunions transfrontalières*, 2007

et dirigé par Danielle Lévy – et une association universitaire, le DORIF-Università l'avait nourri. Le projet pouvait revendiquer son caractère transnational.

2.4 Témoigner des compromis liés au passage du français en anglais

C'était l'objectif même du *Précis* : rendre compte de la complexité des problématiques et des processus de communication et de compréhension dans les contextes plurilingues et pluriculturels, ainsi que de la pluralité des postures disciplinaires et des interprétations scientifiques dans le champ. C'est sa structure particulière, composée sur trois (3) niveaux – structure globale, chapitres et « micro-entrées » – qui a permis sa traduction en anglais, sans moyens avérés. Chaque coordinateur de chapitre a pris en charge sa partie, déléguant parfois à chaque auteur de micro-entrée la prise en charge de la traduction de son texte. Les coordinateurs de chapitres ont signalé dans des *Notes on the English translation of Chapter X* les compromises auxquels ils ont fait face. L'ensemble de ces notes constitue en soi un texte, non seulement parce qu'elles constituent un addendum à la version en français, mais parce que la diversité des compromis y est explicitée. On y lit la délicate transposition de *speaker/actor*, de didactique des langues en *Second Language Acquisition theory,* par exemple dans le chapitre 1 ; le défi des allusions et métaphores (chapitre 2) ; une proposition de catégorisation des traducteurs au début du chapitre 3 ; des compromis de sens entre *diversity* et *plurality* et l'impossible traduction de « laïque » du chapitre 4 ; etc. Dans tous les cas, il a semblé plus rigoureux d'afficher les choix difficiles faits que de les masquer.

2.5 Rendre visibles les débats internes entre auteurs

Le projet a aussi généré des « produits secondaires », un site posté sur le serveur de l'Université de Berkeley a permis de consulter les curricula vitae des auteurs dans une facture plurilingue inédite, à l'initiative de Danielle Lévy (site http://precis.berkeley.edu/index.php/Main_Page). L'expérience singulière des débats non formatés a généré un numéro de la revue *Le Français dans le monde. Recherches et applications*, intitulé *La circulation internationale des idées en didactique des langues,* qui reprenait les principes formulés par Pierre Bourdieu[5], mettait en

---

5 La circulation internationale des idées. *Actes de la recherche en sciences sociales*, Paris, Seuil, 2002/5, n°145. « Le fait que les textes circulent sans leur contexte, qu'ils n'emportent pas avec eux le champ de production (...) dont ils sont le produit et que les récepteurs, étant eux-mêmes

garde sur les détournements de « l'import-export intellectuel » en présentant les ambiguïtés liées à une « circulation internationale des idées (qui) implique leur transformation », et en illustrant le « champ de production » des théories didactiques, dominé par une pensée « occidentale » au cours des siècles précédents et les effets de leur transplantation vers des contextes non-européens. Les alertes lancées par l'article introductif[6] étaient déjà valables dans certains contextes européens. Leur caractère prémonitoire est confirmé au regard des débats actuels en France sur les risques liés à l'utilisation d'une langue unique dans une formation universitaire en sciences humaines et sociales, mondialisée à la sauvette[7].

Avec l'édition d'une traduction en chinois, l'ensemble peut aussi se lire comme un triptyque en français/anglais/chinois, qui constitue finalement un nouveau texte décliné en trois versions. Mais il est aussi constitué de trois histoires singulières qu'il convient de dissocier. Le *Précis/Handbook* a donc généré un triple espace de réflexion sur la spécificité d'une recherche plurilingue et pluriculturelle observable à travers

- une publication francophone : Zarate G., Liddicoat T. *(coord.)* La circulation internationale des idées, *Le Français dans le monde. Recherches et applications*, juillet 2009.
- les avant-propos anglophones de chaque chapitre du *Handbook*, rédigé par les coordinateurs francophones et anglophones ou les traducteurs en charge du chapitre.
- un séminaire franco-chinois, tenu à l'Université des Langues étrangères de Pékin, en septembre 2012 dont il est rendu compte ci-dessous.

Le respect d'une discussion qui approfondit le cadre de la recherche – et non pas qui la donne pour acquise, comme le veulent souvent des projets internationaux lourdement financés – a mis en lumière à quel point les débats sont gagés sur leur contexte de production, en particulier en sciences humaines et sociales, à l'inverse de la croyance en une science qui serait définie par l'universalité de ses concepts. Les échanges ont aussi montré à quel point les catégories de classement en usage flottent pour penser l'enseignement des langues.

---

insérés dans un champ de production différent, les réinterprètent en fonction de la structure du champ de réception, est générateur de formidables malentendus »

6 « Au moment où se met en place un espace européen académique unifié, où l'anglais tend à s'imposer comme la langue unique de l'échange scientifique, y compris dans la réflexion sur l'enseignement des langues et la valorisation du plurilinguisme, il est nécessaire de décrire les traditions qui plaident pour une lecture fondée sur la complexité ». p. 14.

7 Héran F., L'anglais hors la loi ? Enquête sur les langues de recherche et d'enseignement en France, *Population et Sociétés*, INED, prépublication 21 mai 2013.

3 Traduire le *Précis* en chinois, langue « distante » : de nouveaux défis

3.1 La rencontre avec les interlocuteurs de l'Université des études étrangères de Pékin

Si la traduction en anglais, sous le titre de *Handbook of Multilingualism and Multiculturalism* s'est déclenchée sous l'impulsion anglophone, relayée par les pressions d'un espace mondialisé de la recherche, sa traduction en chinois relève d'une logique distincte. Les contacts noués avec le Professeur FU Rong sont initiés dans le cadre de l'équipe de recherche française PLIDAM [8] et s'enracinent dans son expertise en didactique du chinois, en particulier avec les recherches de Joël Bellassen, et de celle de FU Rong, francophone, auteur de la traduction en chinois à partir du français du *Cadre Européen Commun de Référence pour les langues* (CECR) sous le titre «欧洲语言共同参考框架：学习、教学、评估» (ouzhou yuyan gongtong cankao kuangjia : xuexi, jiaoxue, pinggu)[9]. Ce dernier volet du triptyque prend comme point de départ la version en français du *Précis*, ouvre vers un horizon non-occidental ou vers des lecteurs sinophones qui auraient pu lire le *Handbook*, mais, étant dépendants d'une logique mondialisée et anglophone, ne peuvent pas saisir le questionnement sur l'intraduisibilité des concepts et la force des traditions conceptuelles en sciences sociales, puisque l'anglais occupe déjà en Chine des positions indiscutées dans la circulation des idées.

Le colloque *Politiques linguistiques de la France et de la Chine*, organisé à Pékin en septembre 2012[10] dans le cadre des Années croisées France-Chine, a précédé le lancement officiel par les Services culturels français et l'Université des Langues étrangères de Pékin du projet de traduction du *Précis*. Il a donné un cadre introductif au contexte linguistique et politique chinois. Les échanges, à caractère officiel, entre la Commission nationale chinoise des Langues et des Lettres et la Délégation Générale à la Langue Française et aux Langues de France (DGLFLF), ont fait apparaître des jeux d'opposition entre « langues de France » et

---

8 Voir plus haut : EA 4514 *Pluralité des Langues et des Identités : Didactique, Acquisition, Médiations*
9 Traduit par FU Rong, CHEN Liyu, DAI Dongmei, LI Hongfeng et TAN Jia, *Presses universitaires de l'Université des Langues étrangères de Pékin*, Beijing, 2008.
10 Séminaire *Politiques linguistiques en Chine et en France*. Organisé par le Ministère chinois de l'Education et la Commission nationale des Langues et des Lettres ; le Ministère des Affaires étrangères (MAE) et le Ministère de la Culture et de la Communication, le Ministère de l'Education Nationale, l'Ambassade de France en Chine et l'Institut Français.

« dialectes », « rapports de forces linguistiques » et l'« harmonie » que le multilinguisme a vocation à produire en Chine ; les « ethnies » répondent aux « langues régionales et minoritaires » de la politique linguistique européenne ; la langue d'Etat, le putonghua, s'impose face aux « dialectes », plutôt en porte-à-faux avec la vision européenne d'un bi- ou plurilinguisme encouragés.

3.2 La transposition du *Précis* dans le contexte des théories chinoises en présence

C'est donc dans un paysage disciplinaire et culturel très différent des contextes européens/occidentaux que la diffusion en chinois du *Précis/Handbook* opère. Mais cette complexité et cette pluralité, déjà identifiables dans l'*acte de la traduction* entre deux langues perçues « proches » – le français et l'anglais, en tant que « langues occidentales » – se trouve décuplée entre deux langues perçues « distantes » – le français et le chinois, langues « occidentale » et « orientale ». Cet ouvrage est, rappelons-le, lui-même le produit d'une co-construction de chercheurs et d'auteurs aux appartenances disciplinaires, linguistiques, institutionnelles, nationales, etc. diverses qui ne partagent pas forcément toutes les acceptions des concepts qui ont été abordés et discutés même s'ils les utilisent dans leur texte.

Le séminaire sur la traduction du *Précis* en chinois prend place à la suite de ce colloque bilatéral. Il a pour objectif de mener un échange approfondi entre 5 coordinateurs de chapitres et l'équipe des 18 traducteurs, enseignants-chercheurs francophones de l'Université des Langues étrangères de Pékin[11], mobilisée et pilotée par FU Rong. On dispose de trois sources d'informations sur ces débats : un enregistrement vidéo, mis en place à l'initiative de FU Rong, une transcription des parties sonores les plus denses ou les plus audibles de cet enregistrement, effectuées par Shu Shangying, lectrice de chinois et membre de PLIDAM, les notes des discussions et des échanges, reportées sur un carnet de bord par Aline Gohard-Radenkovic.

Dans ce contexte, l'équipe francophone et occidentale de coordinateurs de chapitres s'inscrit dans cette double posture d'observateurs participants et de participants observateurs qui a permis de repérer un certain nombre de processus récurrents dans cette quête collective et terminologique. Quelles stratégies ont été élaborées, consciemment ou non, par les différents participants dans une

---

11 Ce sont CHE Lin, DAI Dongmei, JIN Xiaoyan, LI Yan, LI Xiaoguang, LUO Dingrong, TAN Jia, TIAN Yuan, WANG Jihui, WANG MEI, WANG Kun, XU Yan, XIE Jinhui, YE Sha, YU Chunhong, ZHAO Yang, ZHANG Yingxuan.

interaction, au début hésitante quant à la procédure à mettre en place, qui s'est révélée très vite collaborative ?

3.3 La traduction, processus de remédiations linguistique, disciplinaire et culturelle en miroirs...

3.3.1 Les explicitations d'implicites et d'évidences

Commençons par les évidences propres aux francophones européens : dans les termes employés dans le *Précis*, comme par exemple « Bruxelles » pour « Union européenne » ou encore « Quai d'Orsay » pour « Ministère des affaires étrangères » qui sont des métonymies de lieux politiques, institutionnels, etc. appartenant à la conscience collective d'un peuple, à son histoire et à sa mémoire, sans oublier les nombreux sigles que les représentants francophones ont utilisés de manière abondante, des « allant-de-soi » qu'ils ont dû expliquer aux traducteurs chinois juniors. Ces premières stratégies relèvent de l'explicitation des implicites qui ne sont pas enfouis dans le texte, mais tout de suite repérables à la surface des textes par de non-initiés à la culture implicite partagée d'une collectivité.

Plus difficiles d'accès, car enchâssés dans le texte, sont les références non explicitées, provenant d'univers conceptuels essentiellement occidentaux, issus d'héritages philosophiques, impliquant des références « évidentes » pour les chercheurs francophones, et plus largement occidentaux, à des disciplines et/ou à des concepts. Pour exemplifier, rappelons les termes pointés par nos collègues chinois tels que « décentrage ou décentration » (recours au vocabulaire de la psychologie de l'enfant, Piaget, 2002), «acteur social » (Garfinkel, 1984), « bricolages » (Lévi-Strauss, 1962 ; de Certeau, 1990),« biens symboliques » et « catégories de l'entendement » (Bourdieu, 1982) ; « socialisations premières dans la famille, secondaires à l'école » (notamment Bernstein, 1975) ou encore la « grammaire de Port-Royal » (Lancelot, 1644) qui a dû être remise en contexte à travers l'histoire des différents courants de la grammaire en France.

L'ensemble de ces références implicites pourrait être typifiées, constituant le *sous-texte* d'un texte, notamment lors d'un travail de traduction, comme le souligne Monsacré (2012), le qualifiant de « palimpsestes » tantôt culturels, tantôt philosophiques, tantôt idéologiques, tantôt les trois à la fois.

3.3.2 Les concepts transférables s'appuyant sur des héritages conceptuels

Les intellectuels chinois issus d'une longue tradition de lettrés confucéens ne nous ont pas attendus pour élaborer des concepts comme « appartenances », proche du concept de « rattachements » en chinois (归属 guishu, 附属 fushu), rappelant le terme anglais *affiliations*. Toutefois, nous avons recours, tant en chinois qu'en français, à deux termes qui traduisent bien cette double conception du concept « d'appartenance », exprimant à la fois le rattachement hérité, parfois subi d'un individu à un groupe social et/ou culturel, et celle d'identification, choisie ou revendiquée par un individu ou un groupe selon une conception dynamique co-constructionniste (voir sous « Appartenance (sentiment d'-) de Ferréol et Jucquois, 2003).

Mais attardons-nous un instant sur le concept de « représentations » que l'on assimile souvent dans les textes du *Précis* à celui de « perceptions » parfois de manière indifférenciée. Deux conceptions se sont confrontées dans nos échanges. Ainsi nos collègues chinois ont identifié ce terme, à partir de leur propre bagage conceptuel, en le définissant « d'image mentale, de symbole », à caractère statique, plus proche du terme allemand *Vertretung* que du terme *Vorstellung*, à caractère plus dynamique « d'interface et de relation à... ». Ces deux acceptions sont en fait empruntées à des philosophes allemands. Sous *Vorstellung*, Kant distingue deux catégories : « Au sens subjectif, la représentation est de nature sensible et s'apparente à une image mentale. Au sens objectif, elle n'a rien à voir avec le sensible et est de nature logique. (...) ». (Cassin, 2004, 1073). Husserl, fondateur de la phénoménologie, s'interroge sur ces définitions dichotomiques et développe ses théories représentationnelles, soit une conception dynamique de la relation de l'individu au monde, dont l'appréhension de la « réalité » est sans cesse médiée et remédiée par des croyances et perceptions mentales (Cassin, idem, 1074). Cette deuxième acception est celle qui a été retenue par les chercheurs en didactique des langues. Une longue discussion s'est articulée autour de ce concept et, si les collègues chinois en ont perçu toute la complexité, on peut se demander si tous les participants francophones avaient conscience de ces conceptions sous-jacentes en conflit. Nous avons finalement adopté le sens « d'image mentale, de symbole, de perception » mais à caractère dynamique, c'est-à-dire sans cesse évolutif, soit en chinois : (意象) 表征 (yixiang) biaozheng.

3.3.3 Les appropriations conceptuelles pensables et traduisibles

Contre toute attente, certains termes ont trouvé très vite leur place dans le texte chinois : ceux de « diasporas transnationales » traduit par « groupes nationaux qui habitent à l'étranger » (跨国移居 kuaguo yiju), la notion de « voix/contre-voix » ou encore celle de « polyphonie » (正调-反调 zhengdiao-fandiao), etc.

Plus étonnant a été l'appropriation du terme « entretiens qualitatifs », qui, à l'opposé de l'enquête quantitative par questionnaires « dont les données ont pour fonction de fournir des descriptions fiables de phénomènes collectifs (...) et de vérifier des hypothèses (Bertaux, 2005, 24), ont pour vocation de « donner à voir comment « fonctionne » un monde ou une situation sociale » (...) « ce que l'ethnologue américain Clifford Geertz appelle *thick description*, une description en profondeur de l'objet social » (Bertaux, op. cit., 24–25). Ce choix méthodologique traduit ici une démarche attachée à la recherche qualitative interprétative, adoptée il y a à peine vingt ans en sciences sociales en Europe, notamment en didactique des langues et des cultures. Cette conception commence à faire son apparition dans la formation académique en langues, du moins à l'université Beiwai sur l'initiative du Prof. Fu Rong et à l'Université des Etudes étrangères de Canton, sur l'initiative du Prof. Zheng Lihua, ce qui aboutit à la traduction suivante : 质性访谈 zhixing fangtan, soit un entretien effectué en vue d'une recherche qualitative).

D'autres exemples ont retenu notre attention : le concept de « discours sur la classe/de la classe », binôme pour le moins complexe, car il implique une double « lecture » : celle des discours qui se sont-construits entre les divers acteurs de la classe et celle du chercheur élaborant son propre discours sur ces discours qui circulent dans la classe (discours sur la classe : 关于课堂教学的论述 guanyu ketang jxue de lunshu ; discours de la classe : 课堂话语 ketang huayu) ; le terme d'« alloglottes » – soit « possédant une langue autre que la langue nationale » – a été pensable, appropriable et intégrable dans le nouveau lexique en émergence (会本国语之外另一种语言的人 hui benguoyu zhiwai lingyizhong yuyan de ren).

La notion d'« universel » ne devait pas en soi poser de problèmes à nos collègues chinois, mais les textes du *Précis* offraient tour à tour deux termes, « universalisme » (普遍主义 pubian zhuyi , 普世主义 pushi zhuyi) et « universalité » (普遍性 pubianxing , 普世性 pushixin) – sans jamais vraiment les expliciter. Pourquoi ces différences de termes et que signifient-elles ? Si le premier terme fait référence à la construction d'une idéologie, le deuxième terme traduit davantage un constat, un état de fait. Au-delà de ce qui pouvait apparaître comme un jeu subtil intellectuel, le problème semble avoir été résolu de manière pragmatique par les collègues chinois qui ont adopté le terme de « principes universels » (普遍原理 pubian yuanli).

3.3.4 Les ajustements conceptuels en fonction des réalités contextuelles

Un certain nombre de concepts qui ont été utilisés tout au long des débats, ont dû être ajustés au contexte chinois comme par exemple la traduction, mais aussi la compréhension des rapports entre les termes, comme « pays », « nation », « Etat », « province » qui varient d'un contexte à un autre selon les provenances nationales ou régionales des auteurs ayant contribué au *Précis*. Les traducteurs se sont interrogés sur ces dénominations administratives qui recouvrent aussi des modalités d'organisation politiques. Ils ont dû les rattacher à des conceptions compréhensibles pour le lecteur sinophone, même s'ils ne coïncident pas avec leurs découpages contextuels. Ces concepts sont en effet déterminants pour comprendre les processus de légitimation et de rapports de force analysés dans des contextes politiques et institutionnels précis dans le champ du plurilinguisme et du pluriculturalisme.

La notion de « politiques de littératie » (*literacy policies*), importée récemment de l'Amérique du nord anglophone en Europe, dont le sens est déjà décalé dans sa migration francophone, a été traduite en chinois par « éducation du peuple en lecture, écriture et calcul »(扫盲教育政策 saomang jiaoyu zhengce). Quant à l'expression, « chinois, langue distante », on peut percevoir toute l'absurdité de ce terme dans le contexte chinois. Mais cette incongruité a permis d'introduire le paradigme de la distance *versus* de la proximité (inspirée de Simmel, 2004), qui se trouve au cœur des analyses des dynamiques de contact *versus* de conflit entre les langues et entre les locuteurs. Nos collègues chinois ont traduit cette expression en interprétant « le chinois en tant que langue très éloignée des langues européennes » (汉语，与欧洲语言相隔万里的语言 hanyu, yu ouzhou yuyan xiangge wanli de yuyan).

Le concept de « mobilités » a été un concept difficile à manier. Le terme générique est celui de « déplacement » et sa terminologie va varier selon les publics auxquels on aura affaire. Le terme « mobilités » est arrivé par la petite porte dans le monde académique sous la forme « d'échanges d'étudiants », en vue de développer la mobilité professionnelle dans l'Union européenne, tandis qu'on utilise un autre concept pour migrations, immigrations. On peut se demander quelle place occupe cette notion de « mobilité » ou de « migration » dans l'espace à la fois géographique, historique et symbolique chinois où longtemps la notion de « déplacement » était synonyme de « pauvreté », de « vagabondage », de « sans attaches », ou encore quand cette notion s'inscrivait et s'inscrit toujours dans des règlements stricts de déplacements internes ou externes au pays. Il n'est pas sûr que ce terme puisse être adopté à moins que l'on ne fasse une distinction nette entre la mobilité académique et les autres formes de déplacement, ce qu'Aline Gohard-Radenkovic et Elizabeth-Murphy-Lejeune n'ont pas voulu faire dans le chapitre « Mobilités et parcours ». Mais en chinois, pour enlever toute ambiguïté et souligner qu'il est ici question d'un concept spécifique en Europe, « mobilités » a été traduit par « échanges interuniversitaires d'étudiants » (大学生国际校际交流 daxuesheng guoji xiaoji jiaoliu).

3.3.5 Les questionnements et les vérifications passant par l'anglais, langue tierce

Le passage par la traduction du *Précis* en anglais a été utilisé plusieurs fois quand le terme ou l'expression en français paraissait complexe, obscure, voire opaque, bref semblait nous résister des deux côtés, et dans les explications et dans les décisions.

Ces va et vient entre le texte anglais et le texte français ont été fréquents et ont pu parfois éclairer le sens. Prenons par exemple la notion de « planification linguistique » qu'il ne faudrait pas confondre avec celle de « politique linguistique » car cette dernière n'engendre pas forcement de planification ou d'aménagement des langues, on a trouvé l'équivalent de *language planning* (语言规划 yuyan guihua). De même la question nous a été posée pour celui de « parcours » dont le sens, après bien des tergiversations et explications, serait l'équivalent d'*itinerary*.

Un autre exemple encore : comment mettre en valeur les différences dans le texte français entre « langues et langage » ? On nous demande : est-ce que ces différents termes correspondent à des modes d'expression différents ? Pourquoi faire si compliqué alors qu'un seul terme suffit en anglais *language(s)*, sauf quand il s'agit de la langue maternelle que l'on traduit par *mother tongue* ? En chinois, on distingue facilement « langue » (语言 yuan) de « langage » (言语 yanyu, parole ; 言语能力 yanyu nengli, compétence de parole). Le langage peut d'ailleurs être compris en chinois comme une manière de parler propre à un groupe social ou professionnel ou encore à une discipline, le langage militaire par exemple. C'est donc ici plutôt l'anglais qui poserait des problèmes en chinois puisqu'il a le seul mot *language*.

D'autres questions ont interpellé les traducteurs : pourquoi ne pas utiliser franchement des termes qui font partie des discours officiels de l'Union européenne, des termes comme *ethnic groups* qui sont traduits par « groupes ethniques » ou encore *community languages* (« langues communautaires ») ? Ces termes sont de fait largement empruntés au lexique anglo-saxon et expriment des réalités sociopolitiques et des contextes spécifiques dans le monde, s'inscrivant dans des politiques multiculturalistes. La didactique francophone, marquée par la sociologie et l'anthropologie, mais aussi par l'idée de citoyen universel, les manie en effet avec beaucoup de prudence, même si on les retrouve dans les discours des linguistes appliqués s'appuyant sur le lexique de l'*Applied Linguistics*. Ces concepts sont partie prenante d'une posture plus idéologique que scientifique. Mais d'un point de vue extérieur, les francophones n'affichent-ils pas également une posture plus idéologique que scientifique ? A l'heure où l'anglais est devenue la langue de référence pour le discours scientifique en Chine, et où les discours ethnicisants, culturalisants ou communautarisants prévalent un peu partout dans le monde, quels ont été les choix de nos interlocuteurs ? Il faut reconnaître qu'en Chine, pour des raisons justement politique et idéologique, beaucoup de concepts notamment relatifs à la politique linguistique relèvent plus ou moins d'une posture idéologique, nous pensons ici plus particulièrement aux langues parlées en province chinoise que les autorités prennent toujours soin d'appeler « les dialectes ». Il en est de même pour le terme très sensible « ethnie » qui comporte en chinois, entre autres, le sens de race.

3.3.6 Les contournements face aux concepts difficilement intégrables

Des termes qui ne semblent pas habituels dans les discours scientifiques du domaine de l'apprentissage/enseignement des langues en Chine (et introduits récemment dans le lexique de la didactique des langues) ont été questionnés, mais ils ont pu trouver leur place parce que les traducteurs ont trouvé des équivalents.

Voici plusieurs exemples de cette stratégie de contournement par rapport à des concepts que l'on peut considérer comme gênants, voire difficilement intégrables : « confrontation » (交锋 jiaofeng, 较量 jiaoliang), concept peu acceptable dans les discours académiques chinois dont le sens a été atténué en le traduisant par celui de « confrontation amicale » ou « discussion acharnée, vif débat » (热烈的讨论 relie de taolun); ou encore comme le titre du Chapitre 8 « Histoire, pratiques et modèles » traduit par « Histoire, pratiques d'enseignement et modèles » (历史、教学实践及其模式 lishi, jiaoxue shijian jiqi mushi) car la notion de « pratiques », issue du vocabulaire sociologique, ne pouvait pas suffire à elle seule, et c'est donc l'expression « pratiques d'enseignement », plus spécifique, qui a été retenue révélant un glissement de sens et d'ancrage disciplinaire.

Un certain nombre de discussions ont longtemps tourné autour des dénominations des langues qui mettaient au jour des conceptions et des enjeux autres que purement terminologiques, comme ces questions de nos collègues chinois : comment traduire « patois » et « dialectes », y-a-t-il hiérarchie, et si oui, quelle est-elle ? Pouvez-vous expliquer pourquoi il y a deux mots ? Ou encore : comment traduire une expression comme « idéologies langagières », issue de *language ideologies* (concept très à la mode dans le monde anglo-saxon sous l'influence des *Cultural Studies)*? Cela veut-il dire que ces discours sur les langues recouvrent, voire occultent, des réalités sociolinguistiques différentes ? On peut imaginer que le terme « idéologies » peut avoir une connotation tantôt positive, tantôt négative selon le contexte concerné (意识形态 yishi xingtai).

C'est aussi le terme « chausse-trappes », traduit par 陷阱 xianjing, qui signifie « un trou recouvert cachant un piège pour attraper (des bêtes sauvages) », qui a été source d'étonnement et de perplexité pour nos interlocuteurs. Bien sûr ce n'était pas le terme en soi qui décontenançait mais son usage dans ce contexte scientifique et la dimension subversive qu'il pouvait véhiculer: un discours scientifique pourrait donc en cacher un autre.

3.3.7 Les renoncements face aux concepts difficilement traduisibles, voire intraduisibles

Dans sa *Préface*, Barbara Cassin définit les intraduisibles comme suit : « Parler d'intraduisibles n'implique nullement que les termes en question ou les expressions (...) ne soient pas traduits et ne puissent pas l'être – l'intraduisible, c'est plutôt ce qu'on ne cesse pas de (ne pas) traduire » (2004, p. XV) /2.

Des termes que nous avons repérés dans les échanges, comme par exemple « le politique », « la traduction comme institution », pour ne citer que ceux qui ont particulièrement retenu l'attention, qui ont posé des problèmes à tel point qu'il y a eu renoncement provisoire de leur traduction. Pourquoi la traduction de « la traduction comme institution » a-t-elle fait l'objet d'hésitations ? Cette expression, propre au lexique de l'anthropologie sociale et politique, est subversive car elle sous-tend non seulement l'acte de traduire un ouvrage d'une langue à une autre, mais aussi un ensemble d'acteurs avec leurs enjeux sociaux et contextuels, leurs ancrages institutionnels et disciplinaires, leurs pratiques instituées, ainsi que leurs instances hiérarchiques et éditoriales ayant leurs propres logiques, tous impliqués avec des statuts différents dans le processus de la traduction. Ils sont d'ailleurs perçus avec suspicion dans le domaine des langues et des cultures, même dans un environnement occidental.

Autre exemple, celui de « métalangage », impliquant une posture réflexive sur le fonctionnement de la langue et aussi sur les processus d'apprentissage et d'acquisition, a été une notion longuement discutée, non pas parce que les traducteurs chinois n'étaient pas en mesure de le traduire mais parce qu'ils avaient des difficultés à nous expliquer en français le terme utilisé en chinois. Ici nous ne sommes pas dans une situation de renoncement de traduction d'un concept mais de renoncement à trouver le mot exact en français pour expliquer aux interlocuteurs francophones le terme utilisé en chinois. Dans tous les cas, quelles solutions choisir ?

Garder le terme en l'état, c'est le cas par exemple du terme didactique « approche » par rapport à la méthode, méthodologie et didactique, alors qu'en chinois tous les quatre sont appelés « 教学法 » (jiaoxuefa). Ainsi, en traduisant « approche » en chinois, nous sommes obligés de garder le terme en l'état mais souvent et de préférence avec une note en bas de page pour rappeler la différence entre ces quatre concepts en didactique des langues. Nous pensons ici à un autre exemple aussi très révélateur, il s'agit d'un concept clé en didactique : « complexité », distinct de celui de « compliqué », tandis qu'en chinois, on les désigne avec un seul terme « 复杂性 » (fuzaxing) sans faire distinction de fond. De même, pour être clairs et bien compris dans son vrai sens en didactique, nous devons mettre sa traduction sous forme d'un mot complété entre parenthèses ou d'une note explicative : « (教学法自身固有的) 复杂性 » (jiaoxuefa zishen guyou de) fuzaxing[12].

3.3.8 Les créations et prises de risque conceptuelles

C'est autour du concept de « contrepoint » que les discussions ont été les plus longues et les plus intenses entre les traducteurs chinois, car ce terme utilisé souvent dans le débat scientifique implique une attitude réflexive de distance critique, pouvant remettre en cause les postures développées dans le chapitre dans lequel il s'inscrit. L'équipe de traducteurs recourait dans un premier temps à une traduction calquée sur la métaphore musicale utilisée en français, mais s'en éloignait carrément en trouvant que cela n'avait rien à voir avec ce que veut dire le chinois. Enfin, dans un deuxième temps, nos traducteurs chinois ont retenu une expression chinoise imagée « 争鸣 » (Zheng ming) qui veut dire littéralement que « de nombreux oiseaux sifflotent à qui mieux », mais littérairement, réactions critiques vis-à-vis d'un point de vue avancé.

3.3.9 Les remédiations majeures ou zones-passerelles

On peut en prendre la mesure concrète des débats à travers la transcription ci-dessous des échanges liés au titre de l'ouvrage et aux deux hypermots-clefs

---

[12] La didactique des langues est une discipline qui étonne par sa complexité dans la mesure où, selon Puren, c'est un ensemble de questions complexes pour chacune desquelles, par conséquent, les réponses ne peuvent jamais être que *plurielles, imparfaites, locales* et *provisoires*, alors qu'au niveau méthodologique, toujours selon Puren, c'est un ensemble de questions compliquées, et donc susceptible de recevoir chacune séparément une solution technique appropriée, c'est-à-dire *unique, parfaite, universelle* et *définitive*.

du titre de l'ouvrage « plurilinguisme » et « pluriculturalisme ». Dans un parallèle entre français et anglais, langues officielles du Conseil de l'Europe, le terme « plurilinguisme » fait déjà débat : il a fait l'objet d'une clarification dans le *Cadre européen commun de référence pour les langues* et se construit en opposition avec celui de *multilingualism*[13]. Cette distinction établit deux plans différents pour ces deux termes dont l'un est usité en français (plurilinguisme) et l'autre plus fréquent en anglais (multilinguisme). En choisissant, sans réel débat collectif il est vrai, le terme *multilingualism* pour le titre de la version anglaise, les coordinatrices s'appuient sur l'usage anglais dominant, ce qui occulte de fait la distinction du Conseil de l'Europe. La compréhension du titre par un lecteur potentiel anglophone impose sa loi dans la traduction en anglais du titre. Pour les deux termes « pluriculturalisme » et *multiculturalism*, une autre logique prévaut entre anglais et français. Outre la continuité sémantique entre « pluri » et « multi » appliquée à deux termes s'appliquant au « linguistique » et au « culturel », le terme « multiculturalisme » portait le risque que l'ouvrage soit envoyé aux gémonies par des lecteurs français associant une vision communautaire, contraire aux intérêts de la République française. S'ils n'étaient pas les seuls destinataires francophones de l'ouvrage, ils auraient pu cependant armer un débat franco-français qui emmenait l'ouvrage vers son public sur un grossier malentendu. Le terme « multiculturalisme » était donc exclu pour un titre français, mais celui de *multiculturalism* était bienvenu pour un lectorat anglophone, familier des catégories en usage au Royaume Uni, Australie, Etats-Unis, Canada… Ce débat crucial pour la visibilité de l'ouvrage et sa diffusion en « Occident », comment se profile-t-il en contexte sinophone ?

Dans les échanges, il ressurgit par un détour via le contexte canadien, tel que rapporté par Danièle Moore[14] :

> « C'est vrai que ces questions-là se posaient peut-être comme ça à ce moment-là mais ça a déjà évolué, notamment au Canada, où le terme *plurilingualism* en anglais a vraiment pénétré le marché intellectuel canadien, où justement personnellement moi je suis frustrée que le *Handbook* s'appelle *multilingualism* et *multiculturalism*, justement là les connotations culturelles derrière le *multiculturalism* sont liées à la politique canadienne du « multiculturalisme », donc qui efface le travail conceptuel qu'on essaie de mettre en place. »

---

[13] « On distingue le « plurilinguisme « du « multilinguisme » qui est la connaissance d'un certain nombre de langues ou la coexistence de langues différentes dans une société donnée. On peut arriver au multilinguisme simplement en diversifiant l'offre de langues dans une école ou un système éducatif donnés ». CECR, p. 11.
[14] Professeur à l'Université Simon Fraser à Vancouver.

Pour sortir des impasses créées par les contextes non-chinois, Fu Rong présente le choix suivant :

> (Fu R.) J'ai fait des propositions qui correspondent à peu près à ce que Joël a montré à l'écran. C'est-à-dire, pour le « plurilinguisme », je pense plutôt à une notion, à un concept. Alors que « multilinguisme » c'est plutôt un fait. (...) un constat d'existence de plusieurs langues, alors que « plurilinguisme » c'est plus abstrait, c'est une notion, c'est une vision.
>
> (Danielle M.)... et tout ça on peut le rendre en caractères chinois ?
>
> (Fu R.) Oui en caractères chinois, on dit « yuyan duoyuan 语言多元 », je ne sais pas ... « yuyan duoyuanhua 语言多元化 », ça correspond au « plurilinguisme ».
>
> (Georges A.). En plus c'est musical. (...)
>
> (Fu R.) Oui, mes collègues n'hésitent pas à faire des remarques, même si c'est moi qui l'ai traduit. Je ne suis pas très satisfait maintenant, j'hésite, parce que je dirais, le « plurilinguisme » en chinois on peut dire « duo yuan + isme», « duo yuan zhu yi », « yuyan duo yuan zhu yi ». Parce que c'est « plurilinguisme », on souligne ce « isme », c'est en termes de culture, dans le domaine de la culture, on prétend aussi une certaine pluralité. Mais, je dirais, même en chinois, quand on traduit en chinois, sémantiquement on est fidèle au texte français, mais en chinois, ça poserait peut-être deux problèmes. D'abord, phonétiquement, ce n'est pas très joli, c'est trop long. Ensuite, politiquement, idéologiquement, c'est un peu trop idéologique, quand on dit « isme ».
>
> (Joël B.) Tout à fait.
>
> (Fu R.) Je voudrais atténuer, parce que là c'est plutôt un ouvrage scientifique, une recherche scientifique. C'est pourquoi je préfère, peut-être, une autre option, on abandonne « isme », je dirais « yuyan duoyuanhua 语言多元化 ».5.
>
> (Joël B.) Bien-sûr, il donne plus de dynamique et d'évolution au phénomène, alors qu'effectivement le suffixe « isme » qui a été créé au début du vingtième siècle a permis de décliner capitalisme, socialisme, etc.
>
> (Fu R.) Voilà, c'est très idéologique et politique....
>
> (Joël B.)... et, figer beaucoup en théorie sur ceci cela.

A travers cet échange, le débat s'est donc déporté ailleurs. Il ne s'agit pas seulement de théoriser la pluralité, signifiée par le choix des caractères, mais d'éviter un marquage politique trop systématique et passéiste du terme « plurilinguisme ».

Le débat se poursuit, cette fois sur la dimension « politiquement correcte » de la pluralité culturelle.

> (Fu R.). Par contre, il y a un autre problème, une autre question en chinois, je pourrais dire, « la pluralité linguistique dans les langues », et quand il s'agit des cultures, c'est difficile,

c'est pas très joli de dire « wenhua duoyuanhua 文化多元化 », parce que dans le contexte, on n'aime pas très la « pluralité » lorsqu'il s'agit des cultures, des idées, par contre on préconise, les gouvernements, les autorités chinoises à accepter la diversité culturelle.

(G Z.) Comme chez nous.

(Fu R.) C'est pourquoi j'hésite : est-ce que je peux dire « yuyan duoyuanhua wenhua duoyanghua gailun 语言多元化和文化多样化概论 »[15], « la pluralité linguistique et .... « plusieurs voix », littéralement (...).

(Aline G.) Quoique.... on a créé un terme parce que « pluriculturalisme » ça n'existait pas, c'est le terme « pluriculturalité » qui existait. En fait, à cette occasion-là pour créer une rythmique, on a créé le mot « pluriculturalisme » qui se distinguait en effet vraiment/se démarquait de « multiculturalisme ». Donc on a créé un terme....

(Aline G.) C'est vous qui pouvez décider par rapport aux enjeux de votre contexte. Il n'y a que vous qui pouvez savoir ce qui peut passer.

Dans cet échange où les contextes chinois et français se reconnaissent une solidarité politique inattendue, « pluriculturalisme » apparaît comme une création conceptuelle, ce qui doit aussi générer en chinois une expression *ad hoc*.

La traduction des termes « plurilinguisme » et « pluriculturalisme », au coeur des échanges, pose problème. Les chercheurs chinois sont entrés à leur tour dans les débats concernant les définitions du « plurilinguisme » et du « multilinguisme », directement inspirées de la sociolinguistique et des conceptions du CECR qu'ils ont traduit en chinois. Il s'agissait pour Fu Rong et son équipe de se situer dans le champ des langues et cultures, et davantage encore de se démarquer des discours en circulation, tout en pariant la reconnaissance d'un nouveau champ scientifique en pleine émergence.

Quant au terme de « pluriculturalisme », sa conception est liée à un contexte qui se pense/se pensait comme une entité (« communauté imaginée, communauté inventée » d'Anderson, 2002)... et dans cette communauté qui se pensait homogène surgit « l'étranger ». La question pour les didacticiens à l'heure actuelle est de savoir comment utiliser ce concept pour en faire un concept opératoire dans la formation en didactique de la langue, afin de mieux préparer les étudiants à la communication internationale, mais surtout de travailler sur la « reconnaissance de la diversité » qui met en jeu des zones d'ombre ou « zones blanches » (Bertaux, 2005) des zones où non-dits, implicites et interdits se côtoient.

---

15 Traduction mot à mot : « propos général sur la pluralité linguistique et de la pluralité culturelle ».

L'équipe de traducteurs s'est alignée sur les conceptions propres au *Précis* et propose la traduction du titre de l'ouvrage dans le sens de « Introduction aux idées de la pluralité linguistique et culturelle » (多语言和多文化思想概论 duo yuyan he duo wenhua sixiang gailun). Le terme « idées » qui signifie ici littéralement en chinois, *pensées et réflexions*, est le choix le plus pertinent aux yeux du coordinateur. Il désigne ici le plurilinguisme et le pluriculturalisme en tant que notions, concepts ou visions sur la langue et la culture. Ensuite, linguistiquement parlant, le terme « idées » en chinois s'accorde très bien avec la double « pluri- » (langue et culture). Enfin, de cette façon, le titre en chinois est concis, clair et facile à lire et à retenir.

Quelques processus de remédiations conceptuelles sont ici développés qui se sont traduits par des interrogations, des approximations, des hésitations, des prises de décision mais aussi par des indécisions terminologiques. Avec la distance dans le temps et l'espace, elles ont pu être typifiées en partant de ce qui semblait plus ou moins identifiable, du transposable à l'appropriable, du moins transposable au non traduisible, engendrant des zones franches de transfert, des zones-passerelles de remédiation et des zones blanches de résistance.

4 Une posture spécifique pour les recherches sur le plurilinguisme : penser entre les langues

Le séminaire franco-chinois s'est construit autour de stratégies d'explicitation, de vérification, d'appropriation, d'ajustement, de contournement, de création et de prise de risques, mais aussi des renoncements. Mais il existe certainement d'autres stratégies qu'il reste à identifier. Toutes ont contribué à revisiter les concepts en contexte et à co-construire du sens.

4.1 Des zones d'intraduisibilité entre langues « proches »

Il a pu être observé que ce n'est pas parce que deux langues pouvaient être qualifiées de proches – français, anglais – ou appartenant à la même famille que les univers culturels et conceptuels qu'elles véhiculent sont obligatoirement proches. Ils peuvent au contraire se révéler très éloignés dans leurs « (di)visions du monde ». Lors des débats initiaux, Claire Kramsch (2009) avait bien montré que le terme de « représentations sociales » n'occupe pas autant de place dans les préoccupations scientifiques anglo-américaines que dans celles du monde académique européen. On lui préfère nettement l'analyse des *values, attitudes* (issues de la psychologie interculturelle), alors que les chercheurs francophones voient dans le choix de ces concepts des conceptions essentialistes et fixistes. Un autre exemple peut également être donné à travers le terme de *mobilities* : il n'est généralement utilisé aux Etats Unis que pour caractériser les « mobilités sociales » (Urry, 2005); pour la mobilité académique, on utilise de préférence le terme de *overseas students*, tandis que l'on connaît le succès du terme « mobilités » dans le champ francophone, qui tend à remplacer de manière générique le terme de « mobilité académique » et de « migrations » et à s'intéresser à toutes sortes de publics et de parcours.

4.2 Des zones de traduisibilité entre langues « éloignées »

Par ailleurs, ce n'est pas non plus parce que deux langues semblent éloignées ou distantes qu'elles ne peuvent pas partager des « zones intenses de traduisibilité » (Londei, 2010). En effet, les univers scientifiques marqués par la mondialisation sont perméables à cette constante circulation des idées et de leur(s) traduction(s), notamment grâce à la circulation des chercheurs qui sont aussi des traducteurs-interprètes, mais davantage encore des « passeurs de mondes possibles » selon l'expression d'Aline Gohard-Radenkovic : ils s'imprègnent, s'approprient diverses influences culturelles, parfois en contradiction avec les croyances et les idéologies en place, parfois allant jusqu'au détournement du sens, parfois détrônant les croyances et les pratiques en place avec les concepts venus d'ailleurs.

Ce que nous avons pu apprendre au travers des échanges entre trois langues et plus, c'est qu'à de nouvelles réalités sociales, politiques, économiques et scientifiques, dans toute société en mutation, il faut trouver des mots nouveaux pour le dire... Comme il n'existe pas de génération spontanée de concepts, les choix se font à partir d'héritages, d'un socle conceptuel dans lequel les traducteurs puisent, qu'ils revisitent sous de nouveaux éclairages conceptuels et en regard de nouveaux enjeux scientifiques, mais aussi sociaux, politiques et identitaires.

4.3 Des positions innovantes distinctes pour les lecteurs anglo- et sinophones

Par ailleurs, cette radiographie *a posteriori* des moments-clés de ces journées de dialogue franco-chinois a permis de mettre au jour cette quête à la fois de sens et de consensus à travers des pratiques collaboratives entre l'équipe de traducteurs et celle des auteurs, mais aussi au sein de chaque équipe. Mais elle met les auteurs face à leurs textes, mots, conceptions, postures, lacunes, convictions, évidences, implicites, bricolages... et surtout face à leurs contradictions. Les exemples ci-dessous donnent une idée des bourrasques sémantiques à l'œuvre, dès lors que le chercheur s'aventure hors d'un cadre monolingue ou d'un cadre linguistique qu'il ne maîtrise pas. Dans une nation avec une langue officielle comme la Chine, des rapprochements avec la France viennent à l'esprit, sur la base de ce monolinguisme d'état qui reconnaît cependant le droit des « dialectes » pour la première et des langues « régionales » ou « minoritaires » pour la seconde. Publier un ouvrage « occidental » (mais est-ce le terme juste ?) en Chine le fait entrer dans l'espace politique chinois. La question prioritaire pour un traducteur ouvert à l'innovation francophone est donc : comment faire entendre l'innovation au lecteur sinophone en intégrant les conditions de réception de l'ouvrage ? Traduire en chinois et traduire en anglais un même ouvrage ne relève donc pas de la même stratégie épistémologique. Quand un *global English* a déjà imposé sa loi, le chercheur est tenté de s'affranchir des conditions de réception de son texte en anglais et d'adopter, sans le questionner, de nouveaux systèmes conceptuels dont la circulation est dominante, se soumettant ainsi à la logique d'une « pensée unique » pour décrire la pluralité, une pensée unique fantasmée certes, mais qui a des effets déjà observables sur la légitimité de la didactique des langues et cultures étrangères, champ qui s'est construit dans d'autres langues scientifiques et dans d'autres contextes disciplinaires (Gohard-Radenkovic, 2012). Pourtant il est admis que la recherche a pour mission de déplacer les frontières du savoir, que le répertoire des disciplines s'inscrit dans une évolution scientifique et sociale qui a besoin de repères théoriques, tout en s'ouvrant à de nouveaux objets et questionnements. Si l'on adopte ce point de départ, il convient bien sûr de se positionner à l'échelle de la compétitivité internationale, mais aussi d'admettre que de nouveaux objets et modalités de recherche sont façonnés par l'hybridité des objets transnationaux, que l'internationalisation modifie le rôle social des langues et que la recherche sur les langues est elle-même transformée par un espace renouvelé par de nouvelles légitimités.

Références bibliographiques

Anderson, Benedict. 2002. *L'Imaginaire National. Réflexions sur l'Origine et l'Essor du Nationalisme*. Paris: La découverte/Poche (traduit de : *ImaginedCommunities*, Editions Verso, Londre, 1983).

Bernstein, Basil. 1975. *Langage et Classes Sociales. Codes Socio-Linguistiques et Contrôle Social*. Paris : Editions de Minuit/Seuil. (Traduit de : *Class, Codes*, vol. I, Routledge and Paul Kegan, Lonres, 1971).

Bertaux, Daniel. 2005. *L'Enquête et ses Méthodes. Le récit de vie*. Paris : 128/Armand Colin.

Bourdieu, Pierre. 1980. *Le Sens Pratique*. Paris : Editions de Minuit/Seuil.

Bourdieu, Pierre. 1982. *Ce que Parler Veut Dire. L'économie des échanges linguistiques*. Paris : Fayard.

Bourdieu, Pierre. 1984. *Homo Academicus*, Paris : Editions de minuit.

Cassin, Barbara (dir.). 2004. *Le Vocabulaire de la Philosophie. Le dictionnaire des intraduisibles*. Le Robert/Seuil.

Certeau (de), Michel. 1990. nouv. ed. *L'Invention du Quotidien. 1. Arts de faire*. Paris : Folio/Essais/Gallimard.

Demorgon, Jacques., Will, E. et Carpentier, N. 2007. *Guide Interculturel pour l'Animation de Réunions Transfrontalières*, OFAJ/Saint-Paul.

Ferreol, Guilles. et Jucquois, Guy (dir.). 2003. *Dictionnaire de l'Altérité et des Relations Interculturelles*, Paris : Armand Colin (Appartenance (sentiment d'), 18–25)

Fu R., Chen L., Dai D., Li H., Tan J. 2008. 欧洲语言共同参考框架: 学习、教学、评估 » (ouzhou yuyan gongtong cankao kuangjia : xuexi, jiaoxue, pinggu), Beijing : Presses universitaires de l'Université des Langues étrangères de Pékin.

Garfinkel, Harold. 1984. *Studies in Ethnomethodology*. Cambridge: Polity press

Gohard-Radenkovic, Aline. 2012. « Contre point: Le plurilinguisme, un nouveau champ ou une nouvelle idéologie ? Ou quand les discours politiquement corrects prônent la diversité », in Gohard-Radenkovic, A., Gremion, M., Yanaprasart, P. et Veillette, J. *Alterstic*en°2, août, ARIC /Métropolis/Université Laval, Québec: http://journal.psy.ulaval.ca/ojs/index.php/ARIRI

Kramsch, Claire. 2009. « La circulation transfrontalière des valeurs dans un projet de recherche international ». La circulation internationale des idées en didactique des langues, Zarate G., Liddicoat, T. (eds), *Le Francais dans le Monde*, juillet, 46, 66–77.

Lancelot, Claude. 1644. *Grammaire de Port-Royal. Nouvelle méthode pour apprendre facilement la langue latine*. http://www.google.ch/url?sa=t&rct=j&q=&esrc=s&frm=1&source=web&cd=2&ved=0CCYQFjAB&url=http%3A%2F%2Fwww2.unil.ch%2Fslav%2Fling%2Fcours%2Fa11-12%2FLG%2FCAS-FONC3%2FPR.pdf&ei=FyusU4rGH6TnygOa_IHoCQ&usg=AFQjCNErQK3KG7zxdyLKO3nksaXc16ADiQ.

Levi-Strauss, Claude. 1962. *La Pensée Sauvage*. Paris : Plon

Londei, Danielle. 2010. « Traduire les savoirs pour un savoir culturel mieux partagé », in Londei, D. Et Callari Galli, M. (eds). *Traduire les Savoirs*. Berne : Transversales/Peter Lang. 33–45.

Monsacre, Helene. 2010. « Traduire les savoirs : le point de vue de l'éditeur », in Londei, D. Et Callari Galli, M. (eds). *Traduire les Savoirs*. Berne: Transversales/Peter Lang. 21–26.

Pavic, Milorad. *Le Dictionnaire khazar, Roman – Lexique, exemplaire féminin*, Belfond, Paris, 1988 (traduit du serbe par Maria Bezanovska).

Piaget, Jean. 2002. nouv. ed. *Le Langage et la Pensée chez l'Enfant* (1923). Neuchâtel : Delachaux et Niestlé.

Simmel, Georg. 2004. « Digressions sur l'étranger », in Grafmeyer, Y. et Joseph, I. (ed.) L'École de Chicago. Naissance de l'Écologie Urbaine. Champs/Flammarion, 53–77 (traduit de: *Soziologie,* Leipzig, 1908, 685–691).

Urry, John. 2005. *Sociologie des Mobilités. Une Nouvelle Frontière pour la Sociologie ?* Paris : Armand Colin (traduit de : *Sociology beyond Societies*, Routledge, London, 2000).

Zarate, Geneviève. 2001. « La prise de risque à la frontière des disciplines. Propos en direction des jeunes chercheurs européens », in Paganini, G. (eds), *Distance et proximité culturelles en Europe*. Actes de la journée Jeunes chercheurs. Paris : L'Harmattan. 241-248.

Zarate Geneviève et Liddicoat, Anthony (eds). 2009. La circulation internationale des idées en didactique des langues, *Le français dans le monde. Recherches et applications,* juillet.

Zarate, Geneviève, Levy, Danielle, & Kramsch, Claire (eds). 2011/2008. *Handbook of multilingualism and multiculturalism/ Précis du plurilinguisme et du pluriculturalisme.* Paris : Editions des archives contemporaines.

Autres

Carles, P. *Pierre Bourdieu. La Sociologie est un Sport de Combat.* C-P productions, 2001. Production : Charifi V. et Y., Painchault C., Sasia B.

Synopsis by Claire Kramsch

This chapter reports on a research project on « plurilingualism in the learning and teaching of foreign languages », conducted between 2003 and 2008 by an international group of researchers. The research was published in Paris in 2008 under the title *Précis du plurilinguisme et du pluriculturalisme*, appeared in English translation in 2010 under the title *Handbook of Multilingualism and Multiculturalism*, and is now being translated into Mandarin Chinese. A small group of these researchers met in Beijing with the Chinese translators to discuss the process of translating the book from French into Chinese. Because of their common knowledge of French, the team members had been able to collaborate on this research project, but they faced fascinating challenges when they prepared their findings for a French publisher and, later, when they worked on a translation of the French publication into English for Anglophone readers. The chapter focuses on the difficulties encountered during the translation from French into Chinese for Chinese readers.

Like the chapter by George Lüdi (this volume), this chapter examines what Bourdieu called "the international circulation of ideas" (Bourdieu 1993: 263) and the structural misunderstandings resulting from it. When the lingua franca of international research teams is English, it is easy to dismiss these misunderstandings as cosmetic mishaps in the assumed global consensus on the meaning of scientific concepts and theories. But when the working language is French and the principal investigators are native speakers of French, trained in the French academic research tradition, some of the basic scientific assumptions of the project have to be unpacked, explained, contrasted with similar assumptions made by other non-francophone members of the team in their own scientific language. This imposes quite a different dynamic to research teamwork that presents both challenges and benefits.

The challenges in this case were enormous, for the team here was not only multilingual, but also multicultural and multidisciplinary. Some were anthropologists, others came from the fields of education, linguistics, applied linguistics, or literary and cultural studies. Their academic habitus bore the traces of different institutional histories, different funding policies, different publishing experiences. But the benefits were equally enormous. After the initial shock of realizing that notions that one had always taken for granted did not make any sense to other members of the team, discussions started to slow down, a reflective mood settled in, assumptions had to be made explicit, and the ideological and political bases of one's scientific inquiry had to be acknowledged and subjected in turn to scientific inquiry. The team thus experienced first hand what Bourdieu meant when he wrote about the need "to push further still the effort of reflexivity which seems to me to be the fundamental condition for the progress of scientificity in the social sciences" (p. 274).

This reflexivity is at work throughout the chapter. First in the working conditions of the research team itself. In the desire to free itself from any national or international institutional constraints, the team managed to work for five years without any centralized budget, even though it received financial and political support from a variety of sources including the home universities of the various team members and the France-Berkeley fund. It took great pride in its "intellectual independence" and in its common "critical stance vis a vis a monolingual vision of the teaching of foreign languages where linguistic plurality is conceived mostly under its minimal form, namely the addition of an L2". The global supremacy of English was viewed as "an incontrovertible fact that needed to be discussed with the Anglophone members of the team". What the team wanted to explore were concrete situations in which the teaching of foreign languages, itself a product of globalization, could be seen as counterbalancing the world-wide power of English. "If French was the initial working language, English became the second language. The debates took place at the intersection of these two languages, unequally shared by all." The idea of linguistic power and counterpower is echoed again in the decision by the coordinators to counterbalance the views expressed in each chapter by a counterview, similar to a musical point/counterpoint – a concept that revealed itself extremely difficult to translate into Chinese, that does not share this dialectical view of power relations (*voix* and *contrevoix*) and prefers instead a polyphony of voices.

The authors of this chapter document the strategies used by members of the team to deal with its plurality and its discrepant time-scales: tactics of intercomprehension between etymologically related languages, informal translations with another team member, requests for clarification, group summaries, visual aids, written reports of meetings etc. The negotiations around publishers' requirements and the expectations of a francophone readership with uncertain prior knowledge in a globalized economy illustrated dramatically the challenges of multiplicity today for researchers who choose to publish for a non-anglophone readership.

The decision, in 2010, to translate the book into English represented a second milestone in the life of this research team. The major challenge there was how to translate the word *plurilinguisme* into English. Based on the definition of the *Common European Framework of Reference* (2000), that makes the difference between *plurilinguisme* as an individual phenomenon and *multilinguisme* as a societal phenomenon, the team had deliberately focussed the book on plurilingualism as "the linguistic repertoire [of an individual] in which all linguistic abilities have a place" (p. 5) rather than on multilingualism, seen as the coexistence of different languages in a given society" (p. 4). The term plurilingualism in 2010 was not as well-known in the Anglophone world as the term multilingualism, so the coordinators opted for multilingualism in English, which had the benefit of encompassing both individual and societal linguistic diversity (Weber & Horner 2013). However, in our globalized research landscape, terms quickly change meaning, and plurilingualism has since then been adopted in Canada in the European sense, in part in order to distance itself from the controversial collocation "multilingualism and multiculturalism". Indeed, multiculturalism in France is often seen as undemocratic and a threat to the unity of the French Republic, and in Canada, multiculturalism is associated with Quebec identity politics, as Danièle Moore, a French team member now at Simon Fraser University in Vancouver, remarks:

> "It is true that these questions were framed like that at the time, but it has already evolved, namely in Canada, where the term "plurilingualism" in English has really penetrated the Canadian intellectual market and I am now personally frustrated that the *Handbook* is

called "multilingualism and multiculturalism", precisely because of the cultural connotations behind the term "multiculturalism" that are linked to Canadian politics of multiculturalism, and therefore erases the conceptual framework we were trying to put in place [with our book]."

Similarly, the notion of *mobilité* used by the French to denote the movement of students across Europe (study or work abroad) collided with the English term mobility that connotes upward social mobility, migration and immigration etc. The solution chosen by the French to use the term in the plural (*mobilités*) is awkward in English and doesn't necessarily clarify things.

The decision in 2012 to translate the *Précis* into Chinese came from the efforts of a Chinese team of researchers/teachers from the Foreign Language University in Beijing, directed by Prof. Fu Rong, to translate the Common European Framework of Reference from French into Chinese. Buoyed by their efforts to make the French CEFR accessible to Chinese foreign language educators, Fu Rong proposed to do the same for the *Précis du plurilinguisme et du pluriculturalisme*. The chapter documents this third episode in the life of the research team and the difficulties encountered between some of the team members and the eighteen researchers/translators from China. For these researchers the challenge was not only to find equivalents for notions that were clearly born out of a Western Cartesian tradition of intellectual pursuit and critical language learning, but to adopt a conception of linguistic and cultural diversity that was in part totally foreign to the current linguistic and cultural policies of the People's Republic of China. Finding the words to recast the *Précis* into Chinese was, for Fu Rong's research team, less a linguistic exercise than an exercise in positioning themselves vis-à-vis the current dominant educational discourse in China, and in legitimating a new scientific approach to language education in particular.

The encounter that took place in Spring 2013 in Beijing between the European research team and the Chinese team of scholars/translators had the distinct goal not only of arriving at a satisfactory translation of the *Precis* in Chinese, but of observing and documenting the very negotiation of meaning within and between the teams. This double reflexivity was meant to identify the various linguistic, conceptual, cultural, and epistemological strategies and categorize the processes used by the participants. It is this process-oriented socio-anthropological approach to the study of international research teams and the circulation of concepts across national borders that the authors of this article wish to highlight.

For example, the authors show how certain terms, like *diaspora transnationale* and *voix/contrevoix* were readily translatable as 跨国移居 kuaguo yiju or « national groups residing abroad » and 正调-反调 zhengdiao-fandiao or « polyphony » respectively. But one could argue that such translations gloss over the political debates over whether diaspora Chinese, say in Australia, are Australian or part of a Chinese « national group », and they avoid the problem of dichotomous thinking (voice/countervoice) in favor of harmonious plurality (polyphony). Similarly, the French term *politiques de littéracie* (literacy policies) that is already an American transplant into French got translated into Chinese as 扫盲教育政策 saomang jiaoyu zhengce or « education of the people in reading, writing, and arithmetic », thereby losing some of its policy-related connotations. And the concept of *mobilité* so dear to Europeans got translated into Chinese as 大学生国际校际交流 daxue guoji xiaoji jiaoliu or « interuniversity student exchanges » to clearly demarcate it from other mobilities, such as that of vagabonds and other vagrants from poor backgrounds roaming the Chinese countryside. Finally the Chinese researchers settled for a scientifically legitimate and politically neutral title for the book itself. The title *Précis du plurilinguismeet du pluriculturalisme* was translated as 多语言和多文化思想概论 duoyuyan he duowenhua sixiang gailun or « Introduction to the ideas of linguistic and cultural plurality » which allowed the Chinese to be at once faithful to the French original and to distance themselves from it by reporting on « ideas », i.e., thoughts and reflexions, that were distinctly born elsewhere.

The chapter closes with a reflexion on the very valuable research tools gained in the process of this research project in which translation played such an important role. As the two research teams observed : « It is not because two languages could be considered close to one another, as are French and English, or belonging to the same linguistic family, that the cultural and conceptual universes they vehiculate are necessarily close. They may on the contrary prove to be very distant in the way they 'cut up reality' ». Without the need to identify what was amenable to transposition, translation and appropriation and what needed to remain untransposable or untranslatable, what could be bridged and what could not, this team would not have been able to capture the conceptual mediation and re-mediation processes necessary not only to work in multilingual research teams but to conduct new and innovative scientific research. As Bourdieu remarked : « The implementation of the principle of *reflexivity* is one of the most efficient ways to put into practice the internationalism that science presupposes and promotes. » (1993: 264)

References

Bourdieu, Pierre. 1993. Concluding remarks: For a sociogenetic understanding of intellectual works. In Calhoun, Craig, LiPuma, Edward, & Postone, Moishe (eds.) *Bourdieu. Critical Perspectives*. (pp.263–275) Chicago: U of Chicago Press.

Zarate, Geneviève, Lévy, Danielle, & Kramsch, Claire. (eds). 2011/2008. *Handbook of multilingualism and multiculturalism/ Précis du plurilinguisme et du pluriculturalisme*. Paris : Editions des archives contemporaines.

Larissa Aronin and Ulrike Jessner
11 Understanding current multilingualism: what can the butterfly tell us?

Abstract: Understanding multilingualism has always been a challenge. The reasons are several. Firstly, manifestations of multilingualism at first sight are similar to those of bilingualism, so that often the impression is that it is "just learning an additional language." Secondly, researchers admit it is much too complicated to study compared to bilingualism. In this chapter we will consider the phenomenon of current multilingualism on the background of a significant pool of data collected in multilingualism studies up to now. We will discuss whether there is a need to distinguish between bilingualism and multilingualism, and explain the challenges multilingualism poses to researchers and practitioners by showing how its very nature is complex. Finally we will examine the implications of seeing multilingualism as a complex phenomenon, different from bilingualism in many important ways.

1 Introduction

The study of multilingualism may be thought of as stemming from the study of bilingualism. This is true, but at the same time, multilingualism is a separate field of study with its own subject and methods of research. The three stages of awareness in respect to language, 'monolingual', 'bilingual' and 'multilingual' (Aronin and Singleton 2012), roughly trace the history of coming to grips with the fact that multilingualism is increasingly crucial to contemporary science. The way multilingualism manifests itself now is more informative having emerged from previous appearances that were not always clear. This is due to the property of *liminality*. The term derives from the Latin word for "threshold"- limen. In the context of multilingualism studies the term 'liminality' is used to advert to the fact that many processes and phenomena connected with languages seem recently to have become discernible or noticeable. The realization of their importance derives from the recently linguistically connected events, developments and patterns, which play the role of a 'threshold'. It is the passing of that threshold which makes processes and phenomena visible. (Aronin & Singleton 2012;

Corresponding Author: Larissa Aronin, University of Haifa / Trinity College Dublin, Israel/Ireland, larisa@research.haifa.ac.il

Aronin, Fishman, Singleton & Ó'Laoire 2013: 13). Emergent properties do not exist at a lower level (Checkland 1981) but by now, multilingualism has unfolded to the extent that allows one to see its nature more clearly, to single out many important traits that were previously not discernible.

At present, multilingual practices are in full bloom worldwide, and multilingualism research is rapidly developing. The prevailing official attitude to multilingualism and language diversity is that of encouraging the use and acquisition of languages. It is likewise favourable to language revitalization, and elevating more languages to official status. In practice, multilingualism is still often approached from a monolingual perspective, and its appropriate study is frequently avoided, due to perceived difficulties. It has been noticed, not just once, that multilingualism presents a greater challenge to investigation than monolingualism and bilingualism.

This becomes obvious from the following considerations. If we have one entity for cognition, we can learn about only that one particular object or phenomenon, for example, either about berries or cars or languages. Studying the acquisition of one's first language, say, French, would be contemplating one phenomenon or process. When there are two entities for our cognition, we can compare them, in order to gain a higher level of understanding. Getting to know about blackberries in addition to strawberries or learning a second language, in addition to a first one, in our example, Italian in addition to French, would give us more understanding of berries or languages. With two objects there is a new opportunity for cognitive growth, by comparison, not available when our mind investigates one entity only. On the basis of *two* things, we attempt to make predictions with some confidence. But with *three* things, the possibilities of the human mind penetrating deeper into the matter of things, increase exponentially. The range of findings, outcomes and interconnections opens up. We may realize, for example, that predictions made on the basis of only two things (processes, phenomena) are not unfailing. Or, we may encounter a new manifestation that does not confirm the predictions based on the two systems, which we thought to be a uniform rule. For example, from studying a strawberry and a blackberry, we can assume that berries are rather small in size. But a watermelon is not. To give an example closer to our topic, from learning French and then Italian, we might be pretty sure that languages are written in the alphabetic scripts, but the first experience in learning Korean will demonstrate that Koreans or Chinese do not use alphabetic, but logographic characters for writing, and also that Asian languages are tonal, while Indo-Europeans are not. Having studied English and German, we may learn that in some languages there are many inflections, whereas in others there are fewer. We know of prefixes and suffixes, but until we meet a third language with infixes (an affix inserted inside a word), as in Khmer, we would not know about it. Of course, the order of becoming acquainted with different berries and languages can vary, and one can start one's cognition with very different phenomena, as with English and Chinese, but undoubtedly *three* things under study open up a flood of ways to encounter, compare and categorize, which is not possible with only *two*.

In the field of multiple language acquisition, Flynn, Foley and Vinnitskaya (2004) expressed this difference, and the importance of investigating the third language (L3) acquisition (rather than only L1 and L2) in a straightforward manner stating that "investigation of third language (L3) acquisition by adults and children provides essential new insights about the language learning process that neither the study of first language (L1) nor second language (L2) acquisition alone can provide." (Flynn, Foley & Vinnitskaya 2004: 3). They continue by arguing that "a comparison of L1 and L2 acquisition alone [...] is not sufficient in terms of our understanding of the human capacity for language. We need to investigate the acquisition of a third language (L3) in order to unconfound certain factors left confounded in L1/L2 acquisition. [...] We need to examine L1, L2 and L3 acquisition in close relation. And, in order to determine the degree to which L1 influences subsequent patterns of acquisition in the new target language, we need to consider L3 studies." (Flynn, Foley & Vinnitskaya 2004: 4–5).

But this would not be the only ground-breaking reasoning. Even more importantly, with more ways and items, *the variation* increases exponentially. Grouping and categorization, which is not available between two things becomes an important cognitive tool with three entities. (Of course we do not deny these operations within two language systems, which can be subdivided into subsystems, as grouping of suffixes, kinds of words, etc.). 'Three' allows comparison from various vantage points in contrast to only two. With adding only one additional language to the two, three pairs of comparison (L1–L2; L2–L3 and L1–L3) instead of one pair (L1–L2) appear. This 'two vs. three' common sense and philosophical contemplation is relevant for discussions on the relationship between bilingualism and multilingualism, and on the nature of multilingualism.

In this chapter we shall present some data pointing to the divergence of *bi*lingualism and *multi*lingualism, and then discuss the core feature that makes the two significantly different – complexity. In the last section of the chapter we shall elucidate the implications of treating multilingualism as a complex phenomenon, different from bilingualism in many important ways.

2 Bi- and multilingualism – the same or worlds apart?

There are many characteristics observable "on the surface" that make people think of bilingualism and multilingualism as the same phenomenon. Both are defined as an ability to use at least one more language beyond the mother tongue referring to an individual, or as use or existence of more than one language in a community or a country. Both bilingualism and multilingualism are studied by a number of disciplines from physiological, cognitive, emotional, pedagogical and social points of view. Cenoz (2013: 13) states that "[R]esearch on multilingualism may be seen as heterogenous or even disorganized, because it is based on different theoretical frameworks and uses a wider range of methodological approaches."

The long-standing assumption of laypeople, and even of some researchers has been that processing, acquisition, and use of three and more languages are the same as processing, acquiring, and using only two languages, that it is "just adding one more language". But the increasing amount of data we receive from neurolinguists, psycholinguists, sociolinguistic scholars as well as ordinary daily observations and experiences, do not let us be at ease in thinking so. The data which we cannot ignore indicate systemic and significant differences between bilingualism and multilingualism. By significant difference we mean that there are crucial implications for research and practical dealing with multilingualism – both in the area of language acquisition, and for societal outcomes. To substantiate this claim, first, we shall turn to the discussion of the core properties of multilingualism as a complex and dynamic system.

2.1 Multiple agents, diversity and complexity

Schumann (1997: 26) highlighted the complexity of third language acquisition as a "more complex process, whose complexity derives from the more diversified patterns of acquisition: various sequences of languages learnt, different ages of acquisition, different contexts and functions/domains of language use, varied motivations and attitudes, as well as different linguistic, learning and communicative sensitivity and awareness."

Generalizing neurolinguistic research on multilingualism in an overview, Goral (2012: 721) observes, that "it is plausible that multilinguals are *unique* in their ability to learn an additional language and their ability to activate or inhibit their other languages while communicating in one"(our italics – L.A. and U.J.). In line with many other researchers – not necessarily from neurolinguistics – who are aware of a sharp rise in complexity when adding even one additional language, Goral also points to the reasons for such a supposition. For a neurolinguist, these reasons are that the use of languages beyond two in speakers of three languages "adds to the variability, with multiple permutations of order of learning, levels of proficiency patterns of language use and language mixing" (Goral 2012: 720).

Researchers in structural anatomy such as Crinion et al. (2009: 4108) remind us of regional structural "differences between languages that are likely to have consequences on brain structures and function." Depending on the type of language, whether tonal, such as Chinese, that uses pitch to signal differences in word meaning, or non-tonal European languages, the language network adapts to distinct requirements. Crinion and her colleagues identified "a strong contrast" between Chinese speakers, both native and non-native speakers and speakers of European non-tonal languages in the two brain regions in the vicinity of the right anterior temporal lobe and the left insula (Crinion et al. 2009: 4108) in that "speakers of Chinese had significantly greater gray and white matter density compared with those who did not speak Chinese." This is only one example of how significant, and how infinitely diverse the individual structures of brain are in multilinguals.

Furthermore, clinical studies on aphasia, a disorder caused by damage to the parts of the brain that control language, provide data on the speed, extent and order of the recovery of languages after the impairment. Dissociation of languages, and later their differential recovery are frequently reported in literature (see for example, Goral 2002, Guisani et al. 2007). But no unified picture of language impairment for multilinguals has been found. This also points to the extreme diversity and unpredictability, lack of strict patterns found so far, in how three or more languages are located and processed in the brain.

More recent research in neurolinguistics (Higby, Kim & Obler 2013) more explicitly refer to multilingualism as opposed to bilingualism, stating that "[W]hile some studies of multilingualism have shown similar results to what has been seen in studies of bilinguals, certain unique properties of multilinguals are beginning to be noticed, particularly regarding early language representation, gray matter density, and speed of lexical retrieval." (Higby, Kim & Obler 2013: 68)

2.2 Switching costs and emerging qualities

There are also some puzzling facts discovered with regard to multilinguals which cannot be explained by ways used for bilinguals. The presence of the third language is logically expected to lead not only to qualitative, but to quantitative changes for trilinguals as compared to bi- and rare monolinguals. This is debated in the issue of trilingual *switching costs*. One would expect that trilinguals should need longer response times when switching from one language to the other simply due to the amount of data to be suppressed (languages not used at the moment). Bilingual research supplied evidence that the switching cost in bilinguals is mostly asymmetric: the response time is reported as longer when switching from the L2 to the dominant L1, than to the weaker L2, and not vice versa. It is interpreted as the need to inhibit the dominant L1 more intensively when producing words in the less-dominant language L2 (Kroll et al. 2008 in Goral 2012).

With trilingual participants in tests, the situation with switching cost is different; it is less clear and harder to explain. It seems that switching costs in trilinguals are not so pronounced as could be expected. Goral writes (2012: 723)

> Costa et al (2006) have demonstrated that this asymmetry disappears when non-balanced participants who are highly proficient in their L2 perform the naming task. When trilingual speakers who were proficient in both their L1 and L2 were tested, no switching cost asymmetry was evident between their L2 and the less proficient L3. Furthermore, no asymmetry was found for multilingual participants who were highly proficient in two languages; these participants showed no asymmetry in the switching cost between their highly proficient L1 and a low-proficiency L3, nor between their L2 and L3.

In their turn, Cedden and Şimşek (2012) investigated whether the representation of a third language in the mind provides an advantage in executive control processes compared to bilinguals. 10 high proficient bilingual Turkish–English and 10 high proficient trilingual Turkish–English–German speakers were given a language control demanding task and participants' response times (RTs) and the accuracy of their responses were analyzed. The results showed that the bilingual group responded to their L2 (English) statistically slower than their L1 (Turkish) while the trilingual group did not show any difference in RTs in their three languages. It was also found that the trilingual participants were far more accurate in their responses. Based on these results it is hypothesized that a third language system represented in the mind might have the effect of promoting experience or regulation costs of the executive control system.

Cedden and Şimşek summarize their study as follows:

> We conclude that a third language represented in the mind has the effect of promoting experience or regulation costs of the executive control system which might lead to the development of a more sophisticated and balanced control system. If an additional system expands experience/regulation costs and consequently the organization of the control system evolves into a more effective one, then it might further be hypothesized that the language control mechanism has a dynamic nature.

The somewhat unexpected findings on switching costs in trilinguals elicited a number of explanations. Goral (2012: 723) refers to the review of issues pertaining to switching abilities in bilingual and multilingual speakers by Ansaldo et al. (2008), who suggest that multilinguals may have stronger switching skills by virtue of having to switch between three and more languages, resulting in smaller switching costs in all of their languages. Another neurolinguist, Festman (2012: 209) suggested that the active use of three languages involves the inhibition of two currently unused languages, in order for the third, the current language of production, to be ready for use. In 2009 Festman extended Green's (1986) theory of language processing of two languages to three languages and on these theoretical grounds she believes that the

> additional need to inhibit not only one but two languages requires much mental resources and demands very strong language control abilities for production in a strictly monolingual mode. How demanding trilingualism is, can be different for the individual speaker, depending on a number of factors, such as individual cognitive abilities which shape language processing, the level of language proficiency of each language, the frequency and recency of using these three languages, the speech situation (e.g. formality, feeling at ease, stress, etc.), as well as the requirements in connection with the language output. (Festman 2012: 209).

Strik (2012), in her research into how trilinguals and bilinguals acquire interrogative structures of three languages, is on the same wavelength as neurolinguists in thinking that "the mere presence of a third language creates a different situation compared to bilingual acquisition; more precisely, an additional potential source of cross-linguistic influence." (2012: 49). While exploring acquisition of *wh*-questions, she wanted to find out whether qualitative differences can appear in Dutch wh-questions produced by bilinguals, Dutch-French and trilinguals – Dutch-French-Italian children. She found that "overall, the trilingual children are not at a disadvantage compared to their bilingual peers," and "the trilingual children do not show more difficulties with wh-questions in Dutch than bilingual children" (Strik 2012: 58). Here, as in the above neurolinguistic studies, the same question arises: how is it that with all the complicatedness of the structure of three languages it is not reported that trilinguals have more difficulties? Perhaps it can be argued that multilinguals have additional resources that help them to cope with the acquisition of one more language, without multiplying efforts, time and repeating the same path of acquisition for the third time.

2.3 Multilingual brains, skills and abilities and the M-Factor

There is a good reason for the advance of research into 'multilingual brains,' (term by Festman 2012) and such research is unfolding. An important indicator of increasingly intense research in multilingualism *per se*, rather than studying only two languages in the brain, is the comparison of multilingual speakers to other multilingual speakers by focusing on certain aspects of their multilingual development. Wattendorf et al. (2012), with the help of functional magnetic resonance imaging (FMRI), investigated sentence processing in multilinguals by comparing *early* and *late* multilingual speakers. In her turn, Festman distinguishes between "switching " and "non- switching" multilinguals who are thought to possess weaker or stronger control, and accordingly switch to another language with more or less precision. Indeed, the focus on comparisons of multilingual speakers to other multilinguals is methodologically a crucial step forward (as Festman 2012: 209 points out), if one looks back to the previous decades when research comparing a monolingual to a bilingual group dominated. Comparing bi- to trilingual speakers has been another methodological step in the development of research, as already mentioned.

In the realm of applied linguistics and psycholinguistics, the domain of crosslinguistic influence also uncovers the information compelling us to think about the difference between bilinguals and multilinguals. In her study of non-native lexical transfer De Angelis (2005: 14) analysed data that "illustrates a type of behaviour that speakers of two languages do not display, highlighting the uniqueness of multilinguals' behavior, and the need to view multilinguals as unique learners and speakers, rather than as bilinguals with additional languages." Studying a 50-year old French-Canadian speaker of Italian and ten English L1 university students, learners of Italian as a third language and Spanish as L2, De Angelis obtained evidence regarding the cognitive process of multilinguals "by which a lexical item is transferred from one linguistic system to another, and the speaker later fails to recognize the source of his or her knowledge in the original linguistic system" (De Angelis 2005: 10–11). This led her to propose a 'system shift,' understood as a shift in lexical knowledge from a source to a guest system (De Angelis 2005: 14). She states, then, that "the interaction between non-native languages cannot be assumed to be governed by the same principles that govern the interaction between the native and one non-native languages." (De Angelis 2005: 14).

Evidence from bilingual learners who learn a third language better than monolinguals in Iran comes from Modirkhamene (2011). This investigation explores the extent to which abilities in the previous language(s) predict similar writing abilities in the target language among learners with varying levels of competence attained in the target language. The study involved high intermediate and proficient EFL learners with Turkish and Persian (daily use), versus bilinguals with a Persian and English linguistic family background. Among other things, it revealed that trilinguals performed significantly better in English writing tasks than bilinguals, despite the fact that both bilinguals and trilinguals used the same language, i.e. Persian, as the most frequently referred language.

Moving from abilities to language learning strategies, we here present a study by Kemp (2007), who found very specific tendencies in how multilinguals use language learning strategies. It turns out that the more languages learners knew, a) the greater the number of grammar learning strategies they used, b) the more frequently they used them. Those are the important quantitative data, but they also point to a possible threshold effect for the use of grammar learning strategies which "may mean that, compared to L2 learning, augmentation in number and frequency of strategies used occurs to a greater extent during the acquisition of the third language, increasing more gradually in additional languages." (Kemp 2007: 257).

Neurolinguists, applied linguists and sociolinguists seem to have come to a consensus that with acquisition of the third language important changes occur. Berkes & Flynn (2012) found that the performance of the L3 study group on relative clauses was undeniably better than that of the L2 group and postulated that "results would indicate that enhancement took place in the learners' syntactical knowledge due to multilingual experience" (Berkes & Flynn 2012: 10). This is enormously important in terms of implications of multiple language acquisition for language teaching. In the area of pragmatics and early multilingual development, Safont-Jordà (2012) determined interaction between the three languages, Catalan, Spanish and English in a longitudinal case-study. Importantly she found "quite a different pattern" (Safont-Jordà 2013: 112) in the use of politeness strategies in the third language. The results of this longitudinal study confirmed the dynamic and qualitative change that takes place in third language acquisition. So far, identity modifications of all kinds have been traced. The impact of being trilingual rather than bilingual on education, friends and family interactions are intensively researched (see some of the recent studies such as Lanza & Svendsen 2007, on friends and family; Henry 2011, on L3 motivation).

As a result of this realization, and also by understanding the difference in the nature of bilingualism and multilingualism, specifically multilingual models of third language acquisition have been proposed. These models, although very few so far, explain and demonstrate how and why trilingual acquisition is different from bilingual. The Factor Model put forward by Hufeisen (2005, 2010) is important for understanding multilingualism, because it touches the core of multilingualism theory and introduces a serious argument to the heated discussions: it emphasizes the difference between learning an L2 and an L3. Whereas the learner of an L2 is a complete novice to non-native language learning, in the case of acquiring an L3 a learner already has the experience of learning his first additional language.

Another well-known model for multilingualism, a Dynamic Model of Multilingualism (DMM) by Herdina and Jessner (2002 already mentioned above) explains the individual language learning within the framework of Dynamic Systems/Complexity Theory. As opposed to the traditional visualization of the language learning process as a linear process, this model attempts to explain the actual real life processes of multilingual learning, and explains diversity and individual variability in the process of learning and in language mastery levels.

A dynamic multilingual system has properties that its parts do not have; that is, the acquisition of a further language leads to the development of new qualities in the multilingual system. In the DMM, this emergent quality is referred to as the multilingualism factor or M-factor, which is assumed to consist of multiple components, such as language learning skills, enhanced monitor function and metalinguistic ability, and cross-linguistic awareness (Jessner 2008, 2014). Multilinguals are believed to develop additional (cognitive) abilities that are not found in monolinguals, or at least, not to the same extent. The heightened metalinguistic awareness of bi- and multilinguals "refers to the ability to focus attention on language as an object in itself or to think abstractly about language, and consequently, to play with or manipulate language" (Jessner 2006: 42). This type of acquired awareness has also been observed to influence subsequent foreign language learning. Research on the additive effects of previous language learning on third language acquisition (cf. Cenoz & Jessner, 2000; Cenoz, Hufeisen & Jessner 2001) has linked effective language learning to the enhanced metalinguistic awareness and (procedural) language learning strategies developed in previous language learning. From a multilingual research perspective, metalinguistic awareness is seen as a developmental variable (see also Kemp 2007; Allgäuer-Hackl & Jessner 2013; Jessner 2014).

To sum up: we overviewed a number of studies in neurolinguistics, psycholinguistics, and didactics which point to differences between bi- and tri/multilingualism. These differences, which even given the indubitable similarities in these two phenomena, are significant for dealing with multilingual communities, as well as in language acquisition and teaching, and in education in general.

These, and other studies which have detected "threshold", "system shift," or other qualitative differences, as well as the appearance of theories special to multilingualism, leave little doubt that with more experience in learning an additional language (as opposed to the first experience in learning one) different mechanisms develop that wouldn't exist without having learnt and used the second additional language, that is, L3.

Thus, our answer to the question posed in the section subtitle, as to whether bilingualism and multilingualism is the same, would be: bilingualism and multilingualism are close, and overlapping in many ways but, as a bilingual turns into a multilingual, the phenomenon diverges (bifurcates), quantitative and qualitative differences become deeper, to the extent that the nature of the emerging phenomena changes. The main difference between bilingualism and multilingualism is the degree of complexity. Complexity is not only complicatedness, a matter of many aspects and factors coming together, which is a quantitative feature, but a qualitative transformation, since quantity increase leads to changes in quality. Complexity is very much a quality characteristic, which underlies the nature of multilingualism phenomena. In the next section we will discuss the complex nature of multilingualism in more detail.

3 Multilingualism is complex

One thing transpires very clearly from all the studies discussed above, whether they originate in the social sphere or in the neuroscience domain: an additional language beyond two [languages] crucially raises the level of complexity of learning and using them. That multilingualism and its aspects are complex has been noticed and remarked on by many. At the same time, in daily practice even those who have to deal with multilingualism, such as social workers, doctors, psychologists, administration workers or language teachers, may not perceive the difference between complicatedness and complexity. "Complicated" simply means compiled of many elements, and is therefore not necessarily complex. "Complex" involves multiple active interactions between the parts which lead to countless, often unpredictable, variety of outcomes. It is the interaction, not the mere number of agents, factors or parts that matters in complexity.

3.1 Concepts

Complexity is an increasingly appreciated perspective in different areas of knowledge and also in applied linguistics (see for example, Larsen- Freeman and Cameron 2008, De Bot 2004) and multilingualism. In brief, complexity thinking asserts: (i) that the whole is not the sum of its parts, and (ii) that the world around us is characterized by irregularity, fragmentariness and even chaos (cf. Capra 2005; Cilliers 1998; Dent 1999). The complexity paradigm operates with reference to the concepts of *multiple agents*, *complex interactions*, *'sensitivity to initial conditions*', *chaos*, and *emergent properties*. The presence of multiple agents, 'multiple factors', as they are usually termed in multilingualism (e.g. multiple languages, attitudes to languages programs and aims of language learning, teachers qualifications), are often referred to and enumerated. But the other concepts of complexity view are not so frequently evoked. Thus, even while pronouncing multilingualism complex, researchers and practitioners, in fact, often treat it only as a complicated phenomenon.

There are other, no less important features of complexity which constitute multilingual reality. We will discuss here only some of them. One important feature of the complexity approach is the *interaction* between the constituents of a complex system. "Complexity examines how components of a system through their interaction 'spontaneously' develop collective properties or patterns..." (Urry 2005:5)

An example of such a productive interaction is the recent development of social spaces of variation in the Berlin speech community and polyphony after 1990, involving a traditional Berlin dialect and the emergent ethnolectal variety of West Berlin (Dittmar and Steckbauer 2013). The specific social identity of Turkish-German adolescents, expressed by some markers of identity in oral versions of narratives, is the result of highly sophisticated interacting forces at work, such as attitudes and life views, rather than the mere physical presence of Turkish immigrants in Germany. Therefore, when contemplating multilingualism we have first of all to focus on and emphasize not the constituents (as we traditionally do) but the interaction, flow, and metabolism.

Sensitivity to initial conditions is yet another key feature of complex systems inherent to multilingualism. This feature materializes in the frustration of teachers, parents and language learners when it comes to unpredictability and diversity of results of language learning, the appearance of linguistic minorities and new languages in a society, or new linguistic varieties. In the complexity view, sensitivity to initial conditions is known as the 'butterfly effect' which was modelled by Edward Lorenz for the study of the weather, and the graphic model is therefore also dubbed "Lorenz's butterfly" (see Figure 1).

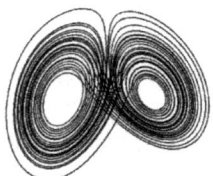

Figure 1: Graphic model of Lorenz's Attractor (Lorenz's Butterfly)

Lorenz's butterfly is a model which demonstrates sensitive dependence on initial conditions, that is, noticeable changes occasioned by the very slightest change. The extreme sensitivity to initial conditions of chaotic systems means that the very slightest change in those conditions can produce radically different results, and thus leads to unpredictability.

We can find a good illustration of sensitivity to specific factors in a study by Trévisiol (2012) of the development of reference to time and space, against the backdrop of the three languages, two of which belong to the same language family, and the third is typologically very different. In his investigation of the acquisition of L3 French after L2 English by the Japanese learners, Trévisiol established that the connection between the three linguistic systems is relative, and concerns various verbal forms in different ways. The interaction between L1, L2 and L3 depends on the particular grammars of the three languages, and the level of learner proficiency. Thus, Trévisiol found, for example, that Japanese learners of French (L3) do not transfer the expression of time references and spatial domain from their native language, rather their L2, English, serves as an intermediate language to construct hypotheses about the target language use. In this particular case L2 English is a better source of transfer, than L1 Japanese in the acquisition of L3 French (Trévisiol 2012: 149–150).

A wide variety of brain surgery outcomes, mentioned in the first section of this chapter, also demonstrate the dependence on the initial conditions, the high volatility and unpredictability of multilinguals' language loss, due to impairment, such as stroke or trauma, and also in recovery patterns. Thus the challenge researchers dealing with any aspect of multilingualism face is interpreting instability in an informed manner (see Jessner 2014).

Multilingualism, like all complex systems, displays situations and processes which can be characterized as *"on the verge of chaotic"*. But 'chaos' does not mean 'randomness', rather it is what Urry calls "orderly disorder" (2005:8). The difference between chaos and randomness, is that randomness follows no discernible pattern, but chaos does. Complexity is not completely unstable, it is irregular, but bounded (Parker &Stacy 1994: 35). Multilingualism in India, for instance, features the uncountable multitude of languages, constellations of languages in use, and patterns of their deployment (see e.g. Mohanty 2010, Kachru, Kachru & Sridhar 2008). It is impossible to deduce strict rules, but it is possible to search for patterns. The implication of the complexity approach in multilingualism is to look for patterns rather than for iron-clad rules, especially on the not- so- rare occasions when language use and acquisition look chaotic to us.

From countless individual interactions *emergent* properties evolve. Emergent phenomena are the products of the interactions between the parts of a system, but they are not only the sum of their parts. Emergent phenomena acquire properties that are different from the properties of their parts. Examples of emergent phenomena are plentiful in organic and physical nature: bacterial infections, and evolution, hurricanes, sand dunes, flocks of birds, schools of fish, communities of ants, and crowds of people – they all show unpredictable behaviour. In the multilingualism domain, emergent phenomena could be the atmosphere in a particular multilingual school, identities of multilinguals, a mini-community of a multilingual family, and also localization and representation in each particular trilingual-multilingual brain. The now confirmed special quality of bilinguals is the addition to their knowledge in their two systems L1, and L2, and the special quality possessed by trilinguals is beyond the sum of their skills in their two previous languages. These are 'emergent' qualities. We could not have expected an emergent property just from looking at individual particles. And so is with the M-factor which has been described as an emergent property of the multilingual system. The varieties of global English (Kirkpatrick 2007) are yet another example of emergent phenomena. It follows from the above that instead of looking for rules and exact predictions, a researcher of complex multilingual reality has to discover the patterns. Researchers have to aim at interpreting instability, rather than looking for stability where there is none. In addition, we have to learn how to detect, to sense the crucial points and thresholds (attractors) after which the bifurcation starts, and the system will change to an emergent one. We have to be able to do this on all levels, from international bodies to teachers at school. How to interpret the patterns- is the next question to be answered. Looking at emergence as a result of irregular patterns of behaviour, it is possible to come to terms with the unpredictability of patterns and discover the new ones.

3.2 Degrees of complexity

For the present discussion in this article it is important to point out that not all the systems are complex in the same way. Different fields of human activity display different kinds of complexity, and use diverse criteria for defining lower or higher levels of complexity. In general, they can be condensed to the number of items involved, such as the number of steps, algorithms, symbols, parts, etc. The intensity of a phenomenon, the amount of effort required, the rate and density of items under review – these are the quantifiable measures that testify to higher or lower degrees of complexity. Thus, in science complexity is ordered in a variety of systems. Quantifiable measures may be "luminosity-to-mass ratio in astronomy; power density in physics; specific radiation flux in geology; specific metabolic rate in biology; and power-to-mass ratio in engineering. "(http://nirmukta.

com/2009/08/29/complexity-explained-3-thermodynamic-explanation-for-the-increasing-complexity-of-our-ecosphere/).

For languages, the aspects that become more dense, or more numerous are many. It might be the number of words for the same situation available for a language user, or the number of grammar options to express an idea. The number of language modes (Grosjean 2001) available for a trilingual is seven as compared to a bilingual's two language modes.

Information theory operates the term of 'information' roughly defining the degree of complexity by "the amount of 'information' needed for describing the structure and function of the system" (http://nirmukta.com/2009/08/29/complexity-explained-3-thermodynamic-explanation-for-the-increasing-complexity-of-our-ecosphere/). Clearly, trilingualism contains more information, as it adds one more 'step' or 'ingredient' – one more language system with accompanying third culture, the third vocabulary set, third culture, one more phonetics system, and also metalinguistic awareness on how this third set of systems relates to the two others, separately and together.

For physics, complexity depends "on the degree of differentiation and integration, where higher differentiation and integration is related with higher complexity." (http://physicalspace.wordpress.com/complexity/) In bilingualism and tri-multilingualism, degrees of integration are profound in cross-linguistic interactions which are, of course, more diverse and numerous with trilinguals than with bilinguals. As for differentiation, this also increases exponentially, paradoxically, also due to cross-linguistic interactions. For example, the specific accent in L3 may be the result of influences from L1 and L2.

Finally, in complexity studies, complexity status is assigned to systems starting with those with three variables. The binary or bivalent systems are treated as simple. Monovalent or binary systems have different natures, and theoretically may be determined by two variables. Their behavior and outcome are theoretically predictable. Starting with systems involving three variables, the outcome is considered inherently uncertain, influenced by spontaneous inner and extrinsic influences.

"Complex order or 'complexity' is thought to be inherent to any multifactorial or multi-agent system, i.e. any system governed by three (trivalent complex order), four (quadrivalent complex order) or more (pentavalent complex order, etc.) variables of whatever kind." (http://www.itmewewhy.com/complex_scientific_method).

Complex systems also possess a quality of non-additivity and emergence, that is, their numerical value is not equal to the sum of values for the component parts, and the result is a new 'thing' (see M-factor in multilingualism, Jessner

2008; 2014). The explanation of this was partially given at the beginning of the chapter where we discussed the two vs. three things (see page 2 MS above).

Overall, the genuine, active move to the complexity paradigm requires three steps: (a) awareness, which will enable the shift in attitude to multilingual phenomena, (b) engaging in complexity approaches while researching or interpreting data of current and previous research and (c) dealing with multilingualism from a complexity theoretical approach.

3.3 Why is a complexity approach useful?

One of the important implications of applying a complexity approach to multilingualism is that it transforms the "black-and white" vision of multilingualism- related phenomena into a truly realistic and sensible, non-threatening, but rather "business-like" view. Things that we see as negative are not negative in the long run, they are just temporary, flowing representations of ongoing processes of change. From this it follows that in addition to the use of traditional methods, multilingualism has to be investigated through complexity methods, and seen via a complexity lens with a complexity approach (Herdina & Jessner 2002; Aronin & Hufeisen 2009).

The complexity approach has a direct reference to the focal topic of this volume: the challenges of multilingualism. What one might perceive as negative under particular circumstances, may be the unintended consequences of human activities, deriving from complexity and the inability to predict. There are issues that we think are problems, but they are not. Consider the statement by Cilliers & Preiser (2010:3) about diversity, its consequences as persistent companion to multilingualism: "Diversity is not a problem to be solved, it is the precondition for the existence of any interesting behaviour." Research has been carried out, which was aimed at revealing and demonstrating the beneficial sides both of individual and societal multilingualism. Indeed many findings persuade us of its positive impact on people's lives and the challenges encountered by individual multilinguals and communities. If we take a sensible view of this complex and multifaceted phenomenon there is a need to consider it not only from an openly pro-multilingualism or anti-multilingualism stance, but to weigh the knowledge accumulated until now in the most unbiased way possible.

How useful is the realization that multilingualism is complex and emergent? Why is knowing this important for us? Firstly, it explains why the double monolingual and bilingual approaches to multilingualism do not suffice, as they generally disregard the complex nature of multilingualism. More importantly, with recognition that multilingualism is complex and emergent, we can apply complexity theory and deploy the methods of study and ways of dealing with multilingual reality that complexity thinking offers. By adopting a complexity perspective, we argue that perceiving the challenges of multilingualism, be it in the domain of language acquisition or in a social sphere, as a function of its inherent complexity, would enable both scholars and practitioners to understand it better, and act appropriately under the circumstances. By thinking in complexity terms we now know better how to study multilingualism, and hope to be more successful in coping with the challenges it presents. Some of the implications of changing the conceptual angle of multilingualism studies to the complexity approach in language learning, teaching and education are shown in Aronin (2015).

Paradoxically, the complexity view, despite its outlandish looking fractals, and peculiar terms like 'attractor', 'Julia set', etc., is, in fact a more realistic approach than the traditional one. Indeed, what is closer to reality? To measure the coastline length from San Francisco to Los Angeles in a traditional manner, as an imaginary line between the two points, or follow each bay and inlet as in complexity measuring? In the latter case, the measurement might increase to 500 miles or more (Garcia 1991: 13). Complexity awareness is critically important for practicing teachers who work with diverse populations of pupils. The awareness will allow learners, educators and parents to reach a more comprehensive understanding of educational processes, and keep up with the new developments in human knowledge. It will enable all those involved to deal with the educational challenges realistically and confidently, rather than being stumped by a reality that does not fit into rigid forms. It will also be instrumental in avoiding the simplistic 'dilemma' of whether multilingualism is 'good' or 'bad'.

4 Conclusions

So what does the butterfly symbolizing a complexity approach tell us? It reminds us of the distinctive nature of multilingualism. From the complexity perspective multilingualism has a higher degree of complexity than bilingualism. In this chapter we have attempted to answer the two core questions on multilingualism: a) whether bi- and multilingualism are the same or different; b) what **is** the specificity and difference of multilingualism?

We have come to the conclusion that bilingualism can be seen as similar to, but also significantly different from trilingualism, yet both as variants of multilingualism. The crucial difference between bi- and tri/multilingualism lies in the degree of complexity. In multilingualism, whether we mean the individual cognitive system, the identity of a trilingual, or the sociolinguistic situation in a trilingual community, the phenomenon is complex and displays all the main characteristics of open complex systems. Like any open complex system, multilingualism in general, and each of its aspects is emergent, characterized by irregularity, fuzziness, sensitivity to initial conditions, liability to predictions of general trends or directions, rather than established exact rule-bound regularities.

The butterfly (complexity approach) persuades us that to understand current multilingualism means, first of all, to accept the fact that it is complex, rather than simply complicated. To this end, simply paying lip-service to the buzz-word complexity is not enough. It is necessary to (a) shift the mental attitude concerning multilingual phenomena, (b) apply complexity approaches to the researching, or (re) interpreting data of current and previous research and (c) treat multilingualism the way complexity phenomena should be treated, focus on new possibilities for research by reflecting on its essential nature, which is distinct from mono- and very often also, from bilingualism.

Acknowledgments

We are most grateful to Philip Herdina and Claire Kramsch for stimulating discussions and to Valentina Pittracher-Terek and Elisabeth Allgaeuer-Hackl for suggestions concerning the text. Thanks also go to Simon Rossmann for the illustration of Lorenz's model.

The research work of the first author of this article was supported by the Visiting Research Fellowship at the Trinity Long Room Hub Arts and Humanities Research Institute. The research work of the second author of this article was supported by the European Union and the State of Hungary, co-financed by the European Social Fund in the framework of TÁMOP 4.2.4. A/2-11-1-2012-0001 'National Excellence Program'.

References

Allgäuer-Hackl, Elisabeth & Ulrike Jessner 2013. Mehrsprachigkeitsunterricht aus mehrsprachiger Sicht: Zur Förderung des metalinguistischen Bewusstseins. In Eva Vetter (ed.), *Professionalisierung für sprachliche Vielfalt* (pp. 111–148). Hohengehren: Schneider.
Ansaldo, Ana Inés, Marcotte Karine, Scherer Lilian, Raboyeau G Gaelle. 2008. Language therapy and bilingual aphasia: Clinical implications of psycholinguistic and neuroimaging research. *Journal of Neurolinguistics* 21(6):539–557.

Aronin, Larissa & Hufeisen, Britta. 2009. Methods of Research in Multilingualism Studies: Reaching a Comprehensive Perspective. In *The Exploration of Multilingualism: Development of Research on L3, Multilingualism and Multiple Language Acquisition*, 103–120. Amsterdam: John Benjamins.

Aronin, Larissa. 2015. Current multilingualism and new developments in multilingual research. In: Safont-Jordà, Pilar and Portoles, Laura (eds.) *Multilingual Development in the classroom: Current Findings from Research* (pp. 1–27). Cambridge: Cambridge Scholars Publishing.

Aronin, Larissa & Singleton, David. 2012. *Multilingualism*. Amsterdam: John Benjamins.

Aronin, Larissa, Fishman, Joshua, Singleton, David & Muiris Ó'Laoire. 2013. Introduction. Current multilingualism: A new linguistic dispensation. In Singleton, David, Fishman, Joshua, Aronin, Larissa, Ó'Laoire, Muiris (eds.) *Current Multilingualism: A New Linguistic Dispensation*. (pp.3–23). Berlin: Mouton de Gruyter.

Berkes, Eva & Suzanne Flynn. 2012. Enhanced L3...Ln acquisition and its implications for language teaching. Danuta Gabryś-Barker (ed.) *Cross-linguistic Influences in Multilingual Language Acquisition*.(pp. 1–22). Berlin: Springer.

Capra, Fritjof. 2005. Complexity and life. *Theory, Culture and Society* 22(5): 33–44.

Cedden, Gülay & Şimşek, Çiğdem Sağın. 2012. The impact of a third language on executive control processes. *International Journal of Bilingualism* 16(3), 1–12.

Cenoz, Jasone. 2000. Research on multilingual acquisition. In *English in Europe: The Acquisition of a Third Language*, J. Cenoz & U. Jessner (eds.), 39–53. Clevedon: Multilingual Matters.

Cenoz, Jasone, Hufeisen, Britta & Jessner, Ulrike. 2001. *Cross-linguistic Influence in Third Language Acquisition: Psycholinguistic Perspectives*. Clevedon: Multilingual Matters.

Cenoz, Jasone & Jessner Ulrike. 2009. The study of multilingualism in educational contexts. In *The Exploration of Multilingualism: Development of Research on L3, Multilingualism and Multiple Language Acquisition*, L. Aronin & B. Hufeisen (eds.), 121–138. Amsterdam: John Benjamins.

Cenoz, Jasone. 2013. Defining multilingualism. *Annual Review of Applied Linguistics* 33: 3–18.

Checkland, Peter. 1981. *Systems Thinking, Systems Practice*, Wiley.

Cilliers, Paul. 1998. *Complexity and Postmodernism: Understanding Complex Systems*. London: Routledge.

Cilliers, Paul & Preiser, Rika (eds.). 2010. *Complexity, Difference and Identity*, Dordrecht: Springer.

Costa, Albert, Santesteban, Mikel. & Ivanova, Iva. 2006. How do highly proficient bilinguals control their lexicalization process? Inhibitory and language-specific selection mechanisms are both functional. *Journal of Experimental Psychology: Learning, Memory, and Cognition*, *32*(5), 1057–1074.

Crinion, Jenny, Green, David, Chung, Rita, Ali, Nliufa, Grogan, Alice, Gavin R Price, Andrea Mechelli & Cathy J Price. 2009. Neuroanatomical Markers of Speaking Chinese. *Human Brain Mapping*. December; 30(12): 4108–4115.

De Angelis, Gessica. 2005. Multilingualism and non-native lexical transfer: an identification problem. *International Journal of Multilingualism* 2(1): 1–25.

Dent, Eric B. 1999. Complexity Science: A Worldview Shift. http://polaris.umuc.edu/~edent/emergence/emerge2-r.htm

Dewaele, Jean-Marc. 2010. Multilingualism and affordances: Variation in self-perceived communicative competence and communicative anxiety in French L1, L2, L3 and L4. *IRAL* 48: 105–129.

Dewaele, Jean-Marc & Li Wei. 2013. Is multilingualism linked to a higher tolerance of ambiguity? *Bilingualism: Language and Cognition* Vol. 16, (1), 231–240.

Dittmar, Norbert & Paul Steckbauer. 2013. Emerging and conflicting forces of polyphony in the Berlin speech community after the fall of the wall: On the social identity of adolescents. In Singleton, David, Fishman, Joshua, Aronin, Larissa and Ó Laoire, Muiris (eds.) *Current Multilingualism: A New Linguistic Dispensation.* (pp.187–229). Boston/Berlin: Walter de Gruyter.

Festman, Julia. 2012. "Multilingual Brains": Individual differences in Multilinguals – a neuro-psycholinguistic perspective. In Braunmüller, Kurt and Christoph Gabriel (eds.) (2012) *Multilingual Individuals and Multilingual Societies.* (pp. 207–220). Amsterdam/Philadelphia: John Benjamins.

Flynn, Suzanne, Foley, Claire & Inna Vinnitskaya. 2004. The Cumulative-Enhancement Model for Language Acquisition: Comparing Adults' and Children's patterns of Development in First, Second and Third Language Acquisition of Relative Clauses. *The International Journal of Multilingualism* Vol.1, No 1, 3–16.

Garcia, Linda. 1991. *The Fractal Explorer* Santa Cruz, CA: Dynamic Press

Giussani, Carlo, Roux, Frank-Emmanuel, Lubrano, Vincent, Gaini, Sergio M. & Bello, Lorenzo. 2007. Review of language organisation in bilingual patients: What can we learn from direct brain mapping? *Acta Neurochirurgica, 149,* 1109–1116.

Goral, Mira. 2012. Multiple Languages in the Adult Brain. Faust Miriam (ed.) *The Handbook of the Neuropsychology of Language.*(pp. 720–737). Blackwell Publishing.

Green, David W. 1986. Control, activation and resource: a framework and a model for the control of speech in bilinguals. *Brain and Language* 27: 210–223.

Grosjean, Francois. 2001. The bilingual's language modes. in: J. Nicol (ed.) *One Mind, Two Languages: Bilingual Language Processing.* Oxford Blackwell, 1–25.

Henry, Alistair. 2011. Examining the impact of L2 English on L3 selves: A case study. *International Journal of Multilingualism 8* (3), 235–255.

Herdina, Philip. & Jessner, Ulrike. 2002. *A Dynamic Model of Multilingualism: Perspectives of Change in Psycholinguistics.* Clevedon: Multilingual Matters.

Higby, Eve, Jungna Kim & Loraine K. Obler. 2013. Multilingualism in the Brain. *Annual Review of Applied Linguistics,33,*68–101.

Hufeisen, Britta. 2005. 'Multilingualism: Linguistic Models and Related Issues', in B. Hufeisen and R. J. Fouser *Introductory Readings in L3*, Tübingen: Stauffenburg Verlag, pp. 31–45.

Hufeisen, Britta. 2010. 'Theoretische Fundierung multiplen Sprachenlernens – Faktorenmodell 2.0' in *Jahrbuch Deutsch als Fremdsprache* 36 (2010), pp. 191–198.

Jessner, Ulrike. 2006. *Linguistic Awareness in Multilinguals: English as a Third Language.* Edinburgh: Edinburgh University Press.

Jessner, Ulrike. 2008. A DST Model of multilingualism and the role of metalinguistic awareness. *Modern Language Journal, 92,* 270–283.

Jessner, Ulrike. 2014. On multilingual awareness or why the multilingual learner is a specific language learner. In Pawlak, Miroslaw & Larissa Aronin (eds.) *Essential Topics in Applied Linguistics and Multilingualism: Studies in Honour of David Singleton.* (pp.175–184). Springer International Publishing Switzerland

Kachru, Braj B., Kachry, Yamuna & Shikaripur N. Sridhar (eds.). 2008. Language *in South Asia* Cambridge: Cambridge University Press.

Kemp, Charlotte. 2007. Strategic processing in grammar learning: do multilinguals use more strategies? *International Journal of Multilingualism* 4(4): 241–261.

Kirkpatrick, Andy. 2007. *World Englishes* : *Implications for International Communication and English Language Teaching* Cambridge University Press.

Kroll, Judith.F., Bobb, Susan.C., Misra, Maya. & Taomei, Guo. 2008. Language selection in bilingual speech: Evidence for inhibitory processes. *Acta Psichologica, 128,* 416–430.

Lanza, Elizabeth & Svendsen, Bente Ailin. 2007. Tell me who your friends are and I might be able to tell you what language(s) you speak: Social network analysis, multilingualism, and identity. *International Journal of Bilingualism, 11,* 275–300.

Modirkhamene, Sima. 2011. Cross-Linguistic Transfer or Target Language Proficiency: Writing Performance of Trilinguals vs. Bilinguals in Relation to the Interdependence Hypothesis. *Journal of English Language Teaching and Learning*.No.7 Year 5/Spring & Summer 2011, 115–143.

Mohanty, Ajit K. 2010. Languages, inequality and marginalization: implications of the double divide and Indian multilingualism. *International Journal of the Sociology of Language.* 131–154.

Parker, David & Ralph Stacey. 1994. Hobart Paper 125. *Chaos, Management and Economics: The Implications of Non-Linear Thinking*. London: the Institute of Economic Affairs.

Safont-Jordà & Maria Pilar. 2012. A longitudinal analysis of Catalan, Spanish and English request modifiers in early third language learning. In Danuta Gabryś-Barker (ed.) *Cross-linguistic influences in multilingual language acquisition* (pp.99–114) Berlin: 2pringer.

Schumann, John H. 1997. *The Neurobiology of Affect in Language*. Malden, Blackwell.

Strik, Nelleke. 2012. *Wh*-questions in Dutch: Bilingual and trilingual acquisition compared. In Braunmüller, Kurt and Christoph Gabriel (eds.) (2012) *Multilingual Individuals and Multilingual Societies*. (pp. 47–61) Amsterdam/Philadelphia: John Benjamins.

Trévisiol, Pascale. 2012. The development of reference to time and space in French L3: evidence from narratives. In Watorek, Marzena, Benazzo, Sandra, and Hickmann Maya (eds.) *Comparative perspectives on language acquisition. A Tribute to Clive Perdue.* pp.133–152. Bristol: Multilingual Matters.

Urry, John. 2005. The Complexity Turn. *Theory, Culture and Society* 22(5), 1–14.

Wattendorf Elise, Festman Julia, Westermann, Birgit , Keil Ursula, Zappatore Daniela, Franceschini Rita, Luedi Georges, Radue Ernst-Wilhelm, Münte Thomas F., Rager Günter & Cordula Nitsch. 2012. Early bilingualism influences early and subsequently later acquired languages in cortical regions representing control functions. *International Journal of Bilingualism* DOI: 10.1177/1367006912456590 pp.1–19. Downloaded from ijb.sagepub.com at Universitaetsbibliothek Potsdam on August 28, 2012

Part V: **Professional and geopolitical challenges**

Lisa McEntee-Atalianis
12 Language policy and planning in international organisations

Multilingualism and the United Nations: Diplomatic Baggage or Passport to Success?

Abstract: This chapter questions whether multilingualism and multilingual provision at the United Nations (UN) is in fact diplomatic baggage or a passport to success. Drawing on an analysis of language policy and practice in the UN-system and a long-term ethnographic and sociolinguistic study of its smallest agency, the International Maritime Organisation (IMO), the chapter highlights the tensions between organisational language policy and micro-language planning and use, in which agency resides with the membership. It is argued that attention must be paid to changing sociological dynamics and the role of member agency in policy development in inter/trans-national contexts. The chapter critiques the call for the implementation of a restrictive multilingual policy and argues that attempts at fostering multilingualism within the UN, and similar sites of international engagement, are better approached through 'bottom-up' field and policy analysis in which processes of overt (planned) and covert (unplanned) policy and planning are assessed, making localised situations the impetus for policy decisions. This may require radically revising current systems in order to foster a variety of language regimes across the ecology of an organisation.

1 Introduction

Within the social sciences increasing debate about the impact of transnationalism and international contact on multilingualism has led to broadly binary analyses of its effects: as a nurturing playground for multilingual diversity leading to the development of complex and fluid language repertoires; or as a stymieing force, making ground for the dominance of linguae francae (see Liddicoat 2009). Themes of power, politics and economics, *inter alia,* play into analyses of different scenarios, with calls for language policy often made to combat inequity and/or to assess the 'cost' (financial and otherwise) of maintaining more than one language (e.g. see Ammon 2006; Fidrmuc 2011; Gazzola 2006; Grin 2008 and van Parijs 2001).

Lisa J. McEntee-Atalianis, Birkbeck, University of London, UK, l.mcentee-atalianis@bbk.ac.u

Traditionally the field of language planning and policy (LPP) has been dominated by models of macro-language planning at the level of the nation, orientated towards a goal-based framework of status, corpus, language-learning and prestige planning, however in recent years ecologically-oriented frameworks and studies, drawing on a consideration of the relationship between social actors and their environment have begun to emerge (e.g. see references in Baldauf 2006). These studies focus on multiple meso- and micro-level scenarios, such as community, family or institutional contexts. Some have taken a critical post-modern stance towards agency in planning, recognising that finding solutions to language problems and influencing changes to policy can emerge from different sources in any ecology. However, "[w]hereas there have been significant developments in the understanding of macro language policy and planning (i.e. at the polity level) [...] much less attention has been paid to micro developments, either in relation to macro planning implementation or in genuine micro-level analysis and action" (Baldauf 2006: 165–6).

This chapter aims to address this gap and demonstrates how LPP research and practice can move beyond a nationalist paradigm to accommodate the networks, structures and flows apparent in post-national societies and inter/transnational contexts. As we move into ever-increasing global connectedness many are now interwoven in professional and personal networks which transcend the nation, leading to complex patterns of interaction. Many are subject to multiple layers of governance and influenced by the burgeoning economic and political might of transnational corporations and supranational organisations, which far exceed the influence of some states. Models of language policy and planning based on the nation no longer necessarily reflect the experiences or needs of individuals and communities operating directly or indirectly inter/transnationally.

Within international organisations we witness the ideological and practical challenges posed by advocating and imposing restrictive 'top down' language policies, developed within a 'nationalist' LLP framework, to a membership whose language use appears at variance to that advocated. In this chapter we explore the difficulties of such an approach and argue against its utility, asserting instead that attention must be paid to changing sociological dynamics and the role of member agency in policy development in a global context. We advocate the perspective (as Baldauf 2006) that micro-language planning should be a field worthy of development and argue that organisational policy should be informed 'bottom-up' via an examination of locally emergent practices and operational constraints. This is demonstrated via the examination of language policy and planning in the multilateral organisations of the United Nations (UN). Drawing on an analysis of the UN-system and a long-term ethnographic and sociolinguistic study of its smallest agency, the International Maritime Organisation (IMO), we highlight the tensions that have emerged between organisational policy (in which agency resides at Headquarters with distant policy-makers) and micro-planning (in which agency resides within the membership). We critique the broadly-conceived aspirational call for the implementation of a restrictive multilingual policy and argue that attempts at fostering multilingualism within the UN and similar sites of international integration are better approached through a stringent process of field and policy analysis in which processes of overt (planned) and covert (unplanned) policy and planning are reviewed allowing localised situations and needs to become the impetus for policy decisions. It is argued that reforms and changes to planning where language problems arise should be carried out via a detailed examination of circulating ideologies/discourses, practices and needs across the various levels and sectors of the organisation, in synergy with a consideration of pressing pragmatic (economic/workload) constraints. This may demand overhauling current systems in order to creatively develop a combination of language regimes and will require the skills of advisors and planners who are adept at understanding the context in which planning is required.

The UN is a unique organisational ecology in which to research and explore these issues, although its daily interactional challenges undoubtedly reflect those of other international organisations and corporations. Its membership includes a diverse group of individuals: those who directly support its functioning (the Secretariat and related support workers, e.g. language specialists); and an elite body of transient international representatives, who, in principle at least, strive to uphold the Organisational precepts of fairness and equality through the development of treaties and resolutions designed to improve conditions for humanity and the environment. Their work demands diplomacy and careful negotiation, for in striving towards these 'common' goals individuals seek to champion national interests and preferences. Where conflicts arise, these often reflect issues developing externally in 'the field', with concomitant power hierarchies played out institutionally. Decisions made and the subsequent enactment of legal instruments create seismic shifts in world politics and global conditions (see Duchêne 2008: 20). The UN is therefore a powerful 'institution' in which language plays an essential role in its functioning and in the construction and representation of its identity (see McEntee-Ataliani 2011, 2013).

Since the first General Assembly Resolution 2 (I) in 1946, the United Nations (UN) has championed multilingualism and cultural diversity through the promotion and support of six official languages and a varied[1] number of working

---

1 The UN in New York supports two working languages (English & French); however their number differs from one UN organisation to the next. For example the UN Economic Commission for Africa (UNECA) proposed the use of Portuguese as a working language within the Commission

languages. However despite this *de jure* set up the *de facto* reality has seen a continued imbalance in the support given to these languages and in the linguistic practices of its membership, who have overwhelmingly favoured English (Piron 1980, 1994; McEntee-Atalianis 2006, 2008, 2010). Attempts have been made at Headquarters to redress this imbalance through rigorous inspections of the status of multilingual implementation across the system and via internal processes of review and reform across its organisations[2], the most recent precipitated by an inspection in 2011. The UN has been vociferous in its continued support of multilingual provision citing its commitment to cultural diversity. However increasing financial and administrative burdens, global challenges and realities have led to the emergence of regulations, recommendations and practices that run counter to this ideal.

The chapter first describes the status of multilingualism in the UN system and problems of its implementation system-wide and specifically in its smallest agency. Drawing on this description it then recommends changes to the practice of review and reform and discusses a transformational model for policy and planning applicable to other multilingual organisations and/or sites of inter/transnational integration.

2 The status of multilingualism in the United Nations System Organisations

2.1 History

The seriousness with which the United Nations has approached the issue of multilingualism and in particular the parity afforded to its official and working languages system-wide has been demonstrated in a number of activities since its inception, including: a series of resolutions supporting multilingualism devel-

---

due to the large number of African member states who use the language. The International Maritime Organisation (IMO) has three working languages – English, French and Spanish. Some organisations support more working than official languages. Note too that the distinction between 'Official' and 'Working' Languages differs from organisation to organisation.

2 'Organisation' spelt with a capital 'O' will be used to refer to the entire UN system (including all of its agencies) and its Headquarters in New York; 'organisation' with a lower case 'o' refers to individual agencies.

oping from its initial resolution in February 1946[3]; internal and external seminars and language days promoting multilingualism; and in 2008 and 2012, the appointment of a 'Co-ordinator', a senior Secretarial official (the Under-Secretary-General for Communications and Public Information, in addition to senior staff in other organisations) to address questions on multilingualism.

In its most recent resolution (65/311: 1) the UN reiterates its commitment to multilingualism, noting that the General Assembly:

'*Recogniz[es]* that the United Nations pursues multilingualism as a means of promoting, protecting and preserving diversity of languages and cultures globally,

Recogniz[es] also that genuine multilingualism promotes unity in diversity and international understanding, and recognizing the importance of the capacity to communicate to the peoples of the world in their own languages, including in formats accessible to persons with disabilities,

[and] stress[es] the need for strict observance of the resolutions and rules establishing language arrangements for the different bodies and organs of the United Nations...'

Throughout its long history the Organisation has struggled to redress what it sees as an imbalance in the use and provision afforded to the official and working languages and in its most recent review of multilingual implementation across the UN network it stresses once more a need for action.

2.2 Contemporary concerns: The 2011 Joint Inspection Report (JIU/REP/2011/4)

In 2010 the Joint Inspection Unit (JIU) of the United Nations[4] was tasked to review the nature of multilingual provision across the UN system in order to (re)assess its

---

[3] These include: 2480 B (XXIII) of 21 December 1968, 42/207 C of 11 December 1987, 47/135 of 18 December 1992, 50/11 of 2 November 1995, 52/23 of 25 November 1997, 54/64 of 6 December 1999, 56/262 of 15 February 2002, 59/309 of 22 June 2005, 61/121 B of 14 December 2006 and 61/236 and 61/244 of 22 December 2006, 61/266 of 8 June 2007, 63/100 B of 5 December 2008, 63/248 of 24 December 2008, 63/280 of 8 May 2009 and 63/306 30 September 2009, 65/107 B of 10 December 2010, 65/245 of 24 December 2010 and 65/247 of 24 December 2010 and 65/311 of 19 July 2011.
[4] The JIU is an independent unit of the UN tasked to monitor service efficiency and financial management. Their mandate is to independently review, analyse and evaluate current systems in order to enhance management and coordination across the UN system.

rationale, strategy and language policies/practices in order to make recommendations with respect to its implementation. 25 organisations participated in the study and the inspectors focussed on five main domains (conference provision; institutional partnerships; outreach; recruitment and training). Their work was published in 2011 and responded to in the General Assembly of June 2012 by the Secretary General of the United Nations on behalf of the United Nations system organizations (A/67/78/Add.1), and also, in light of nuanced recommendations, by the Secretary Generals of its satellite organisations/agencies (see discussion below with respect to the response by the SG of IMO). One of its main objectives was to assess equality in provision and language use among the official and working languages of the secretariats and by members and stakeholders of the organisations. This was explored beyond the purview of budget and entailed a qualitative analysis of the current situation as reported by Secretariat personnel in surveys and interviews.

The report details the widespread use of multiple languages within its organisations, however it stresses the overall dominance of English as a consequence of economic and pragmatic constraints. Whilst failing to acknowledge external pressures, it is critical of the executive heads who it perceives are lacking in their responsibility to ensure parity amongst the official and working languages within secretariats and further expresses disappointment towards the ineffective role of the 'Co-ordinator of Multilingualism', noting a lack of strategy and co-operation among staff in the co-ordination of multilingual policy and objectives. The report emphasises the need for both organisations and Member States to address the increasing hegemony of English and the imbalance between the UN languages, which the authors see as running counter to the founding principles of the Organisation – to ensure participatory equality via linguistic means. Member States and UN staff, the report argues, ultimately must decide whether pragmatism reigns over linguistic rights and the benefits of multilingualism.

Noting the 'piecemeal and fragmented approach' (p.iv) to multilingualism across the UN system, and the fact that not all organisations have a language policy, the document calls for a "One UN policy on Multilingualism" under the institutional umbrella of the United System Chief Executives Board for Coordination (CEB).' (p. iv). This would involve establishing a working group with representation from each UN organisation tasked to identify and solve the difficulties posed by the implementation of a multilingual policy ensuring parity amongst its official and working languages in different domains of use (i.e. the Secretariat; in meetings; documentation; web pages; outreach; field work etc.). The document calls on numerous groups, including UN personnel, Member States, stakeholders, language experts, IT specialists to support and encourage this policy and emphasises the 'collective and shared responsibility' (iv) of all.

Fifteen recommendations were made to improve the current situation; four intended for the legislative bodies of the UN and 11 addressed to executive heads (EHs). These include (in summary):
- the appointment of a 'Co-ordinator for Multilingualism';
- the development of a unified definition of 'official' and 'working' languages;
- staff (dependant on duties) to be fluent in one working language and have 'good knowledge' of a second;
- frequent assessment of user need in the official languages to ensure equitable language use and develop appropriate strategies to support multilingualism;
- development of a working group to support the sharing of resources in order to limit costs and enhance the efficiency and productivity of conference and language services;
- budgetary planning to support language services for any new institutional bodies;
- awareness and compliance with agreements between the UN and the International Associations of Conference Interpreters and Translators;
- ensuring resources for language examination training and succession planning;
- the development of multilingual websites supporting all official and working languages;
- the promotion and support of 'language-related events' to enhance international awareness of the challenges of multilingualism and to encourage partnerships with internal and external parties (e.g. Member States, academia);
- field work (e.g. humanitarian, peace-keeping) to be undertaken and made available in all official and working languages and the beneficiary's local language(s); and
- legislative bodies to support all necessary arrangements to ensure the delivery of 'core' work in all of the working and official languages of the organisation.

In his response to the report (A/67/78/Add.1) Ban Ki-moon, on behalf of the participating UN system organisations, asserts the continued commitment by the UN to multilingualism and notes that despite the report creating an impression of a "broken" (p. 3) system the organisation generally supports the findings and recommendations made. These must however be tempered by a consideration of increasingly reduced or 'stagnant' budgets and therefore should be usefully tested, where appropriate, by a cost-benefit analysis. A resolution (65/311), incorporating many of the recommendations, with additional commitments, was formally adopted by the General Assembly on 19 July 2011.

These recommendations remain untested, and in some instances, aspirational. The following explores their general applicability and potential long-term success to enhance multilingualism in the UN, drawing on data derived from a long-term study of multilingualism within its smallest agency[5], 'The International Maritime Organisation' (IMO)[6]. Via a consideration of IMO's *modus operandi*, and recent reforms to organisational procedures, an evaluation and critique of the recommendations and suggested uniform macro-policy approach to multilingual implementation across the UN system will be explored. We consider how the UN might take forward a more detailed 'organisation by organisation' and scientifically-informed review of current operating conditions and language practices, which in turn will create a more robust and informed platform from which to further develop a nuanced model for status planning in each of its organisations. The latter has implications for further research and application in other international organisations and settings.

3 The International Maritime Organisation (IMO)

3.1 Brief history and background

The 'Inter-Governmental Maritime Consultative Organisation' (IMCO) was formally established in London in 1959, tasked to deal with issues of ship safety and the prevention of pollution at sea. Since then its remit has broadened and in 1982 its name changed to 'The International Maritime Organisation' (IMO). It currently boasts a membership of 170 Member States with three Associate Members; employs approximately 370 staff and has an annual budget of approximately $50,000,000. It is responsible for the development of codes, conventions, recommendations and their implementation. Its mission and strategic plan (2012–2017) is to "... promote safe, secure, environmentally sound, efficient and sustainable shipping through cooperation...." Resolution A.1037(27).

---

[5] Smallest in terms of number of personnel
[6] IMO is reported as participating in the JIU/REP/2011/4 however individualised responses are not available in the report.

3.2 Modus operandi – in principle and practice

3.2.1 Organisational structure

The organisation operates as the UN Headquarters in New York with a hierarchical structure (see Figure 1 below) consisting of: an Assembly (the ultimate decision-making body), Council and five policy-making committees: Maritime Safety (MSC), Marine Environment Protection (MEPC), Legal (LC), Technical Cooperation (TC) and a Facilitation Committee (FC). Subsidiary bodies (subcommittees/working groups) arise as required to service the technical/scientific demands of the work of the Committees (see McEntee-Atalianis, 2006 for more details).

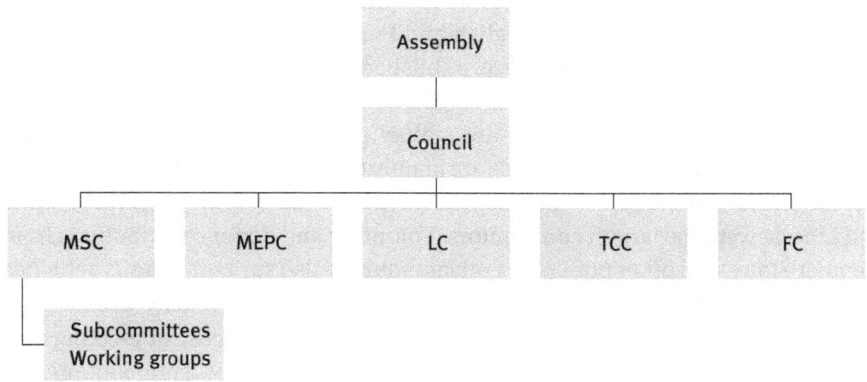

Figure 1: Structure of IMO

The Organisation is managed by the Secretary General, Mr Koji Sekimizu, assisted by six Divisional Directors. Language provision is predominantly the responsibility of the 'Conference Division'.

3.2.2 Language policy & provision

IMO has no official language policy, however in line with the UN (New York) it operates with six 'official' languages: Arabic, Chinese, English, French, Russian and Spanish. In contrast to the UN Headquarters it also boasts an additional working language, Spanish, therefore supporting three with the addition of English and French. All discussion in the Assembly, Council and committees are supported by simultaneous interpretation into the official languages and all documentation for agenda items is provided in the working languages, with the exception of 'information' papers. These can be submitted in one of the official languages, according to the language choice of the submitting delegation. Documents (i.e. recommendations, reports, resolutions) arising from Assembly and its subsidiary organs are first developed in one official language and then translated into the remaining five once agreement on the final form is reached. Interpretation for sub-committee meetings is restricted with provision given only to English, French, Russian and Spanish. Working groups are not supported by interpretation services and predominantly function in English.

Conventions are available in the working languages, with many also available in the official languages; Assembly Resolutions have been available in English and French from 1959, in Spanish (from 1965), in Russian (from 1975), in Chinese (from 1979) and in Arabic, (from 1985). Other IMO documents are generally available in the working languages (English and French from 1959 and Spanish from 1985). National texts of treaties are published in the official language of the country with some also appearing in English, French or German.

Costs within the organisation are mainly shared amongst the 170 Member States and Associate Members. These are mainly calculated in relation to a flat base fee: the tonnage of the States' merchant ships and its ability to pay. In 2012 Panama and Liberia were the largest contributors. Voluntary and donor contributions from Member States and other public and private sources also support various activities of the organisation. Some funding is also generated from the agencies' commercial activities and indirectly from interest on assets. In 2012 the cost of meeting personnel (including interpreters, translators and temporary workers) amounted to approximately £790,000 GBP, constituting 2.6% of the annual budget[7].

As of June 2013, 60 personnel were employed within the 'Translation Services'[8] of the Conference Division with its constituency shown in Table 1.

A further 14 were employed to support the Word Processing Unit: three in the English Unit; five in French and six in Spanish.

3.2.3 Internal language practice

Despite these arrangements ethnographic, sociolinguistic and desk research undertaken to investigate language policy and practice within the organisation over a period of a decade has demonstrated that in practice there is an imbalance

---

[7] Note this excludes other additional costs such as staff training and documentation.
[8] Not all were translators; some were administrators, clerks or word processing operators; others editors and technical writers.

Table 1: Number employed in the Translation Services at IMO (2013)

Terminology and Reference Section	3
Translation Services	
Arabic	4
Chinese	4
English	3
French	13
Russian	6
Spanish	13

in the use and provision of official and working languages, with the majority of employees and delegates exploiting English.

3.2.3.1 Language choice in plenary

In 2006 the language choice of delegates participating in one of the major committees: the 53rd session of the Marine Environment Protection Committee (MEPC) was investigated (McEntee-Atalianis 2006). This committee sat for extended debate (approximately 40 hours of plenary discussion) over a period of a week. 765 delegates attended, including representatives of member states, associate members, UN and specialised agency staff, observers and IMO secretariat staff, the Chair (a Cypriot delegate) and vice-Chair (an Indian delegate).

Of 751 interventions to the plenary discussion, 88% were in English. Excluding the contributions by the Chair and Secretariat, (which were all in English), this figure reduces slightly to 83.5%. Findings revealed that despite the opportunity to exploit simultaneous interpretation by some, delegates chose to function in a lingua franca (notably English); some even code-switched (see Table 2 below, McEntee-Atalianis 2006: 348): 73 member governments and inter/non-governmental delegations made spoken interventions; 34 had the opportunity (theoretically) to use at least one of their national languages and 19 a working language of their organisation (English). Figures of the actual (A) and potential (P) contributions by delegates in one of their national/working languages are presented in Table 3 below[9] (McEntee-Atalianis 2006: 349):

---

9 Certain considerations need to be taken into account when analysing this data however. The Panamanian delegation was represented by an English national and therefore spoke English.

Table 2: Language used throughout plenary

Language	All participants % (Number)	Excluding Contributions by the Chair & Secretariat
English	88.41% (664)	84.15% (462)
Spanish	5.05% (38)	6.92% (38)
Russian	2.79% (21)	3.82% (21)
Chinese	2.26% (17)	3.09% (17)
French	0.79% (6)	1.09% (6)
Arabic	0.53% (4)	0.72% (4)
Russian & English (Code-switching)	0.13% (1)	0.18% (1)

Table 3: Number of potential (P) and actual (A) interventions in an official national/working

Arabic (A/P)	Chinese	English	French	Russian (A/P)	Spanish (A/P)
1. Bahrain (0/1)	1. China (17)	1. Australia (13)	1. France (6)	1. Russia (18/19)	1. Argentina (4)
2. Egypt (2/2)		2. Bahamas (9)		2. Ukraine (3)	2. Chile (3)
3. Saudi Arabia (2/14)		3. Canada (8)			3. Ecuador (2)
		4. Dominica (1)			4. Mexico (5)
		5. Honduras (1)			5. Panama (0/24)
		6. India (28)			6. Spain (14)
		7. Ireland (8)			7. Uruguay (1)
		8. Jamaica (1)			8. Venezuela (9)
		9. Liberia (13)			
		10. Malta (4)			
		11. Marshall Islands (11)			
		12. New Zealand (6)			

Also, it is common practice in Bahrain and Saudi Arabia to conduct business through the medium of English; this may explain the high preference for the use of English by these delegations.

Arabic (A/P)	Chinese	English	French	Russian (A/P)	Spanish (A/P)
		13. Pakistan (1)			
		14. Philippines (1)			
		15. Singapore (18)			
		16. S. Africa (5)			
		17. U.K. (37)			
		18. U.S.A. (32)			
		19. Vanuatu (5)			
		20. 19 International organizations (39)			
Total: 4/17	Total: 17/17	Total: 241/241	Total = 6/6	Total = 21/22	Total = 38/62

English was the national/official language of 19 delegations and the working language of a further 19 inter/non-governmental agencies, (i.e. 52% of those making contributions to the plenary.) Of those delegations (20) for whom a national language was not supported in plenary all used English as a lingua franca. Other languages supported by interpretation were used by comparatively few, as shown in Figure 2 below:

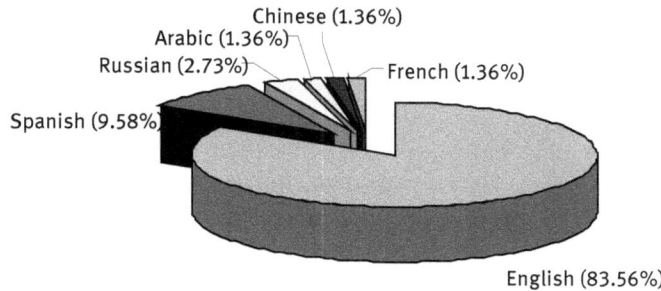

Figure 2: Percentage of delegations using each of the six official languages of IMO in the plenary of MEPC

In addition to spoken contributions, documents were submitted to plenary in support of agenda items. Submissions were made by 62 delegations. Despite the opportunity to submit these documents in the organisation's three working languages 97.3% (145 documents) were originally submitted in English, with the remaining 2.7% (four) submitted in Spanish (by the Spanish, Mexican and

Venezuelan delegations). All submissions by French-speaking nations were in English.

Although restricted from attending working groups, members reported that all groups functioned through the medium of English. The original language of reports arising from these groups was also English.

Observation and qualitative analysis of the debate in plenary (post-2006) also uncovers the 'percolatory' and pervasive dominance of English. For example, discussions which had germinated in working groups through the medium of English continued to be debated in plenary in English; the Chair directed delegates to action points suggested by intercessional and sessional working groups using the 'English version' of working papers; he/the Secretariat drafted and summarised plenary debates using English and this became the source language for final discussion; discussions surrounding the adoption of specific terminology took place in English or demanded a return to the English language version of a submitted document; written documents supporting agenda items, reports from the working groups, and the draft final report of the meeting also appeared in English.[10]

Observations of other Committees since this initial investigation confirm similar patterns of language use and the continued dominance of English.

3.2.3.2 Electronic access to IMO documentation by delegates and stakeholders

With an interest in broadening and enhancing the implementation of organisational instruments internationally, and crucially in reducing the organisational budget, IMO designed a pilot study in order to assess the uptake of IMO texts on-line. The study began in July 2003 and information was gathered over a period of 20 months in two overlapping stages: July 2003–December 2004 and August 2004–February 2005. Throughout the first phase documentation was available initially in English and in the summer of 2004 was made accessible in all of the official languages.

While a thorough analysis cannot be provided here, what is considered are: the languages chosen by users, and the regions which most exploited the service. Throughout the first phase a substantial number of documents were downloaded

---

[10] The latter was introduced into the plenary for discussion in order to ensure that the minutes represented a true reflection of the meeting. The Chair progressed through the English version of the document paragraph by paragraph and invited comments or queries. This was agreed upon – with some minor amendments – by the delegations present and subsequently corrected before translation into the other official languages.

(31,135) by individuals in 166 countries however approximately 66% of downloads were made in only 20 countries (see Figure 3 below).

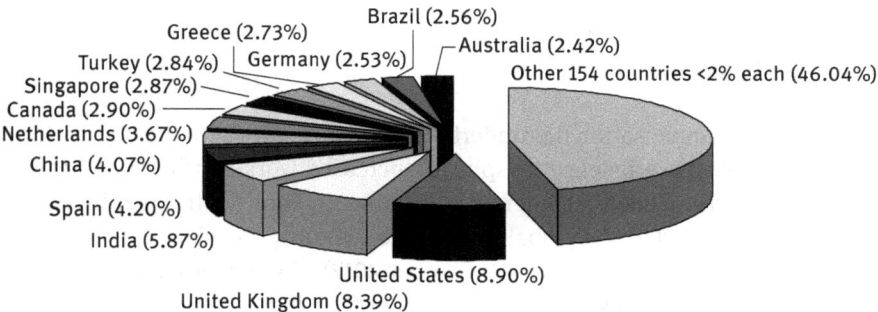

Figure 3: Downloads by country (IMO document: C94/3(e)/3 p. 2)

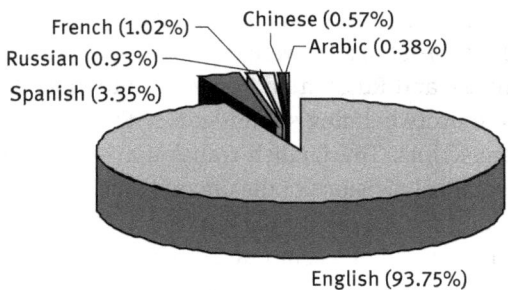

Figure 5: Downloads by language: July 2003-December 2004 (IMO document: C94/3(e)/3 p. 3)

Almost 94% of downloads were in English in the first phase of the study, with comparatively few in the other official languages (3.35% Spanish; 0.93% Russian; 0.57% Chinese and 0.38% Arabic). In the second phase of the pilot study the number of English downloads decreased slightly, to approximately 80%. However English still proved to be the language most exploited by users.

Overall statistical analysis demonstrated that the main users of the on-line resources were those in developed countries (see further discussion below) and from the private sector. Under the direction of the 94th session of the Council it was decided to extend the pilot for a further year, in particular, to assess the impact of moving to on-line resources for developing countries. At the end of the study it was recognised that the maritime administrations of developing countries were somewhat hampered by a lack of computer hardware to enable them to benefit from the free access of material from the IMO web-site. Recommendations were made in the 96th Council (2006) for Member States and donor communities to provide material support (see further discussion below).

3.2.4 Meeting costs

Since 2006 the organisation has undertaken a further wave of 'review and reform' in order to increase efficiency (despite an increased workload[11]) and reduce the cost of resources needed for internal operations in light of stringent budgetary constraints imposed by the global economic downturn.

In the 109th session of Council (October 2012), the operating arrangements and budgets were reviewed in an assessment of the future financial sustainability of the organisation. A large percentage of IMO's annual budget is devoted to the servicing of meetings. These costs include the hiring of external interpreters and translators and it is reported that these have increased over a 15 year period (1996–2011). The number of pages requiring translation has trebled over this time (amounting to 63,500 pages in 2011). 84% of the total were translated into French and Spanish; 14% into Arabic, Chinese and Russian and only 2% into English. The latter once again illustrating the overwhelming submission of English language documents as 'original' manuscripts. The English translation section is noted to increasingly support the technical divisions of the organisation and delegates in editorial work.

The cost of interpreters has also increased in recent years due to a new methodology introduced by the UN Common System (July 2012) for the calculation of interpreter fees and this has placed an additional burden on the organisation's budget.

3.3 Review and reform

Major developments involving recommendations and amendments to rules of procedure for documentation, interpretation and translation services have transpired and these have major implications for multilingual policy, provision and practice (as highlighted in italics) with respect to arrangements for the physical and virtual support of meetings (C110/3/2). These include:

---

11 It was reported at the 109th Council session (C109/3/1) that the number of pages processed by IMO and requiring translation, increased by almost a third over a period of four years – 23,898 (2006) to 31,446 (2011).

i. a reduction in the total number of Council, committee and sub-committee meetings from ten to eight sessions for the majority of committees leading to *a reduction in interpreter and translation costs* (14% reduction in 2012);
ii. limitations imposed on the size of documents submitted in support of meetings – *a maximum of four pages may be submitted for translation* (this may constitute a summary) into the working languages with additional content submitted as an annex in a language (*notably English*) to be used by working groups (this amounted to a 12% reduction in pages translated into French & Spanish in 2012);
iii. only brief summary decisions in all working languages to replace summary documents (including a summary of discussions and positions taken during debate) and stream-line reporting for all meetings. *It is estimated that this could amount to £30,000 and reduce the translation burden by 35%*;
iv. Chairmen of correspondence, drafting and working groups are no longer to provide a verbal summary of reports to Council; 'summary of decisions' arising from these meetings are taken as read. Therefore *no interpretation provided in the meeting* for such reports;
v. it is also proposed that summary documents for working and drafting groups should be attached to reports rather than contained in the main text, *reducing the amount of translation by approximately 60% and enabling a saving on overtime payments*;
vi. meeting decisions are cross-referenced in order to *reduce 're-translation' costs*;
vii. loan of laptops to delegates in support of paper-free meetings;
viii. *audio-recordings* of Council, Assembly and Committee meetings made *available in the official languages* via the IMO web-site; and in adherence with the UN's 'Paper Smart Initiative' (Circular Letter No. 3087) a movement away from the availability of hard copies of pre-/in- and post-session papers; instead these are available on IMODOCS (IMO website)[12]. The Secretariat is also reported to be moving towards paper-free operations (C110/3/2 p. 3). The introduction of the Digital Recording System is reported to have led to an 84% in reduction of the costs of hiring précis-writers and 61% in printing volume of meeting documentation;
ix. increased use of virtual meetings and video-conferencing for inter-sessional and correspondence groups reducing transport costs and the carbon footprint. Such meetings will operate via *a lingua franca*;

---

12 In addition to notes verbales; circular letters; communications with respect to 'entry into force' of legal documents and final committee and sub-committee reports.

x. Translation data bases and software, including terminology in the six languages of the organisation, are to be made available to delegates. This includes a multilingual document repository of previously translated texts.

Implementation of a large proportion of these proposals across 2011–2012 is reported to have led to an 11% reduction in costs with an increasing reduction projected over the coming years.

3.4 Review & reform: An evaluation

In his response (C 109/12(b)) to the recommendations made in JIU/REP/2011/4 the SG of IMO affirms his organisation's commitment to multilingual provision and training and supports maintaining linguistic diversity through the appointment of a multilingual co-ordinator, the employment of a multilingual work force and the support of the organisations' official and working languages. However he also emphasises the need for cost-saving measures, outlining some of the actions summarised in 3.2.4 above. His response presents a diplomatic gloss over a very difficult and complex situation.

While it cannot be denied that the official and working languages are available and used in some sectors of the organisation, in particular at higher levels of functioning (i.e. plenary meetings of Assembly, Council and Committee meetings) the issue of 'equity' and 'opportunity' for multilingual functioning across the various layers of the organisation appears limited and requires further scrutiny, for the majority of the recommendations for reform appear to foster an increasing use of English as a lingua franca even at the highest levels. For example, in developing work which is finally discussed and debated in plenary, initial negotiations, discussions and recommendations are developed through correspondence and working groups which have no access to interpreter provision and predominantly function in English. A number of delegates reported that they often experienced difficulty contributing to discussions and negotiating decisively in working groups and/or understanding other delegates who may have limited command of English. Previously, if a delegate had been unable to fully contribute to such meetings a further layer of interpretation/translation was guaranteed once summaries of discussions were introduced into plenary via the Chair of the group (and/or translated into the organisation's working languages in summary documents). However now only brief summaries of decisions are introduced verbally or in writing in the working languages and the majority of content appears in English as an annex to documents. Should delegations wish to translate the annex, the burden of effort, time and cost will fall on them, by which time the opportunity for negotiation may be missed.

As illustrated in the account of the plenary meeting of MEPC (see section 3.2.3.1 above) agenda items arising from working/drafting groups/documents often continue to be discussed in English by the Chair and meeting members. Moreover, once a draft of the meeting minutes is circulated in plenary in the working languages, it is often the English version which is used as the main reference for further deliberation and checking. Some delegates who have the opportunity to use an official language (other than English) choose not to do so since they feel able/compelled to accommodate to the debate in the majority language making interventions in English. Some note (e.g. French speaker representative of Vanuatu, pers comm) that it is easier and more efficient to continue the discussion in the majority language.

Further, while full access to plenary meeting recordings in the official languages on the IMO website appears to support access to the full repertoire of official languages and the entire debate by all meeting members, the difficulties experienced, particularly by developing countries with regard to access to on-line resources (as discussed section 3.2.3.2 above) remains intractable to date. A 'recording-only' policy in place of meeting minutes also places any subsequent translation costs squarely at the door of those delegations which may need to translate material for their Governments or stakeholders. Once more this burden of effort and cost will fall unequally, predominantly on non-English-speaking nations and participants[13].

It appears that the measures taken by the organisation to enhance efficiency and reduce financial and administrative pressures post-the JIU report may shift the burden of cost (financial and otherwise) unfairly onto some delegations and deepen the divide between the UN principle of support for multilingualism and the pragmatic reality of the reduction of communication to a lingua franca. Despite an over-arching rhetoric encased in a discourse of egalitarian 'linguistic human rights' (see Grin 2005) the reality is the continued and arguably enhanced *de facto* dominance of a lingua franca. Both economic and pragmatic considerations favour parsimonious solutions leading to a reduction in the amount of interpretation and translation services offered, despite the fact that these services actually constitute only a small percentage of the overall organisational budget. In order to fully participate at all levels within the organisation English appears to be a minimum requirement. This therefore calls true 'equity' into question.

---

13 Note too that audio-recordings may prove to be inaccessible to the Deaf and hard-of-hearing contravening Resolution 65/311: 1, see p. 295 above.

4 Review and reform – an alternative approach

While micro-language planning appears to have moved in the direction of lingua franca communication, interviews and questionnaires returned by twenty delegates in 2013[14] reveal a consistent picture in which a desire for multilingualism remains apparently unquestioned. The motivation for some is political; they see it as important to maintain and support the democratic right of those nations with access to interpretation/translation (including themselves in some instances) to enjoy access to meetings and documentation in their national languages, albeit recognising that true democracy cannot be reached unless all language groups within the organisation have such privileges. It is also recognised that the strength of English as a lingua franca is not the consequence of organisational constraints alone but a reflection of larger socio-economic and political forces in which English is a powerful global language commanded by many participating in global networks who use it as a lingua franca for their work in global shipping[15] and for travel and social engagement outside of the organisation.

Those delegates who enjoy the benefits of interpretation and translation at IMO reported that they did not wish to see this regime altered, despite the fact that they themselves might choose, on occasion, to engage in English in debate or negotiation, reporting the ability to accommodate to their interlocutor as an important rhetorical device; noting too the added advantage of efficiency and expediency (even when consulting documentation). They note however that diplomats will converge to other linguae francae (particularly French and Spanish), where appropriate, in informal meetings/discussions outside of plenary. The latter notwithstanding, some reported that they found participation in working and correspondence groups more difficult when having to converse in English and this obviously creates restrictions around access and participation.

When asked if the organisation should expand its language provision beyond the six official and three working languages, all noted, without exception, the limitations of the organisational budget and unwelcome increases in administrative burdens.

---

14 In order to protect their anonymity it is not possible to reveal the name of delegations or delegates, however representatives from Arabic (1); Chinese (1); English (3); French (2); Russian (2); Spanish (5) and 'other-language' (6) nations participated. Space does not permit a full analysis of the questionnaire data here.

15 Note that IMO has been responsible for the development of laws and instruments to support Maritime English as a global lingua franca for communication at sea. Support for an international language of communication has arisen from a desire to combat weaknesses in the 'human factor' leading to shipping accidents (see Bocanegra-Valle, 2010).

How then might we account for the apparent contradictions between a stated desire for multilingualism and the reality of lingua franca dominance?[16] These may have transpired as a result of the direct method of elicitation used (respondents providing what they perceived to be a 'desired'/'politically correct' response). Alternatively, the direct elicitation approach may serve to elicit, and reproduce, broader ideologies and discourses in support of multilingual policy – ideologies which may be keenly felt and supported. In this sense firmly held principles may appear at odds with actual practice. The challenge for planners is therefore to reconcile the tension between widely-shared principles and practice and the tension between collective and individual interests/needs. Research in national language planning has illustrated the futility of imposing policies which run counter to social flows or individual demands (Wright 2004).

Current practice certainly restricts/impedes ease of access and full participation for some and therefore influences the democratic process of ideological agenda setting, negotiation and ultimately the democratic evolution of the organisational work programme, including the development of legal instruments. Full participation in the work of IMO requires not only attendance but also thorough preparation of the known facts of agenda items including knowledge about their evolution; awareness of the position(s) taken by one's own delegation and that of other delegations, and subsequently the ability to negotiate in order to contest, influence, and shape the development of ideas and instruments. This demands a high level of linguistic and political competence and preparedness. The current regime is one in which the principle of multilingualism is upheld in policy but a 'free linguistic market' (see Tonkin 2004) and restricted multilingual provision across the organisational ecology enables English to dominate.

Assuming that the UN's commitment to multilingualism holds fast, how might it be further enhanced and supported at IMO, especially for meetings? Ethnographic observation and data collection has demonstrated the 'percolatory' and penetrating effect of English; its dominance appears to have developed through organisational practice, arising 'bottom up' through the discussions and reports emanating from working and correspondence into plenary debate, in addition to external forces, as communicative currency in the profession of shipping and the global linguistic marketplace. A practice has emerged in which English has become the dominant default code. For changes to occur it is contended that a more radical proposal (than that currently suggested in the recommendations made at UN headquarters) for reform should be made based on: a review of current and potential interlingual practices; a consideration of the tension between collective

---

16 I would like to extend my thanks to Leigh Oakes for his provocative thoughts on this.

and individual interests/needs; and economic/workload constraints. This calls for a thorough policy analysis to explore alternative 'language regimes' (Grin 2008) which cater for the realities of the globalised world. Two broad proposals present themselves which in turn may encompass various regimes:
1) lingua franca usage to become the 'norm'[17] with appropriate compensatory schemes employed to enable delegations/the Secretariat to train personnel and/or take advantage of nuanced ('requested') translation/interpreter provision as/when needed for communication inside and outside of the organisation (e.g. to stakeholders), and/or
2) expansion of multilingual provision across the organisational ecology, enabling greater flexibility and choice of provision (as/when required), and support for the enhanced (re-) distribution of resources. A complex combination of mono/multilingual regimes under these conditions may offer alternative modes of operating conditions (e.g. 'interpretation/translation on demand') and nurture a culture of multilingualism that is not artificially restricted to higher-level functioning but one which becomes a feature of all domains.

These proposals have both strengths and limitations, however they, in different ways, prioritise the agency of the 'language user' emphasising flexibility over rigid and restrictive language choice and/or the constant provision of unexploited multilingual resources within limited domains. These proposals, *inter alia*, demand a transformational re-modelling of current policy ('official' or 'non-official'), calling for a restructuring of current provision, and the creative remodelling of resources and costs (e.g. reviewing the possibility of further/changed income streams) to accommodate complementary and multiple scenarios of interlingualism. Rather than imposing or enforcing a 'top down' policy (as called for by the current system and noted to be unenforceable: see criticisms of SGs and Language Co-ordinators on p. 296 above) these regimes nurture and support a dynamic ecology. The benefit of a policy analysis is that it addresses two issues of importance to the UN (as any organisation with limited budgets): "resource allocation" (the 'efficient use of scarce resources') and "resource distribution" (net gains and losses) (Grin 2008: 75), whilst acknowledging the global pull toward lingua franca communication.

The proposals outlined here require the development of robust theoretical and analytic frameworks and methodologies appropriate to review all UN organisa-

---

[17] Where, as Ammon (2006) suggests, selection of named linguae francae could be made according to their international standing and the number of native & non-native speakers within the organisation.

tions and capable of modelling different scenarios of monolingual/multilingual provision and practice (e.g. see Ammon 2006; Fidrmuc 2011; Gazzola 2005; Grin 2008 and Pool's 1996 work on the European Union and Fettes's 2004 interlingual models) in order to explore the possibility of developing language regimes which are capable of prioritising and appealing to different, and sometimes opposing priorities (e.g. cost; equality/democracy; changing demo-linguistic constitution of personnel; group size; expediency/urgency of debate; 'field' contingencies/needs; capacity for interpretation/translation facilities; preferred lingua franca communication). These regimes should be sensitive to changing priorities and "policy goals" (Grin 2008: 73) and the fluid configuration and language choices of delegates/Secretarial members/stakeholders. No one scenario may be appropriate for any one domain or work programme; rather a variety of scenarios and multilingual/monolingual regimes may be required/desired at different levels of functioning (e.g. Secretariat meetings; working groups; plenary; field practice) and on different occasions, remembering that both the diplomatic community and work programme priorities are constantly changing.

As a starting point one could develop a model in which configurations of regimes vary according to the number and type of official and working languages, the number and direction of translation and interpretation, and the language learning needs of personnel. A summary of some possible regimes for IMO (adapted from Grin's 2008: 78 consideration of the EU, based on previous work by Pool 1991 and Gazzalo 2005) is detailed in Table 4 below:

Table 4: Possible language regimes

Regime	Number of Official & Working Languages	Type	Direction of translation & interpretation	Language learning needs
Monarchic	1	English	0	English by non-Anglophones
Oligarchic	3	English, French & Spanish	6	English, French or Spanish
Panarchic	6	All official & working languages	$n(n-1) = 6 \times (5) = 30$	None
Hegemonic	6	All official & working languages	$2(n-1) = 2 \times (6-1) = 10$	None
Triple symmetrical relay	6	All official & working languages	$r(2n-r-1) = 3(2 \times 6-3-1) = 24$	None

A 'Monarchic' regime would support the use of English-only and this could be expanded to three languages (the current working languages), if the Oligarchic system were to be adopted. The current regime in place in Assembly, Council and Committee meetings is represented by the Panarchic regime in which all languages are provided with interpretation and translation facilities. Variations in translation and interpretation provision are illustrated by the 'Hegemonic' and 'Triple symmetrical relay' regimes, in which all languages are also recognised as official, however translation and interpretation takes place through a pivot language, such as English (Hegemonic) or three working languages (Triple symmetrical relay). In the latter three cases further reductions in provision could occur if demand for translation/interpretation were not needed.

It is contended that any proposals for change in status planning across the UN system will only succeed through a pragmatic and nuanced consideration of current and emergent language dynamics in individual agencies, taking into account user preferences/needs/trends, in conjunction with a consideration of economic and operational constraints. This will enable a review of official and working languages and the feasibility of multiple language regimes operating within and across different agencies of the UN. An analysis of language scenarios in consultation with the O/ (o)rganisational membership also has the benefit of influencing political will which may counter any tension between informal and emergent micro language planning and policy (in which agency rests with the membership) and macro-level policy imposed 'top down' from UN-system Heads. In addressing the former, one might, as illustrated in the study of IMO, appeal to the methodological and analytical tools developed in the fields of ethnography, sociolinguistics and social-psychology in order to determine the success/limitations of current language practices (including macro-linguistic studies of language choice and attitudes to language use across and within domains and micro-interactional analyses of mono and multi-lingual communication) and informant attitudes towards the political, cultural, social and economic costs of multilingualism.

In order to counter any potential managerial bias in prioritising stringent economic constraints in decision-making, and cater for the reality of economic thresholds, (as emphasised by Ban Ki-moon and Koji Sekimizu), an analysis of practice and attitudes should be merged with methods recently developed in 'Language Economics' (see Grin 2001, 2006; Grin & Vaillancourt 1997, Grin, Sfreddo & Vaillancourt 2010) in order to calculate the costs and benefits (financial/material and non-financial/non-material) of proposed scenarios and regimes. Consideration of reported attitudes and practices can facilitate the measurement of qualitative, symbolic and quantitative variables (e.g. democracy, prestige; efficiency;

production).[18] Whilst this should not determine policy; it can make a significant contribution to informing it and aid in the consideration of feasible interlingual scenarios, in addition to how costs for support might be spread across contributors to the Organisation, including the possibility of a 'language tax' to be levied on members on an annual basis. The ratio of costs to be borne by members to be decided on an organisation basis, for example, in the case of IMO in relation to the tonnage of the States' merchant ships and its ability to pay (in line with current contributions to IMO, see p. 300 above) and/ or as proposed in the case of the EU (e.g. Ammon 2006), by those who benefit the most from lingua franca use, as a form of compensatory tax. Contributions may be supplemented from other sources, voluntary or otherwise (see p. 300 above). A balance of lingua franca communication and multilingual provision might enable costs to be harnessed more effectively and prudently. As noted by Gazzola (2006) in his study of the European Parliament, multilingualism does not necessarily have to imply an unsustainable expansion in cost.

5 Multilingualism – Diplomatic baggage or a passport to success?: Implications for multilingual organisational policy

Analyses of the reported status of multilingualism across the UN network, supplemented by an empirical study of language policy and practice in one of its agencies, suggests that the Organisational ecological principle of language diversity and equality is significantly challenged by global, pragmatic, practical, political and economic factors, and that the movement towards ever greater lingua franca usage may be accelerating as a consequence of measures to counter budgetary constraints. Nevertheless, support for 'multilingualism' (encased in a discourse of 'language rights') is weighing heavily on the shoulders of those responsible for its implementation and function. Calls for Executive Heads and Language Co-ordinators to over-see and bear responsibility for its implementation across the network appear fruitless, unless changes are made to the current system through detailed scientific modelling of alternative language regimes and a creative exploration of individual and group interests, economic and labour constraints,

---

18 For example see Nelson's (1987) account of the success of a novel approach to the drafting of the 'UN Convention on the Law of the Sea' in which the Committee created language groups for multilingual drafting of the Convention.

and recognition of the impact of global forces. As recommended in this chapter, methods are available to undertake an extensive review of organisations, capable of modelling different scenarios of interlingual practice suitable for bespoke organisational application and these may not necessarily involve additional economic hikes in current contributions once trade-offs and efficiencies have been calculated. It must be remembered that economic arguments for reductions in translation/interpretation are not necessarily warranted given the small percentage of budget often devoted to these.

As a deliberative starting point the UN, as any international organisation, might first benefit from critiquing its organisational philosophy and priorities. 'Equitability' is prevalent in UN discourse but it is necessary to problematize the agent(s) to which this applies. In its current form 'equitability' relates to the equal provision of a specific number of official or working 'languages' (in a restricted number of organisational domains). However as contested in this chapter 'equitability' might be better conceived in relation to the language user, such that a principle of equitable language provision becomes one of user choice/ need (with in-built restrictions) across domains of use. Extensive research on language maintenance, shift and revitalisation, has demonstrated that unless languages are maintained in a number of domains in any language community they will be subject to attrition. Although the UN body does not constitute a 'language community' under threat, patterns of language use and arguments based on a premise that 'multilingualism equates to unsustainable costs' foster and contribute to a culture of parsimony. On the other hand, arguments rejecting lingua franca usage on the basis of hegemony or dominating ideologies need to be questioned by policy makers in international organisations attended by the global elite. Members are not necessarily 'coerced' into use but responsive to its advantage and instrumental in its development. Arguments used for the preservation of language(s) in a national context (e.g. cultural maintenance) may not be appropriate for transnational connectedness. English has become an established lingua franca in global political, economic and business contexts allowing individuals to transcend group or national boundaries. Some would argue (see Wright 2004: 246) that use of English in global networks and in a post-national period mirrors behaviour in the "multi-layered authority" of pre-national Medieval society, in which European clergy and scholars communicated in a lingua franca. Language policy, however conceived, cannot restrain the forces of globalisation.

Although this chapter has focussed on an analysis of the UN system, it has far-reaching implications for research, policy and practice in other contexts of international and transnational integration. In a world now influenced by global flows and complex language repertoires, post-national models of language policy and planning need to accommodate fluid and alternating regimes of interaction in international networks and systems.

References

Ammon, Ulrich. 2006. Language conflicts in the European Union. *International Journal of Applied Linguistics* 16 (3): 319–338.
Baldauf, Richard. 2004. Rearticulating the case for micro language planning in a language ecology context. *Current Issues in Language Planning* 7 (2 & 3): 147–170.
Bocanegra-Valle, Ana. 2010. Global markets, global challenges: the role of Maritime English in the shipping industry. In Angeles Linde Lopez, Rosalie Crespo Jimenez (eds.) Professional English in the European Context: The EHEA Challenge, 151–174. Peter Lang: Switzerland.
Duchêne, Alexandre. 2008. *Ideologies across Nations: The Construction of Linguistic Minorities at the United Nations*. New York: Mouton de Gruyter.
Fettes, Mark. 2004. The geostrategies of interlingualism. In J. Maurais and M. Morris (eds.) *Languages in a Globalising World*. Cambridge: Cambridge University Press, 37–46.
Fidrmuc, Jan. 2011. The economics of multilingualism in the EU. Economics and Finance Working Paper Series. Brunel University.
Gazzola, Michele. 2005. "La gestione del multilingualismo nell'Unione Europa". *Le sfede della politica linguistica di oggi. Fra la valorizzazione del multilinguismo migratorio locale e le istanze del pluringuismo europeo*. Augusto Carli (ed.) Milano: Franco Angeli, pp17–117.
Gazzola, Michele. 2006. Managing multilingualism in the European Union: Language policy evaluation for the European Parliament. *Language Policy* 5:393–417.
Grin, François. 2001. English as economic value: facts and fallacies. *World Englishes* 20 (1): 65–78.
Grin, François. 2005. Linguistic human rights as a source of policy guidelines: A critical assessment. *Journal of Sociolinguistics* 9 (3): 448–460.
Grin, François (2008). Principles of policy evaluation and their application to multilingualism in the European Union. In Xabier Arzoz (Ed.), *Respecting linguistic diversity in the European Union* (pp. 73–83). Amsterdam: Benjamins.
Grin, François, Claudio Sfreddo & François Vaillancourt. 2010. *The Economics of the Multilingual Workplace*. New York/London: Routledge.
Grin, François & François Vaillancourt. 1997. The economics of multilingualism: overview and analytical framework. *Annual Review of Applied Linguistics* 17: 43–65.
Liddicoat, Anthony. 2009. Language planning and international collaboration: a current issue in language planning. *Current Issues in Language Planning* 10 (2): 163–165.
McEntee-Atalianis, Lisa. 2006. 'Geostrategies of Interlingualism': Language policy and practice in the International Maritime Organisation, London. UK. *Current Issues in Language Planning* 7 (2 & 3): 341–358.
McEntee-Atalianis, Lisa. 2008. Diplomatic Negotiation in an International Organisation: An Exploration of Expert Status and Power. *The International Journal of Diversity in Organisations, Communities and Nations* 8(3): 265–271.
McEntee-Atalianis, Lisa. 2010. An Investigation of Argumentational Discourse Units in Diplomatic Negotiation. *Sociolinguistic Studies* 4 (3): 553–568.

McEntee-Atalianis, Lisa. 2011. The Role of Metaphor in Shaping the Identity and Agenda of the United Nations: The Imagining of an International Community and International Threat. *Discourse and Communication* 5 (4): 393–412.

McEntee-Atalianis, Lisa. 2013. Stance and Metaphor: Mapping Changing Representations of Organisational Identity. *Discourse and Communication* 7 (3): 319–340.

Nelson, L. D. M. 1987. The Drafting Committee of the Third United Nations Conference on the Law of the Sea: The implications of multilingual texts. *British Yearbook of International Law*. 57 (1): 169–199.

Piron, Claude. 1980. Problèmes de communication linguistique aux Nations Unies et dans les organisations apparentées. *Language Problems and Language Planning* 4 (3): 224–236.

Pool, Jonathan. 1991. "The Official Languages of the European Communities.' Manuscript, Center for the Humanities, University of Washington (Seattle).

Pool, Jonathan. 1996. Optimal language regimes for the European Union. *International Journal of the Sociology of Language* 121: 159–179.

Tonkin, Humphrey. 2004. The search for a global linguistic strategy. In J. Maurais and M. Morris (eds.) *Languages in a Globalising World*. Cambridge: Cambridge University Press, 319–33.

Van Parijs, Philippe. 2002. Linguistic justice. *Politics, Philosophy & Economics* 1 (1): 59–74.

Wright, Sue. 2004. *Language Policy and Language Planning: From Nationalism to Globalisation*. New York: Palgrave MacMillan.

Elizabeth Ellis
13 Challenges within the ecology of multilingual interactions in Aboriginal cultural tourism in Central Australia

Abstract: This chapter explores some of the sociolinguistic issues raised by multilingual language use and interpreting in tourism services in a key Aboriginal-owned culturally significant site: Uluṟu in Central Australia. It reports on a project which investigated the challenges presented by different modes of foreign-language tour guiding, commenting on the accuracy, cultural appropriateness and semantic nuances of information given to visitors in different languages. It documents the complexities of this multilingual situation and discusses how the challenges are met from the perspective of ideologies about language, different understandings of interpreting and translation, and the nature of cross-linguistic interaction.

1 Introduction

Key tourist sites are locations where languages mingle, cultures cross, and identities are performed. Tourists speak many languages and varieties; tourism providers make efforts to provide for those languages; these both interact with the local language ecology in multiple ways. There are affordances and misunderstandings: understandings are reached or are elusive; people strive in good-humoured or impatient ways to get their needs met; humour is shared across languages and even in the absence of a common language. In tourism interaction there is a "quickness" – an energy, freshness and life in meaning-making across languages (Phipps 2007). Language in tourism is grossly under-studied (Cohen & Cooper 1986; Dann 1996; Huisman & Moore 1999; Phipps 2007). Phipps (2007: 1) bemoans the fact that "... in the research into tourism we find a massive multilingual phenomenon boiled down to a few articles bemoaning the lack of language skills in its servants, and a few more critically assessing the patterns of discourse and the potential symbolic violence inherent in such representations".

Tourism locations however are fertile sites for studying language use – they are where we find purposeful uses of language in a range of genres. Such sites attract people from many places and of many language backgrounds. Bryant

Elizabeth Ellis, University of New England, Australia, liz.ellis@une.edu.au

(1992) used this fact to her advantage when she positioned herself at the Australian War Memorial in Canberra to gather data on lexical variation in Australian English, secure in the knowledge that visitors from every town and suburb in Australia, from Oodnadatta to Weipa would eventually pass through. One reason perhaps for the lack of research into language in tourism, particularly into spoken language, is that the very nature of tourism renders it difficult to study. Tourists are mobile, here today, gone tomorrow, and their interactions are fleeting, ephemeral, and principally verbal. Tourism is a commercial enterprise – time is money and tour operators and tour guides keep long, busy hours with few breaks, creating problems for researchers with audio recorders and clipboards. Tour guiding is perhaps the most mobile aspect of the industry, and, at least in Australia, the most unregulated. Most tour guides in Australia learn on the job (Boyle & Arnott 2004), move between employers, and form short but intense relationships with each of their tour groups which are potentially threatened by researcher presence.

Yet tour-guiding holds undiscovered riches for linguists, and multilingual tour-guiding even more so. It is a purely spoken genre in which every encounter is intercultural; in which cultural, historical, geographical, and social knowledge is articulated, and in which the communicative functions of informing, directing, reassuring, advising, warning, entertaining, are performed. The tour guide must adapt her spoken language to tourists' different ages, genders, cultural backgrounds, expectations, physical condition, and background knowledge. She accommodates linguistically in form and content to the characteristics which she perceives in a particular tour group: reserved or outgoing, conservative or liberal, adaptable or rigid, humour-loving or dour. She must assume at different times the role of leader, parent, nanny, teacher, and even counsellor (Dann 1996: 168). When multiple languages are in play: those of the host culture, those of the tourists, and those of the tour guide herself, it is clear that numerous challenges will be presented which must be overcome or at least met in real time in commercial and time-constrained circumstances.

In this chapter I first outline the Central Australian context, then explain how the languages of tour-guiding fit into the local language ecology. I then describe the challenges of multilingual language use and the different views and practices in the local tourist industry. The sociolinguistic issues highlighted by these practices are identified and I describe how they are investigated by the current research project. The remainder of the chapter presents findings of the research project thus far, in the form of interview data from key stakeholders and tour guide commentary in two languages.

2 Uluṟu context

Uluṟu and Kata Tjuṯa (formerly known as Ayers Rock and the Olgas), located in the centre of the Australian landmass, are important cultural sites for Australian Aboriginal people and attract some half a million national and international visitors per year. These spectacular rock formations sit within the Uluṟu-Kata Tjuṯa National Park (henceforth UKTNP or "the Park"), which is 1325 square kilometers in size, and which was in 1985 formally handed back by the Australian Government to the Aboriginal people who are the traditional custodians of the area – the Aṉangu. Today the Park is acknowledged as being Aboriginal land, and is managed by a Board of Management consisting of 8 Aṉangu elders (four male and four female) and 4 non-Aṉangu Park staff. Uluṟu and Kata Tjuṯa are the sites that most tourists come to see, but the arid semi-desert area of Central Australia contains many other spectacular and scenic sites including those around the town of Alice Springs, the West MacDonnell Ranges, and the East MacDonnell Ranges. A typical trajectory for an international tourist is to fly into Ayers Rock Airport, tour the Park for one or two days, travel by bus to Watarrka National Park (Kings Canyon) then on to Alice Springs (a total of 750 km), spend a couple of days there and fly from Alice Springs airport to one of the major Australian cities. In discussing how tourism is enacted and managed in Central Australia, and hence how tourists are guided and kept safe, it is important to understand the nature of the landscape, the harshness of the climate, and key aspects of Aboriginal culture. Distances are vast and apart from the major highways, roads are unsealed, dusty, and subject to potholes and washaways. The population of Alice Springs (450km from Uluṟu) is 25,000 and most other settlements count a population only in the hundreds. The cities of Darwin (North) and Adelaide (South) are each 1500km away. Temperatures range from 47 degrees Celsius in summer down to minus 7 degrees Celsius on winter nights. The average annual rainfall is a mere 300mm and humidity is hence extremely low. The aridity means that humans can dehydrate to a dangerous degree very rapidly and are advised to drink 1 litre of water per hour in warm weather. This is a key aspect of tourist safety as will be discussed further below.

The culture of the Aṉangu people rests on *Tjukurpa*, described in the *Uluṟu-Kata Tjuṯa National Park Visitor Guide* by Aṉangu themselves thus:

> Just as a house needs to stand on strong foundations, so our way of life stands on *Tjukurpa*. *Tjukurpa* has many deep, complex meanings. *Tjukurpa* refers to the creation period when ancestral beings created the world. From this came our religious heritage, explaining our existence and guiding our daily life. Like religions anywhere in the world, *Tjukurpa* provides answers to important questions, the rules for behaviour and for living together. It is the law for caring for one another and for the land that supports us. *Tjukurpa* tells of the

relationships between people, plants, animals and the physical features of the land. It refers to the time when ancestral beings created the world as we know it. Knowledge of how these relationships came to be, what they mean and how they must be carried on is explained in *Tjukurpa*. *Tjukurpa* refers to the past, present and the future at the same time. This knowledge never changes, it always stays the same. (Department of Sustainability, Environment, Water, Population and Communities 2012: 10)

3 Language ecology

First the Aboriginal language situation of the region is described, then the English varieties which are spoken, and thirdly the languages which feature in the local tourist industry.

Of some 250 Aboriginal and Torres Strait Islander languages estimated to be spoken in Australia at the time of white settlement, only approximately 20 are considered to be in common use by a sizeable community in recent times (Walsh 1993). The situation is complex, though, and while traditional languages are in decline, new creoles are emerging. For a general introduction to language in Aboriginal Australia, the reader is referred to Walsh and Yallop (1993) and for more recent work on language revitalisation to Walsh (2005), on bilingual education to Simpson, Caffery and McConvell (2009), and on children's multilingualism to Simpson and Wigglesworth (2008).

The main languages spoken by the Anangu people in the area around Uluru-Kata Tjuta are Pitjantjatjara, Yankunytjatjara, Ngaanyatjarra, and Ngaatjatjarra, all of which form part of the Western Desert Language group, but people may speak several other languages as well such as Luritja or one or more of the Arandic languages from the Alice Springs area: (see Figure 1). Most Anangu speak some English, but proficiency may vary from native-speaker proficiency to minimal. According to Eades' extensive writings on Aboriginal ways of using English, "the majority of Australian Aboriginal people speak some kind of English. But often this is not quite the same as English spoken by other Australians" (Eades 2013:1). It is widely recognised that many Aboriginal people, even those who no longer speak an Indigenous language, are bidialectal in Aboriginal English and Standard Australian English, switching with ease according to context and interlocutor (Eades 2013). In Australia generally, English – Standard Australian English (SAE) – is the national language and functions as the de facto official language (Pauwels 2006). Australian English (AE) is commonly thought to fall into three groupings: Broad, General and Cultivated, with "general" equating with SAE. "Broad" is most commonly, but not exclusively, found among those of lower socio-economic status, manual workers and speakers in remote areas.

While intelligible to native speakers of other major Englishes, broad varieties of Australian English do pose problems of comprehension for speakers of other languages who have learned British or American English. This becomes relevant in the tour-guiding context as discussed below. (For more information on Aboriginal languages see http://www.ourlanguages.net.au/)

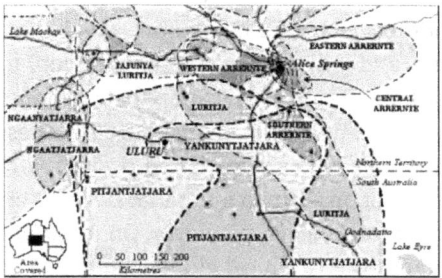

Figure 1: Map of Western Desert languages http://www.environment.gov.au/topics/national-parks/uluru-kata-tjuta-national-park/culture-and-history/anangu-language

Thus far, then, we have identified the presence of traditional Indigenous languages Pitjantjatjara, Yankunytjatjara, and others, the Arandic languages around Alice Springs, and varieties of English spoken in Australia: Aboriginal English, General or Standard Australian English and Broad AE. We now look at how other languages feature in the tourist industry.

This study focused on tourists from overseas non-English-speaking countries who travel to Central Australia in an organised group – what Dann (1996: 95) calls the "organized coach tour". The largest such groups visiting in 2012 were Japanese and German, with smaller numbers coming from Italy, China, France, and other countries in Europe, Asia, and South America.

For these non-English speaking groups, guiding services of three main types are available.

Multilingual guides: locally-based Australian citizens or residents who are either native speakers of English fluent in one or more languages, or native speakers of another language (e.g., German, French, Japanese) with a near-native level of English. Many multilingual guides working in Central Australia have a high level of fluency in 3 or 4 languages. Multilingual guides live in Central Australia, have accreditation to work in Uluru-Kata Tjuta National Park and undergo regular professional development through their company and/or National Parks. Experienced guides are promoted as having a deep understanding of the spiritual, environmental, and geological aspects of the country built up over years, and claim to be able to accurately and sensitively convey complex aspects of Aboriginal culture, history and beliefs, in the visitors' own language.

Foreign tour leaders (also called foreign tour escorts): foreign nationals who accompany a group of tourists on their entire itinerary throughout Australia and usually other destinations (New Zealand, Bali, Singapore etc.) Their main role is to facilitate the group's travel between destinations, deal with hotels, baggage, give general information on each destination such as where to shop and eat, and solve problems the group may encounter. They will be a native speaker of, for example, German, French or Japanese, and will speak some English too, to enable them to deal with Australian hotels and airlines. Some foreign tour leaders conduct the same tour many times, and develop knowledge about particular sites: others are office-based travel agency employees who are rewarded occasionally with the "perk" of acting as a foreign tour leader on a trip to Australia. Hence their expertise in English, local knowledge and experience vary widely. On arrival in a location they usually (but not always) hand over to a local guide who has local expertise and provides the specialist commentary on, for example, Uluṟu or the Sydney Opera House.

Indigenous tour guides: may be Aṉangu elders who live near the Park, and who lead walks which trace the journeys (*iwara*) across the land of the ancestors, describing the physical features (*Tjukuritja*) left by these journeys and telling of relevant flora and fauna. An Aṉangu tour guide is usually a speaker of Pitjantjatjara and English, but may also speak other Aboriginal languages, dialects and creoles. Aṉangu guides may give commentary in English or prefer to speak in Pitjantjatjara and work with a Pitjantjatjara-English interpreter. Where the group is, for example, French, there may be, then, an Aboriginal elder speaking Pitjantjatjara, an interpreter conveying his/her talk in English, and a multilingual guide or tour leader converting this commentary into French. A very small number of local multilingual guides can interpret directly from Pitjantjatjara into Japanese, German, and French. In Alice Springs Indigenous tour guides may be Arrente speakers who have traditional custodianship of various sites or give tours about Aboriginal culture generally. Some may come from other parts of the country, in which case they will usually make it clear that there are limitations on what they are permitted to share of local Arrente stories.

Three examples of common guiding patterns are given.
1. A group of 40 tourists travels from Colombia on a 4-week tour of Australia and New Zealand, accompanied by a Spanish/English speaking Colombian tour leader. They arrive at Alice Springs airport and are met by an Australian English-speaking coach driver and a local multilingual (Spanish-English-speaking) guide. During the 3 days in the area, the local guide provides all

commentary in Spanish, with the tour leader taking a back seat and simply dealing with personal issues the group may have.
2. As above, but in this case a local guide is not hired, and the Colombian tour leader conducts all commentary in Spanish. Clearly this is only possible or desirable when the tour leader has in-depth familiarity with the area from many previous visits – however this is discussed further below.
3. A group of 15 German tourists from a walking club in Bavaria arrive without a tour leader. The tour operator has booked the services of a local multilingual guide company which provides a small bus and a German-English speaking multilingual driver/guide.

Any of the above may also choose to engage an Indigenous tour guide for a specific aspect of the tour.

4 Literature review

While there is substantial research on tourism, the vast majority focuses either on business and marketing aspects or takes a cultural studies approach. There is an extraordinary dearth of research on languages in tourism (Cohen & Cooper 1986; Dann 1996; Huisman & Moore 1999; Oenbring 2011), very little on the role of tour guides in tourism, with the notable exception of a recent overview (Weiler & Black 2014), and virtually none on the languages of tour guides.

Dann's 1996 book was perhaps the first thorough investigation of language in tourism, and he claimed that "no-one has comprehensively analysed this language as a phenomenon in its own right ...[no study] has systematically examined tourism as a language per se. This book intends to remedy that deficit" (1996: 2). While tour guides feature frequently in Dann's analysis of tourism, there is no examination of bilingual/multilingual guides and the only item relating to foreign languages is "languaging" which is not related to Swain's use of the term (Swain 2006) to mean the creation of meaning through the process of producing language, but instead refers to the "borrowing" of terms from the local language in travel writing to give the impression of "insider" status (Dann 1996: 183). Much of the literature on language in tourism which can be found focuses on written or visual language; the language of promotional literature (Salim, Ibrahim & Hassan 2012); translation of tourist informational texts (Agorni 2012); of tourism publicity material (Zhang 2012); signage in tourism destinations (Blommaert 2010); labelling of souvenirs in Sámi tourism (Pietikäinen & Kelly-Holmes 2011); the linguistic landscapes of postcards (Jaworski 2010).

Of research located which focused on spoken language, key concerns were: the poor state of language training for the tourism industry in Australia and New Zealand (Marriott 1991; Watts 1994; Watts & Trlin 1999); the lack of awareness among tourism authorities of the need for language proficiency in the UK (Russell & Leslie 2006); and the importance of English proficiency in the development of the tourist industry in Romania (Otilia 2013). Jaworski (2009) investigated greetings in tourist-host encounters, while Piller (2011) employs the lens of intercultural communication to analyse tourism interaction examples such as those taking place in multilingual tourist information call centres and offices.

Cohen and Cooper (1986) provide a scholarly and in-depth sociolinguistic overview of verbal encounters in tourist situations which furnishes a typology of tourist roles, proposes "tourist talk" as a variation on "foreigner talk" and introduces the notion of "language brokerage". In elaborating this term, the authors explain that their analysis in the majority of the paper has been on direct interaction between tourists and locals, but they now examine "...interaction mediated by a variety of bilingual individuals such as guides, tour leaders, professional natives, hustlers, ... taxi-drivers and other individuals lurking around hotels and offering their services ... [t]hey may collectively be called *language brokers*" (Cohen & Cooper 1986: 556–557). There is much that is of value and relevance in their discussion, but there are several factors that limit its value in understanding the Central Australian context. The paper is now nearly 30 years old; professional tour guides would be horrified to be lumped in with "hustlers"; and the authors' study sites are tourist destinations in Thailand. The context in which the theoretical framework is outlined then is a developing country where Thai-speaking hosts who constitute the majority culture but are often of low socio-economic status provide services to much wealthier foreigners from the USA, Australia, and Europe, with English as the lingua franca. Verbal interactions examined include those of persistent touts promoting services and wares to passing tourists; English conversation between Thai "bar girls" and Western potential sexual clients; the antics of local children who shout foreign words at tourists to engage their attention. These contexts are simply irrelevant to Central Australian tourism in the 21st century.

The communicative competence of American, French, and German tour leaders in the US Southwest was investigated by Leclerc & Martin (2004), who found that the different national groups had different expectations of verbal and non–verbal communication of their tour leaders. Tour guide training was the focus of Boyle & Arnott (2004) in a context similar to that of this paper: Kakadu National Park in the Northern Territory of Australia – also an Aboriginal-owned site with major safety issues such as tropical heat and prolific crocodiles. The authors characterise the role of the tour guide as being "... [to] enhance the experience of the visitor through information and its understanding, given in an interesting, informative and culturally sensitive way" (Boyle and Arnott 2004: 86).

5 Central Australian tour guide training

Tourism to Uluṟu developed haphazardly from the 1950s onwards (Bradley 2009). The early years were characterised by a free-for-all approach with no regulation and where tour operators could set up business and take tourists anywhere with little regard for Aboriginal sensitivities or for the need to treat the environment with respect. While no doubt many tour guides acted responsibly, there are also accounts of abuse (Kerle 1995) such as tour guides throwing water on ancient rock paintings to illuminate the colours, or permitting tourists to swim in rock pools now recognised as sacred. The establishment of Aboriginal ownership and the joint management process in 1985 led to the development of much improved protocols about how tourists and tourist operators could access the fragile sites. Tourist accommodation and roads were moved away from the Rock itself (the local colloquial term for Uluṟu), access to sacred sites was restricted and photography of them banned, and a system of entry permits for approved tour operators was put into place. Concerns remained, however, about the quality of tour-guiding commentary. Tour guides ran the gamut from highly experienced professionals, to inexperienced backpackers. As a result in 2009 a training course "Knowledge for Tour Guides" (KTG) was introduced and became compulsory in 2011 for tour guides to work inside the Park. It consists of one university unit (course) of approximately 100 hours, delivered online in English only. Its description reads: "This entry-level training covers the key areas of visitor safety, understanding the parks' natural and cultural values and history, minimising environmental impact and legal compliance" (Department of the Environment 2014a). The rationale for the course's compulsory status is that "[t]he information presented to visitors by tour guides *directly impacts on visitor safety and experience* … [the training uses] information collected by Parks Australia *on behalf of the Aboriginal traditional owners* … [and that] *[g]uides need knowledge specific to each park* to maximise safety, compliance and the accuracy of information provided to park visitors …" (Department of the Environment 2014a, emphasis added).

Selected words are italicised in the above excerpt to emphasise that the major concerns are for visitor safety, legal compliance, and for the accurate and appropriate conveying of Aboriginal knowledge. Over the past 3 years several hundred tour guides have successfully completed the KTG course and achieved the necessary accreditation. Parks and University staff have therefore gone to great lengths to ensure that information available in English is accurate, complete, sensitive, and appropriate for public dissemination. However there is little consensus on how this information can best be conveyed in tourists' languages, beyond a common desire that it (foreign language commentary) should meet the same high standards. It is important to note that this accreditation requirement meant that foreign tour leaders accompanying a group could only continue to give foreign language commentary (as outlined above) if they had completed the KTG course.

When the issue of foreign language tour guides was raised at an UKTNP Tourism Consultative committee meeting in 2011 an Anangu Board member was later quoted as saying it was acceptable for tourist commentary to be given in foreign languages "as long as they [tour operators] can guarantee it's accurate". The sentiment is indisputable but it is not clear how it might be assured that foreign language commentary does indeed meet the required standards of accuracy, completeness, and cultural sensitivity.

This chapter attempts to examine how this might best be assured, drawing on sociolinguistic theory, interpreting and translation theory, and with an awareness of prevailing language ideologies.

6 Research design and methods

6.1 Researcher background

I first became aware that there was an interesting sociolinguistic situation that warranted a systematic qualitative inquiry in 2011 when the implementation of the Knowledge for Tour Guides (KTG) accreditation was starting to affect the ways in which tour operators catered for their foreign-language speaking visitors. In 2009 and 2010 I was on leave from my university and had worked as a Spanish-speaking tour guide in Central Australia. During that time I made many contacts in the local industry, completed the KTG course myself along with undertaking other practical training with UKTNP and multilingual tour operators. I also had other experience in the tourist industry. As an applied linguist with an interest in social attitudes to language and languages, some experience in translating and interpreting, and as an accredited Spanish-speaking tour guide in Central Australia, I was in an ideal position to investigate the challenges of multilingual tour guide provision in this context. Without that insider knowledge of both the local context and the wider tourist industry, its assumptions and practices, it would have been much more difficult to gain access to stakeholders, and to understand the complexities of the industry and of the provision of language services within it.

6.2 Data gathering

Data gathered was of two main kinds: interviews, and the recording of tour commentary. Interviews were held with representatives of different stakeholder groups.
- Anangu elders
- Management and visitor services officers in UKTNP
- Tour operators who cater for multilingual groups
- Multilingual tour guides
- Tour operators who cater for English-speaking groups
- English-speaking tour guides
- English-speaking bus driver-guides
- Indigenous tour guides from both Pitjantjatjara and Arrernte language groups
- Tourism industry representatives
- Professional interpreters

Interviews were conducted using a semi-structured questionnaire, and the entire interview was audio-recorded, with the respondent's permission, and then transcribed.

The recording of tour commentaries is ongoing. Thus far the data set comprises one tour commentary in English, one in German and one where the information is presented by an English-speaking Indigenous guide, and translated by a French-speaking local multilingual guide. The recording of tour commentary on tour is problematic. First, tour guides' commentary and expertise is their livelihood and their intellectual property, as well as being the source of their professional identity. As a result they are both proud of their commentary and reluctant to have it recorded, in case it might be used by rival companies or other tour guides, or held up to negative comment. Second, even having secured the tour guides' agreement and having negotiated informed consent consistent with the Ethics approval obtained for this study, practical problems emerge. Tour guides speak on buses which are noisy, using an internal PA system. Recording the ambient sound means including the noise of the bus's engine and air-conditioning as well as the passengers' chat. The researcher usually has to sit near the back, since the forward seats are naturally prized by the paying passengers. Fitting the tour guide with a body mike linked to a receiver carried by the researcher gives better sound, but it is common for the guide to knock the "off" button or otherwise disable it unwittingly, losing many hours of data. Tour itineraries are hectic, and stopping the guide more than once or twice to check that the device is functioning is not well received, especially since the device is wired up inside the shirt, presenting issues of modesty in checking it. Once off the bus, the tour guide walks from point to point, stopping to provide commentary. The body mike works well here, but a hand-held one is more reliable, not being prone to the above mishap. However, being close to the tour guide is a position favoured by many tourists, and if a researcher usurps this position, it can cause resentment which threatens the project. A third problem is that there is an awareness among tour operators and guides that some models of providing foreign language commentary are better than others, and so there may be reluctance to allow a researcher to record instances of the models which may be thought to be inferior, albeit prescribed by circumstance or by cost constraints.

6.3 Ethical considerations

Three separate levels of Ethics clearance were applied for and granted. The first two were the UNE Human Research Ethics applications, first for working with non-Indigenous respondents and the second for working with Indigenous respondents. A Research Permit Application was lodged with the Uluṟu-Kata Tjuṯa National Park. This was considered first by the Tourism Consultative Committee of the Board of Management and then by the Board itself. The system of requiring a permit for any research undertaken in the Park is consistent with Parks Australia's view of its management responsibilities as: "maintaining and respecting local indigenous culture while accommodating the interests of non-Aboriginal people. ... Parks Australia has obligations to protect local Aboriginal law and lifestyle and the integrity of the World Heritage natural and cultural values of the park" (Department of the Environment 2014b).

While entry to the Park on each occasion was provided by the Permit, I also carried my UKTNP Tour Guide accreditation card and further bought a tourist entry permit. (The latter two were not really necessary, but I wished to avoid any impression that I was gaining entry to the Park gratis while others have to pay, and since I was not actually working as a tour guide, the accreditation card was not appropriate). While these measures may seem excessive, it is important to conform exactly to protocols of research which involve Aboriginal people. There exists a sorry history of researchers and others misusing or misrepresenting their respondents and their data, and so in order to gain trust and co-operation it is crucial to be transparent and to follow all ethical protocols.

7 Findings

In this section are presented views from various stakeholders in the Central Australian tourist industry and extracts from tour commentary. In the Discussion section I draw out key themes from the findings and discuss their implications for understanding the challenges of providing multilingual tour guiding services.

7.1 The Anangu elders

The single thing most stressed by the Anangu elders interviewed for this project in and outside the park was that the information received by visitors should be the *right* information, in the sense that it should be accurate and sanctioned by Anangu themselves. Information is not neutral in the Aboriginal worldview: in an oral culture, knowledge is imparted in accordance with age and education in traditional ways. The stories of *Tjukurpa* are revealed by elders in increasing complexity as children mature and take on adult roles. Men's business and women's business are separate and secret from each other. It follows then that it is appropriate only to share certain information with visitors, and it is the role of Parks (UKTNP) to mediate this, passing it on according to Anangu wishes.

> I think it's very important to give the right information – and how it is really – that's really important. The kind of information about the land and how important it is to, to us, and special and sacred ... by coming through Parks to get the right information, yeah (Elder)

Within these limits, elders stressed that they want visitors to understand their culture and their ways. They see the visitors to their land as embarking on a process of learning, understanding, and coming to respect a different way of life and worldview. Talk about learning is often prefaced with "sit down", referring to the common practice in Central Australia and elsewhere of sitting on the ground to talk and/or to conduct business. "Sitting down" seems to emphasise willingness to engage, to take time, and to listen with respect.

> [we want tourists] to come and sit down and talk to Anangu people, Aboriginal people and to get the right story about that history with the hunting and gathering and all that.
>
> And [we want to] tell them about it, 'cause they really want to hear everything and listen ... and listen and understand. (Elder)

Asked about the effectiveness of different kinds of tour guides, elders again referred to the need to ensure that they are giving the right information, and stressed the role of Parks in working together with the tour industry to make sure the right information is out there.

> Well, you always wonder if they, if they not giving the right information and where they're getting it from.
>
> I think there should be more work, um, doing it to get it right. And like, you know, Park is there, our key organisation, 'cause it's right there, got a lot of information and rangers and, you know, people working with Anangu people, traditional owners and that. Yeah, more training I'd reckon, working together we call it "Tjungu" work, working together. And that way you can, you know, you can get the right information.
>
> [visitors must] respect the Park manager ... Park[s] Australia looking after country on behalf of us ... they're not making their own rules, they're making it through Anangu voice. (Elder)

Elders recognise that tour guides are key to the conveying of the right kind of information: although many would like to see more Indigenous guides, Aboriginal communities are small and could not provide guide services for the hundreds of thousands of visitors from around the world. Hence they see Parks' role as critical in ensuring tour guides are accredited and only give the sanctioned information. Another important aspect of the Anangu worldview is that they only tell stories which relate to their land. Many of the ancestral beings in *Tjukurpa* travelled far beyond Anangu land, but the telling of their stories must stop at the point where the beings pass into the land of a neighbouring group. It is important for tour guides to know this and not to "over-tell" stories.

> No, we don't, we don't expose any secret business ... like I explained we can only give – because some of them are sacred dances, important dances, so we can only give an overview, like pick bits out, you know, where the story – where we're following the travelling, you know Tjukurpa? To another land then cut off ... up to our boundary, yeah ... So everybody knows where to speak and where, um and where they stop and another clan group takes over. (Elder)

Men and women can only tell stories appropriate to their gender:

> I can only speak on the ladies' side. (Elder)

Throughout their talk there is constant reference to respect for the land. Many tourists like to climb Uluru, and although this is not banned, Anangu try to educate visitors as to why this is not a good thing to do: because of its sacred nature, and for safety reasons. Here an elder emphasises how having respect for the land and traditional ways is part of *Tjukurpa* law which is ancient and immutable, unlike Western practices.

> so you have to respect the land and the people. And the rules of the land. 'Cause Anangu rules don't get changed like government rules or European [ones] do.
>
> Tour guides or tourists, you're coming to one law country. That'll never, ever, ever change ... yes, so it just goes on and on and on ... so some people look for easy rules or bending rules, but we can't do any of them. No negotiations. That's it, that's the law of the land. (Elder)

7.2 Multilingual guides and foreign tour leaders

"Multilingual guide" is the term for those residents in Central Australia who work with incoming groups in their first or second language(s). They pride themselves on extensive local knowledge of Aboriginal culture, geology, flora and fauna, and history as well as the broad knowledge of Australian society and institutions needed to answer tourist questions. Here we must examine one of the peculiarities of the tourist industry: there are different understandings in the tourist industry, in the general population, and among linguists, of the meaning and use of the terms "interpreting" and "translating".

Among linguists, and among informed members of the public, interpreting refers to the conveying of oral language from one language to another, while translating means rendering written text in one language into another language. Linguists recognise the complexity of both tasks, and the need for professional accreditation for those who perform them. In Australia standards are set, and accreditation provided, by the National Association of Accredited Translators and Interpreters – NAATI. Members of the public may have much less understanding of both, and in some cases may perceive them as simple and routine processes of exchanging one word for another in a spoken or written text (Hale 2007).

In the Australian tourist industry, changing verbal information given in one language into another language is called *translating*.[1] The term *interpreting* refers to explaining key cultural, geological, and biological information about a particular site in a full, accurate, and sensitive manner to visitors. This may be done verbally, for example by a National Parks Ranger, or via *interpretive* signs, brochures, exhibitions or interactive multimedia installations.

---

[1] The tourist industry use of these terms will be distinguished by the use of italics.

Hence local multilingual guides see themselves as *interpreters* because they are the source of the information gained from their own training, reading, and experience, as this long-term guide explains:

> We're interpreters – even the Australian Tourism award is called "interpretive guide" and that has nothing to do with language – it's interpreting your own information in the language that's been booked ... see that library over there? [pointing to her shelves of books] – that whole library is just about Central Australia"(Multilingual Guide)

Multilingual guides take a very dim view of foreign tour leaders providing their own commentary in the foreign language, maintaining that because they visit only irregularly, they cannot possibly build up the specialised knowledge, skills, and vocabulary possessed by the local multilingual guides who are constantly on the ground and regularly apprised of changes by Parks and other authorities.

The practice which appears to raise most sociolinguistic concerns and the ire of multilingual guides, though, is that of an incoming foreign tour leader *translating* commentary from an English-speaking bus driver. Since the introduction of the Knowledge for Tour Guides accreditation, Parks has approved this as an alternative to hiring a local multilingual guide. Parks' view is that as long as the English-speaking driver is accredited, a Japanese tour leader can simply *translate* his or her commentary: "Alternatively, a foreign language speaking guide translating information from an accredited guide is acceptable" (Department of the Environment 2014a)

An interesting and informed view on this practice was obtained during the study from a former local multilingual guide who is also a qualified Level 5 NAATI interpreter (in the linguistic sense).

She points out that in order for a *translator* to perform to a reasonable standard he or she must have an in-depth knowledge of the content being *translated*.

> in my view, the local knowledge is of utmost importance – you have – to be a good one, you have to be a local – you have to know about the conditions of the area that you talk about – therefore I would not dream myself .... to do the same job in an area that I don't know. Because it's not only a matter of translating as you are saying – it's not only a matter of telling bla bla bla what the other person is saying in bli bli bli – it's a matter of putting out the conditions of the area that you are exploring. And only the local will know that. (Multilingual guide and professional NAATI interpreter)

She goes on to point out the importance of understanding subtle concepts of culture, and how it is impossible to "translate" these without that understanding:

people also ask often about kinship – and this has been for me one of the hardest things to explain – even though there are books explaining how to project the concept of kinship and moitiés and – the generational groups and so on ... and people are amazed, and they don't understand and then we say it again a bit later when we talk and walk – and it's interesting but– it's not the work of a translator – it's the work of somebody who has acquired the knowledge of the region. And if you don't know it you'd better shut up! (Multilingual guide and professional NAATI interpreter)

if whoever – at Yulara [the resort at Uluṟu] or wherever if you just take a person ... who speaks a language of her own country and then ask them to be the translator for an accredited tour guide of a specific region – that person knows **nothing** about the subject matter of that tour guide. If you don't know the subject matter, you cannot be a good translator. (Multilingual guide and professional NAATI interpreter)

Information to be given to visitors in Uluṟu-Kata Tjuṯa is complex and specialised, relating to the geology, biology, ontology, history, and culture of land and peoples. In Aṉangu society this information is seen as interrelated rather than as belonging in separate silos, and conveying such complexity even in one's native language is a challenge. To do so in a second language requires the novice to spend considerable time preparing terms and explanations using dictionaries and official information sources and consulting with native speakers over problematic terms before a tour guiding assignment.

Australian English terms such as "whitefella", "bush tucker" or "swag" are not part of everyday vocabulary likely to be known by those who have learned English overseas. Nor are other terms essential to explaining the Central Australian context, such as "traditional custodians", "arkose", "alluvial fans" or "kinship systems". The *Uluṟu Tour Operator Workbook* devotes 55 pages to explaining the complexities of Aboriginal society, and it would be naïve to think that the subtleties therein can be easily translated into another language "on the spot". Translation of specific terms used in the *Tjukurpa* stories into another language requires careful preparation and much thought. Otherwise, information given to visitors can be superficial, inaccurate, offensive, simplistic, and even dangerous.

Suggestions that foreign tour leaders may not always give accurate information came from Parks staff, as well as from local multilingual guides:

The other thing is it's really hard for us to ascertain what information is being given to foreign-language guests by their tour guides, so we don't know whether they're being presented with the correct information a lot of the time ... we had a French group come through that were talking about an author called (name)[2] and the fact that Aboriginal people had extra-sensory perception. Their whole group was talking about that – it was obviously their tour guide – had encouraged that particular way of thinking (Parks staff member)

The guy can translate but I don't know what he's telling them! He could be telling them yeah Ayers Rock is six hundred and seventy meters high or, two and half thousand meters high, I wouldn't know. That's the thing about, translating off a, off a driver you know, the driver that's supposed to hear it he – he doesn't understand it so, he doesn't know what the guide is telling them! So that's pretty stupid, I reckon. (Local multilingual guide and driver-guide)

The following example of a multilingual interaction comes from a tour commentary recording where a French group, guided by a local multilingual French-speaking guide, is undertaking a tour segment offered by an Aboriginal company. The commentary is given in English by an Aboriginal guide "Chris", and *translated* into French by "Marie". This is a different context, though, from the *translations* provided by foreign tour leaders, since Marie has 25 years experience of guiding in French and English and thus has a wealth of content knowledge.

Hence where Chris refers to something which Marie knows the French tourists will not know about, she takes it upon herself to expand upon it and give background information to make sense of it.

Chris explains that he never knew his Aboriginal mother as a child:

Chris: *I don't know what happened but I was institutionalised when I was 2 years old.*

Marie: *Donc il fait partie de ce qu'on appelle La Génération Volée, à deux ans ils l'ont mis dans une institution.*

[So he is part of what we call the Stolen Generation, when he was two years old they put him in an institution]

There is also a skilful interplay between the two tour guides: both experts, they negotiate about what Marie knows the tourists have already seen and been told, and what Chris wants to relate:

Chris: *see from Kings Canyon we could walk all the way to Uluṟu because there is a map that will make us get there*

---

[2] This author has published inaccurate and offensive information about Aboriginal people's belief systems. One language group has gone to some lengths and expense to correct this, and I have no wish to give the author publicity by naming him or her here.

Marie: (aside, to Chris) *I talked, I talked to that – the way you can find your way from Kings Canyon – I told that, when I was in Uluṟu I explained. But they didn't see it (KC) so you can explain, but ...*

Chris: *to get the map, what people needed to do was to create stories*

Marie: *donc pour faire leur carte, il fallait une histoire, parce que ils la mettent dans la tête parce qu'ils n'écrivaient pas, alors l'histoire dans la tête c'est comme ça on fait la navigation*

(so to make their map, they needed a story, because they keep it in their heads, because they didn't write, so the story [is] in your head – that's how you navigate)

Here Marie expands on Chris' words, to ensure the tourists understand the point that this is an oral culture and that knowledge of how to travel safely through the harsh evironment is passed down through the memorisation and enactment of stories. The 'map' which Chris refers to is a metaphor for this mental knowledge held in the form of stories – it is not a printed representation as Western society understands a 'map' to be.

8 Discussion

This chapter began by pointing out that language in tourism is a fertile, but still under-studied area, and that tour-guiding interactions have as yet attracted very little researcher attention. The practice of tour-guiding is a complex activity enacted through language. Guides in Central Australia face the challenge of *interpreting* 40,000 years of Aṉangu culture in an accurate and complete fashion to visitors who fly in and out in 2 or 3 days. They need to respond to questions on Australian history, geography, politics, society and ethnic relations with accuracy and respect, avoiding stereotypes. They need to construct informative itineraries in 45-degree arid desert conditions, and to keep visitors safe and entertained in an environment whose dangers they little appreciate. Multilingual guides do all this in two or more languages and furthermore tailor their commentary and approach to the cultural idiosyncrasies of groups from different countries.

The language ecology of the area is complex, including several Aboriginal languages spoken in the area, the interplay of Standard and Broad Australian English, Aboriginal English and the Englishes of visitors, and the interaction of these with the foreign languages spoken by visitors. Multilingual guides must negotiate these interactions, drawing on much local knowledge and experience but also adapting to the moment and the interlocutor.

It is clear, then, that multilingual challenges exist in abundance in such a context. Here we have a meeting of multilingual members of the world's oldest continuous culture (the Anangu) with tourists speaking multiple languages, catered for by both Australian-based multilingual tour guides and by foreign tour leaders with various language proficiencies and varying degrees of specialised local knowledge. These interactions are mediated via an English-speaking dominant host culture with a recognised monolingual mindset (Clyne 2005; Ellis 2006; Ellis 2008). The term "monolingual mindset" was coined by Clyne (2005) to refer to the tendency to ignore or downplay the roles played by languages other than the dominant, and to see everything in terms of the one language known by the monolingual speaker. While this mindset has largely been characterised as being one of the English-speaking world, Australia's monolingual mindset has also been compared with that of Germany (Ellis, Gogolin & Clyne 2010). Although Australia prides itself on being multicultural, it is far from being widely multilingual. Immigrants tend to experience language shift by the second generation, so multilingualism is generally confined to remote Indigenous populations and first generation immigrants. Foreign languages are not widely taught, with less than 10% of school-leavers taking a foreign language in their Higher School Certificate (final exam). The consequence of this for the present project is that speaking two or more languages is regarded as something unusual by many Australians. There is certainly no overall requirement for tourism industry employees to speak a second language, as there is in Europe, a fact bemoaned by Watts (1994) and Marriott (1991). A further consequence is that matters surrounding second language use and bi/multilingualism are not well understood by the average Australian. Language practices such as code-switching, interpreting and translating or functioning in different languages in different domains are simply out of the range of experience of monolingual Australians who form the bulk of the population (Clyne 2005). Hence the sociolinguistic issues which are raised by this study may be viewed by some from a naïve and limited perspective. Little thought is given in the tourist industry in general to the level of proficiency of a speaker, and it is assumed that if one speaks a foreign language one can automatically *translate* to and from it with no preparation. There is little understanding of the tendency of bilinguals to possess strengths in different domains, and of the need to develop vocabulary in a new domain when the situation calls for it. Australians in general have very little understanding of the interpreting and translating professions, and assume both are technically simple processes of substituting one word for another in a different language.

There is widespread agreement among Anangu people, the Park and professional tour operators and tour guides, that it is essential that tourists receive accurate and complete information. The basis for achieving that is the carefully-produced information produced under the auspices of the Board of Management and, importantly, the introduction of accreditation for tour guides.

The introduction of the 'Knowledge for Tour Guides (KTG)' course was an important step in assuring the quality of provision. However views gleaned from Anangu elders, some of whom are quoted above, make it clear that simply doing the KTG course is insufficient, particularly if undertaken online from outside the area. Anangu stress the importance of 'sitting down' in the country and listening and learning. There is no substitute for personal experience of the people, the landscape, the flora and the fauna. Anangu talked of the importance of all the senses – touching, listening, smelling, tasting and seeing, and all these facets of experience are included in the workshops and training courses offered by Parks, but which foreign tour leaders do not have the time to take.

There is little consensus about how quality information should be provided to tourists who do not speak English. Local multilingual guides have long experience in and knowledge of the area, and understand the difference between "*interpreting* the landscape" in another language and simply "*translating*" the words of another guide. Their language abilities and content knowledge permit them to do both effectively as the situation warrants. Several companies which provide multilingual guides provided ongoing training and development for years before accreditation was introduced. It is less clear how the quality of commentary of foreign tour leaders might be assured. If they *translate* from an English-speaking driver or guide, it is possible that complex concepts of Anangu society and worldview may be dealt with only simplistically, since such vocabulary is not readily available to those not familiar with the area. It seems, then, that local knowledge and engagement with Anangu elders and an ongoing relationship with Parks is the key to effective language work. Supporting and developing the capacities of local multilingual guides who have a commitment to the area and to Anangu is critical. Developing a common language to deal with the differing concepts of interpreting and translation (in linguistics) and *interpreting* and *translation* (in tourist industry parlance) could help negotiate misunderstandings about the role of language in effective tour guiding provision. A planned outcome of this study is to produce a report for the Central Australian tourist industry outlining the sociolinguistic issues touched on here, in the hope that this can be used to improve training and practice in the cross-linguistic provision of tour-guiding. This stands to benefit visitors as well as those professional multilingual tour guides who take their work seriously, strive to continually update and improve their knowledge, and develop respectful relationships with the Anangu traditional custodians.

References

Agorni, Mirella. 2012. Tourism communication: The translator's responsibility in the translation of cultural difference. *Pasos: Revista de Turismo y Patrimonio Cultural* 10(4), 5–11.
Blommaert, Jan. 2010. *The Sociolinguistics of Globalization*. Cambridge: Cambridge University Press.
Boyle, Alicia & Allan Arnott. 2004. What tour guide stories can tell us about learning, education and training: A case study in the top end of the Northern Territory [online]. In Chris Cooper (eds.), *CAUTHE 2004: Creating Tourism Knowledge*, 86–94. Brisbane: Common Ground Publishing.
Bradley, Edna. 2009. *A Rock to Remember: A memoir from early tourism to Uluṟu*. Alice Springs: NT Print Management.
Bryant, Pauline. 1992. Regional variation in the lexicon of Australian English. Canberra: Australian National University PhD thesis. Retrieved from http://hdl.handle.net/1885/8744
Clyne, Michael. 2005. *Australia's Language Potential*. Sydney: UNSW Press.
Cohen, Erik & Robert L. Cooper. 1986. Language and tourism. *Annals of Tourism Research*, 13(4). 533–563. http://dx.doi.org/10.1016/0160-7383(86)90002-2
Dann, Graham M. S. 1996. *The Language of Tourism: A Sociolinguistic Perspective*. Wallingford Oxon: CAB International.
Department of Sustainability, Environment, Water, Population and Communities. 2012. *Palya! Welcome to Aṉangu land: Uluṟu-Kata Tjuṯa National Park*. Visitor Guide.
Department of the Environment. 2014a. *National Parks: Tour guide training FAQ*. http://www.environment.gov.au/national-parks/tour-guide-training-faq
Department of the Environment. 2014b. *National Parks: Uluṟu-Kata Tjuṯa National Park: Permits*. http://laptop.deh.gov.au/parks/uluru/management/permits.html
Eades, Diana. 2013. *Aboriginal Ways of Using English*. Canberra: AIATSIS.
Ellis, Elizabeth M. 2006. Monolingualism: The unmarked case. *Estudios de Sociolingüística* 7(2). 173–196.
Ellis, Elizabeth M. (ed.). 2008. Monolingualism. [Special issue]. *Sociolinguistic Studies* 2(3).
Ellis, Elizabeth M., Ingrid Gogolin & Michael Clyne. 2010. The Janus face of monolingualism: A comparison of German and Australian language education policies. *Current Issues in Language Planning* 11(4). 439–460.
Hale Sandra Beatriz. 2007. *Community Interpreting*. Palgrave Macmillan, Basingstoke, UK
Huisman, Suzanne & Kevin Moore. 1999. Natural language and that of tourism. *Annals of Tourism Research* 26(2). 445–449. http://dx.doi.org/10.1016/S0160-7383(98)00083-8
Jaworski, Adam. 2009. Greetings in tourist–host encounters. In Nick Coupland & Adam Jaworski (eds.), *The new sociolinguistics reader*, 662–679. Basingstoke: Palgrave Macmillan.
Jaworski, Adam. 2010. Linguistic landscapes on postcards: Tourist mediation and the sociolinguistic communities of contact. *Sociolinguistic Studies* 4(3). 569–594. doi: 10.1558/sols.v4i3.569
Kerle, Anne. 1995. *Uluṟu: Kata Tjuṯa and Watarrka National Parks* (National Parks Field Guides). Sydney: University of New South Wales Press.
Leclerc, Denis & Judith N. Martin. 2004. Tour guide communication competence: French, German and American tourists' perceptions. *International Journal of Intercultural Relations* 28(3–4). 181–200. doi: http://dx.doi.org/10.1016/j.ijintrel.2004.06.006

Marriott, Helen E. 1991. Language planning and language management for tourism shopping situations. *Australian Review of Applied Linguistics*. Series S(8). 191–222.
Oenbring, Raymond. 2011. Review of Crispin Thurlow and Adam Jaworski, *Tourism Discourse*. Houndmills, Basingstoke, UK. Palgrave Macmillan, 2010. *Discourse and Society*, 22(4). 491–493.
Otilia, Simion Minodora. 2013. English: The language of communication in tourism. *Analele Universităţii Constantin Brâncuşi din Târgu Jiu : Seria Economie* 1(1). 306–309.
Pauwels, Anne. 2006. Australia and New Zealand. In Ulrich Ammon, Norbert Dittmar, Klaus Mattheier & Peter Trudgill (eds.), *Sociolinguistics: An International Handbook of the Science of Language and Society*, 2nd edn., 2025–2034. Berlin: De Gruyter.
Phipps, Alison. 2007. *Learning the Arts of Linguistic Survival: Languaging, Tourism, Life*. Clevedon: Channel View Publications.
Piller, Ingrid. 2011. *Intercultural Communication: A Critical Introduction*. Edinburgh: Edinburgh University Press.
Pietikäinen, Sari & Helen Kelly-Holmes. 2011. The local political economy of languages in a Sámi tourism destination: Authenticity and mobility in the labelling of souvenirs. *Journal of Sociolinguistics* 15(3). 323–346.
Russell, Hilary & David Leslie. 2006. The importance of foreign language skills in the tourism sector: A comparative study of student perceptions in the UK and continental Europe. *Tourism Management* 27(6). 1397–1407. http://dx.doi.org/10.1016/j.tourman.2005.12.016
Salim, Muhammad Arfin Bin, Noor Aireen Binti Ibrahim & Hanita Hassan. 2012. Language for tourism: A review of literature. *Procedia – Social and Behavioral Sciences* 66(0). 136–143. http://dx.doi.org/10.1016/j.sbspro.2012.11.255
Simpson, Jane Helen, Jo Caffery & Patrick McConvell. 2009. *Gaps in Australia's Indigenous Language Policy: Dismantling bilingual education in the Northern Territory* (AIATSIS Research Discussion Paper No. 24). Canberra: AIATSIS.
Simpson, Jane Helen & Gillian Wigglesworth (eds.). 2008. *Children's Language and Multilingualism: Indigenous language use at home and school*. London: Continuum.
Swain, Merrill. 2006. Languaging, agency and collaboration in advanced language proficiency. In Heidi Byrnes (ed.), *Advanced Language Learning: The Contribution of Halliday and Vygotsky*, 95–108. London: Continuum.
Uluṟu tour operator workbook: Uluṟu-Kata Tjuṯa National Park. 1992. Darwin: Australian Nature Conservation Agency.
Walsh, Michael. 2005. Languages and their status in Aboriginal Australia. In Michael Walsh & Colin Yallop (eds.), *Language and Culture in Aboriginal Australia*, 1–14. Canberra: Aboriginal Studies Press.
Walsh, Michael. 2005. Will Indigenous languages survive? *Annual Review of Anthropology* 34. 293–315.
Walsh, Michael & Colin Yallop. 2005. *Language and Culture in Aboriginal Australia*. Canberra: Aboriginal Studies Press.
Watts, Noel R. 1994. The use of foreign languages in tourism: Research needs. *Australian Review of Applied Linguistics*, 17(1), 73–84.
Watts, Noel R. & Andrew Trlin. 1999. *Utilisation of Immigrant Language Resources in International Business, Trade and Tourism in New Zealand*. Massey University Palmerston North: New Settlers Program.
Weiler, Betty & Black, Rosemary. 2014.*Tour Guiding Research: Insights, Issues and Implications*. Clevedon: Multilingual Matters.

Zhang, Baicheng. 2012. On Chinese-English translation of culture-loaded tourism publicities: A perspective of cultural manipulation theory. *Theory and Practice in Language Studies* 2(11). 2342–2348.

Claire Kramsch
Afterword: Challenging multilingualism

The pluridisciplinary perspectives offered in this book make it possible to view multilingualism in complex ways that don't necessarily get highlighted when campaigning for linguistic rights or when making the case for raising multilingual families, making accommodations for a multilingual workforce, or praising the polyglottism of the European elites. Such complexity puts into question the invisible complacency that settles in when language becomes transparent, our words seem to be one with the world and with our thoughts, and communication is taken as a straightforward packaging of thought into speech. With multilingualism, the dream of a monolingual Garden of Eden is shattered. For multilingual speakers, not only does thinking-for-speaking replace thought-for-speech (Slobin 1996), but choosing-for-speaking replaces the taken-for-granted use of a shared linguistic code. Among multilingual interlocutors, speakers have to consciously tailor their utterances to speakers of languages that carry other memories and associations. Language choice carries the weight of a multilingual family's history, of national allies and enemies, of happy and painful memories.

Several themes emerge in this book that serve to remind us of the sociopolitical tensions presented by linguistic diversity in everyday life.

1 Between memory and imagination

Much has been written about the negotiation of identity that immigrants to a new country have to go through in order to regain a sense of self-respect and the respect of others, and the obligatory cultural change that accompanies the acquisition of a new language. From a psychological perspective and in the context of immigration, this process has been mostly seen as one of loss, journeying and redemption whose happy ending provides legitimacy to the travails endured (e.g., Pavlenko & Lantolf 2000). The metaphor of a "journey" is a spatial metaphor that stresses change and transition, but ultimately continuity.

But beside the geographical distance of immigrants from their country of origin, there are also generational and historical discontinuities that the new language brings about in the delicate linguistic balance of multilingual immigrant families. Suddenly youngsters cannot talk to their grandmothers any more, parents cannot understand their children; every misfortune, every failure is attributed to a linguistic inferiority that saps one's self-esteem (e.g., Norton 2000). This sense of inferiority is not only linked to a lack of proficiency in the new language; it is caused also by the temporal disjuncture of what has to remain untranslated, indeed untranslatable and therefore unsayable. Li Wei and Zhu Hua (Ch. 1 this volume) describe the loss of "cultural memory of linguistic practices" experienced by an old Chinese couple now living in the U.K. The Chinese language spoken by young Chinese is comprehensible to them, but they no longer understand the context of its use, because China has changed so much since they left. This makes them feel doubly alienated from their original country. Young Chinese in the U.K. live in a global present in which their ability to use multiple languages will allow them to shape a future that they yet have to imagine. Some Chinese of Korean descent now living in Britain have decided to emphasize their Korean ethnicity rather than their Chinese nationality. Multilingualism for transnationals, Li Wei and Zhu Hua conclude, is a constant "tension between memory and imagination" (Li Wei & Zhu Hua p. 35).

This tension is also felt among the French youngsters enrolled in a Breton immersion program in Brittany. Osterkorn and Vetter (Ch. 5 this volume) show how the laudable historical motivation behind the decision to institute such monolingual immersion programs, namely to redress the national monolingualism imposed by the French Revolution, can backfire. Youngsters, forbidden to speak anything but Breton on the school grounds, find all kinds of imaginative ways to fulfill their emotional needs … in French, thus reinstating a multilingualism that the teaching of Breton was supposed to bring about. Here too we have the tension between multilingualism as historical legacy and multingualism as personal experience.

2 Between multiplicity and intensity of experience

Intimately linked to the temporal/historical dimension of multilingualism is its cultural dimension. Many of the papers in this volume express a fear of a loss of local cultural identity brought about by a global multilingualism that assimilates all languages to mere "modes of communication". Indeed, in his latest book *Communication Power* (2009), Manuel Castells, who defines culture as "the set of values and beliefs that inform, guide, and motivate people's behavior" (p. 36) writes the following about the global culture in which we live :

> What characterizes the global network society is the contraposition between the logic of the global net and the affirmation of a multiplicity of local selves … The common culture of the global network society is a culture of protocols of communication enabling communication between different cultures on the basis *not of shared values but of the sharing of the value of communication*. (pp. 37–38, my emphasis)

Multilingualism seen as number of languages mastered, frequency of postings, number of hits, volume of information bites, risks displacing multilingualism as intensity of experience, complexity of thought, and depth of cultural values.

Multilingualism as multiplicity itself raises both the need for English as shared global language and the fear that English brings people together only to better divide them along social and economic lines. The chapter by Pilar Safont (Ch. 2 this volume) is a dramatic illustration of this dilemma. English superimposes itself as a global language on a decade long struggle for Catalonian autonomy and for the recognition of Catalan as the official language of Catalonia. But in so doing it changes the delicate balance of power between Spanish and Catalan and between the languages of local political legitimacy and the language of global economic opportunity. Spanish parents who choose to have their children learn English instead of Catalan are trying to reduce the linguistic multiplicity in response to the economic argument. Some, who decide to let go of multilingualism altogether, respond to the widespread folk belief that "monolingualism may cure language impairment" (Safont ch. 2 this volume). The challenge is how to hold on to the old political imperatives while grasping at the new economic world order; how to fulfill the expectations of a nation-state and of a global economy – a tension that Duchêne and Heller characterized as a tension between pride and profit (Duchêne & Heller 2011). We find that same tension in the chapter by Lisa Atalianis on the work of diplomats at the United Nations, where the convenience of using English to exchange information trumps most of the time the use of other national languages that could provide a greater depth of understanding of national cultures, attitudes and beliefs (see Ch. 12 this volume).

The chapter by Baider and Kariolemou (Ch. 8 this volume) reminds us that, of course, national cultures are not as homogeneous as U.N. diplomats represent them to be. Their study examines the importance of the dominant languages: Greek-Cypriots speak Greek, Cypriot-Greek, and English, the enclaved Arab-Cypriots speak Turkish and Cypriot Turkish, as indicators of power, affluence and influence in their local context. But the examples of the Armenians and Arab-Cypriots in Cyprus show that learning languages may become linked to the history of emotional trauma in the context of ethnic conflicts and postcolonial societies. Ideology – defined here as "a set of dominant or subaltern ideas, discourse, and signifying practices used to acquire or maintain linguistic power (Woolard 1998,7)" – shapes the acceptance or the reluctance of Cypriots to learn, hear or speak the dominant language and live their sameness/ strangeness and estrangement. And, as ideologies, language policies work at the intersection of theories common to gender, class, and ethnicity issues.

3 Between transmission and mediation

Multilingual individuals are well acquainted with issues of legitimacy, loyalty, and (im)posture (Kramsch 2012). In chapter 4, Kramsch and Zhang describe the particularly vulnerable position of foreign born language instructors, who are hired to teach their native language at academic institutions in the U.S. These individuals are highly educated, and with a highly developed sense of mission to serve as bilingual/bicultural ambassadors or mediators between their own and their host culture, yet their academic legitimacy rests only on their monolingual purity and authenticity. Well-experienced in the challenges of multilingualism, they could be of great help to their students if they could develop together with their students a pedagogy of mediation rather than one of transmission. A glimpse at such a pedagogy is given by Heidenfeldt (Ch. 3 this volume) in his study of a Spanish teacher who focuses explicitly on issues of legitimacy and illegitimacy in her classroom lesson on Cortez' multilingual mistress, *La Malinche*. Heidenfeldt shows how a bold, politically inclined Spanish teacher uses her feminist leanings to discuss with the students the social and political legitimacy of a trilingual like *La Malinche* under the difficult conditions of colonization. The original question: *"Fue La Malinche una mujer buena o una mujer mala?"* (was La Malinche a good woman or a bad woman?) turns into a discussion of the challenges faced by multilingual individuals among people with monolingual national ideologies.

The dilemma has to do with the subject position of the multilingual mediator that Elisabeth Ellis (Ch. 13 this volume) takes up explicitly in her chapter on the Australian Aborigines who deal with international tourists at their sacred sites. While on the one hand, they wish to have a voice on how these sites are understood and interpreted by foreign visitors, on the other hand the Aboriginal translators/interpreters fear that translation will silence them by making communicable what should not be communicated to outsiders. Their fear is not only that their culture cannot totally be expressed in other languages, but that by transmitting the knowledge of their ancestors, they are opening the door to misinterpretation and thus to misrepresentation, trivialization and abuse. Here, multilingualism is silencing the very people to whom it is supposed to give a voice. Ellis' chapter offers a dramatic illustration of the political paradox of multilingualism. But this paradox plays itself out on a much larger historical scale as well, as discussed below.

The interest in learning foreign languages ushered in by the advent of the steam engine at the end of the 19th century, the new ease of travel across borders, and the growth of the tourism industry in the late 1800s, combined with the desire for peace after WWI, led the European elites in the 1920's to see in multilingualism the hope of world peace and prosperity. By promoting the teaching of foreign languages in schools, by facilitating researcher mobility and the means of collaboration across national boundaries, through commercial exchanges and scientific competition, multilingualism was seen as enabling a variety of intellectual traditions and styles to be heard and to enrich one another. But there was also a dark side to this utopia. In his chapter on the multilingual policies of the Third Reich, David Gramling (Ch. 7 this volume) sounds a note of caution against too romantic a view of the multilingual euphoria that prevailed between the two world wars, and that was based on the dream of global mediation that multilingualism could bring about between workers and researchers across national boundaries. The Third Reich quickly reframed multilingual mediation into the transmission of *Reichsdeutsch*, the global language of its empire, and made linguistic diversity, as we all know, into the multilingual inferno of the concentration camps.

4 Between scientific knowledge and scientific legitimacy

Shocking as it is today to realize that the Third Reich had indeed a policy of multilingualism, the link between knowledge and power is never far under the surface of well-intended efforts to promote multilingualism. This is particularly true of the work of international research teams, who seek to further knowledge by collaborating multilingually on scientific research projects. Such a collaboration can make researchers realize as never before how much their scientific knowledge is anchored in the language they use to express it. George Lüdi describes in Chapter 9 how having to conduct the team's research and to publish exclusively in English is feared to sever the link to the local language that was used to frame the local problems that the researchers seek to solve. The future of scientific knowledge itself depends on keeping multilingual channels of communication open. However, the multilingual scientific game makes apparent the linguistic relativity of cognitive categories, classification schemes, logical arguments, scientific concepts and notions, and their symbolic power. Researching multilingually requires a metapragmatic awareness that needs to be developed; language ceases to be transparent, professional expertise can no longer be taken for granted. And the need to explain oneself at every turn slows down the process of discovery and risks threatening one's scientific legitimacy. But, as both Lüdi (Ch. 9) and Zarate et al. (Ch. 10) show through ample examples, ultimately the process can have its own scientific rewards. What gets lost in chronological time might be gained in experiential time through unexpected scientific insights.

The delicate position of the scientific translator is illustrated with particular force in chapter 10 where Geneviève Zarate, Fu Rong and Aline Gohard-Radenkovic describe how they engaged with Chinese translators of the French *Handbook of Multilingualism and Multiculturalism*. The challenges were at first sight of a linguistic and cultural nature. For example, the notion of *voix/contrevoix*, that comes from a Western musical art of the fugue and is used in the *Handbook* as a metaphor for the oppositional structure of an argument, was found to be foreign to Chinese expository prose and had to be translated by "polyphony". But the challenges were also of a political nature. Thus the idea of a "handbook" about multilingualism, presented as the sum of attested facts and universal knowledge, did not sit well with the representation that China has of itself, nor with the Chinese perception that multilingualism itself is originally a Western concept. Hence the translator's compromise in choosing the Chinese title: "Introduction to the ideas of linguistic and cultural plurality". Through this title, the Chinese translator managed to retain his distance from the object of translation and to keep a Chinese voice within the translation from the French, thus enacting the kind of savvy in-between-ness that Georges Lüdi notices in multilingual research teams within the DYLAN project (Lüdi, Ch. 9 this volume).

Multilingualism also presents a challenge to traditional, linear, cause-and-effect approaches to the study of language acquisition and learning. If, as Aronin and Jessner show in chapter 11, multilingualism is radically different in nature from bilingualism, if it has to be seen as a complex, emergent, non-linear, unpredictable process, then the very development of multilingualism in the individual is the mirror image of the complex, emergent, decentered social processes that are taking place on the social local and global levels today. Complexity, that as Aronin and Jessner point out, is quite different from "complicatedness", is ultimately what makes multilingualism both a source of excitement and a source of anxiety. Multilingualism as complexity raises both the thrill and the fear of scientific knowledge itself, based as it is on the notion of linear progress toward a universally recognized truth that can be discovered through rigorous categories and logical arguments. If this categorization and logic are themselves put into question, then what multilingualism does is remove, but also reveal, "the fundamental codes of our (scientific) culture" (Foucault 1970:xx). Such a post structuralist stance requires the researcher to objectify him/herself as a participant in the scientific project, a point that Ellis makes in her chapter (Ch. 13).

5 Between monolingual and multilingual discourse

Ultimately, multilingualism confronts us with a challenge that is greater than the sum of its multiplicities. The cross-disciplinary perspective that we have adopted in this book enables us to understand multilingualism as a far more complex phenomenon than just the use of several codes in everyday life. If, according to the definition given in our introduction, it encompasses also the use of various modes (e.g., verbal, visual, acoustic, gestural) and modalities (e.g., spoken, written, virtual), within a global economy and global technologies that erase the boundaries of time and space, and blur the distinction between the real and the imagined, then the multilingual challenge is a discourse challenge. How can we know the universe at once monolingually and multilingually? Indeed, how can we remain knowing subjects if we are challenged to express our knowledge of our multilingual selves in a single language and through the monolingual knowledge that others have of us?

This dilemma is nowhere more acute than in the representation of multilingualism through the essentially monolingual discourse of literature. In Ch. 6, Brian Lennon addresses the fascinating paradox of monolingual U.S. publishing houses having to represent multilingual characters such as in Hemingway's *For Whom the Bell Tolls* for a monolingual Anglo readership – the fear of deterring the monolingual reader if the book is too multilingual, but the danger of trivializing, exoticizing the Spanish if Spanish is used only for local color. Lennon's chapter raises other, equally disturbing questions. Given the argument that literature as we know it is the product of fundamentally monolingual nation states and their national publishing industries, is the growing marginalization of literary studies as compared to communication studies in academia today related in any way to the growth of multilingualism around the world? Is multilingualism responsible for the growing lack of interest in acquiring any in-depth knowledge of any one particular language? And what then is the future of verbal art itself under multilingual conditions?

Ironically, the answer to that question might be suggested to us by narrative discourse itself. In a Special Issue of *L2Journal* on multilingual writers, Adrian Wanner (2015) passes in review translingual writers who deal with the paradox of their multilingual condition through narrative (see, e.g., Kellman 2000, 2003). Wanner tells the story of the multilingual Russian-American writer Steyngart (2012) who, like Sheherazade staving off the time of death through her 1001 Arabian Nights, staved off social death upon his arrival as a young Russian immigrant to the United States. Ridiculed and bullied by his peers, he was given the opportunity by a substitute teacher to tell his story in English in front of the class. His humorous and translingual way of telling his story both suspended and reconfigured time at that moment in the class and won him the sympathy of his peers. Steyngart remarks that self-deprecating humor has always been a Jewish mode of survival – putting a distance between you and your words. The very suspension of time and space brought about by computer technologies might create the psychological distance necessary for humor and irony, metalingual reflection and fantasy, that lie at the core of literary narrative. Multilingualism, conceived as heteroglossia and translingualism, might indeed bring us closer to literary discourse than we think.

And yet the fact that a bilingual writer like Ariel Dorfman, despite his repeated attempts at "heading South" to Chile and Argentina and "looking north" to the U.S. in his Spanish-English "bilingual journey", ultimately decided to write this memoir exclusively in English and to publish it in the United States raises serious questions about the future of a truly multilingual literature in an era of globalization. It is fine for applied linguists to call for disinventing languages and their institutional boundaries (Makoni & Pennycook 2007), and for rejecting intercultural strategies in favor of hybrid forms of communication (e.g., Canagarajah 2013), it is fine to acknowledge the need for multilingual repertoires (Blommaert 2005) and translanguaging practices (e.g., Garcia 2009), and even to praise the creativity of metrolingual verbal art (Otsuji & Pennycook 2010), but when it comes to the large scale publication of works of literature, multilingualism presents a challenge of overwhelming proportions.

6 Conclusion

Choosing to title this afterword "Challenging multilingualism" has meant benefiting from a pun made possible through the grammar of English. This pun refers to the challenge that multilingualism represents for individuals and societies, but it also exhorts us to challenge the traditional view of multilingualism as the mere juxtaposition of linguistic codes under the motto "the more the merrier".

Multilingualism, as multiplicity of codes, modes, voices and perspectives, combined with the superdiversity brought about by globalization and social networks, and magnified by the virtual worlds created by the computer, is indeed a challenge to individuals and societies. The papers in this collection have all addressed this challenge as it appears at various sites and under various forms. But these papers have also provided a beginning of a response to this challenge by challenging in turn the unitary view of multilingualism as mere polyglottism. If we consider multilingualism as heteroglossia (Blackledge & Creese 2014, Weber & Horner 2012), as complexity (Morin 2005), and as a dynamic system (Larsen-Freeman & Cameron 2008, Aronin & Jessner this volume) which realigns our conceptions of time, space, and reality (Kramsch 2009: Ch. 6), then we are drawn through multilingualism to forms of experience that realign the axes of our human existence.

And this is where poetry and narrative come in. Whether these forms of verbal art match the monolingual literary productions of yesteryear is an open question. The multilingual imagination is sure to be different. After the dream of a common, transparent language, that has been ours since the Enlightenment, multilingualism once again foregrounds the materiality of language and the opacity of meaning, the historical density of words and their symbolic power. That is the narrative of our times that verbal art can help us deal with in families, communities, schoolrooms and boardrooms.

References

Blackledge, Adrian & Creese, Angela (eds.). 2014. *Heteroglossia as Practice and Pedagogy.* Berlin: Springer.
Blommaert, Jan. 2005. *Discourse.* Cambridge U Press.
Canagarajah, Suresh. 2013. From intercultural rhetoric to cosmopolitan practice: Addressing new challenges in Lingua Franca English. In Diane Belcher & Gayle Nelson (eds.) *Critical and Corpus-Based Approaches to Intercultural Rhetoric* (pp.203–226). Ann Arbor: U. of Michigan Press.
Castells, Manuel. 2009. *Communication Power.* Oxford: Oxford U Press.
Duchene, Alexander & Heller, Monica. 2011. *Language in Late Capitalism. Pride and Profit.* Routledge.
Foucault, Michel. 1970. *The Order of Things. An archaeology of the human sciences.* New York: Vintage.
Garcia, Ofelia. 2009. Education, multilingualism, and translanguaging in the 21st century. In Ajit Mohanty, Minati Panda, Robert Phillipson, & Tove Skutnabb-Kangas (eds.) *Multilingual Education for social justice. Globalising the local* (pp.128–145). New Delhi: Orient Blackswan.
Kellman, Steven 2000. *The Translingual Imagination.* Lincoln, NE: U of Nebraska Press.
Kellman, Steven (ed.). 2003. *Switching Languages. Translingual writers reflect on their craft.* Lincoln, NE: University of Nebraska Press.
Kramsch, Claire 2009. *The Multilingual Subject.* Oxford: Oxford U Press.
Kramsch, Claire. 2012. (Im)posture. A late modern notion in poststructuralist SLA research. *Applied Linguistics* 33:5,483–502.
Kress, Gunther. 2010. *Multimodality. A social semiotic approach to contemporary communication.* Routledge.
Kundera, Milan. 2007. Reflections. Die Weltliteratur. *New Yorker* Jan.8.

Makoni, Sinfree & Pennycook, Alastair. 2007. *Disinventing and reconstituting languages.* Clevedon, UK: Multilingual Matters.

May, Stephen (ed.). 2014. *The Multilingual Turn. Implications for SLA, TESOL and bilingual education.* Routledge

Morin, Edgar. 2005. *Introduction à la pensée complexe.* Paris: Seuil

Norton, Bonny. 2000. *Identity and Language Learning.* London: Longman.

Otsuji, Emi & Pennycook, Alastair. 2010. Metrolingualism: fixity, fluidity, and language in flux. *International Journal of Multilingualism* 7:3, 240–254.

Pavlenko, Aneta & Lantolf, Jim. 2000. Second language learning as participation and the (re)construction of selves. In Lantolf, James (ed.) *Sociocultural Theory and Second Language Learning* (pp.155–178). Oxford: Oxford U Press.

Slobin, Daniel. 1996. From "thought and language" to thinking for speaking. In Gumperz, J.J. & Levinson, S.C. (eds.) *Rethinking Linguistic Relativity* (pp.70–96). CUP.

Wanner, Adrian. 2015. Writing the translingual life: Recent memoirs and autofiction by Russian-American and Russian-German novelists. L_2 *Journal* 2015/7, 141–151.

Woolard, Kathryn A. 1998. "Introduction: Language Ideology as a Field of Inquiry". *Language Ideologies: Practice and Theory,* In Schieffelin, Bambi B., Kathryn A Woolard and Paul Kroskrity (eds.). 285–316. Oxford University Press.

Index

Aboriginal
– culture 325
– languages 326
Arab Cypriot 189–191, 195–199
Armenian Cypriot 189–191, 200–205
attitudes, *see* language attitudes
authenticity 88

bilingual speech community 40, 55
bilingualism *see* difference between bi- and tri/multilingualism

Chinese communities
– in Britain 24–26
circulation internationale des idées 246–247
code-switching 145
commodification of language 7, 66, 83, 85
communicative strategies 213, 216–217
comparative literature 155
competence, *see* linguistic competence, multicompetence, symbolic competence
complexity 53, 121, 274–275, 281, 347, 352
– approach 286–287
– concepts 281–284
– degrees of 284–286
cosmopolitanism 150, 155–157
cultural legitimacy 100–102
cultural politics, *see* foreign cultural politics

difference between bi- and tri/multilingualism 274, 287–288
discontinuities 347
diversity 274–275, 286
– challenge 5–8
– opportunity 2–5
– transnational families 35–36
– *see also* super-diversity
DMM 43, 57, 280
DYLAN 213

early multilingualism 56
ecology, *see* language ecology
economic opportunity 5, 349
– *see also* language economics

English medium education 214
epistemological legitimacy 102–106
equitability 320
estrangement 185–186, 201, 349
– *see also* strangeness
ethnic narratives 185–186

family
– dynamics 21
– interaction 22, 27
– language decisions 28
– transnational 23–24
foreign cultural politics 169–172
foreign tour leaders 328, 338
– *see also* tour guides

generation 21, 163, 206, 342
geopolitics 170–174, 180
globalization 22, 35, 87, 112, 266

identity 24, 28, 43
– construction 186, 199
– politics 206
– production 43, 50–51, 56
ideological legitimacy 108–111
ideology 43, 57, 89, 186, 214, 349
immersion 42, 49–50, 124, 130
– schooling 115–117, 122–123
immigration 347
IMO, *see* The International Maritime Organization
indigenous tour guides 328
– *see also* tour guides
integrated multilingualism 121, 133–134
– *see also* separated multilingualism
interculturality 161–162
intercultural competence 161, 164, 168
interpreting 179, 323, 337, 341, 343
– *see also* translating
intersubjectivity 217, 222, 224, 230

Joint Inspection Award, *see* United Nations

Korean 26–28

language
- attitudes 43–45, 56
- ecology 323, 326, 341
- economics 318
- maintenance 26, 35, 320
- planning 254, 296, 315
  - micro 295–296, 314, 318
- policy 130, 295–296, 319–320
  - macro-level 318
  - micro 318
  - *see also* policy analysis
- proches vs distantes 261
- regime 115, 316–318
- shift 34–36
- teacher identity 70, 85
- teaching 84, 89, 175–177, 266
legitimacy 88–89, 99, 111–112
- cultural, *see* cultural legitimacy
- epistemological, *see* epistemological legitimacy
- ideological, *see* ideological legitimacy
- linguistic, *see* linguistic legitimacy
- political, *see* political legitimacy
- professional, *see* professional legitimacy
- symbolic, *see* symbolic legitimacy
liminality 271
lingua franca 216, 266, 313
- English 6, 214, 229–232, 312, 314, 320
linguistic
- competence 51, 122
- legitimacy 100–102
- minorities 185, 187, 205, 282
  - socio- 191–193
literature 353–354
- *see also* comparative literature
loyalty 350
LPP 296
- *see also* language planning, language policy

M-Factor 278
macro language policy, *see* language policy
micro language policy, *see* language politics
micro-level language planning, *see* language planning
migration 35, 89, 268

minority languages 57, 74, 121, 188, 202
- *see also* linguistic minorities
minority language education 115, 123
- *see also* multilingual language teachers
mixed teams 215
monolingual
- discourse 353
- mindset 15, 342
- *see also* national monolingualism, space
multicompetence 3–4, 217, 229
multilingual
- competence 74, 199, 214
- development 3, 39, 50–53, 56, 279
- guides 327, 337–338
- practices 1, 213, 272
- reasoning 227–229, 233
- repertoires 67, 219, 354
- schools 136, 284
- subjects 84, 112, 115–116, 120–121, 126, 136
- teachers 67–68, 83, 87–88, 112
multinational multilingualism 156
multiplicity 1, 267, 348–349, 354

national literature 143–145, 152
national monolingualism 156, 348
National Socialism 161–167, 180–181
native instructors 87, 89–100
- *see also* multilingual language teachers

paradox 89, 98, 125, 350, 353
- of legitimacy 100
parent's beliefs 44–45, 51–53, 56–57
- *see also* language attitudes
plurilanguaging 214, 217–218, 229–232
policy analysis 295, 297, 316
- *see also* language policy
political legitimacy 349–350
professional legitimacy 106–108
propaganda 167–169

researching multilingually 170, 243, 351

scientific knowledge 216, 351–352
separated multilingualism 121, 128, 133
- *see also* integrated multilingualism

space 117–120
– monolingual 126
strangeness 185–186, 201, 349
– *see also* estrangement
super-diversity 120–121
– *see also* diversity
switching costs 275–277
symbolic competence 24, 73, 112
symbolic legitimacy 111

teaching, *see* language teaching, multilingual teachers
threshold 271, 279–280
The International Maritime Organization
– history 302
– organizational structure 303
– language policy 303–304
– language choice 305–308
– meeting costs 310
Tjukurpa 325–326

tour guides 15, 328
– training 331–332
tour-guiding 324, 341–343
tourism 329–330
transcultural competence 4, 98
translating 337–338, 342–343
translation 152, 155, 167, 179
translational mimesis 148–149
translingual competence 4, 98
transnational families, *see* diversity, family
trilingualism 44, 277, 285
– difference to bi/ multilingualism 287–288

Uluru-Kata Tjuta National Park 325–326
United Nations 297–298
– history of multilingualism 298–299
– Joint Inspection Award 300–302

zone de traduisibilité vs d'intraduisibilité 262–263

www.ingramcontent.com/pod-product-compliance
Lightning Source LLC
Chambersburg PA
CBHW050850160426
43194CB00011B/2100